involving even Rome: the Abbelen Memorial episode, the parochial school dispute, the problem of German succursal parishes, opposition to the erection and operation of the Catholic University of America and disagreement over episcopal appointments coveted by both factions. What happened in the years of dissension until conciliation makes fascinating and revealing reading.

Particularly valuable is the author's vindication of the much-maligned Peter Paul Cahensly, the German merchant whose efforts to provide for the temporal and spiritual welfare of the German immigrants en route to and after arrival in America resulted in the founding of the St. Raphael Societies. Growing in size and range and administered by Catholics in the Fatherland, these societies became a factor, innocent no doubt, in the animosity that followed.

Excerpts from old documents, personal letters and manuscripts which the author painstakingly unearthed in his research in libraries and archives both here and in Germany and Rome high-light the major developments in the long controversy and provide telling insights into the actions and intentions of influential personages involved. In addition, the important documents which led to the most publicized episodes are printed in full in the Appendixes.

This history objectively presents the whole era of rash statements, misjudgments, ecclesiastical intrigues, sensational journalism, *faux pas,* invective, suspicions, and dangerous national frictions along with its dramatic climax, the appointment of an apostolic delegate to the United States and Rome's pronouncement, Leo XIII's historic *Testem Benevolentiae.*

Peter Paul Cahensly, as papal chamberlain
di spada e cappa, 1907

The Catholic Church and German Americans

COLMAN J. BARRY, O.S.B.

THE BRUCE PUBLISHING COMPANY
MILWAUKEE

Imprimi potest:

✠ Baldwin W. Dworschak, O.S.B.
Abbot of St. John's Abbey

Nihil obstat:

John Tracy Ellis
Censor deputatus

Imprimatur:

✠ Peter W. Bartholome
Coadjutor Bishop of St. Cloud

January 21, 1952

Made in the United States of America

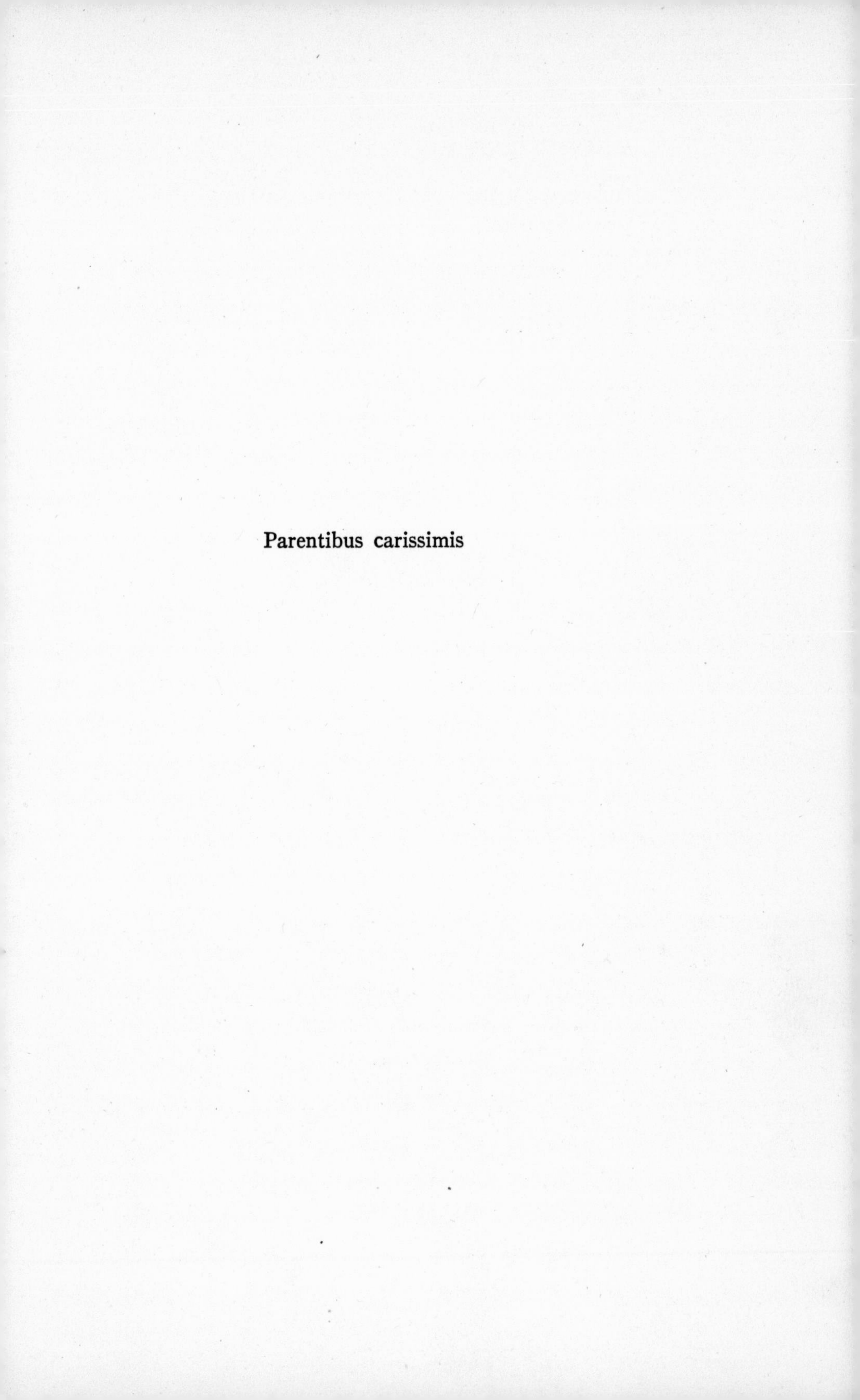

Parentibus carissimis

Key to Abbreviations

ARCHIVES

AAB — Archives of the Archdiocese of Baltimore
AABo — Archives of the Archdiocese of Boston
AAM — Archives of the Archdiocese of Milwaukee
AAMe — Archives of the Abbey of Metten
AANY — Archives of the Archdiocese of New York
AASP — Archives of the Archdiocese of St. Paul
AASPOW — Archives of the Abbey of St. Paul Outside the Walls
ACHSP — American Catholic Historical Society of Philadelphia
ACUA — Archives of the Catholic University of America
ACV — Archives of the Central Verein
ADC — Archives of the Diocese of Cleveland
ADCV — Archives of the Deutsche Caritasverband
ADL — Archives of the Diocese of Limburg
ADR — Archives of the Diocese of Richmond
AHSRV — Archives of the Hamburg St. Raphaelsverein
ALH — Archives of the Leo House
ALMV — Archives of the Ludwig Missionsverein
APF — Archives of the Paulist Fathers
APM — Archives of the Pallottine Mother House, Limburg
ASH — Archives of the Stone House, Limburg

PERIODICALS

ACQR — *American Catholic Quarterly Review*
AER — *American Ecclesiastical Review*
AVG — *Annalen der Verbreitung des Glaubens*
BLS — *Berichte der Leopoldinen Stiftung*
C — *Caritas*
CBSJ — *Central Blatt and Social Justice*
CE — *Catholic Encyclopedia*
CHR — *Catholic Historical Review*
CUB — *Catholic University Bulletin*
CW — *Catholic World*

DAB	—*Dictionary of American Biography*
DGH	—*Der Grosse Herder*
FR	—*Fortnightly Review*
HRS	—*Historical Records and Studies of the United States Catholic Historical Society*
LfThK	—*Lexikon für Theologie und Kirche*
LHB	—*Leo Haus Blatt*
RACHS	—*Records of the American Catholic Historical Society of Philadelphia*
SRB	—*St. Raphaels Blatt*

Preface

AMONG the varied nationalities which comprise the Catholic Church in the United States, the German people justly occupy a leading and honorable place. Immigrant Catholic Germans of the nineteenth century brought to American shores a firm loyalty to their religion, masterly organizational techniques, and a strong community pattern of worship, culture, and social action. From the days of the first Pennsylvania settlements of the mid-eighteenth century, German Catholic leaders insisted on separate treatment and recognition as a minority group. Their demands in the following century for language rights, national parishes, and proportional representation in the hierarchy were defenses against attacks by liberal German Americans and others, as well as insurance that their faith would be maintained intact.

Simultaneously, leading Catholic churchmen and laymen, following the splendid pioneer example of Archbishop John Carroll, were working throughout the nineteenth century to instill devotion to American constitutional and political ideals among immigrant Catholics. Accordingly, toward the end of the century, differences over procedure and practice brought robust Americanizing and German elements into an open conflict, a conflict which centered around the efforts of Peter Paul Cahensly and the international St. Raphael societies for the protection of Catholic immigrants. Several German Catholic leaders and newspapers, supported at times by some French, Polish, and Italian representatives and organs both at home and abroad, accused the Americanizers of striving to break down in a precipitate fashion all traditions and customs among Catholic immigrants. The Americanizers were also accused of causing a loss of religious faith and creating an undue attachment to American secular trends. On their side, the Americanizers, represented by such men as James Cardinal Gibbons, Archbishops John Ireland and John J. Keane, Bishop Denis J. O'Connell, the Paulist Fathers, and some of the professors in the Catholic University of America, were wedded to the vision of traditional Catholicism formed in an American mold and based on a fusion of all national groups. In the end the latter group succeeded in achieving their aim without compromise of doctrine and without sacrificing proper European national customs and traditions.

Both sides in the question drew closer together, especially after Leo XIII issued his tempering letter, *Testem benevolentiae,* to American Catholics in January, 1899. Eventually Cahensly's name was cleared of the charges of conspiracy, and a number of programs very much favored by the Germans were generally adopted, such as colonizing societies for Catholics, a strong parochial school system, and German Catholic organizational techniques. German American Catholics, on their side, came to view the United States more sympathetically as their homeland, and recognized the traditions of other elements in the American Church, while their own mother tongue gradually gave way to the English language.

Accordingly, the Catholic Church in the United States proved to be an effective "melting pot" for immigrants where incoming European nationals learned to live together. In the Catholic climate of the American Church they found a unity which today is the special pride of both Church and State. The Catholic Church encouraged the Americanization of the immigrant and loyalty to democratic values in the realm of politics; thus it played a significant role in the maturing of a united nation. The fervent and heated stages of this prolonged process are sometimes forgotten as one surveys the accomplishment of the present day. In this study the Americanization of the German Catholic immigrant is detailed as evidence of the vision, and at times the painful effort, that helped to fashion the final achievement. During the period tempers ran high on both sides, and it is unfortunate that the name and work of Peter Paul Cahensly were impaired. For that reason a belated recognition of his rightful historical position has been attempted here.

It is difficult to express in an adequate way the gratitude the author feels to the many who have supplied assistance, encouragement, and guidance in the preparation of this work. A statement of obligation can only partially fulfill so heavy a debt. Access to archival deposits was made possible through the kindness of: Right Reverends Corbinian Hofmeister, O.S.B., of Metten Abbey; Hildebrando Vannucci, O.S.B., of the Abbey of St. Paul Outside the Walls; John J. Duggan, chancellor of the Archdiocese of Baltimore; James H. Moynihan of Incarnation Church, Minneapolis; Vincent J. Balmat, former chancellor of the Diocese of Cleveland; Walter J. Leach, vice-chancellor of the Archdiocese of Boston; Reverends Bartholomew F. Fair, custodian of the collections of the American Catholic Historical Society of Philadelphia; Leo J. Brust, of the Archdiocese of Milwaukee; Jeremiah J. Brennan, archivist of the Archdiocese of New York; Friedrich Fröhling, S.A.C., secretary general of the St. Raphaelsverein, Hamburg; Willibald Mathäser, O.S.B., of the archives of the Ludwig Missionsverein, Munich; Peter Schupp, S.A.C., of the Pallottine mother house, Limberg; Joseph I. Malloy, C.S.P., of the Paulist Fathers; the Sisters of St. Agnes, of the Leo House, New York; Ernst Grandpré, of the Stone House, Limburg; Cyril Echele, of the Central Verein, St. Louis; and Karl Becker, of the Caritasverband, Freiburg im Breisgau.

For hospitality and personal help, Benedictine confreres are to be thanked at the Collegio di Sant' Anselmo, Rome, and at the Abbeys of St. Paul Outside the Walls, St. Jerome, Einsiedeln, Metten, St. Boniface in Munich, Beuron, Maria Laach, Neuburg, Mont César, Downside, Buckfast, St. Mary's in Newark, St. Anselm's Priory in Washington, and at St. Anselm's and St. Benedict's Churches in New York. Professor John J. Meng, of Hunter College, and Reverend Peter Leo Johnson, of St. Francis Seminary, gave valuable suggestions. To the staffs of the Mullen Library of the Catholic University of America, the Library of Congress, the New York Public Library, the libraries of the Universities of Freiburg, Heidelberg, Munich, Rome, Louvain, and the Vatican the author is also sincerely grateful. Among many friends who contributed of their knowledge and time in assisting the author in one way or another were Kurt Kreisler, Philip Des Marais, John Simons, Reverends Casimir Peterson, S.S., Patrick H. Ahern, Damian Baker, O.S.B., Kenneth Wimsatt, O.S.B., Gunther Rolfson, O.S.B., Ralph Eisenzimmer, O.S.B., Callistus Edie, O.S.B., and Miss Emma Messner.

Reverends Aloysius K. Ziegler and Henry J. Browne, of the Catholic University of America, critically read the entire manuscript, generously offered many valuable suggestions, and balanced the author's every conclusion. Special thanks are likewise due to the Catholic University of America for granting the author a Penfield Fellowship to enable him to pursue his research in Europe. A most particular debt of gratitude is owed to Reverend John Tracy Ellis, of the Catholic University of America, who took the greatest possible pains in directing this study. Father Ellis' unstinted generosity at every stage of the work proved an unforgettable inspiration. The author also wishes respectfully to record his gratitude toward the memory of the late Right Reverend Alcuin Deutsch, O.S.B., to Right Reverend Baldwin Dworschak, O.S.B., and the community of St. John's Abbey for the opportunity afforded him of ample time free from teaching duties to complete the necessary research. In its original form this work was submitted as a doctoral dissertation at the Catholic University of America.

COLMAN J. BARRY, O.S.B.

St. John's University
Collegeville, Minnesota

Contents

THE CATHOLIC CHURCH AND GERMAN AMERICANS

Chapter I

Background and Beginnings, 1800–1884

The Catholic Church in the United States has been in large measure an immigrant institution. The tide of immigration which brought millions of settlers to American shores created a phenomenon for the Church which was unparalleled in its history. Peoples of different races and nationalities, of distinct traditions and prejudices, came individually or in groups to establish new homes in a strange country. While the founding fathers of the American republic wished that the oppressed of all nations should find freedom and opportunity in America, yet none could have realized the magnitude or the complexity which the fulfillment of their vision was to entail. To make a homogeneous people out of such a vast number, differing in language, customs, and religion, proved to be an experiment never before attempted on so vast a scale. To this experiment the Catholic Church made a major contribution. For over 40 per cent of the immigrants the first bond of union was their common Catholic faith. It may consequently be maintained that the work of Americanizing the foreigner, especially from the Catholic countries of Europe, was accomplished in great part through the Church. This was achieved along with her primary mission of saving souls of the immigrants, and of building a flourishing, closely knit ecclesiastical organization in the new world.

This double task of creating simultaneously a religious and national unity among the immigrants reached a climax during the years between the War between the States and World War I. It centered especially around differing opinions among the two leading immigrant Catholic peoples in the United States — the Irish and the Germans — concerning leadership in the Church, as well as the traditions and customs of religious observance. After a prolonged period of stress and strain it was resolved in the Catholic climate of the Church through the attainment of a gradual understanding of pluralistic, mutual differences, and a compromise of nonessentials in favor of true Christian unity.

German immigration to the United States was given a new impetus following the close of the War between the States. In the first year after peace had been declared, 50,000 German immigrants entered New York harbor alone, and by 1867 the number had risen to over 117,500 new arrivals.[1] The rapid recovery of the North encouraged this movement, especially the industrial and commercial progress of that region. The advancement of world communication at this time also contributed favorably to the movement. In 1866 the first trans-Atlantic cable brought Europe closer to America. Three years later East and West were more closely linked by the completion of the first railroad to the Pacific Coast. This not only opened the central and Pacific Coast regions to settlement and development, but also opened a new and much faster route to the Orient.

But conditions in Germany itself were, perhaps, far more influential in encouraging this new and larger tide of German emigration to the United States. The movement toward unification of the German peoples entailed in its wake political conditions which drove many citizens from their homeland. Jealousy and antagonism between Prussia and Austria, the two leaders of the Germanic Confederation established after the Congress of Vienna, came to a head in 1866 in the Seven Weeks' War from which Prussia emerged the victor. As a result, Austria was excluded from the Confederation and Prussia took the leadership in the formation of a new North German Confederation in 1867, which opened the way for the formation of the German Empire four years later. Militarism became the keynote of the new regime, especially with the rise to power of Count Otto von Bismarck as chancellor, and taxes for the upkeep of this military state became increasingly heavier. When the German and French empires clashed in 1870, universal military service was instigated and established as a

[1] "Einige Gründe der Massenauswanderung aus Deutschland," *SRB,* I (Jan., 1886), p. 3. For German emigration statistics, cf. *Statistische Jahrbücher für das deutsche Reich,* 1880–1939–1940; E. V. Philipowitsch, *Auswanderung und Auswanderungspolitik in Deutschland. LII Schriften des Vereins für Socialpolitik* (Leipzig, 1892); Johannes Müller, *Deutsche Bevölkerungsstatistik* (Jena, 1926); Roderich Sternberg and Hermann Schubnell, "Die räumliche Bevölkerungsbewegung," *Grundriss der Bevölkerungswissenschaft* (Stuttgart, 1950), pp. 462–528. On American immigration statistics, cf. *A Century of Population Growth, 1790–1900* (Washington, 1909); *Emigration Conditions in Europe,* Vol. IV of *Reports of the United States Immigration Commission* (Washington, 1911); *Statistical Review of Immigration, 1820–1910*; *Distribution of Immigrants, 1850–1900,* Vol. III of *Reports of the United States Immigration Commission* (Washington, 1911).

permanent policy in Germany. With the decisive victory of Prussia and the establishment of the German Empire in 1871, Germany was politically unified, and the iron control of north German statism extended throughout the country.

A further motive for German emigration was the economic conditions resulting from this new order. Many people, unable to find work in Germany and feed their families, left for the United States in the hope of bettering their conditions. Eighty per cent of the German population at this time was composed of small landowners or farm hands, domestic hand workers and small shop owners. As the new German government directed the change to a military-industrial society the small farmer found his market prices decreasing steadily in competition with the large and more scientifically managed farm units. On the other hand, the small hand worker had the choice of becoming a factory hand or of being crowded out by large industries. Thus both the farm hand and the independent artisan saw their only hope of self-sufficiency and independence in emigration.

Catholics made up a large section of these German people who turned their backs on a society that had sacrificed life and material prosperity for national honor. (See Tables I and II, which cover the nineteenth century and include totals for immigrants from European countries by decades, as well as totals for Catholic immigrants from the same countries.)[2] But more important than these factors for the Catholics of Germany was the *Kulturkampf*.[3] This religious persecution was waged in an attempt to suppress all religious differences in the twenty-six confederated states of Germany. It reached its peak in the May Laws of 1873, which practically annulled papal jurisdiction over German Catholics, abolished religious orders, and fined and deposed resisting German bishops. But the Catholics of the Rhine provinces, Bavaria, and Prussian Poland combined under the leadership of Ludwig Windthorst, who directed his famous campaign by "passive resist-

[2] These tables were compiled on the basis of United States Government immigration publications and the findings of Gerald Shaughnessy, *Has the Immigrant Kept the Faith* (New York, 1925).

[3] *Webster's New International Dictionary* (Springfield, 1941), p. 1377, defines *Kulturkampf:* "A name originating with Virchow (1821–1902), given to a struggle between the Roman Catholic Church and the German government, chiefly over the latter's efforts to control educational and ecclesiastical appointments in the interests of the political policy of centralization. The struggle began with the passage by the Prussian Diet in May, 1873, of the so-called May Laws or Falk Laws aiming at the regulation of the clergy. Opposition eventually compelled the government to change its policy, and from 1880 to 1887 laws virtually nullifying the May Laws were enacted."

TABLE I. IMMIGRATION FROM EUROPEAN COUNTRIES

Decade Ended	*Total Immigration*	*Net Immigration*	*Net Catholic Immigration*
1830	143,439	121,925	54,000
1840	599,125	509,255	240,220
1850	1,713,251	1,456,263	700,777
1860	2,598,214	2,208,000	985,157
1870	2,314,824	1,800,000	741,340
1880	2,812,191	1,190,000	604,000
1890	5,246,613	3,600,000	1,250,000
1900	3,844,420	2,538,000	1,225,000
1910	8,795,386	4,696,000	2,316,000
1920	5,735,811	2,000,000	1,202,000
Total	33,803,274	20,119,443	9,318,494

TABLE II. NET CATHOLIC IMMIGRATION FROM MAJOR EUROPEAN COUNTRIES

Decade Ended	*Austria-Hungary*	*Switzerland*	*Germany*	*Ireland*	*Italy*	*France*	*Great Britain*	*Spain and Portugal*
1830		961	2,197	35,356	316	5,736	641	2,006
1840		1,435	38,876	144,545	1,725	33,867	1,927	2,261
1850	535	1,382	110,831	530,890	1,431	25,000	6,809	1,691
1860		13,989	244,887	602,000	7,061	58,414	5,977	5,150 2,500
1870	31,000	9,000	210,000	371,000	6,000	14,400	6,500	900
1880	46,000	8,800	175,000	180,000	27,000	4,000	11,000	2,000 4,000
1890	134,000	10,500	400,000	300,000	130,000	15,000	23,000	1,000 8,000
1900	232,000	10,000	105,000	40,000	390,000	4,000	5,000	1,800 14,000
1910	553,000	10,000	36,500	10,000	802,000	26,000	10,130	14,000 30,000
1920	239,000	7,000	10,000	70,000	275,000	18,000	5,500	27,000 16,000
Total	1,235,535	73,067	1,333,291	2,383,791	1,640,533	204,417	76,484	132,308

ance" in the Prussian Chamber of Deputies and the Reichstag of the new empire.[4] The Catholic Church in Germany then experienced one of its most glorious hours, highlighted by such noble ecclesiastics as Wilhelm von Ketteler, of Mainz; Mieceslaus Ledochowski, of Gnesen-Posen; Matthias Eberhardt, of Treves; Paulus Melchers, of Cologne; and such splendid Catholic laymen as Hermann von Mallinckrodt, Peter and August Reichensperger, Burkhard von Schorlemer-Alst.

[4] Charles Poulet, O.S.B., and Sidney A. Raemers, *A History of the Catholic Church* (St. Louis, 1937), pp. 404–413, 454–461.

Nonetheless, many priests and nuns were forced to flee, and their plight, in turn, brought a large number of German spiritual leaders to America. Many of the common people among Germany's Catholics, wearied by the liberal campaign of vilification in newspapers, and the constant pressure against their faith by their political masters, also turned their eyes toward foreign lands. In 1883 an agent of the St. Raphaelsverein in Hamburg asked a Catholic tenant from the Rhineland why he and his family were emigrating to the United States. His answer was indicative of the thoughts of thousands of others:

> My landlord gave us free lodging and 23–30 pfennig a day for wages. For this my whole family had to labor on Sundays as well as weekdays. We were obliged to do our own chores during free hours and on Sunday afternoons. If we asked permission to go to Church on Sunday, then the man abused us . . . every time and said: "You won't always need to be running after the priest if you find yourselves in the alms house." And so I am going to America. My acquaintances write from there that they have such good conditions, and on Sundays as many as wish to may go to Church. My children shall not imitate my slavery.[5]

Catholics made up an average of over 35 per cent of the total German immigration to the United States during the years after the War between the States. They totaled around 700,000 in number from 1865 to 1900,[6] and became the largest Catholic immigrant group arriving in the States. Between 1830–1870 Irish immigrants had come in the largest numbers, up to 50 per cent above the German totals. But by 1865 the Germans had equaled the Irish influx and, from 1870–1890, the Germans led the field until Italian immigration began in earnest in the last decade of the century and thence continued as the dominant immigrant movement in the Church of the United States for many years (see Table II).

Germans who came after 1865 generally settled in the same regions as earlier German immigrants. As in the eighteenth and early nineteenth centuries German settlers had chosen land best suited for farming, so in the last half of the nineteenth century they selected agricultural areas, which in time became known as "the German belt." This zone lay between the northern boundaries of Massachusetts and of Maryland, spread westward through the Ohio river basin to the Great Lakes and out into the prairie states beyond the Mississippi river. Germans settled in the Mohawk Valley, eastern Pennsylvania, all along the shores of the Ohio and the Great Lakes, and down the Mississippi to

[5] *SRB,* I (Jan., 1886), p. 7.
[6] Cf. Shaughnessy, *op. cit., passim.*

New Orleans. In the triangle embracing Cincinnati, Milwaukee, and St. Louis, the German population was especially dense.[7]

On his homestead and in the city the German settler enjoyed an excellent reputation among his neighbors for industry, thrift, and dependability. Many states, companies, and agents offered special concessions to attract German immigrants. They were, for the most part, with the exception of liberals and socialists who came in the late 1840's and 1850's, a conservative force in the community. They seldom became a burden upon the neighborhood, were better educated on the average than other immigrant groups, orderly, law abiding, and of good moral character. Frank H. Mason, American Consul-General at Berlin, reported to Washington: "The general character and peculiarities which distinguish the average German emigrant are so well known as to require no elaborate description. They have long been recognized as among the most valuable elements that our country has derived from any foreign source during the past half century"[8]; while Oscar Bock wrote from the United States Consulate in Nuremberg:

> The Bavarians are, much more than the North Germans, accustomed to a very modest mode of living. They can all read and write, are good natured, and, in my opinion, their diligence and ability can only add to the general prosperity of the United States. They may be considered desirable immigrants. Those presenting themselves at the steamship offices here are mostly strong, healthy persons, with habits of cleanliness, which they derived from their service in the army. If others appear, they get a warning from the agents not to risk emigration. Beggars or bad individuals do not register here for emigration.[9]

Catholic German immigrants were concerned in great part not only with their material well-being in the new world, but primarily with their spiritual life. This may be deduced from the fact that among

[7] Albert B. Faust, *The German Element in the United States* (New York, 1927), II, p. 581. Many Germans also remained in the larger metropolitan areas. The ten American cities with largest German populations were: New York, Chicago, Philadelphia, St. Louis, Milwaukee, Cleveland, Cincinnati, Buffalo, San Francisco, and Baltimore. Close behind in totals were Detroit, Newark, Pittsburgh, Jersey City, Rochester, St. Paul, Louisville, Toledo, Allegheny, Hoboken, Boston, New Orleans, Indianapolis, Syracuse, Minneapolis, and Dayton.

[8] *Special Consular Reports,* Vol. XXVII of Department of Commerce and Labor Bureau of Statistics (Washington, 1903), Nov. 2, 1903, p. 39.

[9] *Ibid.,* Oct. 19, 1903, p. 46. For treatments of the German immigrant in American life, cf. Carl Wittke, *We Who Built America* (New York, 1940), pp. 187–262; *Katholisches Deutschtum in den Vereinigten Staaten von Amerika,* ed. George Timpe, S.A.C. (Freiburg i. Br., 1937); Rachel Davis-Dubois and Emma Schweppe, *The Germans in American Life* (New York, 1936).

their first interests was the erection of a church and a school. Fresh from Germany and feeling isolated because of their language differences, the German Catholics in the United States from the outset insisted that separate churches were an absolute necessity for themselves. The German Catholics settled together in colonies whenever possible, often by their own choice, more often under the direction of a zealous German priest or missionary. They desired to have churches of their own in which their traditional religious observances and customs would be carried out, where they could hear sermons in their mother tongue, go to confession as they had learned to confess from early childhood, and take an active part in parish life through their beloved societies. They wanted the order and discipline of parish life as they had known it before coming to the United States.[10] To their English-speaking neighbors this attachment to the customs of their fatherland by the Germans was often misunderstood. But since the Irish and English Catholics had no language problem of their own, the German immigrants felt their new coreligionists could not properly understand the close bond which

[10] Reverend Friedrich Fröhling, S.A.C., present director of the St. Raphaelsverein with headquarters in Hamburg, in an interview with the author stated that German Catholic emigrants were always characterized by a special attachment to their native region, their diocese, their own parish. This was especially true of the German Catholic farmer who, along with craft laborers, made up the large majority of German Catholic emigrants after 1865. Reverend Albert Hammenstede, O.S.B., former prior of Maria Laach, also emphasized this deep love of the German fatherland, which meant an attachment for living as the emigrant had lived in Germany. The love of God and the love of the fatherland were mystically united, and had been deepened by Protestant and liberal attacks throughout the century which protested that German Catholics could not be true Germans because they were Catholics. The German emigrant to the United States had been brought up, he stated, on the tradition that "there is no better or higher culture than German, and the practice of religion by a German must be the best of the world." German priests understood this, and knew that many of the German emigrants felt that if they could not practice their faith in the German way when they came to America, then they would not practice their faith at all. This was why the mother tongue was stressed, the *vereins* encouraged, and the traditions fostered. All were kept together by the mother tongue. Furthermore, the German was accustomed to authority, and when he came to a strange land the only real authority for him naturally was German authority.

Reverend Willibald Mathäser, O.S.B., archivist of the Ludwig Missionsverein in Munich, confirmed these two statements. Loss of language meant loss of faith and traditions, as ample documentation evidenced. The German did not claim that German was the language of his faith, but that it was his best means for keeping the faith. He employed an analogy between the German emigrant and a farm boy who left the country: on his farm he had his traditions; in the city he found a new environment with people not living together in the community spirit he was accustomed to. In the United States, likewise, the German, alone in a new environment, was constantly tempted to move into the liberal or Protestant German circles if he could not enjoy a Catholic German milieu.

existed in the German soul between the practice of his faith and these traditional customs which were deeply rooted in the centuries-old Catholic culture of the German fatherland.[11]

During the nineteenth century the German spiritual leaders in the United States were insistent upon these special provisions because they had witnessed immigrants turning to non-Catholic churches, especially Lutheran, where they felt more at home because they could hear their mother tongue spoken. Editors of the German American press, liberals and freethinkers of the *Achtundvierziger* type, as well as influential German societies were all leading a concerted campaign to preserve the German language and German culture in the new world. German Catholics, both in Germany and the United States who were judged to be hyphenated Germans because of their allegiance to Rome, realized they would be open to cynical attack if they should diminish their efforts to preserve *das Deutschtum* in the new world. And many of the common people among the German Catholics, timid and homesick in a new environment, would be easy prey to such charges.[12]

For these reasons leading German Catholic missionaries spoke out for the preservation of German culture, customs, and language under the slogan of "Language Saves Faith." Father Francis X. Weninger, the famed Jesuit missionary among German immigrants on the frontier, defended this position strongly, and attributed the phrase to Bishop John Martin Henni, of Milwaukee. Bishop Joseph Nepomucene Neumann, of Philadelphia, also insisted that adoption of the English

[11] The Belgian provincial of the Redemptorists summed up this same position on his return from the United States when he said: "The erection of new missions for German Catholics becomes more urgent and pressing each day. German immigration will increase each day, yes, considerably every month and every week. Thus the problem is for the Germans to preserve German, and this can only come about if they are snatched from the pernicious influence of American morals and habits of life through religious unity under the direction of German priests. Unfortunately, experience teaches only too well that where there is no German priest, the German parents preserve only very poorly those good civil and religious qualities which, in a more pious German fatherland, they sucked in with their mothers' milk. The children in every respect are lost, and soon, without Catholic German services and schools, they necessarily succumb to the American spirit . . ." (*ALMV,* Friedrich von Held to Director of Ludwig Missionsverein, Munich, Nov. 3, 1845).

[12] Reverend Joseph Prost, C.Ss.R., answered such charges and raised the effort to preserve the German language to a much higher motive: "We are apostles to bring the people to Christ . . . not to maintain or implant a nationality or to spread a language. . . . How laughable it is, therefore, for the German farmers and laborers to wish to establish a Deutschtum in America" ("Geschichte," *Wuest, Suppl. I,* p. 228). Cf. also Emmet H. Rothan, O.F.M., *The German Catholic Immigrant in the United States* (*1830–1860*) (Washington, 1946), p. 150, and Carl F. Wittke, *Refugees of Revolution* (Philadelphia, 1952), *passim,* for a thorough treatment of the German Forty-Eighters.

language and conformity to the American way of life would have to be a slow process for the German immigrant. The German language was necessary, he contended, during the years of transition, and failure to realize this always contributed to the loss of souls.[13] King Ludwig I of Bavaria, patron of the missions and benefactor of the German Catholics in the United States, advised the first group of German school sisters sent out through his munificence in June, 1847: "I shall not forget you, but stay German, German! Do not become English." In June, 1850, he again wrote to the Ursuline nuns in St. Louis when he forwarded 10,000 gulden for their new convent: "I am very, very anxious that only Germans enter the convent as sisters, and that the instruction should be only in German, both to be perpetual."[14] The Bavarian monarch advanced these warnings because he wanted a constant supply of German religious leaders to be prepared for the incoming German immigrants. Sarah Worthington King Peter, outstanding convert and lay apostle in the American Church, commented on this tendency of the German Catholics in the United States to her friend Abbot Bernard Smith, consultor to the Congregation of the Propaganda Fide at Rome:

> The Germans among us avowedly desire to keep their people apart from Americans, with a view the more surely to separate them from Protestants and infidels — and this necessarily excludes the hope of many conversions. . . . I have observed in Cincinnati the same thing. Our Catholics seem to forget their duties toward unbelievers, and to shut themselves up within themselves. It is my only hope, by means of the religious houses, which by the favour of God, I hope to aid in planting there, that candid Protestants will be won by the good examples and conversations of our religious, and that conversions to the truth may follow. After all that our people try to hope and claim, it is lamentable that we have so *very few* conversions from Protestantism; and I must think that much of this failure is owing to the mistaken ideas of our Catholics.[15]

But German Catholic leaders had consistently held this position from the days of the pioneer settlements in the American colonies.

[13] Weninger to Ludwig Missionsverein, *AVG,* XXVI (1858), pp. 283–301; Neumann to Leopoldinen Stiftung, May 4, 1841, *BLS,* XVI (1842), p. 86.

[14] K. Winkler, "König Ludwig I von Bayern und die deutschen Katholiken in Nordamerika," *Historisch-politische Blätter für das katholische Deutschland,* CLXIX (1922), p. 706.

[15] *AASPOW,* Peter to Smith, Vienna, Nov. 26, 1857. Mrs. Peter was in Austria at that time appealing for money and sisters for a convent in Cincinnati.

Two Jesuit fathers, Theodore Schneider and Wilhelm Wappeler, came to Pennsylvania as early as 1741 to care for the growing number of German Catholics who desired to use their native language, especially for devotions and confession. These two missionaries, enlisted by their confreres of the English province to care for settlers whom the English-speaking members could not assist, were the first of a long line of noble priests who ministered to the spiritual needs of the small German colonies and isolated settlers of Pennsylvania, New Jersey, and New York.[16] These people were visited for the most part by itinerant priests, while centers were established whenever possible, such as those at Goshenhoppen and Conewago, from which the missionaries could extend their labors. But the first national or racial church in the country came about as the result of fractional difficulties in St. Mary's Parish in Philadelphia, spurred on by two German Capuchin brothers, Fathers John and Peter Heilbron. In 1788 Father John Carroll, the Prefect Apostolic of the United States, gave permission for the establishment of a new national parish at Holy Trinity Church, since the feeling in Philadelphia was that German Catholics ought to form a congregation of their own, in which the language and customs of the fatherland would be maintained and where their children could be instructed in the tongue of their own people.[17] In 1808 the German Catholics of New York likewise addressed a petition for a German pastor to Carroll, who in the meantime had become the first bishop of the United States.[18]

It is not within the scope of this work to trace the development of German Catholic settlements, churches, priests, and apostolic labors in the United States.[19] The purpose here is to study German na-

[16] The sacrifices and accomplishments of these early German priests cannot be discussed in detail here. For a general treatment of this effort, cf. Lambert Schrott, O.S.B., *Pioneer German Catholics in the American Colonies (1734–1784)* (New York, 1933), pp. 1–139.

[17] Peter Guilday, *The Life and Times of John Carroll, Archbishop of Baltimore (1735–1815)* (New York, 1922), I, p. 292.

[18] *HRS,* II (1901), pp. 194–195. Cf. also Guilday, *ibid.,* II, p. 628.

[19] Cf. Schrott, *op. cit.;* Guilday, *op. cit.;* Rothan, *op. cit.;* Timpe, *op. cit.;* Beda Kleinschmidt, O.F.M., *Das Auslanddeutschtum in Übersee und Die katholische Missionsbewegung mit besonderer Berücksichtigung von Deutschland u. Österreich von 1875 bis 1925* (Münster, 1926); Mathew Pekari, "The German Catholics in the United States of America," *RACHS,* XXX (1925), pp. 305–358; Theodore Roemer, O.F.M.Cap., *The Catholic Church in the United States* (St. Louis, 1950); Karl Algermissen, *Der deutsch-amerikanische Katholik* (Cincinnati, 1887); John N. Enzlberger, *Schematismus der katholischen Geistlichkeit deutscher Zunge in den Vereinigten Staaten Amerikas* (Milwaukee, 1892); Beda Kleinschmidt, O.F.M., *Auslanddeutschtum und Kirche,* 2 vols. (Münster, 1930).

tional consciousness in its relation to American Catholicism and as it existed among German Catholics in the United States. This consciousness was present in the first immigrants and continued throughout the whole period of immigration. As the German immigrants migrated into the West, following the opening of the Northwest Territory for settlement in the early 1830's, the need of priests and religious of the German tongue became more pressing. The early American bishops were, indeed, conscious of the problem and continually strove to supply the demands of the German immigrants, but their efforts to find such pastors in Germany itself were never entirely adequate. Spiritual and material aid for the German immigrant did come from the two well-known German mission societies founded to advance the missionary activities of the Church in North America. The *Leopoldinen Stiftung,* established in Austria in 1829, and the *Ludwig Missionsverein,* founded in 1838 in Bavaria through their charitable and financial support of the American missions, exercised a major influence on the growth of Catholicism in the new world.[20] The burden of multiplying churches was heavy, however, and the American bishops often used funds from these societies, as well as from the older Lyons Society for the Propagation of the Faith, for non-German or non-French projects. The erection of churches, rectories, or charitable institutions, as well as the financing of seminaries and schools were some of the needs into which these funds were channeled. Consequently, many struggling German priests and missionaries did not feel that they were receiving as much money from the donations of German Catholics as it was the latter's intention to direct to their fellow German Catholics abroad. Complaints reached the headquarters of these missionary organizations, and an especially strong remonstrance was carried to Munich in 1840 by Reverend Benedict Bayer of Baltimore. This memorial, termed a "diatribe" by one historian of the movement, was an open attack upon the administration of the Church in North America, with special emphasis placed upon the undue influence of the Irish Catholics in matters of Church leadership.[21] A much more temperate, albeit critical, report was made to

[20] Benjamin J. Blied, *Austrian Aid to American Catholics, 1830–1860* (Milwaukee, 1944); Theodore Roemer, O.F.M.Cap., *The Leopoldine Foundation and the Church in the United States (1829–1839)* (New York, 1933), and *Ten Decades of Alms* (St. Louis, 1942).

[21] Severus Brandus, *Die katholische-irische-bischöfliche Administration in Nordamerika* (Philadelphia, 1840). A critical analysis of this work with European reaction to it was furnished by James E. Corenan, a New York student at the Urban College in Rome (*AANY,* Corenan to "Dear and Respected Friend," Rome, Mar. 22, 1841).

the Ludwig Missionsverein in 1845 by the provincial of the Belgian Province of the Redemptorists after a visitation tour of the society's American stations:

> In all these stations in which the Congregation, through its priests, cares for souls and establishes schools, no other source of financial assistance can be relied on except from the societies of the faith in Europe and from the Catholics of those missions. The American bishops have to provide so much for the American and Irish Catholics under their care that they can do nothing, even with the best of will, for the German missions. They consequently abandon the building of churches and schools as well as the support of religious exercises for the Germans. . . .[22]

As a result of these charges, Canon Joseph Salzbacher, of Vienna, came to the United States in 1842 as a representative of the Leopoldine Foundation to investigate conditions and to learn the truth of these accusations. In his interesting travelogue-report he reached the conclusion that only a continuous supply of priests acquainted with the

---

Cf. also, for further complaints of this kind, Willibald Mathäser, O.S.B., *Der Ludwig Missionsverein in der Zeit König Ludwig I von Bayern* (Munich, 1939), pp. 162–167; John M. Lenhart, O.F.M.Cap., "German Aid to the Church in America," *CBSJ,* XXXII (Nov., 1929), pp. 237–238.

[22] *ALMV,* Friedrich von Held, C.Ss.R., to Director of Ludwig Missionsverein, Munich, Nov. 3, 1845. Abbot Boniface Wimmer also discussed this subject with the former abbot of Metten, then Archbishop of Munich: "If German Catholics are to be helped with the German mission donations, this can only be achieved if the German religious orders and German bishops in America receive them. The English do not do one thing for them; they always spend it first of all for the English and leave the Germans to provide for themselves. . . . A recognized and worthy Prelate, the Archbishop of Baltimore [Francis P. Kenrick], when he was Bishop of Philadelphia, had neglected the German Catholics to such an extent that the present good Bishop Neumann (Redemptorist) who followed him in Philadelphia, had to act primarily on this problem" (*AAMe,* Wimmer to Gregory Scherr, St. Vincent's Abbey, Mar. 10, 1856).

Bishop William G. McCloskey, of Louisville, answered criticism on this score by protesting to his Roman agent, Abbot Bernard Smith. He had been accused by "Dutch and Belgian influence" of spending too much money on the property of the seminary and of squandering mission money. McCloskey considered this report which had been made against him to Rome to be a hampering of a bishop's governance of his diocese and, if it continued, a bishop, he thought, could do "little real good." He stated that if Rome continued to listen to unworthy priests, that bishops would be led "to take little interest in that financial support of the Holy Father which they formerly felt so deeply interested in . . . " (*AASPOW,* McCloskey to Smith, Louisville, Mar. 30, 1876).

But not all Germans agreed with these complaints. Joseph Prost, C.Ss.R., wrote to Brother Friedrich Roeder, C.Ss.R., from Pucheim on June 10, 1875, and stated that the contributions received from German Catholics in the United States were only a small percentage of what was needed for the Church there, and that the American bishops were not the only cause of this situation (Wuest, *Suppl. I,* pp. 230–231).

German tongue offered the real solution to German Catholic needs in America.[23] There was no doubt that the immigrant Germans needed help, and more help than they were receiving. But for some German Catholic priests and laity to attempt to direct the American bishops in the distribution of the missionary funds and in the organization of their parishes was understandably regarded as unwarranted interference, and there were some bishops who associated such procedure with the trusteeism difficulties which were disturbing the American Church at that time.

Reports and petitions of this kind continued to flow to Rome and Germany throughout this whole period. It was natural, of course, for German Catholics to complain of what they considered their grievances to their homeland and to the central authority of the Church. Many of them did not look upon the United States with the same nationalistic viewpoint as the native-born Americans, while at the same time they often felt that the English-speaking bishops did not fully understand their particular needs. As early as 1836 the Germans of Philadelphia wrote to the Leopoldine Foundation in Vienna, asking that the directors use their good offices in Rome to obtain a German bishop for them.[24] Baron Heinrich von Schröter, a promoter of St. Mary's German colony in Pennsylvania, also appealed to King Ludwig I of Bavaria to use his influence to persuade the Holy See to appoint German-speaking bishops in areas which the German immigrants were populating. He suggested John N. Neumann, C.Ss.R., of Pittsburgh, Nicholas Balleis, O.S.B., of Newark, and Bishop John Laurent, the exiled Vicar Apostolic of Luxembourg, as qualified to govern dioceses in which Germans were settling. Ludwig sent this memorial to his ambassador at the Vatican, Graf von Spaur, who was a personal friend of Pius IX and an organizer of a group of papal Zouaves. Spaur

[23] Joseph Salzbacher, *Meine Reise nach Nord-Amerika im Jahre 1842* (Vienna, 1845). In the preface of his report Salzbacher stated that he had not gone to the United States with a desire to control or direct the expenditures of the Leopoldine Foundation, and that there was no reason to doubt that the subsidies granted to the German Catholic missions were conscientiously and properly applied. The annual reports to the Leopoldine Society furnished minute details concerning the American dioceses and these reports were published.

Reaction was not slow in coming from some of the American bishops in regard to this visitation tour of Canon Salzbacher. "It is really humiliating to be subjected to such espionage," said Bishop Richard Miles, O.P., to Bishop John B. Purcell, of Cincinnati (Miles to Purcell, Pittsburgh, May 7, 1842, as quoted from the Archives of the University of Notre Dame, Purcell Papers, in Michael J. Curley, C.Ss.R., *Venerable John Neumann, C.Ss.R.* [Washington, 1952], p. 433). Cf. also Michael O'Connor to Purcell, Pittsburgh, Feb. 13, 1844, as quoted in Curley, C.Ss.R., *ibid.*

[24] Peter Guilday, *The Life and Times of John England,* 2 vols. (New York, 1927), II, p. 383.

gave a digest of the memorandum to the Propaganda in 1846, spoke emphatically to the Holy Father of the lack of interest shown by the Irish bishops in America for the condition and needs of the five million German Catholics, and recommended the appointment of German bishops.[25] During the following year the Propaganda advised Archbishop Eccleston, of Baltimore, that when names of candidates were submitted for vacant sees in which a large portion of foreign-born Catholics lived, attention should be given to the fact that those proposed have a knowledge of the language of the foreign-born element in the region. This was particularly necessary in a diocese containing a large German population.[26] When Neumann, Bohemian-born provincial of the Redemptorists in the United States, was appointed fourth bishop of Philadelphia in 1852, and became the first German-speaking bishop to rule an eastern diocese, Graf von Spaur informed his sovereign that he had been instrumental in great part in securing this appointment.[27] Actually, Bishop Kenrick had recommended to Rome that his successor be one acquainted with the German language, since so large a population in the Diocese of Philadelphia spoke that tongue, and with that in mind he had nominated Neumann in first place as his successor.[28]

Father Boniface Wimmer, O.S.B., founder of the American Benedictines, also called on his close friend Ludwig I of Bavaria, not only for funds, but also for his support and influence at Rome when Wimmer found himself at variance with Bishop Michael O'Connor, of Pittsburgh. Wimmer had come to the United States with the excellent and farsighted project of starting an abbey which would provide seminary training in the new world for candidates who could

[25] Willibald Mathäser, O.S.B., "König Ludwig I von Bayern als Förderer des Deutschtums und des Katholizismus in Nordamerika," *Gelbe Hefte,* I (1924–1925), pp. 616–649.

[26] Donald Schearer, O.F.M.Cap., *Pontificia Americana* (Washington, 1933), p. 248.

[27] Mathäser, *op. cit.,* p. 633.

[28] Cf. John Berger, *Leben und Wirken des hochwürdigen Johannes Nep. Neumann* (New York, 1883), and Michael Curley, C.Ss.R., *op. cit.*

Bishops James Van de Velde, of Chicago, and John Hughes, of New York, had both considered it necessary that the next Bishop of Philadelphia should speak German (*AAB,* 29-C-2, Van de Velde to Kenrick, Chicago, Oct. 27, 1851; *AAB,* 29-H-9, Hughes to Kenrick, New York, Oct. 27, 1851). Bishop Ignatius Reynolds recommended Neumann to Kenrick because of his personal piety (*AAB,* 31-G-2, Charleston, Oct. 28, 1851). Bishop O'Connor wrote to Bishop Purcell after he learned of Neumann's appointment: "I do not know how to explain this decision except that in their anxiety to impose some German blood into the episcopal body they laid hold of the first German name that presented itself . . ." (O'Connor to Purcell, Pittsburgh, Mar. 3, 1852, as quoted from the Archives of the University of Notre Dame, Purcell Papers, in Curley, C.Ss.R., *op. cit.,* pp. 434–436).

speak the German language and care for the German immigrants. The King and the Ludwig Missionsverein were behind the project, and Wimmer felt confident that his foundation would in time be self-sufficient through the efforts of his new Benedictine family. Although accepted into the Diocese of Pittsburgh by Bishop O'Connor, Wimmer soon found himself in difficulties with the Ordinary over the important question of whether or not his new foundation could be canonically erected with the status of an abbey and with himself as an independent abbot. There were further differences over a brewery, which in the old Bavarian tradition he maintained at Indiana, Pennsylvania, under the management of a relative. Wimmer proceeded to enlist the support and protection of his patron, the King of Bavaria, who, in turn, ordered his ambassador at the Holy See to intervene with the Pope and the Propaganda in favor of the abbot's petitions. Wimmer informed Ludwig:

> The ecclesiastical condition of America is still in its infancy; the will of the bishop is the only law. The bishops can expect no support from the state against refractory priests, and much less from the Protestant, or better, atheistic state and the democratic inclination of its citizens. Accordingly they are naturally mistrustful of every attempt to deprive them more or less of their unrestricted power, or to insure oneself against their arbitrariness.[29]

Upon learning this, Ludwig instructed Spaur to appeal to the Holy See for the status of an independent abbey for St. Vincent's in Westmoreland County, Pennsylvania, and for permission to operate a brewery near the abbey. In a short time independence was granted and permission to brew and distribute beer wholesale was given to Abbot Wimmer. However, Wimmer discontinued the business a short time before this decision was communicated to him.[30]

Bishop O'Connor, a representative of the Irish temperance movement, of which Father Theobald Matthew, O.F.M.Cap., was the leading figure, stood out against this German custom of operating a brewery, since he felt American churchmen should abstain from alcoholic beverages and, too, because he feared the bigotry of Protestant temperance fanatics. The details of this incident cannot be entered into here, but it is interesting to note how the conflict in the new world of Irish and German customs was beginning to take shape. O'Connor

[29] Wimmer to Ludwig I, St. Vincent's, Feb. 13, 1852, in Mathäser, *op. cit.*, p. 34.

[30] *Ibid.* Pages 34–44, 61 contain a complete documentation of this transaction. At Metten abbey in Bavaria, from which Wimmer had come, a brewery had been in operation since 1322, and it was difficult for Germans to understand why Americans should become excited over what was to them such a commonplace practice.

forwarded a protest to his Roman agent, Abbot Smith, with instructions to present his position to the Propaganda. In this early letter there was found for the first time an attitude which would grow with the years and would be repeated many times in the conflicts which lay ahead:

> I hope that instead of a mitre and a crozier he [Wimmer] will get what he wants much more badly, a good lesson on the shameful manner in which he has acted, disregarding all I could say to him. It would be a poor encouragement for us to stand out for defending the liberty of the Church from secular power to find out that we are only exposed by our independence to the interference of foreign secular powers. If seculars are to dabble in our affairs it would be much better for us to have to deal with those we know and whom we could call to an account, than to have German princes dabbling in our affairs. If I were but to apply to our Secretary of State he would be only too glad to be asked to write a letter to Rome that would rebut this gentleman's interference; but thank God I would scorn to do so no matter how it ends. But all may not do as I will, and if these things are repeated we may find the most deplorable results. If the Sacred Congregation has any regard for our welfare it will give these people a lesson that will teach them to mind their own business and let us alone. If you communicate this sentiment, take care not to give it the shape of anything like a threat. It would be the farthest thing from my thoughts so to speak or think. I only mention it with the melancholy conviction of the consequences of such proceedings. One of the many evidences of the imprudence of these German priests and religious is their dragging in these people into our disputes whereas the knowledge they *ought* to have of the country should convince them that nothing is more disastrous.[31]

A few years later a strong difference of opinion arose within the Redemptorist community in the United States, which up to that time had particularly devoted its efforts to the care of German Catholics. One of the American-born Redemptorists, Reverend Isaac Hecker, a convert from Congregationalism, along with four of his native-born brethren who were also converts, had for some years been giving missions in English-speaking parishes. Gradually they came to feel that they had a special vocation to work for the conversion of American Protestants and other non-Catholics. The five priests ultimately withdrew from the Redemptorist congregation, and Hecker in 1858 ob-

[31] *AASPOW,* O'Connor to Smith, Pittsburgh, Aug. 13, 1851. For Wimmer's opinion on this subject, cf. Archives of the Archdiocese of Dubuque, Wimmer to Loras, Latrobe, Feb. 8, 1856.

tained permission from Piux IX to found a new religious society. Thus was born the Missionary Society of St. Paul the Apostle, the first American foundation of a new religious body for men. Father Hecker and his companions, through preaching, publishing, and the use of techniques aimed at attracting native-born Americans, strove to present the Church as a universal body which had definite characteristics consonant with American democratic ideals rather than merely a European body. This break from an old and tried religious congregation as well as a new presentation of the truths of the faith brought much criticism upon the Paulist community and upon its founder in particular, differences which years later would culminate in charges and countercharges of "Americanism." Many Germans and conservative non-German Catholics found the Paulist program tinged with a false type of native Americanism. However, prelates like John Hughes, Michael O'Connor, and later James Cardinal Gibbons, Archbishops John Ireland and John Keane, as well as Bishop Denis O'Connell did not feel that the Paulists' Americanism was anything improper, but rather that it was the type of sentiment which any American ought to have for his country. O'Connor informed Smith of his regret that Hecker had withdrawn from the Redemptorists, since, as he said, he would have preferred if the Redemptorists had adapted themselves to the usages of the country rather than have a precedent established for founding American houses as such. He told the Abbot:

> I think they [Redemptorists] are too tenacious of their German habits, etc. But I think also that the whole order should move together in any contemplated change. Gradually they would be as complete as would be desirable, and as all persons and things in this country Americanize themselves sooner or later it is a question of time when they will do it also. There may be some evils in it happening too soon, but then another in it being deferred too long. They have already done much and in spite of themselves they are moving. A German religious order will be the last to yield. The Jesuits have gone on the way, the Dominicans and so with the rest, but an American section or separation on any basis would, I think, be injurious to both parties. . . . You will be glad to hear that the Benedictines are getting on well. They, too, had their German notions to contend with. They are far from being over them, but they, too, are getting Americanized. . . .[32]

Such were some of the *ante-bellum* characteristics and general

[32] *AASPOW,* O'Connor to Smith, Pittsburgh, Dec. 6, 1857. Archbishop Francis P. Kenrick also wrote to Smith concerning the Paulists: "I consider the movement as unfortunate, originating in a feeling rather national than religious, or in zeal not according to knowledge. As they are all converts, I am not without apprehensions for the result" (*AASPOW,* Baltimore, Sept. 10, 1858).

developments among the German Catholic immigrants to the United States. After the War between the States, and stimulated by the cheap land opened through the Homestead Act of 1862, new and larger waves of German Catholic settlers entered the country. The problem of spiritual care for these people was broadened and multiplied across the country, and differences over procedure and techniques which had developed in earlier years were now accentuated in practically every diocese of the country. The American bishops were fully occupied in finding priests who could care for the German immigrant as he needed to be cared for, speak to him in his mother tongue, and guard him from becoming a victim of indifference, carelessness, or unbelief. They were never able to meet this need adequately, and consequently the attitude developed of becoming concerned over the immigrant's spiritual care only after he had settled in a diocese. This was a major difficulty and deficiency in the American Church up to the 1880's. No organizations had been set up at any of the provincial or plenary councils of the American bishops to care for the immigrant from the time he arrived on American shores, to assist him in transit, and to direct him to areas where priests of his own nationality were already settled. Neither had any effort been made to unite on an even broader scale with episcopal bodies in the European countries of origin through which the immigrant could be protected and assisted from the time he left his home parish, in the port of departure, on the sea, at the landing docks and through the new country until he reached a Catholic colony or settlement. No Catholic German society in the United States during the years preceding the War between the States had undertaken the task of providing and caring for the newcomers, nor had the hierarchy of Germany through its many organizations given support to such a program. Perhaps, the lack of such systematic efforts was beyond the realm of possibility due to pioneer conditions and to the religious persecution in Germany. But, in any case, its absence would serve to explain in great part the losses to the faith which the Church suffered in the immigrant movements during this period.

In the early 1860's a young German Catholic layman of extraordinary vision and apostolic charity took up the cause of the European emigrant, and for some sixty years thereafter he devoted the greater part of his time and fortune to aiding and directing "the poorest of the poor," as he called them.[33] The efforts and program of this man,

[33] Peter Paul Cahensly, *Der St. Raphaelsverein zum Schutze katholischer deutscher Auswanderer* [*Caritas-Schriften,* 5 Heft] (Freiburg i. Br., 1900), p. 1.

Simon Peter Paul Cahensly, merchant of Limburg an der Lahn, became the focus for the nationality question in the United States which culminated in the so-called "Cahenslyism" struggle of the 1890's.

Cahensly's father, Peter Paul Cahensly, Sr., had been born in Seth, Switzerland, and had inherited the old "Stone House" in Limburg an der Lahn in the Rhine province of Nassau. The elder Cahensly moved to Germany and established a wholesale grocery business in the Limburg Stone House. After the death of his first wife the elder Cahensly married a daughter of the large merchant family of Stöck from Bernkastel. Four children were born to this second marriage, of which Peter Paul, born on October 28, 1838, was the youngest. When he was seven years old his father died, and his mother took over the growing business of the firm until Peter Paul was old enough to take charge. He was given a good education to prepare him for commerce, first in the Volksschule and Realschule in Limburg, and later at the Realgymnasium in Trier. His mother sent him to the large firm of Karl Martens in Cologne as an apprentice and, after traveling widely in Germany, Switzerland, France, England, Belgium, and Holland, he went to the port of Le Havre in 1861 as a journeyman to study freight and shipping techniques. After the death of his mother, in 1868, Cahensly inherited the thriving grocery business of P. P. Cahensly in Limburg. He built up an excellent business in low-priced Brazilian coffee, developed his own roasting process for Java and Ceylon coffee, expanded petroleum consumption, and increased the volume of sales in imported merchandise.[34]

Cahensly entered the field of immigrant welfare as a result of his activity in the St. Vincent de Paul Society. At the time when he was studying his trade at Le Havre he became conscious of the thousands of German emigrants who were embarking from this port to North and South America. After long, tiresome low-class rail journeys these people arrived exhausted and frightened in a strange port town with-

[34] Wilhelm Nathem, S.A.C., *Peter Paul Cahensly. Ein Gedenkblatt zu seinem 100. Geburtstag. 1838* 28. October *1938* (Hamburg, 1938); *Zur Erinnerung an das 40. jähr. Geschäftsjubiläum zugleich an den 70. Geburtstag des Herrn Kommerzienrat Peter Paul Cahensly in Limburg a. d. Lahn* (Limburg, 1908); Hans Pabst, "Grosskaufmann und Laienapostel," *Limburger Bistums-Kalendar* (Limburg, 1951), pp. 75–77; "Peter Paul Cahensly," *DGH* (Freiburg i. Br., 1933), II, p. 1726; "Peter Paul Cahensly," *LfThK* (Freiburg i. Br.), II, p. 691; *Zur Geschichte des "Steinernen Hauses" zu Limburg a. d. Lahn. Besitzer: Kommerzienrat Peter Paul Cahensly* (Limburg, 1908); "Peter Paul Cahensly," *Das katholische Deutschland. Biograph-bibliographisches Lexikon* (Augsburg, 1933), I, p. 300; "Peter Paul Cahensly," *C,* XLIII (Dec., 1930), pp. 364–367; *ADCV,* George Timpe, S.A.C., "Der St. Raphaelsverein. Sein Gründer und seine Arbeit."

out knowledge of the French language. Cahensly watched them fall into the hands of unscrupulous agents, landlords, and innkeepers who tricked and robbed them in many cases of both their spiritual and material goods. The religious care of these unfortunate people had been almost entirely neglected until Archbishop Henri Bonnechose, of Rouen, answered the appeal of the St. Vincent de Paul Society for a German-speaking priest to provide for the German emigrants, and in 1859 appointed Father Lambert Rethmann of the Picpus Fathers as missionary in Le Havre. Cahensly became acquainted with Rethmann and soon a close friendship evolved. Cahensly helped the priest hang signs in the lodging houses directing the emigrants to Father Rethmann, announcements of church services in his small chapel, and instructions on how to prepare for the dangerous trip that lay ahead. Along with other volunteers, Cahensly visited the emigrants on the morning before they sailed and invited them to attend the final religious exercises which Father Rethmann always held just before the boats departed.[35]

Cahensly boarded many ships in the harbor of Le Harve and obtained firsthand knowledge of the miserable conditions in which the emigrants were forced to travel. At this time the majority still crossed the ocean in sailing ships which carried cotton or tobacco between Philadelphia, New Orleans, New York, and Le Havre. The emigrants went steerage, and Cahensly could scarcely believe the conditions he discovered.[36] Available space was utilized to the last corner, while boards were placed in double rows to be used as beds. Each of these beds was assigned to two, and more often to three, people. As Cahensly later described the scene:

> A person could climb only with the greatest difficulty to the upper and rear places because of the small amount of free space which was usually barricaded with boxes and trunks. Besides, there was almost total darkness, and I became frightened when I thought that in these small rooms of indescribable disorder and darkness hundreds of people should spend weeks and months. By dividing the sleeping places, difference of sex was almost absolutely neglected, and it is not surprising

[35] Peter Paul Cahensly, *Der Auswandererapostel Pater Lambert Rethmann und die Anfänge des St. Raphaels-Vereins* (Freiburg i. Br., 1909). Cahensly gave a description of the missionary techniques and solitary labors of Rethmann, as well as his many differences with ship companies, agents, and landlords. The history of the "Chapelle Allemande" and Rethmann's work are also detailed in "Havre in den Jahren 1853–1907," *SRB,* XXII (Oct., 1907), pp. 523–526.

[36] Peter Paul Cahensly, *Der St. Raphaelsverein,* p. 3.

that under such circumstances immoral situations developed which defy description.[37]

Aroused by what he had seen, Cahensly began to collect data on the conditions prevalent on these ships. Reverend John C. Albrinck, German pastor of SS. Peter and Paul Church at Reading in the Archdiocese of Cincinnati, wrote of conditions on the *Deutschland:*

> There was not the least interest shown in the separation of the sexes in the steerage, and all lay across one another like cabbage and turnips. Sexual intercourse was unlimited. The common people not only acted in this way with depraved women, but more than once I saw the women's room of the steerage become around eleven o'clock the sleeping quarters for women with the higher officers. It was a real Sodoma.[38]

Leopold Kist summed up his impressions of steerage deck conditions aboard the *Saxonia* to New York in August of 1868:

> The steerage is a pig stall, a robber's den, a cut-throat and poisonous abyss. Truly, I wonder that this swimming hell is not regularly swallowed up by the deep.[39]

Even after he had returned to Limburg and found himself preoccupied with the management of his new firm, Cahensly was still fired by his zeal to better the conditions of the emigrant. With the encouragement of Father Rethmann, of officers of the St. Vincent de Paul Society in Paris, Brussels, and Antwerp, and especially with the assistance of Mother Francesca Schervier, superior general of the Franciscan Sisters in Aachen, who had experienced the ocean crossing while visiting her convents in the United States, Cahensly resolved to lay the case before the yearly assembly of the Catholic societies of Germany. Rethmann accompanied him to the 1865 assembly at Trier. These *Katholikentage* were characteristic German Catholic public demonstrations by both clergy and laity for the protection of their religious interests and for "the establishment of the correct approach to cultural, civic, economic, and social life."[40] They were begun in 1848 at Mainz

[37] *ADL,* Peter Paul Cahensly, "Kirchliche Fürsorge für die Auswanderer." Cahensly sent this thirty-two page summary along with a nine-page letter to all members of the German hierarchy.

[38] *ADL,* Albrinck to Cahensly, Reading, Mar. 6, 1866. Reverend L. W. Brandt, pastor of St. Mary's Church, Madison, Indiana, informed Cahensly: "If I were asked to give a description of the immorality it would stand your hair on end" (*ADL,* Brandt to Cahensly, Madison, Mar. 1, 1869).

[39] *ADL,* Peter Paul Cahensly, "Kirchliche Fürsorge für die Auswanderer," p. 15; cf. also *Der St. Raphaelsverein,* pp. 4–7, for further testimonies.

[40] *DGH,* "Katholikentag," VI (Freiburg i. Br., 1933), pp. 1192–1193.

and Limburg under the title of *Pius Verein,* in honor of Pius IX, and gradually their activities were broadened in an effort to win a wider influence for Catholicism in the liberal atmosphere and to defend the Church during the persecution of the Prussian state. Cahensly hoped to win support for his plan to aid the emigrant and in this way to obtain official endorsement from the Church in Germany.[41]

The Trier assembly was receptive to Cahensly's suggestions due to the recent sinking of the American steamship *William Nelson* on June 25, 1865, which had carried 438 emigrants to their death. Cahensly presented a lengthy defense and explanation of his program, the first of his many speeches for this cause. He stated that he wished to broaden former discussions of the problem to the area of action, described in detail the conditions he had seen, and pointed out that the state and the shipowners had no interest in the protection of these people, since they both judged them only from the standpoint of freight. Protestants, he said, met the emigrants at foreign ports and proselytized them. There was constant danger of the emigrants losing their faith and morals due to the frightful conditions in passage. He proceeded then to state his first figures on the number of Catholic emigrants to America who had lost their faith and, quoting the president of the St. Vincent de Paul Society in Paris, Monsieur Baudon, he asserted that "scarcely half after a generation have kept their faith." He asked the Catholics of Germany not to allow their youth and their good work to be thus dissipated, but to put a halt to conditions which, as an insult to what he called "our Christian century," had continued for years. He then said:

> Without doubt the German emigrants to America have a providential importance; to serve as a means of spreading and strengthening Christianity and civilization in this important body of people. Shall this effort even before the work is done be rendered useless? It is our duty to do what lies in our power for our separated German children whom

[41] The ground had been prepared to a degree for Cahensly by four earlier reports submitted to the General Assembly on the emigrant situation. The Katholischer Verein in Rottenburg made a report at the second *Katholikentag* at Breslau in 1849; a Le Havre shipowner by the name of Marzion had submitted an exposé at the 1858 and again at the 1864 assemblies in Cologne and Würzburg; Reverend Modeste, of the *Josephsverein* in Aachen, had also spoken in 1864 on the needs of Germans abroad, and he had declared that the *Josephsverein* should work for Germans in Paris, London, and Le Havre who were selling their own and their children's faith to proselytizers for bread.

Cf. also Lorenz Werthmann, "Die Auswandererfürsorge der deutschen Katholiken seit 1865," *Das Auswandererproblem VII. Fünfzig Jahre Raphaelsvereins* (Freiburg i. Br., 1919).

we cannot keep in the fatherland, and to give them the best possible preparation and equipment for keeping their faith by establishing large missions which they may find in the new hemisphere.[42]

Cahensly and Rethmann presented three resolutions at Trier as first steps in a solution of the problem: first, an address should be made to the governments of the four ports of Bremen, Hamburg, Antwerp, and Le Havre to separate the sexes. Second, the St. Joseph's Society of Aachen should establish a mission in Hamburg to begin this work. Then, as a third point, and this was noteworthy in the light of what followed, Cahensly moved for international co-operation and unity of action in emigrant care by suggesting that the Belgian Catholics be asked to co-operate with them in this matter, as well as that the St. Vincent de Paul Society in New York be approached to care for the incoming settlers, in order to counsel and direct them to districts where other Catholics already lived. He then concluded:

> The war in America is over, and a million lives have been given as an offering. But it almost appears that, as men hurry from the old world, they can repair this loss, since from all sections emigrants swarm to the ports.[43]

The general session unanimously accepted these three resolutions, and the project was launched.

From the very outset Cahensly assumed leadership by contacting port and governmental authorities and by giving regular reports to the deputy chairman of the General Assembly of German Catholic Societies at the *Katholikentage.* He soon discovered that the work would entail many difficulties which would postpone the desired reform. The French Minister of Interior answered his address through the French embassy in Berlin to the effect that laws were already in operation for the separation of the sexes. Cahensly and Rethmann knew that in reality the law was not being observed, so they proceeded to contact the French Commissariate for Emigrants in Le Havre and asked for explanations of existing evils. This board advised that German emigrant contracts be co-ordinated with French forms so that the directive could be generally enforced to the effect that only persons of the same sex should sleep in the same beds, and that agents could not place people who came together by chance on the same contract. It was at least a beginning. In Bremen, likewise, the Senate in-

[42] *Verhandlungen der 17. General-Versammlung der katholischen Vereine Deutschlands in Trier, 10–14. September 1865* (Trier, 1865), p. 85.

[43] *Ibid.*, p. 90. For the complete text of Cahensly's speech, cf. pp. 79–90.

formed Cahensly that a new emigration law of July 9, 1866, would take care of the bad conditions. However, he traveled personally to Hamburg and Bremen, examined all the ships anchored in those harbors, and then went directly to the *bürgermeister* of Bremen and the head of the Emigration Commission with his findings. They were astounded at his discoveries and did everything in their power to remedy the situation.[44]

Neither the Belgian Catholics nor the St. Vincent de Paul Society in New York answered the communications that had been sent to them. After the Trier meeting Father Rethmann made a trip to the United States in 1866 to study conditions at firsthand, traveling both ways on emigrant ships. His observations strengthened the two men in their determination to publicize the abuses. Rethmann had been hopeful that a bill which had passed the House of Representatives at Washington, and which had incorporated ample provisions for the protection of morality on board the ships, would become law. But, unfortunately, it was defeated in the senate on a technicality.[45]

In 1867 the Catholic societies of Germany and Austria convened in a joint *Katholikentag* at Innsbruck. Dr. James Marx, of Trier, deputy chairman of the German General Assembly who had been working with Cahensly, distributed a printed report on advances made in emigration matters, and then proposed two motions on the floor which were accepted. The first was that the convention should prepare an address to the Archbishop of New York, asking him to give every possible protection to the immigrants landing in New York and direct them to neighborhoods where they could practice their faith. This motion was presented as a result of the visit of Archbishop Purcell, of Cincinnati, to Le Havre where, accompanied by Father Rethmann, he was shown the conditions of emigrants setting out for America. But Archbishop John McCloskey, of New York, did not answer this petition.[46] The second resolution was that a compressed

[44] Adolph Stadtländer, retired passenger director of the Nord Deutscher Lloyd, Bremen, declared in an interview with the author that Cahensly was the greatest single influence in improving conditions on board ships during these times. Whenever Cahensly discovered anything wrong, he went directly to the officials and demanded changes. Whatever Cahensly desired, Stadtländer declared, he always endeavored to fulfill because he felt he was doing this work solely for the welfare of the poor emigrants.

[45] *Der St. Raphaelsverein,* p. 12.

[46] *Verhandlungen der 18. General-Versammlung der katholischen Vereine Deutschlands in Innsbruck, 9–12. September 1867* (Innsbruck, 1867), p. 167. Reverend Max Gärtner, American missionary, wrote to the assembly and invited German Catholics to come to Wisconsin. He stated that more and more Germans were settling between

report should be drawn up of the dangers to which the emigrants were submitted on the sea and upon landing in New York, and that remedies should be listed so that the people could protect themselves.

It was agreed that, since no answer was received from McCloskey, the German Roman Catholic Central Verein of the United States of America should be approached to take an interest in the immigrant problem.[47] The Central Verein, at its thirteenth General Assembly in May, 1868, had already evidenced its interest in the immigration problem at American ports by electing Joseph Kölble, since 1842 a member of the first German Catholic Verein in New York, as agent of the Central Verein for the port of New York, and Christian Bitter, of Baltimore, as its agent for that port. These gentlemen were to be salaried and were to meet all incoming ships, care for the German Catholic immigrants, help and support them where necessary, and send them to their destination as soon as possible so that swindlers could not take advantage of them. Cards were sent to various Catholic societies in Germany to be distributed to emigrants for the United States which they could wear in their hats and thus be recognized by the two agents on the docks of New York and Baltimore. Within a few months, in 1868–1869, over 16,000 Catholic immigrants made American landings with these cards.[48]

Kölble came to Germany in 1868 to report to the Bamberg ***Katholikentag*** on American work for the German emigrant. It was at this same meeting of the General Assembly that the first major step was taken in the creation of an independent organization for the protec-

---

Lake Michigan and the Mississippi River. He quoted the Yankees as saying to the Germans: "Go ahead and dry it up." Gärtner further stated that the Germans had already half-won the area (cf. p. 55).

[47] The Catholic Central Verein of America was established by German Catholics of the United States in Baltimore on April 15, 1855, to unite all the Catholic benevolent societies; to aid the German immigrant to withstand the attack of his radical non-Catholic brethren in the United States; to safeguard the faith and rights of German Catholics from the Know-Nothing movement; and to sponsor a broad, social action program of spiritual perfection, charity, reform of society, credit unions, guilds, rights of workers, and social studies courses. Cf. Rothan, *op. cit.,* pp. 110–111; Mary Liguori Brophy, *The Social Thought of the German Roman Catholic Central Verein* (Washington, 1941); Alfred Steckel, "German Roman Catholic Central Society of the United States of America," *RACHS,* VI (1895), pp. 252–265; *ACV, The Central Verein: History Aim and Scope* (St. Louis, n.d.).

[48] *ALH,* L. Schwenninger, "St. Raphaels Verein — Röm-kath. Central-Verein Einwanderung. Zur Orientirung." Cf. also *Verhandlungen der 19. General-Versammlung der katholischen Vereine Deutschlands in Bamberg, 31. August–3. September 1868* (Bamberg, 1868): Central Verein to General Assembly, New York, Aug. 5, 1868, p. 218. Rev. Anthony B. Schwenniger, editor of the Cincinnati *Wahrheitsfreund,* was president of this new Committee of Immigration of the Central Verein and one of the Catholic leaders in this work in the United States.

tion of the Catholic emigrant. A committee was set up, entitled *Das Comité zum Schutze katholischer Auswanderer,* with a membership composed of Karl Fürst von und zu Isenburg-Birstein; Reverend Ibach, of Limburg; Graf Felix von Loë; Joseph Lingens, lawyer of Aachen; Canon Prisac, of Aachen, and Peter Paul Cahensly, merchant of Limburg.

Cahensly had reason for optimism at this point. A German society was in operation, an Immigration Committee was functioning in the United States, and both were under central organizations in their respective countries. For the next four years, from 1868–1871, he and his companions worked within the framework of the committee to better the cause of the German Catholic emigrant. All the bishops of Germany were notified of the existence of the new committee, and Bitter addressed each of them, describing the work begun in America, asking them to instruct their priests to send emigrants to either Kölble or himself, and assuring them that the German Catholics in the United States desired to help those coming from the homeland.[49] In 1869 the committee suggested to the American Central Verein that a church be established in New York City near the debarkation point, but the American group did not have funds for such a project. Cahensly continued to work for better emigration conditions at Bremen and Hamburg, while supporting strongly the pending negotiations between the North German Confederation and the United States for regulation of emigration matters. Nothing came of this discussion, since the Bismarck regime was most reluctant to take any position on emigration. Officially, Bismarck's government was, and remained throughout the whole period, positively opposed to emigration from the fatherland since it would drain man power and weaken the national potential. Emigration was unpatriotic, and any assistance to the emigrant was looked upon as co-operation to the detriment of the nation. Thus Cahensly's work did not receive official favor, and later positive action was taken against him by Bismarck and his ministers. It was decreed that emigrants could not hold public office if they returned to Germany. Furthermore, no public law was enacted for regulating emigrating until 1897, which, accordingly, came too late to be of assistance to the greater part of the German emigrants. Private agencies were forced to work alone and under the heavy frown of the state.[50]

[49] *ADL,* Bitter to Bishop Peter Blum, Baltimore, Sept. 1, 1868.

[50] *ADCV,* Lorenz Werthmann, "Der Raphaelsverein aus der Geschichte der kathol. Auswandererfürsorge."

At the Düsseldorf *Katholikentag* in 1869 Cahensly stated that the committee had proved to be only a temporary expedient and, with a view to securing more funds and a permanent source of income, he recommended that the General Assembly of Catholic Societies establish a new society under the patronage of St. Raphael for the protection of the emigrant. In this way the work would be fully incorporated in the official union of Catholic societies, and have a regular source of income from collections taken up throughout the dioceses of Germany. Cahensly's motion was tabled, however, because the assembly felt that religious brotherhoods and fraternities were multiplying too fast. It was recommended instead that the committee address itself to the St. Joseph's Society in Aachen.[51] But this society refused to assume the work for the emigrants on the ground that such activity was outside the scope of its statutes.

The next two years proved to be the ebb tide in Cahensly's endeavors for the Catholic emigrant. He and the committee convened four times a year, but in between sessions they carried on their efforts by correspondence to arouse interest for the cause among bishops and public officials. Their supply of money, however, was dependent on voluntary donations of which the committee itself provided the greater part. One of their members, Canon Prisac, died; the 1870 *Katholikentag* was not held because of the bitter *Kulturkampf;* and no extension of the work was foreseeable.[52]

It was at this point that Cahensly was able to win the support and interest of Paulus Melchers, Archbishop of Cologne. The Archbishop offered to approach Bismarck himself concerning the sad conditions aboard emigrant ships and promised to support the movement among his colleagues in the hierarchy. Karl Klein, later Bishop of Limburg, also supported the committee, and by the time of the 1871 *Katholikentag* in Mainz the stage was set for the organization of the St. Raphaelsverein.

After Cahensly had made his report at Mainz, a new resolution was introduced on the floor and carried unanimously that a society

[51] *Verhandlungen der 20. General-Versammlung der katholischen Vereine Deutschlands in Düsseldorf, 31. August–3. September 1869* (Düsseldorf, 1869), pp. 194–202. In his plea for a church at Castle Garden in New York City, Cahensly stated his first figure on losses in the American Church when he asserted that there were three million Catholics less than there should be.

[52] The secretary's minutes supply a complete account of the efforts of the committee during these years. Cf. Theodore Meynberg, *Berichterstattung des "Comite zum Schutze katholischer Auswanderer" über seine bisherige Wirksamkeit* (Luxembourg, 1875).

be formed for the welfare of the Catholic emigrant under the protection of St. Raphael the Archangel, patron of travelers. This society, *Der St. Raphaelsverein zum Schutze katholischer deutscher Auswanderer,* had a three-point program: to help the emigrant in every possible way before he sailed, during his voyage, and at the ports of debarkation. The central committee of the society consisted of Karl Fürst von und zu Isenburg-Birstein, as president; Graf Felix von Loë, as vice-president; Peter Paul Cahensly, as secretary; and a membership of Joseph Albers, merchant of Münster; Graf Ludwig von Arco-Zinneberg, in Munich; Joseph Lingens, a lawyer of Aachen; and Graf Praschma zu Falkenberg, in Silesia.[53] It was a distinguished array of German Catholic lay leadership. Prince Isenburg-Birstein was named because of the prestige of his noble name, although it was Cahensly who carried the burden of responsibility and work. Because of his modesty and what he considered to be his lack of higher education he could not be prevailed upon to assume the presidency of his organization until he was forced to do so upon the death of Isenburg-Birstein in 1899. No clerics were included in the general committee because of the existing opposition to the Church meddling in public affairs, by the regime, although the hierarchy of Germany now solidly backed the work and were official sponsors of the society.

The first task of the St. Raphaelsverein was to obtain financial support from the dioceses whose bishops had agreed to sponsor the organization at the *Katholikentag.* Statutes were drawn up for the new society and submitted to all the bishops for their approval, after which diocesan and parish representatives were appointed.[54] Local units were organized on a voluntary basis, membership being limited to from seven to twelve persons. Contributing members paid 10M ($2.50) each year and honorary members donated 6–24M ($1.50–$6.00) a year. Several of the bishops also organized annual collections in their dioceses for the society's work.[55] The St. Raphaelsverein then directed its efforts to the accomplishment of its first aim, namely,

[53] *Verhandlungen der 21. General-Versammlung der katholischen Vereine Deutschlands in Mainz, 10–14. September 1871* (Mainz, 1871), pp. 187–192, 318.

[54] *ADCV, Satzung des St. Raphaelsverein.* Twelve statutes were drawn up under the headings of purpose, membership, organization, officers, subscriptions, meetings, and privileges.

[55] A thorough study could be made on a diocesan level from the large archival collections in Cahensly's own Diocese of Limburg on the efforts of the St. Raphaelsverein to win support from the ordinaries of Limburg during these years, through such items as pleas for money, pamphlets printed, reports of national committee meetings, letters of Limburg diocesan priests on the progress of Raphaelsverein activity in their respective parishes, and the like.

the erection of spiritual missions or stations at the major European ports to care for both the moral and material needs of the emigrants. Cahensly prepared a brochure on their needs, the first of many pamphlets and broadsides the society would print in the coming years,[56] and these were distributed widely throughout Germany. Because money and members were still wanting, Cahensly appealed to the General of the Society of Jesus in Rome to assume the responsibility of supplying priests for these projected emigration missions at the ports.[57] The Jesuits being unable to accept the assignment at the time, the central committee decided in 1872 to appoint a layman, Theodore Meynberg, as its first *Vertrauensmann,* or agent, and to station him at Hamburg. He was given a fixed income, worked under the supervision of the diocesan priests in Hamburg, and devoted all his time and energy to the service of the emigrants arriving there. The next year Archbishop Melchers of Cologne again came to the aid of the society and gave one of his priests, Reverend Schlösser, for the second mission at Bremen. In quick succession agents were then appointed for Antwerp, Rotterdam, Liverpool, and London. Along with Father Rethmann at Le Havre, who had affiliated himself with the society as one of its agents, the St. Raphaelsverein could count seven agents in the field within six years.

The success of the movement was so notable that the Prussian regime eyed the whole enterprise with increasing suspicion and hostility. A campaign of propaganda against the society was begun in the liberal and antireligious press, obstacles were placed in the way of St. Raphaelsverein agents whenever possible, and their activity was branded as unpatriotic. Liberal magazines accused them of ferreting out the Catholics from Germany and aiding them to emigrate from Germany in order to avoid the effects of the *Kulturkampf.*[58] Joseph Lingens, the only member of the committee who was also a member of the Reichstag at that time, frequently complained on the floor of the imperial diet against this unjust treatment, but to no avail. The Prussian Central Intelligence Bureau for Emigration consistently opposed all social betterment of emigration conditions.[59]

[56] Peter Paul Cahensly, *Kirchliche Fürsorge für die Auswanderer* (Soest, 1873). This excellent tract has been translated by John Lenhart, O.F.M.Cap., and appears with commentary in "Historical Studies and Notes," *Social Justice Review,* XLIII (Feb., 1951), pp. 348–352; XLIII (Mar., 1951), pp. 383–386.

[57] *ADL,* Cahensly to Bishop Peter Blum, Limburg an der Lahn, Mar. 9, 1872.

[58] *ADCV, Beiträge zur Auswandererfrage und Rechenschaftsbericht* (Vienna, 1907), p. 22.

[59] The persecution of the St. Raphaelsverein by the state came to a head for the first time in October, 1881, when two editors at Heinsberg and Geilenkirchen were

Although standing entirely alone in this new field of endeavor, the St. Raphaelsverein did not lose heart. Instead, using one of the Prussians' maxims that a strong offense constitutes the best defense, Cahensly and the central committee presented a detailed petition to Bismarck himself, reminding him that the chancellery had stated in answer to their petition of 1868 that it was willing to take up a discussion of international legislation for betterment of emigration conditions. They pointed out that President Ulysses S. Grant, of the United States, had asked for better immigration legislation and a redress of abuses on board ships in his message to the American Congress of May 14, 1872.[60] The committee further informed Bismarck that they felt Germany should assume this leadership, and that the prestige of the empire among the nations of the world demanded that these abuses be abolished. Germans by custom seldom complained about conditions, were unacquainted with the English law and language, and consequently were not able to express themselves before English or American courts. This was the reason why the government received so few complaints, not because the evils did not exist. The

---

prosecuted by the state on the grounds that they published advertisements of the St. Raphaelsverein and, accordingly, broke a law of May 7, 1853, which forbade promotion of emigration. At the publishing house of the Bachem family in Cologne, members of the Center Party and friends of Cahensly, as well as publishers of the noted Catholic paper, *Kölnische Volkszeitung,* a number of cards for the emigrants were also confiscated. The case was thrown out of court by the district court at Cologne on the grounds of no cause, on January 23, 1883. The appeal board sustained the decision on March 27, 1883. Then the attorney general appealed to the imperial court in Aachen where the original decision was again sustained because the society, according to its statutes, had only the aim of caring for the religious and moral needs of the emigrant at its mission stations. On another appeal to the supreme court of final appeal in Berlin decision was given again in favor of the St. Raphaelsverein. But the supreme court decided that any proffered information about emigration was punishable, and accordingly the society was forced to discontinue all publication of the names of its agents. This greatly impaired the effectiveness of its work.

On February 3, 1883, one of the liberal representatives, Doctor Kapp, for many years a member of the Board of Directors of the Deutsche Gesellschaft in New York, defended Cahensly and his work, complained against this persecution by the regime, stated he knew Kölble in New York and praised his work. Cf. *ADCV, Rechenschafts-Bericht 1882,* p. 1; also Tarsicius Wolf, "Der St. Raphaelsverein."

[60] President Grant, in his Message of December 6, 1869 (*Messages of the Presidents,* James D. Richardson, ed. [New York, 1897], IX, pp. 4120–4121), also had asked for uniform international regulations for construction of ships, quantity and quality of food, medical care, rules of ventilation, protection of females, and establishment of tribunals in several countries to enforce these regulations. Here he mentioned the earlier proposition of the North German Confederation for an emigrant convention between the United States and Germany which had not materialized because it was felt it should include other countries on an international basis. But Grant's appeal, like the earlier German appeal, did not materialize.

last obligation of the German Reich to the departing emigrant, the committee courageously stated, was to care for them as for people who had fulfilled their duties as citizens.[61]

Needless to say, this petition went unheard. The committee, nevertheless, remained undaunted; more than that, they proceeded to address a second petition to President Grant, and a third to every member of the hierarchy of the Church in the United States.[62] This was certainly broad-visioned procedure for the St. Raphaelsverein in its second year of existence. These two documents, along with the above-mentioned petition to Bismarck, proved to be pathfinding efforts in the field of emigrant and immigrant social welfare. The hierarchy of the United States was asked to support the St. Raphaelsverein petition to President Grant, and to assume leadership themselves in accomplishing the second and third aims of the program, namely, of protection, both material and moral, for the emigrant on the sea and in the ports of arrival in the new world. But, like the overture to Bismarck and the German government, President Grant's petition was not answered, and to render the silence from across the ocean complete, no recognition or reply was received from any of the members of the American episcopate. The first movement for co-operation between Germany and the United States on this issue had been rejected on all fronts, and thus Cahensly and his committee were forced to fall back upon a far narrower radius than they had at first contemplated.

But work they did. It is unfortunate that a more complete description of their early activities in the major ports of Europe cannot be detailed here. It is a stirring chapter in the history of the Church of the nineteenth century which still remains to be written. The suspicion, prejudice, and chicanery of emigrant agents, lodging proprie-

[61] *ADL,* Petition of the Central Committee, St. Raphaelsverein, to the High Praesidium of the Confederacy of German States Chancellery, Offenbach am Main, Dec. 28, 1872, copy.

[62] *ADL,* Petition of the Central Committee, St. Raphaelsverein, to His Excellency the President of the United States, Mr. Grant, Offenbach am Main, Jan., 1873, copy; Petition of the Central Committee, St. Raphaelsverein, to the Most Reverend Archbishop (Bishop), Offenbach am Main, Mar., 1873, copy. Because of their significance as pioneer Catholic efforts for the international care of emigrants, and also because of their importance in relation to the charges of Cahenslyism in the years ahead, both documents are included in their entirety in Appendixes I (pp. 278–285) and II (pp. 286–288). The assembled German Catholic Societies at Vienna in 1853 had also drafted an appeal to the American hierarchy which was sent in 1854, and which was not answered. Thus the St. Raphael petition of 1873 was the second address from German Catholics to the American hierarchy, but the first overture to both German and American governments, as well as to the American hierarchy.

tors, local police, unscrupulous ticket agents and money changers, as well as representatives of some ship lines against the St. Raphaelsverein agents were incredible. Only gradually did the unselfishness and obvious religious character of the agents make headway against this concerted opposition and win for the St. Raphaelsverein a respected position on the water fronts. The construction of chapels, lodging houses, and express agencies; the creation of a banking and deposit service; the mailing, letter writing, and message distribution; the counselor facilities; and, most important of all, the thousands of religious services, Masses, sacraments, and spiritual solace that were offered to the departing emigrant in his mother tongue — these were but the high lights of a program the effects of which can never be adequately evaluated. It was these activities which justly won for Peter Paul Cahensly, "der kleine Cahensly" as he was called because of his small physical stature, the title of "Father of the Emigrant."

Cahensly, indeed, bore the burden of organization, contact, and control of this ambitious project. He denied himself the joys of family life by remaining unmarried, journeyed to and from the different missions, answered many of the emigrants' letters personally, while all the time directing his personal business which would have been a full-time occupation for most men.[63] He even made a trip incognito by steerage in 1874 to Baltimore and return, the better to acquaint himself with the needs of the emigrant. While contributing his time and what his relatives considered too great a portion of his wealth to emigrant work, Cahensly also entered upon an active political career on local, regional, and national levels. For many years he was an elected member of the town council of Limburg, served in the college of city commissioners of which he was president after 1903, and acted as vice-president of the Limburg chamber of commerce. He was a member of the district assembly and, from 1885 to 1915, served in the Prussian House of Delegates as representative of the election district, first of Montabaur-Wallmerod and later of Limburg. Besides this he was elected to membership in the Reichstag, the Imperial Diet of Germany, in 1898, and served until 1903 as a member of the Center Party, while acting as president of the Nassau election caucus of that party. Cahensly was a personal friend of Windthorst, who often visited at his home in Limburg, and he voted

[63] Cahensly also served on the central committee of the *Katholikentage* and acted for many years as treasurer. He was a member of the board of directors of the *Volksverein* for Catholic Germans; the *Albertus Magnus Verein* for Catholic students; and the *Fürsorgeverein* for discharged convicts.

generally with the left wing of the Center along with his friends Dr. Ernst Lieber, Georg von Hertling, and Felix Porsch. In both the Prussian Landtag and the Reichstag his main interest was to support the Church and to fight the policies of the regime according to the program of the Center.[64] He was not a leader in Center Party activities, but he was always a solid party member.

In his St. Raphaelsverein activity, Cahensly during these years became more and more engrossed in dealings with city and port officials, consuls, and ship captains. He made yearly reports to the *Katholikentage* and strove to spread a knowledge and support of the movement in the Catholic body of Germany. As individual parts of the society's first two aims in its program began to be realized, Cahensly turned his interest to the third point, namely, the care of the emigrant at the port of arrival in the new world. Canada, South America, Australia, and the United States entered more prominently into his plans. At the Bonn *Katholikentag* in 1881 he asserted that one third of all German Catholics lost their faith after arriving in the United States because they settled in areas where there were no German churches and schools. He suggested that the emigrants go to Minnesota, Kansas, Nebraska, and Illinois rather than into the larger cities in the East. In the western states colonies existed for the emigrant, and Cahensly recommended the settlements made by the Benedictine Fathers and the one sponsored by Bishop John Ireland in St. Paul. Little did he dream at the time that his chief American antagonist in future years would be this same Bishop Ireland. His report of 1881 concluded:

> The St. Raphaelsverein embraces the poor emigrant with charity; its agents assist him without charge in all ports on his journey so that he may arrive at his new settlement without peril of body and soul. This is done so our separated countrymen may have a blessed remembrance of the German fatherland, and upon their arrival on the other side of the ocean they may remain true children of the holy Catholic Church. May God dispose it.[65]

Cahensly had reason for concern over the growing emigration movement to the new world, and especially to the United States to which 90 per cent of the Germans migrated. From Hamburg and Bremen

[64] Cf. Lorenz Zach, *50. Jahre Zentrum. Wirtschafts und Socialpolitik im Reichstag 1871–1921* (Berlin, 1921), p. 129; Karl Bachem, *Vorgeschichte, Geschichte und Politik der deutschen Zentrumspartei,* VII (Cologne, 1930), pp. 237, 484.

[65] *Verhandlungen der 28. General-Versammlung der katholischen Vereine Deutschlands in Bonn, 4–8. September 1881* (Bonn, 1881), pp. 221–223.

alone, in the two years 1880–1881, 203,067 emigrants departed, of whom the society's agents cared for 31,705.[66] In order that the German Catholic leaders could obtain a better understanding of conditions in the United States, and especially as they related to German Catholics, J. B. Müller, editor of the German Catholic weekly in Detroit, *Die Stimme der Wahrheit,* was invited to come to Frankfurt to address the general assembly of the 1882 *Katholikentag.*

Müller used the opportunity to present a picture of the American Church to his fellow Catholics in Frankfurt. Since he had been in the United States sixteen years, twelve of which had been spent as editor of a German Catholic paper, he felt competent to give an analysis of conditions. He began with a survey of Catholic life from colonial days and then described German Catholic conditions in particular. One hundred Catholic papers were being published in the United States at that time, he said, of which twenty-eight were German. The only Catholic dailies were four German papers. He emphasized the influence of German societies as the chief characteristic of German Catholic life in the new world; there were a number in every parish, and they were the main means of keeping the emigrants good Catholics, as well as of opposing the Freemasons and liberals who were as strong there as in Europe and who were endeavoring to create a modern humanitarianism in the United States. As for priests, he was proud to report that there were over 300 German-speaking priests, of whom 100 were from Germany itself. The University of Louvain since 1857 had helped the Church by training priests for the American missions in the American College there. Already there were five German bishops in the American hierarchy. He singled out especially the work of St. Vincent's Abbey, "the Monte Cassino of America," as he called it, and its head, Abbot Boniface Wimmer, O.S.B., whom he entitled "the Patriarch of German Catholic America."

The German Catholics in the States were distinguished especially for their generosity and good taste. Müller said:

> The German churches in America are already the most beautiful, evidencing taste and practicality with no overloading. The German cloisters are constructed of stone and are the finest; the German schools, the most practical. The German Catholics have given an eminent service with their schools. While the Catholics of other nationalities, namely those immigrant brothers from the green island, have a strong dislike for schools, the Germans have accomplished a great deal. Bishops must inflict penalties on parents who do not send their children to Catholic

[66] Cahensly, *Der St. Raphaelsverein,* p. 25.

> schools. I know only a few German parishes which do not have a thriving school, because the Germans, whenever a parish is formed, endeavor first to build a school, before they build a church. For they are convinced that, if a school is lacking, the church is only a passing thing, because when the parents pass away the children will no longer desire a church. Without a school children become totally ignorant or, what is worse, unbelievers, Godless, and immoral. In the American state schools there is no religion, and Catholic parents consequently do not send their children there. Because of this the Germans have always been first to erect schools.[67]

It was unfortunate in many ways that such reports as these were made to the Catholic leaders of Germany by a resident of the United States. While it was natural that a German American should be called upon to give them, yet at the same time a decidedly one-sided impression was thus created of the status and efforts of the German Catholics which in future years would be a source of difference between the Germans and their coreligionists of other nationalities in the United States. No mention was made by Müller of American nationality or of the necessity for immigrants to become a part of this new nation. The state was presented as godless if not antireligious, and losses in the Church were pictured in the darkest hues. This report reflected, unfortunately, a typical journalistic summary of the position of the German Catholic press of the United States. If it would have been accepted as only press opinion and nothing more, many exaggerated viewpoints could have been avoided.

In comparison with Müller's report, a much more temperate, balanced, and objective analysis of the Church in the United States was given three years later to the 1885 *Katholikentag* at Münster by Bishop Martin Marty, O.S.B., Vicar Apostolic of the Dakotas. He began with high praise for German Catholic efforts in the United States, called the country a German missionland, and said the progress which the Church had made was chiefly due to German priests, colonies, prayers, and donations. "It will be the glory of the German nation," he said, "if the Catholic Church in the United States flowers and continues to grow." He praised the work of the two major mission societies, pointed out that the major religious orders were German for the most part (Franciscans, Redemptorists, Jesuits, and Benedictines), and had words of praise for the German Catholic schools, press, societies, parishes, and social work. But then the bishop went

[67] *Verhandlungen der 29. General-Versammlung der katholischen Vereine Deutschlands in Frankfurt a. M., 11–14. September 1882* (Frankfurt, 1882), pp. 191–206.

on to point out that the work of the American Church had been chiefly that of two nations, the Germans and the Irish. The Irish came first; they were really a nation of missionaries. As Ireland had Christianized France, Germany, and Italy in the sixth and seventh centuries, with Irish missionary priests occupying several German episcopal sees, so after a glorious resistance during the Protestant Revolt the Irish had passed to the new world as missionaries, with English as their mother tongue. Marty characterized the Irishman in the United States at that early time as firm, generous, industrious, ready to die for his Faith and to resist Protestant attacks on the Church even to the shedding of his blood. He then said:

> But today that is no longer necessary, and the missionary work and growth of the Church in the United States, through the efforts of the Irish, through their colonies, has universally a peaceful nature. They amalgamate easily with the Americans, and the influence which they exercise is always for the welfare of the Church. . . .
>
> In earlier times there existed a species of mistrust from the side of the Irish against the Germans; but since the Germans likewise suffer persecution and maintain their faith, they are accepted by the Irish as peers in the faith.[68]

Mistrust, according to Marty, was entirely gone between the two races, as the unity of the Third Plenary Council of Baltimore evidenced in the address of Irish bishops to the German hierarchy. The Irish were represented as beginning to imitate the German custom of building schools in their parishes. For hundreds of years in Ireland Catholics were not allowed to have schools, and thus the Irish were not accustomed to building them. Children were trained at home, and upon coming to the new world it was easy to send their children to the state schools as their mother tongue had become English. Now, however, they were following the lead of the Germans and the encouragement given on this subject by Pius IX and Leo XIII.

Marty's outlook on Protestants and native Americans was much more favorable. He claimed that there were no more real Protestants

[68] *Verhandlungen der 32 General-Versammlung der katholischen Vereine Deutschlands in Münster i. W., 9–12. September 1885* (Münster i. W., 1885), p. 249. Cf. pp. 245–252 for Marty's speech. Marty also gave his estimate on losses to the Faith in the United States. Of fourteen million who had emigrated since the Revolution, he stated, there were only seven million Catholics to be found. This loss of seven million could be explained by a lack of priests, lack of schools, Freemasons who took away thousands through their efforts and through their pension system. Thousands of emigrants worship the dollar and refuse to support the Church, he continued, "and in America it is no small matter to be a Catholic; it costs money, much money, to satisfy one's obligation as a Catholic."

in the United States; there were only those who were not Catholics. He stated:

> The American is reasonable in his judgments; he is not intolerant; he does not believe that he knows and understands everything; he willingly listens and accepts things from others. . . . The American, because he has freedom, is a lover of order, a friend of law; accordingly he observes that the Catholic Church adheres to principles and has laws which have universal worth. . . .
>
> The American is an empirical man of experience, not of theory. He sees effectiveness, results. If he realizes that the Catholic Church really makes men better, then he will also be a Catholic. . . .[69]

The St. Raphaelsverein was likewise becoming interested at this time in the Italian Catholic emigrants, both those who went to the new world and the many who came north into Germany for seasonal labor. Their plight was equal to, if not worse than, that of the German emigrant. Cahensly determined, therefore, to go to Italy in 1882 and to discuss the needs of the Italian emigrant with leading Catholic social workers. On this trip he made several contacts, particularly in Genoa, but this initial venture to establish an Italian branch of the St. Raphaelsverein failed. Since Leo XIII had granted special indulgences to the society as early as 1878, as well as a plenary indulgence to all Catholic emigrants who performed the necessary conditions on the day of their departure and in case of shipwreck, Cahensly determined to approach the Holy Father and to explain the work they were attempting to accomplish. The Pope received him in special audience, blessed the endeavor, expressed the wish that an Italian branch of the society be established, and recommended that the work become international in character. Giovanni Cardinal Simeoni, prefect of the Congregation of the Propaganda, also received him cordially and seconded the Pope's suggestion that the work be internationalized.

At the Düsseldorf general assembly in 1883, Representative Lingens had moved that a member of the society go to the United States to examine the situation there and to take measures for the protection of the emigrant in the new world. This motion was passed, and arrangements were made for Cahensly to represent the society on a visitation tour. Accordingly, upon the recommendation of the Holy Father, Cahensly left in an attempt to internationalize the St. Raphaelsverein, but only after the *Katholikentag* had authorized the

[69] *Ibid.*

move. This also occurred two years previous to his entrance into national politics as a member of the Prussian Landtag.

There was also an American reason for Cahensly's trip. The working agreement between the agents of the Central Verein and the St. Raphaelsverein had broken down because the former, in its twenty-second general assembly at Cleveland in 1877, had voted to disassociate itself formally from immigrant work. Complaints had been growing from members of the different societies which constituted the Central Verein that the poor people alone were supporting this effort, while the wealthy German Catholics did nothing because they did not belong to the member societies. It was decided that an immigration committee should be established at each of the main ports of the United States and that these member committees, rather than the Central Verein itself, should assume responsibility, collect money, and solicit support from any local societies of the Central Verein which would implement the plan. This decision considerably curtailed the activity of the agents, and soon Joseph Kölble in New York was the only agent in the work. However, he had a scant $500 yearly salary for himself and the work he was trying to do at Castle Garden.[70]

In August, 1883, Cahensly embarked from Bremen for the United States. He found the steerage of the steamer most unsatisfactory as far as accommodation and morals were concerned. Of a total of 1200 passengers, 849 were in steerage with only four crew members assigned to their care. Cahensly traveled incognito and he landed in New York on August 17, where he began at once to examine conditions at Castle Garden and in the immigrant lodging houses. Supplied with a warm letter of introduction from Cardinal Simeoni, he presented himself to Coadjutor Archbishop Michael A. Corrigan, of New York. Cahensly explained the purpose and efforts of the St. Raphaelsverein, and the Archbishop seemed favorably impressed with the project.[71] They agreed to meet again when Cahensly returned from the western states. After meeting the leading German Catholic clergymen of New York and several prominent German Catholic laymen, he moved on through New York State and out across Ohio into Indiana to be present at the twenty-eighth general assembly of the Central Verein at Evansville in September. Cahensly addressed the gathering and urgently requested that the delegates take up col-

[70] *ALH,* Schwenninger, *op. cit.,*

[71] *AANY,* Simeoni to Corrigan, Rome, July 17, 1883. Simeoni also asked Corrigan to introduce Cahensly to other bishops in the United States in whose diocese immigrants lived.

lections in their respective societies to support the Catholic immigrant. He also asked the delegates to become members of the St. Raphaelsverein.

From Evansville the visitor went on to St. Louis, which he termed "the headquarters of Catholic Germanism."[72] Here he met German priests, editors, and leaders, then toured through Arkansas, Kansas, and Minnesota, regions which he considered to be the chief sections settled by Germans. His return trip to New York took him to Milwaukee, Cincinnati, Baltimore, and Philadelphia. Back in New York, Cahensly was ready to present to Corrigan the plan that had been germinating in his mind as he viewed the condition of the Germans in the United States. He suggested that an American branch of the St. Raphaelsverein be established to care for the German immigrants when they reached this country, thus attempting to achieve the third aim of the society. He had secured Bishops Louis Fink, O.S.B., of Leavenworth, Rupert Seidenbusch, O.S.B., of northern Minnesota, and August Toebbe, of Covington, as patrons of his society in the West, and in the East Bishop Winand N. Wigger, of Newark, had shown great interest. Corrigan agreed that St. Raphaelsverein activity in New York would be beneficial to the German immigrant, and thus the society was established with Bishop Wigger as president.

The American society was the first daughter branch of the St. Raphaelsverein, and in the years to come it would be the center of the society's greatest trials. But at this time Cahensly was overjoyed at what had been accomplished. He felt certain that the new society would help to alleviate the conditions he had discovered on his trip of several months. He was more convinced than ever that the efforts of the society could not cease at the European ports, or even at the harbors of the new world. The immigrants badly needed protection when they landed, on their journeys to new homes, and also in the places where they settled. Thus he broadened the original scope of the St. Raphaelsverein, but to Cahensly it was a natural extension. In his report to the *Katholikentag* he noted that there were twelve Protestant missionaries in Castle Garden waiting to help the more than 1000 immigrants who came in each day, while the Catholics had but one layman, Joseph Kölble. The ministers distributed Bibles, tracts, calendars, and had even put these objects in the hands of Cahensly himself. Catholic immigrants were taken to large Lutheran lodging houses where over 10,000 passengers were given accommodation free of charge every year. The immigrants were not familiar with the language,

[72] Cahensly, *Der St. Raphaelsverein,* p. 28.

were swindled of their money, and, worst of all, they were not directed to Catholic colonies where priests were already stationed. Kölble could not begin to do more than attempt to meet a small number of the incoming Catholics, let alone direct them to Catholic colonies. Cahensly said:

> What will it avail our Catholic emigrants if, after we have conducted them safely to the ship, they run into the danger on the other side of the ocean of losing the greatest treasure they have, their holy Catholic faith.[73]

Returning to the question of Protestant proselytism, Cahensly stated that it was an undeniable fact that the number of Catholics in the United States, considering the large immigration movement, should be much larger than it was. He quoted Richard F. Clarke, S.J., from *Month* magazine, saying that there should be thirteen million Catholics instead of the seven and a half million who were counted in the United States. The reason for the loss of five and a half million to the Faith was due, as he expressed it, "to the peculiar, extremely independent, and unrestrained American conditions," as well as to the fact that the immigrants were neglected by Catholic officials who had failed to channel them to places where pastoral care had already been established. On his trip through the western states he had learned that there were thousands of Catholics who had settled in localities visited by priests only a few times a year. Parents partially preserved their faith, but what would become of children who grew up without the benefit of school or priest? Cahensly surmised that only too quickly they would fall into religious indifference.[74]

Cahensly had high hopes in 1883 that the new St. Raphaelsverein in New York would meet these problems. In retrospect, and in the light of what was to happen, it is noticeable and regrettable that, with the exception of Archbishop Corrigan, he had limited himself on this first journey exclusively to German contacts and impressions. He did not introduce himself or his cause to the leading archbishops of the country; nor did he consult on a broader basis than the German Catholic community for a program of action which would be consonant with American susceptibilities. Perhaps this would be asking for too much, since he had come for the welfare of the German Catholic

[73] *Verhandlungen der 31. General-Versammlung der katholischen Vereine Deutschlands in Amberg, 31. August–4. September 1884* (Amberg, 1884), p. 157.

[74] *Ibid.*, pp. 150–158; *Rechenschafts-Bericht des St. Raphaelsvereins für das Jahr 1883;* Cahensly, *Der St. Raphaelsverein,* pp. 27–32.

immigrant exclusively. But the Church in the United States was a body composed of more than Germans, and if the St. Raphaelsverein had been formed with broader co-operation and advice, its history might have been more pleasant and worthy of the noble intentions of its founder.

CHAPTER II

The German Triangle of the West

NO DECADE in the history of the Church in the United States evidenced a more gradual yet relentless build-up of tension and emerging conflict than the years of the 1880's. During this period procedural and racial differences on a practical level, though seemingly unrelated, crystallized the basic issues which were to occupy Catholic leaders both clerical and lay in the years ahead. These issues broadened and intensified until by 1891 they broke forth in charges and countercharges of Americanism and Cahenslyism. When these procedural and racial differences of the 1880's were combined in the 1890's with supposed doctrinal errors relating to the school question, Heckerism, liberalism, and minimism, a major controversy ensued which has been termed "Americanism."[1] Throughout the entire period, and perhaps basic to its development, were German organization on a national scale,

[1] Different phases of "Americanism" have been treated by Frederick J. Zwierlein, *The Life and Letters of Bishop McQuaid,* 3 vols. (Rochester, 1927), Vol. III; Robert H. Lord, John E. Sexton, and Edward T. Harrington, *History of the Archdiocese of Boston,* 3 vols. (New York, 1944), Vol. III; Daniel F. Reilly, O.P., *The School Controversy (1891–1893)* (Washington, 1943); Henry J. Browne, *The Catholic Church and the Knights of Labor* (Washington, 1949); Henri Delassus, *L'Américanisme et la conjuration antichrétienne* (Paris, 1909); Abbé Félix Klein, *Souvenirs,* Volume IV, *Un hérésie fantôme. Américanisme* (Paris, 1949); Jules Tardivel, *La situation religieuse aux États-Unis. Illusions et réalité* (Montréal, 1900); John Tracy Ellis, *The Formative Years of the Catholic University of America* (Washington, 1946); Patrick H. Ahern, *The Catholic University of America, 1887–1896. The Rectorship of John J. Keane* (Washington, 1948); Peter E. Hogan, S.S.J., *The Catholic University of America, 1896–1903. The Rectorship of Thomas J. Conaty* (Washington, 1949); Colman J. Barry, O.S.B., *The Catholic University of America, 1903–1909. The Rectorship of Denis J. O'Connell* (Washington, 1950); Charles Maignen, *Le pére Hecker — est-il un saint?* (Paris, 1898); Vincent F. Holden, C.S.P., "A Myth in 'L'Américanisme,'" *CHR,* XXXI (July, 1945), pp. 154–170; Thomas T. McAvoy, C.S.C., "Americanism, Fact and Fiction," *CHR,* XXXI (July, 1945), pp. 133–153; John J. Meng, "Cahenslyism: The First State, 1883–1891," *CHR,* XXXI (Jan., 1946), pp. 389–413; "Cahenslyism: The Second Chapter, 1891–1910," *CHR,* XXXII (Oct., 1946), pp. 302–340; John Tracy Ellis, *The Life of James Cardinal Gibbons,* 2 vols. (Milwaukee, 1952).

and the growing demands of the Germans resulting from their mounting immigration to the United States.

This fermentation process of the 1880's began in the so-called "German triangle of the West," which embraced the areas centering around Milwaukee, Cincinnati, and St. Louis. In all three localities the Church had been organized into provinces with archiepiscopal sees. The first public indication of dissatisfaction within this triangular region came from Milwaukee in 1878, where Archbishop John Martin Henni, the first ordinary of that jurisdiction, petitioned the Holy See for a coadjutor with right of succession. After a long and fruitful tenure, which began in 1843, growing infirmity of body compelled him to seek assistance, and he submitted to the Congregation of Propaganda the names of Bishops Michael Heiss, of La Crosse, Joseph Dwenger, C.PP.S., of Fort Wayne, and Francis Xavier Krautbauer, of Green Bay, as his three choices. He also notified the other American archbishops of his decision and requested them, according to one of the regulations of the Second Council of Baltimore, to submit their opinions to Rome on the Milwaukee succession.[2]

Even before Henni had made this move a number of priests of Milwaukee had written to Archbishop James Gibbons of Baltimore and had requested him to consider their position in this matter. Reverend George L. Willard, pastor of St. Joseph's Church, Fond du Lac, Wisconsin, drew a picture of the Church in that area for Gibbons. He explained that he himself was a convert from Protestantism, an American whose ancestors had settled in the country before the Declaration of Independence and had fought in the American Revolution. Willard was now very anxious that the powerful organization of German priests in the Archdiocese of Milwaukee, whom their good archbishop had induced to come there, should not be successful in securing a German as successor to Henni. Owing to the feeble health of the Archbishop, these priests, he explained, had been more assiduous in their efforts and more importunate in their demands to have Bishop Heiss transferred from La Crosse to Milwaukee and Reverend Kilian Flasch, rector of St. Francis Seminary in Milwaukee, appointed as bishop of La Crosse. He said that the American and Irish priests had remained quiet up to then, thinking there could scarcely be a possibility of another German bishop in Milwaukee, but they now felt they must act. He stated:

> I have said Holy Mass, that God would direct me to write the truth

[2] *AABo,* Henni to Williams, May 10, 1878.

> in all charity to you. I think my mind is wholly divested of hatred to the Germans. I wish them all well, but would rather see them, like St. Paul, become all things to all men. Not that I love the Dutch less, but I love our Holy Religion more.[3]

Whenever one or two German families settled, he continued, a mixed congregation was formed according to the opinion of the German priests of Wisconsin, and this congregation then had to be presided over by a German priest even if there be one hundred or more Irish families in the same place. This was the foundation for Archbishop Henni's frequent statement that he must have all German priests for his diocese. The basis of Willard's objection was, as he said, that:

> these German priests have frequent meetings, the principal and ulterior object of which is to perpetuate a young Germany here. . . . These priests seem to forget the Unity and Catholicity of the Church to perpetuate the curse of Babel in *Language.* Their great endeavors are to make everything foreign and German, to make them obnoxious to Americans. So long as the priests care more for sauerkraut and its concomitants than they do for the souls of the Americans, they are not very likely to convert them. And thus practically one great object of the existence of the Church of God here is frustrated. Over one half (by far) of the inhabitants of the state are Catholic. The great majority of the Catholics speak English. Only a small minority in comparison are real Germans. The work of the Church here is twofold: to convert the Americans and preserve our own. By this way of acting neither of these objects can be well gained.[4]

On the following day Archbishop Gibbons received another letter from a committee of Milwaukee priests made up of Reverends P. F. Pettit, pastor of St. Raphael's Church, Madison; H. F. Fairbanks, pastor of St. Patrick's Church, Whitewater; James J. Keogh, St. John's Cathedral, Milwaukee; Thomas Fagan and James J. Keenan, St. Francis Seminary and Pio Nono College respectively; and again George L. Willard, Fond du Lac. They asked for a remedy of what they considered to be existing evils and stressed the danger of the appointment of a German coadjutor archbishop. They asserted that there had not been one English-speaking bishop or ecclesiastical official in either Milwaukee or the two suffragan sees of the state, La Crosse and Green Bay. They further claimed that the English-speaking Catholics were the most numerous and that nearly all others

[3] *AAB,* 73-5-1, Willard to Gibbons, Fond du Lac, May 7, 1878.
[4] *Ibid.*

understood English, the language of the country. Despite this fact, St. Francis Seminary in Milwaukee had German officials and only two of the thirteen professors were English-speaking; in the Dioceses of La Crosse and Green Bay there were only five and four English-speaking priests respectively; the School Sisters of Notre Dame, who taught in the parochial schools of the area, were thoroughly German in their spirit and rule. These priests were worried about the future of the Church and the Catholicity of the children under what they termed the "thorough and complete rule of one nationality, which chance has placed in its possession, and a seeming determination on the part of that nationality to keep all the influence and authority in its own hands, and within the province of Milwaukee, to build up a new Germany in the Church." They asked that consideration be given to the vast population outside the Church which was English-speaking, since the Church had always in every state taken cognizance of the language of the country.[5]

Archbishop Gibbons wrote to Archbishop John J. Williams of Boston after receiving these letters and explained that he was anxious to gratify the venerable Archbishop of Milwaukee by recommending his names, but at the same time he felt that the memorial of the Milwaukee priests was worthy of some consideration. Williams concurred with Gibbons and suggested that the whole case should be stated clearly to the Propaganda. To Williams the most prudent decision would be to have someone appointed who would be both satisfactory to the German element while at the same time taking an interest in others not German. To the English convert, James F. Wood, Archbishop of Philadelphia, such a choice would be Bishop Dwenger, of Fort Wayne, since he was born in America of German parents, and had a perfect knowledge of both German and English. Wood felt that the statistics advanced by the Milwaukee priests gave substance to their complaints, and he continued:

> The whole Province seems to be pretty thoroughly *germanized.* Now if this defect could be corrected or even mitigated by the choice of a future Archbishop in the person of a coadjutor *cum jure successionis,* it would certainly be very desirable. . . . The appointment of either of

[5] *AAB,* 77-5-2, Committee of Priests of Archdiocese of Milwaukee to Gibbons, Milwaukee, May 8, 1878. These priests based their figures on the United States census of 1870, in which Wisconsin's population was around 1,050,000. Of this figure, 690,000 were native born and 360,000 foreign born. According to their calculations, about 120,000 were Irish and of Irish descent, about 117,000 were German and of German descent, and the remaining 50,000 were of French, Polish, and other national descents.

> the others named, would confirm, perpetuate, and intensify the *germanizing* process *usque ad infinitum*. I think we know that this would be a *calamity* for the English speaking portion of the population.[6]

When the Congregation of the Propaganda received Archbishop Henni's *terna* they informed him that he had not followed the directives of the Second Council of Baltimore, since he had not asked the advice and opinion of his suffragan bishops in this matter. Accordingly, the bishops of La Crosse, Green Bay, St. Paul, and the vicariates of North Dakota and Marquette were assembled in Milwaukee on September 4. Bishop Thomas L. Grace, of St. Paul, reported to Gibbons on the results of the meeting. He stated that it was only with great difficulty that he succeeded in obtaining the consent of the other bishops present to have the name of an American prelate proposed as a candidate for the appointment. Grace supported Bishop John Lancaster Spalding, of Peoria, who spoke both German and English and who had created a favorable impression in Milwaukee following his lectures he delivered there. Catholics and non-Catholics, both English and German-speaking, said Grace, had expressed the highest esteem for Bishop Spalding.

On the evening before the meeting the Vicar-General of Milwaukee, the Very Reverend Martin Kundig, visited Grace and urged him for the sake of religion to do all in his power to have Spalding's name on the list of candidates. Kundig had assured him that it was a false impression that the German people would not be satisfied with any other than a German bishop, since there was an intelligent and influential group among the German Catholics who leaned toward Spalding. Kundig feared there would be no change in policy if either of the German candidates on the list should receive the appointment as coadjutor. Kundig stated that fervent prayers were being offered through his urgency in several religious communities and pious societies of laymen for Spalding's nomination. At the meeting itself Grace was able to persuade the bishops to place Spalding's name third on the list, following Bishop Heiss in first place and Bishop Krautbauer in second. "The opposition to Rt. Rev. Spalding on the part of three Bishops," he told Gibbons, "had no other ground than that the Bishop was not a German."[7]

[6] *AABo,* Gibbons to Williams, Baltimore, May 16, 1878; *AAB,* 73-T-4, Williams to Gibbons, Boston, June 7, 1878; 73-S-15, Wood to Gibbons, May 25, 1878.

[7] *AAB,* 73-W-3, Grace to Gibbons, St. Paul, Sept. 8, 1878. Vicar-General Kundig, along with Reverends Patrick J. Donahoe, James J. Keogh, and Edward P. Lonigan, also wrote to Gibbons in support of Spalding and declared that he would make the

While this new *terna* was being forwarded to Rome the whole matter entered the public forum in the Milwaukee area with unfortunate results. The German professors at St. Francis Seminary were accused of having petitioned Rome for a German coadjutor, while extreme and intemperate individuals, like the Irish priest, Thomas Fagan, representing a minority of two on the seminary faculty, took what they considered their complaints against Bishops Heiss and Krautbauer into the secular papers and held up their characters and actions to ridicule. Fagan asserted that Heiss could not write grammatical English and that he blundered in public addresses, while Krautbauer could not get along in his own diocese. The two local Catholic weeklies, the English language *Catholic Citizen* and the German language *Columbia,* clashed in editorial battle over nationalistic attitudes toward the succession. The rumor that the seminary priests had petitioned Rome proved baseless, but not before the editor of the *Catholic Citizen* went to the extreme of sending the seminary professors a document to sign, denying that they had prepared a petition. The *Columbia* claimed that all this talk of a plot was really an attempt to distract attention from the real conspiracy on the part of English-speaking Catholics to end German "rule."[8]

Archbishop Henni finally felt constrained to issue a strong circular to his priests condemning this public agitation. He reminded them that Rome was to make the ultimate decision, and that any discussion in public print could only bring discord and disgrace to their archdiocese. He branded the charges against the seminary professors as entirely false and as a slander to his dearest institution. Then he went on to condemn those priests who had heaped insults upon his close friend, former secretary and faithful colaborer, Bishop Heiss of La Crosse, a man who was, he contended, distinguished for his piety, deep learning, and ardent zeal for religion.[9]

This, fortunately, put an end to public commotion. All waited throughout the spring of 1879 for the decision from Rome. On May 17 Giovanni Cardinal Simeoni, prefect of the Congregation of Propaganda, wrote again to Archbishop Henni and informed him that the cardinals of the Propaganda had met on the question of the Mil-

---

Church attractive to the non-Catholic Americans, who were numerous, well-disposed and on the threshold of the Faith, but ignored up to then. No effort had been made for their conversion, they stated, except by individual priests (*AAB,* 73-W-10, Sept. 23, 1878).

[8] *Columbia,* Dec. 26, 1878; Jan. 16, 1879.

[9] *AAM,* Archbishop John M. Henni to Priests of the Archdiocese of Milwaukee, Jan. 19, 1879.

waukee coadjutorship. They did not feel that Heiss should be transferred from La Crosse because of the condition of his own health and, too, because such a move would be detrimental to that diocese is so far as they could not easily find a suitable successor. Simeoni asked Henni again about his opinions on the succession of Bishop Spalding to Milwaukee, and stated that he would have been appointed if it had not appeared from the Archbishop's letters that this would be less satisfactory to him. The Archbishop was also asked to present names of suitable priests for the position, since the congregation was not favorable to transferring bishops from one see to another.[10]

Documentary evidence is not available on the details of this matter, but one year later, on April 9, 1880, Bishop Heiss was transferred from La Crosse to Milwaukee, and Very Reverend Kilian Flasch, rector of St. Francis Seminary, was appointed Bishop of La Crosse in June of that year. When Heiss succeeded to the metropolitan see of Milwaukee, following the death of Archbishop Henni, the Coadjutor Bishop of St. Paul, John Ireland, delivered the sermon at the conferring of his pallium on April 23, 1882. Six days later, when the new Archbishop received a public welcome at Notre Dame Convent, the chaplain of the sisters, Peter M. Abbelen, gave the address of welcome.[11] This man, soon to become the vicar-general of Archbishop Heiss, and Bishop Ireland, soon to be metropolitan of the new archiepiscopal see of St. Paul, would clash publicly over the German question long before the ten-year administration of Heiss was completed. At that time the question of Heiss's successor would divide the American hierarchy even more decidedly.

Meanwhile in the St. Louis sector of the triangle no difficulties appeared over succession to that metropolitan see, as Archbishop Peter Richard Kenrick continued his long administration which had begun in 1841. Serious differences, however, came to a head at this time concerning a matter of parochial procedure which Kenrick had established in the early years of his regime. He had declared that the German, Bohemian, and Polish parishes in the city of St. Louis did not enjoy all the rights and privileges of English-speaking parishes, that they were succursal churches or chapels of ease for the use of their respective nationalities. Pastors of these parishes were to enjoy full pastoral rights in regard to their own people, but they were not juridical pastors, despite the fact that in many cases the parishes,

[10] *AAM,* Simeoni to Henni, Rome, May 17, 1879.
[11] *Catholic Citizen,* Apr. 29, 1882; *Daily Sentinel,* Apr. 24, 1882.

German especially, were larger and more active than other parishes of the city. Archbishop Kenrick had acted in this way since the legislation of the Council of Trent was always considered as promulgated in the St. Louis area, and, in keeping with Trent's decrees, in 1842 he had issued a pastoral declaring that in one given parochial territory a division of authority was not admissable. Consequently only the English-speaking parishes had parochial rights. Friction arose between the clergy of the different parishes as a result of this ruling, especially in reference to the fact that some of the English-speaking pastors were administering sacraments to Germans. But the foreign nationality parishes gradually came to be regarded as parishes in a practical sense until, in 1884, the whole question was raised in public and aired in journals when Kenrick's pastoral was exhumed and published in the press. Reverend David S. Phelan entered the field of battle through the columns of his weekly paper, *The Western Watchman,* and Reverend William Färber took up the cause of the German Catholics in the monthly theological magazine for the clergy *Das Pastoral Blatt.*[12]

During the summer previous to this controversy in St. Louis, John Gilmary Shea, the noted historian of the American Church, published an article in the *American Catholic Quarterly Review* entitled "Converts — Their Influence and Work in This Country." He described American converts to the Church as isolated among their foreign-born brethren in the Faith, especially among the German Catholics where a Catholic found himself lost unless he acquired the language and identified himself with the hopes and desires of the

[12] *The Western Watchman* first appeared as the weekly, *Edina Watchman,* in 1865 when Phelan was pastor in that town. The name of the paper was changed to *The Western Watchman* and transferred to St. Louis in 1869 after he became pastor of the Church of the Annunciation in St. Louis. It remained the private paper of Phelan and was never the official journal of the Archdiocese of St. Louis, although recommended by Archbishop Kenrick. Its life span was one of continuous and active controversy due to Phelan's delight in debate, militant defense of the Church, definite ideas on "Cahenslyism," "Americanism," and the school question. He was often intemperate and brought upon himself five condemnations by bishops and one by the apostolic delegate. But he submitted to authority each time and continued publishing, much to the distress of his opponents. The paper was Democratic in its political leaning.

Archbishop Heiss established the *Pastoral Blatt* in 1866, and Reverend Henry Mühlsiepen of St. Louis was its first editor, while the German priests of St. Louis pledged support. Professors at St. Francis Seminary in Milwaukee contributed to the magazine. In 1873 Father Färber took over the editorship, and under him the publication entered more actively into the problems agitating the Church in the United States at that time. He also stressed historical studies of German Americans and their contributions.

Germans who, it was said, made in their German Catholic papers "the most contemptuous allusions to American and Irish Catholics." Shea insisted that to foster such national feelings was a great mistake because it would breed animosity, and since the rising generation would be American in feeling they must look upon the United States as their own country. If religion remained a matter of nationality it would expire with that nationality. He asserted that many were daily falling away without any effort put forth to save them, and he termed the whole matter a "canker eating away the life of the Church in the United States." Shea wrote:

> Those who labor mainly among Catholics of foreign birth, as well as such Catholics themselves, rarely form a conception of the extent to which we Catholics, as a body, are regarded by the people of this country only as a sort of foreign camp in their midst, who will in time scatter and be lost in the mass of the Protestant, or at least non-Catholic population. Though the census will show that the Catholic far exceeds the foreign population, only part of which is Catholic, it is not easy to convince or disabuse them. Many things which they see and know, keep up the delusion. A Protestant will point to the map and say: "Where are your American Catholics? The whole country is laid off in dioceses, as though you owned it, but how is it that your Popes have never found an American Catholic fit to occupy a see west of the Mississippi and Lake St. Clair? There are thousands of miles where no American-born bishop has ever been seen."[13]

The *Pastoral Blatt* was not slow to take up these charges. Father Färber was joined by Reverend Innocent Wapelhorst, O.F.M.,[14] and two articles of rebuttal appeared which in 1884 were published as a brochure.[15] They branded Shea's article as Nativism or Know-Nothingism, an exclusive spirit against foreign nationalities in the social life of the Union, and they charged him with insulting prelates who

[13] *ACQR,* VIII (July, 1883), pp. 509–529.

[14] Father Innocent Wapelhorst had been professor and rector at St. Francis Seminary in Milwaukee, where the St. Louis seminarians for the most part received their training. In 1879 he joined the Franciscan Order and received the name of Innocent. He taught in the Franciscan house of studies in St. Louis, wrote a celebrated *Compendium sacrae liturgiae,* and helped Heiss work out plans for the *Pastoral Blatt,* contributing articles to it on the rights of German Catholics. He also was a frequent contributor to the Milwaukee German Catholic paper, *Nord Amerika.*

[15] *The Future of Foreign-Born Catholics; and Fears and Hopes for the Catholic Church and Schools in the United States* (St. Louis, 1884). Cf. also *Pastoral Blatt,* XVII (Nov., 1883), pp. 121–131; XVIII (Apr., 1884), pp. 37–49. These articles appeared a month after Cahensly's visit to St. Louis, but this is no evidence that he inspired or was associated with them in any way. He did meet and speak with all the German leaders, clerical and lay, in St. Louis, learned their position on Church affairs in the United States, but nothing more can be adduced from his visit.

Le porteur de cette carte est un émigrant protégé par la Société allemande de St. Raphael et comme tel, nous le recommandons tout particulièrement à la bienveillance, à la charité des catholiques auxquels il pourra s'adresser en pays étranger.

Geleitskarte des deutschen St. Raphaels-Vereins zum Schutze katholischer Auswanderer.

Die Herren Vertrauensmänner des St. Raphaels-Vereins werden gebeten, dem Inhaber dieser Karte jeglichen Schutz zu gewähren.

Peter Paul Cahensly,
Präsident.

Für

aus

ausgestellt durch

The owner of this Card of Recommendation is patronised by the German, „St. Rafael Society", and he is as emigrant, recommended to the brotherly love and assistance of his compatriots, as well as to all brethren of the Roman Catholic church in foreign countries.

Man trage bei Ankunft diese Karte **sichtbar.**

Ratschläge für den Auswanderer.

1. Bei Ankunft am Bahnhofe oder am Landungsplatze der Hafenstadt trage der Auswanderer diese Karte sichtbar und benutze unter **keinen Umständen** Adreß- oder Wirts-Karten, die ihm von anderer Seite angeboten werden.

2. Sollte der Vertrauensmann am Bahnhofe oder am Landungsplatze nicht anwesend sein, so wende man sich an den Polizeibeamten und erfrage denselben.

3. Kein katholischer Auswanderer unterlasse es, vor einer so wichtigen und gefahrvollen Reise im Hafenplatze dem Gottesdienste beizuwohnen und die hl. Sakramente zu empfangen.

4. Klagen über Behandlung, Beköstigung oder Unsittlichkeit während der Seereise wolle der Auswanderer unter Vorzeigung dieser Karte dem Kapitän u. nach Ankunft dem Vertrauensmanne im Ein- oder Ausschiffungshafen mitteilen.

5. Wer sich den Schutz des Deutschen Reiches sichern will, versäume nicht, am Bestimmungsorte sich gleich in die Liste des nächsten deutschen Konsulats eintragen zu lassen.

☛ **Der Vertrauensmann trägt als Erkennungszeichen ein goldenes Ankerkreuz.**

Der hochwürdige Klerus wird dringend gebeten, die kathol. Auswanderer zu veranlassen, alles, was die Reise betrifft, brieflich mit dem Vertrauensmann zu beraten. Der Vertrauensmann gewährt auf Ersuchen **unentgeltlich** Rat und Schutz in allen Angelegenheiten der Reise: Auswahl einer guten Schiffslinie, des Logierhauses, Ueberwachung der Einkäufe, des Geldwechsels, Begleitung zum Gottesdienst, Empfehlung an überseeische Vertrauensmänner usw. — Der Auswanderer muß, um vor Schaden bewahrt zu bleiben, die Ratschläge desselben aufs genaueste befolgen.

Alle Dienste der Vertrauensmänner geschehen **unentgeltlich.**

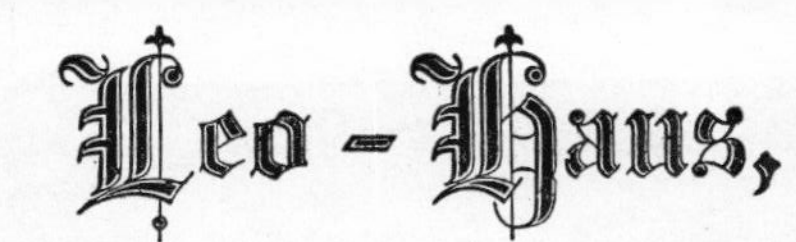

No. 6 State Str., New-York,

für

Katholiken;

unter

dem Patronate des St. Rafael-Vereins zum Sch[illegible] katholischer Auswanderer;

Vertrauensmann: Der katholische Missionär für Auswanderer,

Hochw. F. W. Wayrich.

N. B.—Derselbe ist erkennbar an einem goldenen Ankerkreuz, welches er am Landungsplatze (Ellis Island) an der Brust trägt.

Am Landungsplatze (Ellis Island) trage man diese Karte am Hut oder vor der Brust als Erkennungszeichen.

☞ **Billette von und zu allen Häfen und Eisenbahn-Stationen des In- und Auslandes werden vom Leo-Hause besorgt und jde Auskunft wird bereitwilligst ertheilt.**

↑ St. Raphael Society Immigrant Card

← St. Raphaelsverein Emigrant Card

James Cardinal Gibbons

Most Rev. John Ireland

Most Rev. Denis J. O'Connell

Most Rev. John J. Keane

Most Rev. Michael Heiss

Rev. Peter M. Abbelen

Most Rev. Michael A. Corrigan

Most Rev. Sebastian G. Messmer

The First Provincial Council of the Archdiocese of Milwaukee
May 23–30, 1886

(1) Thomas Fagan, Milwaukee. (2) Lawrence Conrad, Milwaukee. (3) F. John Gaffron, O.S.F., praeses of the Order of Franciscan Brothers. (4) William Corby, C.S.C., superior of Congregation of Holy Cross. (5) Charles Becker, Milwaukee. (6) John H. Niehaus, Milwaukee. (7) J. Adolph Birkhaeuser, Milwaukee. (8) John Shanley, St. Paul. (9) Leonard Batz, vicar-general of Milwaukee. (10) Charles F. X. Goldschmidt, La Crosse. (11) Kilian Flasch, bishop of La Crosse. (12) John Morrissey, Milwaukee. (13) Joseph Rainer, Milwaukee. (14) John Vertin, bishop of Marquette. (15) Frederick Eis, Marquette. (16) Rupert Seidenbusch, O.S.B., vicar apostolic of Minnesota. (17) Unknown. (18) William Neu, Milwaukee. (19) Michael Heiss, Archbishop of Milwaukee and praeses of the council. (20) Peter M. Abbelen, Milwaukee. (21) Stanislaus Lalumiere, S.J., superior of the Jesuits. (22) John Ireland, bishop of St. Paul. (23) James J. Keogh, Milwaukee. (24) Anselm Leiter, S.J., superior of the Jesuits. (25) Martin Marty, O.S.B., abbot of the Benedictine Order and vicar apostolic of Dakota. (26) Otto Zardetti, Milwaukee. (27) Dominic Thill, Milwaukee. (28) Frederick X. Katzer, adm. of Green Bay. (29) J. M. Naughtin, Milwaukee. (30) Elzear De Wilt, Green Bay. (31) August Zeininger, rector of St. Francis Seminary. (32) Nicholas July, Green Bay. (33) James Schwebach, vicar-general of La Crosse. (34) Simon Lebl, Milwaukee. (35) Unknown. (36) George L. Willard, vicar-general of Sioux Falls. (37) Edward Jacker, Marquette. (38) Francis Haas, O.F.M.Cap., provincial.

labored amid unspeakable hardships when no native-born priests could be found in the West. They stated that while he had not gone on to suggest practical conclusions as to eliminating the "canker eating away the life of the Church in the United States," others would and were doing so at that time. In this way they associated the succursal church situation in St. Louis with the Shea article and they proposed to answer those who claimed that German churches and German parishes must be looked upon as makeshifts to be removed and restricted. The authors stressed three points: that souls were at stake in this matter, that the fear of a new Germany or the perpetuation of un-American clannishness by German Catholics was altogether without foundation, and that forcible Americanization would be most dangerous. It was said:

As a rule, the German in this country soon makes himself at home, and becomes as good an American citizen as those of any other nationality. He has as much love for free American institutions; there is certainly no danger that the German Catholics will prefer the hegemony of Prussia and of Bismarckism to the greatest and freest republic in the world, with its flag of stars and stripes and its glorious constitution. German children are known to learn the English language very fast; and if a German school wishes to thrive, it must teach English thoroughly. Should the managers of the school, through national prejudice, neglect to have English taught, the parents would insist upon having it taught, as regard must be had to the imperative necessity for business purposes. Let us, therefore, allow things quietly to take their course, and to develop themselves in a natural manner. How in future the different nationalities will unite harmoniously in one people, what is to become of the different languages, of the German churches and schools, will all be arranged later on. Forcible, premature interference is always dangerous. "In nature there is no leap"; this also holds good in the natural development of things, social, political, and religious. Let us cheerfully permit our descendants to settle those questions. When once immigration has entirely ceased, and there lives a generation that has been reared up with its priests, the English language will also be gradually adopted in the Churches. Even now, to many a German priest brought up in this country the giving of instructions and of preaching is easier in English than in German. The best policy for the present would be, that as children of our Mother, the Catholic Church, we should live together peaceably, like true Catholics, according to the spirit of the Church (where there is neither "Greek nor barbarian"); that all, bishops, priests, and people, should become large-hearted; that they should not be first American, Irish, or German, and then Catholic; that they should be more solicitous for the salvation of souls

> than for the preservation of the German or English language; and that no one should disregard the words of the Chief Pastor of souls, Jesus Christ: *"Quaerite PRIMUM regnum Dei et justitiam ejus et reliqua adjicientur vobis."* It would be very dangerous, through zeal for one's mother-tongue, to disregard this admonition of the Eternal Wisdom; it would be *dangerous* and *foolish* to wish, at present, forcibly to solve these delicate questions and complications by suppressing, slighting, disfranchising the people of any nationality.[16]

To the *Pastoral Blatt* the "canker" was rather the want of Catholic schools and the predominance of what were called "godless or so-called public schools." Father Wapelhorst adduced sources and statistics to maintain his position that losses to the Church in the United States had totaled eighteen million souls, and that the destructive influence of the public schools was in great part the basis of this loss. All other causes he held would mostly disappear of themselves if, with a properly regulated care of souls, the children were brought up according to the spirit of the Church in good Catholic schools. This article was a clear and positive statement of the German position on parochial schools, and it became one of the primary sources in the conflict over the Faribault school plan in the years ahead.

Three months after the second of these articles appeared, on July 31, 1884, eighty-two priests of the diocesan and religious clergy of St. Louis drew up a petition on the matter of succursal parishes and presented it to Cardinal Simeoni of the Propaganda. This was done in their name by Very Reverend Henry Mühlsiepen, vicar-general for German, Bohemian, and Polish Catholics in St. Louis.[17] They stated

[16] *Ibid.*, pp. 12–14. The London *Tablet* agreed with the two authors in their plea to let the transition from mother tongue to English be in a "natural manner." The work was termed one replete with much advice, and if its warnings were heeded much good could be accomplished. The English Catholic weekly believed that its arguments were truthful and timely, a warning to imbibe the true spirit of Catholicity instead of losing it in spiteful bickering of foreign importation.

But in the monthly journal for priests, *The Pastor* of Nov., 1884, an entirely different critique was given. Here it was stated that there was no ground for the monstrous charges made in the injudicious pamphlet. If retorts were provoked against German priests being placed in charge of Irish-American congregations, the editors of *The Pastor* held that the *Pastoral Blatt* would itself be to blame.

[17] Vicar-General Mühlsiepen was a native of Cologne, pastor of St. Mary's Church in St. Louis and acted as the Archbishop's director of German, Bohemian, and Polish Catholics in the archdiocese. He helped in the establishment of the *Pastoral Blatt, Amerika,* and the *Herold des Glaubens.* He was a defender of the Catholic parochial school, brought many teaching sisters to America, and placed convents in new parishes as they were founded in the diocese. In time he came to be known as the "unconsecrated bishop of St. Louis," or again as the "apostle of the Germans in Missouri." Cf. Kleinschmidt, *op. cit.*, pp. 274–276, and John E. Rothensteiner, *History*

that, since the republication of the statute of 1842, which had been unknown to nearly all of the undersigned and considered obsolete by those few who had known of it, several English-speaking pastors had conducted themselves as the rectors of German Catholics, although the archbishop was said to be displeased with such an application of the pastoral statute. They claimed their ecclesiastical status was both dangerous and disastrous for German Catholics under their care as well as humiliating and intolerable for themselves. They feared that this arrangement would become firmly established, be extended beyond St. Louis, and receive sanction or at least toleration at the approaching third plenary council to be held in Baltimore. They accordingly requested that equal and independent rights be granted them in their pastoral office.[18]

Father Färber was in Rome during that summer of 1884 and pushed the petition at the Propaganda. Vicar-General Mühlsiepen also wrote to Archbishop Anton Maria Graselli at Propaganda to assure him that there was not the least dissatisfaction evidenced by this petition toward Archbishop Kenrick who had always provided for German Catholics just as well as for others, but that there seemed no reason for keeping up the 1842 decree. Simeoni referred the matter to the archbishops of the United States for opinions, and it was in this way that they heard of it for the first time. Only when Färber informed Mühlsiepen of this fact did the latter write to Archbishop Gibbons on the matter and enclose a copy of the petition, while expressing the hope that it would not be misunderstood as implying any kind of accusation against Kenrick.[19] Gibbons regretted that the step had been taken and that Mühlsiepen had endorsed it, because he considered the complaint, as he said, "at least exaggerated," while Archbishop Patrick J. Ryan, of Philadelphia, who had formerly been vicar-general for English-speaking Catholics in St. Louis, maintained that the Germans had not been better treated in any diocese of the country than they had been in St. Louis. But he felt that it would be better to define the rights of German and other non-English pastors at the coming council so as to prevent collisions in the future. He had

---

of the Archdiocese of St. Louis (St. Louis, 1928), II, pp. 222, 225, 245, 301, 324, 410, 416–418, 429.

[18] *Relatio de Questione Germanica in Statibus Foederatis a Rev. P. M. Abbelen, Sac. Milw. conscripta, a Rmo. et Illmo., M. Heiss, Archiep. Milwauk., approbata, et Sacrae Congr. de Propaganda Fide mense Novembri 1886, submissa. Sequuntur objectiones plurimorum Rvmorum Praesulum eidem S. Congr. propositae, e lingua Gallica in Anglicam translatae.*

[19] *AAB,* 78-R-18, Mühlsiepen to Gibbons, St. Louis, Oct. 20, 1884.

written these sentiments to Simeoni and expressed the opinion to Gibbons that Rome desired some definite action in the council on this matter because similar complaints had come from other quarters.[20]

Gibbons wrote to Simeoni and, in his capacity as apostolic delegate to the coming council, he acknowledged receipt of the documents on the St. Louis complaints. He regretted that the quarrel had been aired in the German language papers, stating:

> It would have been enough to bring this matter to the notice of the Sacred Congregation of the Propaganda by letter, as it was afterwards done, or to reserve it to the notice of the Fathers of the Third Plenary Council of Baltimore. In this way a remedy, if it were necessary, would have been arrived at without jealousy and envy emerging and without the archbishop being subjected to so much reproach. From my knowledge of my own and other dioceses, even the diocese of St. Louis, I greatly fear that questions of this kind are exaggerated and amplified out of due proportion. As soon as the Archbishop of St. Louis comes here I shall meet him and we shall discuss better plans to meet this matter whatever they might be. Then in as far as I am able I will see to it that all these things will be provided by the Fathers of the Council so that the just desires of the Germans and other nationalities in this matter may be satisfied.[21]

Kenrick arrived in Baltimore a few days later to be the guest of Gibbons at his residence during the meetings of the council. Archbishops, bishops, religious superiors, and theologians from across the country were gathering in the premier see city during those days to assist at the Third Plenary Council of Baltimore, called by order of the Holy See with a view to enacting national legislation on ecclesiastical administration for the growing Church in the United States. As early as the fall of 1883 the archbishops of the country had gone to Rome to confer with the officials of the Propaganda on the subjects to be presented to the council. Topics were distributed among the archbishops as a result of these preliminary Roman meetings, and each metropolitan along with his suffragans was charged with preparing a prospectus on such titles as Catholic faith, divine worship,

[20] *AANY,* Gibbons to Corrigan, Baltimore, Oct. 21, 1884; *AAB,* 78-S-3, Ryan to Gibbons, Philadelphia, Oct. 22, 1884.

[21] *AAB,* Letterbook of James Gibbons, Oct. 23, 1884. On October 27 Gibbons forwarded to Simeoni the letter which Mühlsiepen had sent to him. Ella B. Edes, unofficial Roman agent of Archbishop Corrigan, also placed an article in the November 28, 1884, issue of *Osservatore Romano* against the demands of German Catholics and in defense of Irish Catholics in the United States. On October 24, 1885, she expressed to Gibbons her appreciation of the approval he had given the article (*AAB,* 79-T-20).

education, ecclesiastical persons, Church property, and the like. The title, *De colonis et advenis,* which concerned the problem of immigration was assigned to Archbishop William H. Elder and his suffragan bishops of the Province of Cincinnati. Elder informed Gibbons that he felt the bishops of seaports would be more suited to recommend measures for the care of immigrants than he would and, furthermore, there were few immigrants in Cincinnati because all public land had been occupied.[22] But Gibbons asked him to retain the chapter assigned him because he feared it was too late to transfer it to another metropolitan with preliminary discussions already in progress. Cardinal Simeoni had written a special letter to Gibbons on March 6, 1884, in which he had requested him to consider and prepare legislation on the question of the immigrant, especially Italians. He was particularly anxious for a remedy to the sad conditions experienced by the immigrants in transit and for some provision to give them direction to areas of the country where their spiritual care would be assured. For this reason Gibbons wanted something prepared on the subject, although he felt, as he said, that "there is very little to be said about it, & its study involves very little labor." This was unfortunately representative of the episcopal attitude in the United States over which Cahensly was becoming more concerned. The Archbishop of Baltimore based his opinion on the thesis that it was impractical to establish colonies for Italians, as nearly all of them congregated in cities and did not adapt themselves to farming. The local ordinary, he felt, could provide a priest for them whenever their numbers demanded one of their nationality. He informed Elder, who had not gone to Rome in 1883, that the American prelates there had proposed it as most expedient that societies be established in the sea-board ports and the leading cities of the West modeled after the St. Raphaelsverein, "which is doing so much good for the Germans." It was also recommended that corresponding societies for the Italians should be established in Genoa, Naples, and similar ports in Italy, and that these European societies should correspond with sister societies to be established in the United States. Simeoni had promised the American bishops that he would bring this matter to the attention of the ordinaries of Genoa, Naples, and other port cities.[23]

Elder agreed to retain his title and proceeded to prepare possible decrees on Italian immigration, with the active assistance especially of Bishop Richard Gilmour, of Cleveland. When this matter was pre-

[22] *AAB,* 78-B-4, Elder to Gibbons, Cincinnati, May 6, 1884.
[23] *AAB,* Letterbook of Gibbons, May 8, 1884.

sented to the assembled churchmen at the council Archbishop Corrigan, of New York, suggested that the report had not adequately stressed the extent to which the Italians were victims of the "padrone system," as well as their lack of religious instruction. He was seconded by Bishop Bernard J. McQuaid, of Rochester. Bishop Spalding thought that something of the report could be salvaged, and that the Italians should be directed into the West, but Corrigan adduced statistics to show that of approximately 50,000 Italian Catholics in New York City only a small percentage attended Mass. Bishop Francis S. Chatard then moved that the whole title be rewritten, and Archbishops Patrick W. Riordon, of San Francisco, John B. Lamy, of Santa Fé, along with Corrigan, McQuaid, and Spalding prepared a new prospectus. They reported out of committee that they could only speak disparagingly of the Italian immigrants and, accordingly, they changed the title to immigration in general, while recommending nothing concerning the Italians except that societies should be established in Italy to help meet the problem. Praise was given to the St. Raphaelsverein and the Irish Immigration Society for their labors among immigrants, while colonies were strongly urged for Catholic settlers rather than the existing practice of mass congregation in cities.[24]

Thus was the immigration problem resolved in the council sessions at Baltimore between November 9 and December 7, 1884. In regard to the St. Louis succursal parish situation, since the matter had come to his attention so late, Archbishop Gibbons assigned it to a commission established to care for all new business which might come before the council, and composed of Archbishops Williams, of Boston, Feehan, of Chicago, and Heiss, of Milwaukee. What was decided between Kenrick and Gibbons is not known, but Gibbons declared he had placed the petition of the St. Louis German priests in the hands of the Commission on New Business because Archbishop Heiss was on that board and was best suited among the archbishops to deal with the matter. Nothing was reported on the floor of the

[24] "De zelo animarum, Caput I, De colonis et advenis," *Acta et decreta concilii plenarii Baltimorensis tertii* [private edition] (Baltimore, 1884), pp. 76–77. Archbishop Gibbons and Bishop Thomas A. Becker, of Wilmington, sent a private letter to Cardinal Simeoni after the council ended and detailed the conditions and statistics of Italian immigrants in the United States. Archbishop Corrigan had helped and advised them on this matter (*AAB,* 79-B-2, Gibbons and Becker to Simeoni, Wilmington, Jan. 6, 1885, copy). Cf. *SRB,* I (July, 1886), pp. 33–35, for Cahensly's praise of the bishops' Council action in reference to the St. Raphaelsverein. Cf. also Henry J. Browne, "The 'Italian Problem' in the Catholic Church of the United States," *HRS,* XXXV, pp. 46–72, for a study of Italian nationality and American Catholicism.

council by this commission on the St. Louis petition, and no action was taken accordingly at the council itself. In future years when some German Catholics publicly questioned this lack of action the archbishops were not slow to answer that Archbishop Heiss as well as all the German bishops present had initiated no discussion of German demands and had remained silent on this subject throughout all executive and public sessions.[25]

At the conclusion of the council its decrees were carried to Rome for approval by a committee appointed by Archbishop Gibbons, which consisted of Bishops John Moore, of St. Augustine, and Joseph Dwenger, C.PP.S., of Fort Wayne. Reverend Denis J. O'Connell, pastor of Sacred Heart Church, Winchester, Virginia, accompanied them as secretary and assistant in guiding the matter through Propaganda and securing recognition especially of decrees concerning ownership of Church property and the establishment of diocesan consultors rather than cathedral chapters. Bishop Gilmour, of Cleveland, went to Rome later in the spring to assist the committee in its mission, and it was at this time that a new phase in the German nationality tension developed.

In discussions with officials of the Propaganda, Gilmour and Moore discovered that petitions and letters had been coming from German Catholics in the United States in which they requested the Holy See to safeguard their interests from the aggressions of English-speaking and Irish Catholics. It was this movement which Bishop William G. McCloskey, of Louisville, asked his Roman agent, Abbot Bernard Smith, O.S.B., to watch when he told him at this time:

> There is evidently a powerful German influence active in Rome. My own impression is that it is exercised by the Cardinal Hergenröther, especially in the matter of the appointment of German Bishops to sees in this country. The breach between the nationalities is widening every day, and if the German influence at Rome is allowed to hold sway, it will, I fear, be the entering wedge of a grave breach in the unity of action & feeling & purpose which has hitherto existed in the American Church. The feelings of parties are already deeply roused. . . .[26]

Besides the eminent historian, Josef Cardinal Hergenröther, there were in Rome the Jesuit Cardinal Johann Baptist Franzelin and two exiled German archbishops, victims of Bismarck's *Kulturkampf,* namely, Paulus Cardinal Melchers and Mieceslaus Cardinal Ledochowski. It was natural that these cardinals in the Roman Curia

[25] *AAB,* Letterbook of Gibbons, Dec. 17, 1886.
[26] *AASPOW,* McCloskey to Smith, Louisville, Mar. 20, 1885.

should heed protests of their German brethren in the faith from across the ocean. At one conference Franzelin told Bishop Moore that German Catholics in the United States were "neglected and the priests oppressed." At Propaganda the American bishops found a like spirit, and they determined to draw up a memorial to explain their position in this matter and to answer charges on the condition of German Catholics in the United States. They were moved to do this especially after the Secretary of Propaganda, Archbishop Jacobini, wrote a public letter to the president of the Central Verein of the United States in which he stated that a cardinal protector would be appointed for German societies, to which he added: "The Holy Father has not concluded whether it will be Cardinal Franzelin or Melchers."[27]

The memorial of Bishops Gilmour and Moore was drawn up and printed in the fall of 1885. Not only did the two bishops present a copy to the Propaganda, but they also presented one to Ludovico Cardinal Jacobini, Secretary of State to His Holiness, with a request that he place it before the Pope. Copies were likewise distributed to the cardinals in the curia, as well as to such Roman agents as Abbot Smith and the new Monsignor, Denis O'Connell, when the latter was established as rector of the North American College in Rome. In the United States the ordinaries of New York, Baltimore, Louisville, and Rochester likewise received copies. In their memorial Gilmour and Moore asserted that in localities where Germans had settled in sufficient numbers to form parishes, maintain priests and schools, the course they advocated was irreproachable and should be maintained. But the difficulties arose when a smaller number of German Catholics attended the same church as Irish or French or other nationalities. It was then that, in the opinion of the two bishops, German egoism became apparent and in such cases it was said:

> The Germans demand absolutely that the priest and the school should be German. To keep the peace with the Germans, injustice is often done to other nationalities. In such circumstances the Irish usually submit, while the French generally cease going to church. The number of German priests is far greater than the number of German Catholics requires. In the Provinces of Cincinnati and Milwaukee there are seventeen Bishops, of whom nine are German and only one Irish, whilst at least half of the Catholic population in these two Provinces is Irish. Efforts have been made to remedy this injustice. Irish priests were

[27] *AASPOW,* Gilmour to Smith, Cleveland, Jan. 8, 1886; *AAB,* 82-H-10, Gilmour to Gibbons, Cleveland, Dec. 20, 1886; *ADC,* Gilmour to Moore, Cleveland, Jan. 22, 1887, Feb. 4 and 28, 1887, copies.

placed on the lists of candidates for the vacant bishoprics of Nashville, Covington, and Grand Rapids. They were at the head of the lists, but in every case a German priest — the last on the list — was chosen.[28]

The two authors claimed that a spirit of nationalism was being introduced into the Church at home by deliberate effort, and that a sad conflict would result with a consequent loss to religion and piety, while Catholics of all nationalities would become ridiculous in the eyes of the non-Catholic population of the United States. They were convinced that the Germans were attempting to form themselves into a distinct nationalizing movement, and that this would be more harmful to the Church than a renewal of the Know-Nothing attacks of thirty years previous.

The preparation and presentation of this memorial were not generally known throughout the Catholic body in the United States. It was intended primarily for the eyes of the curial officials at Rome and, when the next aspect of the mounting tension crowded closely upon this action, both Bishops Gilmour and Moore were gratified that they had presented their point of view when they did.[29]

Cardinal Simeoni, apparently desiring to obtain information from all sides before taking any action, instructed Archbishops Williams and Gibbons to give careful consideration to the request he was about to make. The cardinal prefect stated that at the time the decrees of the Third Plenary Council were before the congregation they had received a letter from "a certain bishop" in the United States asking for a decision in regard to the relationship between independent parishes and the succursal national parishes which he had erected within the same neighborhood. In this letter, obviously from Archbishop Kenrick, two doubts had been presented: first, whether in the same neighborhood several independent parishes for different nationalities could be erected; second, whether a bishop offended against the law and mind of the Church if he demanded that children of parents in one parish should remain members of that same parish until they had attained their majority or contracted marriage? Simeoni also stated that other questions of this kind had previously been submitted and careful deliberation must, therefore, be given before an answer could be made.[30]

[28] *Memoriale sulla questione dei Tedeschi della Chiesa di America* (*Denkschrift über die deutsche Frage in der Kirche Amerikas*).

[29] *AANY,* Gilmour to Corrigan, Cleveland, Jan. 23, 1887; *AASP,* Gilmour to Ireland, Cleveland, Feb. 14, 1887; *AAB,* 82-H-6, Moore to Gibbons, St. Augustine, Dec. 19, 1886.

[30] *AABo,* Simeoni to Williams, Rome, Dec. 15, 1885.

The Archbishop of Boston responded affirmatively to the first question and maintained that an affirmative reply to the second query was the most probable answer. If one parish was made principal and the other succursal in a designated territory, Williams felt, jealousies of different nationalities would be aroused. In Boston, he stated, independent parishes for Germans, French, Italians, and Portuguese existed, and all lived at peace with their neighbors. Children of parents belonging to foreign language parishes, as well as the parents themselves, would in time desire to become attached to English-speaking parishes, since the children gradually lost their maternal language and their nationality in the new milieu of the United States. Archbishop Gibbons responded in like manner. He saw no reason why independent parishes could not be established for both English-speaking and non-English-speaking Catholics. In Baltimore such parishes existed, and he felt that parishes for immigrants should be established as long as immigration continued, while irremovable rectors should be appointed to these parishes on a *pro rata* basis. It would be difficult to keep children in these parishes, he continued, because of the tendency to adopt the language of the country, of government, and of business. In Baltimore such children were free to be baptized or married in either German or English parishes, but it was impossible to bind them entirely. Gibbons felt that if both parents were German, then the children should be baptized in a German church; however, if the parents desired that their children attend an English-speaking school, they should not be prohibited from enrolling them there.[31]

These opinions were most reasonable and may well have ended the problems had not another development come about at this time which proved to be the most serious disruption of harmony and trust to date on the question of nationality. A priest of the Archdiocese of Milwaukee, Peter M. Abbelen, in the fall of 1886, wrote to Gibbons, who by this time had been created a cardinal, and informed him that after repeated requests of German priests throughout the country and with the permission of Archbishop Heiss, he was going to Rome to present certain propositions to the Propaganda concerning the relationship of German and Irish parishes and the complete independence of each from the other. Cardinal Simeoni had informed him that he would receive a representative, and Abbelen, therefore, requested a letter of recommendation from Gibbons, attesting to the fact that he was a trustworthy person and, as he said, "sufficiently American-

[31] *AABo,* Williams to Simeoni, Boston, Feb. 18, 1886, copy; *AAB,* Letterbook, Gibbons to Simeoni, Baltimore, n.d.

ized not to be a one-sided partisan in this question." Abbelen felt that, unless this problem were settled by the highest authority, it would continue to agitate the minds of many in the future. He maintained that there was a tendency on the part of many Irish priests to consider German parishes subordinate to theirs, that German priests had no parochial rights, and that the sooner German parishes disappeared the better it would be for the Church. The clearest expression of this tendency was the postulate that there should be only one parish in each district with all others its dependencies. Abbelen quoted canonical authorities to disprove this and he continued:

> All direct and violent efforts to deprive the Germans of their language and customs, to "americanize" them in a quiet way, are nothing but fatal means of leading them away from the Church. Let us leave this "americanization" to its natural course, to a gradual amalgamation. It will come of itself, especially when and where immigration ceases. Self-interest is its more potent, irresistible factor. But let no one force it, and least of all, a Catholic bishop and priest. The German is tenacious; the German Catholic is proud of his country, especially since the glorious *Kulturkampf;* the German Catholic — unlike the Irish — is surrounded by countrymen, who, as Protestants, Infidels, Secret-Society men, do everything in their power to allure him away from his church. If they could taunt him with being considered, here in America, only as a second-rate Catholic, etc. — the consequences Your Eminence would be too sad to think of.[32]

Father Abbelen had been Archbishop Heiss's theologian at the Third Plenary Council of Baltimore and in that capacity he was already known to the cardinal. Gibbons sent him a letter of recommendation just before he sailed from New York on October 12 aboard the *City of Rome*. When other members of the hierarchy, after news of the mission became public, questioned why he had given this recommendation, Gibbons maintained that he believed that Abbelen was going to Rome on a matter concerning his own diocese only and with the permission of his ordinary. But the cardinal did not take the opportunity to inform Abbelen that this matter was in the process of being determined, something which he could have done without violating any confidence in regard to the correspondence of himself and Archbishop Williams with the Propaganda.

[32] *AAB,* 82-B-1, Abbelen to Gibbons, Milwaukee, Oct. 4, 1886. The Abbelen Papers are at present in the archives of the School Sisters of Notre Dame, Milwaukee, Wisconsin. In response to a request for permission to use Monsignor Abbelen's papers so that both sides of this question could be adequately presented, Mother M. Andrina, S.S.N.D., Commissary General, replied on Aug. 27, 1950, that "we regret that we have nothing which might be of assistance to you."

The Abbelen mission, as well as the memorial he carried with him in the name of priests from the Milwaukee, St. Louis, and Cincinnati areas, became a storm center of misunderstanding from the very beginning. The Milwaukee priest had informed Gibbons that he planned to reside while in Rome with the newly appointed rector of the American College, Monsignor Denis J. O'Connell, who had been one of his fellow notaries at the plenary council. O'Connell, in turn, informed Bishops John Ireland and John J. Keane that Abbelen was with him as an ambassador from the German bishops and priests of the United States, demanding equal rights for German parishes and people. Ireland and Keane were at that time in London, en route to Rome to discuss and make plans for the establishment of a national Catholic university at Washington. Bishop Ireland set out immediately, traveling day and night, for Rome, where he was able to obtain a copy of the Abbelen memorial and to secure permission from the Propaganda to have it printed and rushed back to a chosen number of the bishops in the United States. Keane joined him soon afterward, and the two bishops, together with O'Connell, began to send a veritable barrage of cablegrams and letters concerning this memorial to all archbishops and a number of carefully selected bishops who they knew would react at once to what they considered a grave danger. As Bishop Keane informed Henry Edward Cardinal Manning:

> On our arrival we found ourselves faced by an unexpected question far surpassing in importance that of the University. Some German ecclesiastics, using the poor old Archbishop of Milwaukee as a tool, had *secretly* sent an emissary to represent the Hierarchy of the United States as hostile & unjust toward the German Catholics, their language, customs, etc., & demanding special legislation of the most ruinous character for their protection. We found, too, that before sending their ambassador, they had for years prepared the mind of the Propaganda by systematic representations of a similar sort. The train was already laid for what would have been an explosion disastrous to the unity of the Church in the U. S. — for the introduction of Germanism and *nationalism* in general. We had a terrible fight on hand — to check the action of Propaganda, to let the Bps. of the U. S. know what was going on, to rouse them to necessary action, & to crush out the strife which we had feared but did not know the time or manner of . . . the *social* question & the *German* or *nationalist* questions, are the two wedges with which the devil is trying to destroy the unity of the Church in our country. Pray that he may not succeed. . . .[33]

[33] Manning Papers, Keane to Manning, Rome, Feb. 10, 1887, copy.

For Keane, Ireland, and O'Connell to term Abbelen's memorial a secret mission was not a true version of the facts. Abbelen had informed Cardinal Gibbons of his intention, had written to Propaganda and received clearance to present it, and had taken up residence at the American College in Rome while executing his mission. Abbelen further insisted that he went with the permission of his own archbishop who had read the memorial, as had a number of other German bishops in the United States. Thus the memorial was secret only in the sense that those opposing it had not seen it before it was presented at the Propaganda, secret in the same partisan manner as Gilmour and Moore's memorial of the year previous. What was unfortunate about the Abbelen petition was its timing and the fact that these grievances could have been brought before the fathers at Baltimore when they were convened in council and there resolved openly and by majority decision. Then such legislation as they had agreed upon could have been forwarded to Rome for approval, with the other decrees, rather than to picture the situation as Abbelen did in terms of a series of unjust restrictions imposed on the German minority by an Irish majority.

But in that winter and spring of 1886–1887 no calm and judicious evaluation was given to the case. Keane first informed Gibbons of the memorial and characterized it as "a more villainous tissue of misstatement I have seldom read." He drew the Cardinal's attention to the fact that Abbelen had made accusations against the synodal legislation of the Archdiocese of Baltimore itself as being prejudicial to German Catholics. Then Keane stated: "Yet we are informed that this secret emissary of a clique of German Bishops among us, comes to the Holy See with a letter of commendation from your Eminence! No wonder the Propaganda is puzzled!"[34] Abbelen had quoted the Baltimore synod of 1876, which had not given German priests exclusive jurisdiction over children of German parents. Upon hearing Keane's version of events, Gibbons rushed a response to Rome and pointed out that the Baltimore synodal decree which Abbelen had quoted had been replaced by a decree of the synod of September, 1886, which had given German pastors exclusive rights in regard to baptism, first Communion, and matrimony in cases where the consent of parents was needed. He admitted that the decree of 1876 could be interpreted by a stranger just as Abbelen had done, but the constant and invariable interpretation which the Cardinal as well as his two predecessors had given to this decree was the same as that described in the last

[34] *AAB,* 82-G-4, Keane to Gibbons, Rome, Dec. 4, 1886.

synod. Gibbons was hurt and astonished that such a report had been submitted on his administration, and he was stung to action. "The only way to correct evil at the beginning," he said, "is to absolutely refuse to recognize any distinctions in our government of the Church, for if any one nationality is accorded special privileges, other nationalities will thereafter demand the same."[35]

As a next step Ireland and Keane cabled all of the archbishops and several bishops in the United States, informed them of the memorial and asked them to unite immediately against the Abbelen petition. Meanwhile the two bishops presented a lengthy document to the Propaganda, begging for delay until the archbishops could be heard and outlining their own views on the subject.[36] They won their point and discussion of the whole topic was set back to the January 3, 1887, congregation of the Propaganda officials. Their next step was to write a letter to all who had previously received cablegrams, to explain the situation more in detail and to ask that cablegrams and letters be forwarded to them which they could submit to the Propaganda to sustain their position. The two bishops stated:

> The document [Abbelen's memorial], you will perceive, opens with a petition for the equality of German & English parishes — a thing simple enough, & which practically has never been denied. But this leads up to various accusations against the non-German clergy, & to certain demands, the granting of which would be disastrous to the Church in America. This written document has, furthermore, given occasion to numerous viva voce statements by F. Abbelen, & to numberless private letters from parties in America. There is a conspiracy wide-spread & well organized against English-speaking bishops & priests. The Consultors & Cardinals of the Propaganda, especially the Germans, have been filled with charges against them, as persecuting the Germans, depriving them of their rights, etc.[37]

After Bishop Gilmour learned of what had happened in Rome he told his friend Bishop Moore: "The question is now fairly sprung & should be as fairly met. *We* know what can be done by push. A word

[35] *AAB,* Letterbook, Gibbons to Keane, Baltimore, Dec. 22, 1886. Gibbons also was indignant that Abbelen had written as though the English-speaking clergy of Baltimore were Irish, and had left the impression that the conflict was between two foreign nationalities. He asserted that in truth only fifteen of the Baltimore clergy were Irish, and these fifteen had all been educated in the United States as well as being American in habit and thought. The remainder of the English-speaking clergy were American by birth (*ADC,* Gibbons to Gilmour, Baltimore, Dec. 23, 1886).

[36] Because of their importance, the text of the Abbelen memorial and the letters of Bishops Keane and Ireland in answer to it are included in Appendix III (pp. 289–312).

[37] *AABo,* Ireland and Keane to Williams, Rome, Dec. 10, 1886.

if you please."[38] Bishop McCloskey rushed a note to Abbot Smith, who was a consultor at the Propaganda, in which he said:

> If these German Prelates are allowed special legislation as Germans, great injury is likely to follow to the interests of religion. We will be looked upon as a *German Church* in an *English-speaking country*. Let the Italians fancy a German element in the Church of Italy, riding rough shod over the Italians. How would your Cardinals & the Pope fancy it?[39]

Even Bishop McQuaid, who did not believe in eliminating German language and customs too quickly, joined in the chorus of protest. He told Gilmour:

> The power now at work will never rest until it has got complete control of the Church in the Mississippi Valley and all other parts of the country worth having . . . it would be a dangerous precedent to set, to let nationalities legislate through Rome, in an underhand way, without the knowledge of the other bishops of the country.
>
> Of course, the Germans have one grievous cause of complaint, the way they are treated in the English churches. How many just complaints the English have in some other dioceses, it is not for me to say. . . .[40]

Meanwhile the archbishops were joining ranks for action. Ryan, of Philadelphia, feared that they had a conflict of nationalities on their hands and that they must be prepared to act prudently and firmly in this matter.[41] Archbishop Corrigan in New York suggested to Cardinal Gibbons that he invite all the archbishops to assemble as soon as possible so that they could, as he expressed it, "state *our* side of the question, as the German Bishops have (surreptitiously) already stated *theirs*. We do them no harm, and seek only to ward off evil from Holy Church."[42] Gibbons chose Philadelphia as their place of meeting and informed the eastern archbishops of the assembly

[38] *ADC,* Gilmour to Moore, Cleveland, Dec. 10, 1886, copy.

[39] *AASPOW,* McCloskey to Smith, Louisville, Dec. 16, 1886.

[40] Zwierlein, *op. cit.,* III, p. 41. The volume of correspondence which passed between the bishops of the United States on this question was very large. For interesting comments on the question in two diocesan archives, cf. *AAB,* 82-H-6, Moore to Gibbons, St. Augustine, Dec. 19, 1886; 82-4-5, Gilmour to Gibbons, Cleveland, Dec. 20, 1886; *ADC,* Corrigan to Gilmour, New London, Connecticut, Dec. 11, 1886; McCloskey to Gilmour, Louisville, Dec. 27, 1886; Gilmour to Williams, Cleveland, Dec. 31, 1886, copy; Gilmour to Elder, Cleveland, Jan. 7, 1887, copy; Gilmour to Moore, Cleveland, Jan. 22, 1887, copy; O'Connell to Gilmour, Rome, Feb. 22, 1887; McQuaid to Gilmour, Rochester, Feb. 20, 1887.

[41] *AAB,* 82-G-3, Ryan to Gibbons, Philadelphia, Dec. 10, 1886.

[42] *AAB,* 82-H-1, Corrigan to Gibbons, New London, Dec. 11, 1886.

on December 16. Baltimore, Boston, New York, and Philadelphia were present; Archbishop Elder could not come on from Cincinnati because of sickness, but he sent his opinions by mail to the cardinal.[43] The archbishops named Corrigan to formulate their position, and he had the Latin document aboard the following Saturday's steamer bound for Europe. Corrigan denied to Simeoni that there had been any unfair treatment of any language group in the United States. He admitted that St. Louis had an exceptional arrangement, but he reminded the Cardinal that this matter could have been brought up at the recent plenary council. The German bishops, however, had remained silent. Now the archbishops wished to ask in what they had offended. Corrigan stated that in some places the English language was not yet spoken as generally as English in England or Italian in Italy, and that the bishops fully realized that it would be folly to attempt to uproot these customs. In fact, their synodal laws had favored the immigrants who were given churches whenever they could show some hope of supporting them. In Philadelphia the Church of St. Mary Magdalen de Pazzi was given to the Italians, but its rector protested when English-speaking Catholics avoided it, since he could not find support without them. At St. Joseph's Church in Washington, a mixed congregation for Germans and English, the people left whenever German was preached, but stayed when the sermons were in English. And these people, the archbishop stated, were second generation Germans. Holy Innocents' Parish in New York City had two German parishes within its boundaries, one Franciscan and the other Capuchin. Most of the people attended Holy Innocents', and the superior of the Capuchins informed Corrigan that

[43] *AAB,* 82-H-9, Elder to Gibbons, Cincinnati, Dec. 20, 1886. Gilmour wanted the bishops called together in council or in a simple conference and, if necessary, he wished to take the matter directly to the Holy Father. If that was not done, in twenty-five years he prophesied it would be too late and "the Church in the Mississippi Valley would be bound hand and foot to the wheel of Germanism" (*AAB,* 82-H-10, Gilmour to Gibbons, Cleveland, Dec. 20, 1886). Elder was more sympathetic to the German position, and recommended, not "special legislation" by Rome, but measures in the dioceses of the country to forestall special legislation. He did not feel that German pastors and congregations should be placed on an unequal basis with others, but that they should have the rights of rectors, have complete control over their congregations, and that the same principles be applied to all nationalities. Otherwise, he believed, one nationality would be set above another. At the same time, he protested against the method of the German memorial and recommended that a remonstrance be sent to the bishops concerned so that, as he said, "they should be made aware of how unfair has been their conduct in this matter; and how grievous injury it threatens to our peace & unity, & consequently to the deepest interests of religion" (*AAB,* 82-J-6, 82-K-7, Elder to Gibbons, Cincinnati, Dec. 28 and 30, 1886).

after hearing confessions for many hours on one day only one had been in the German language.[44]

Gibbons assembled the judgments on the question which were sent to him and he then forwarded them with one of his own to Bishops Ireland and Keane in Rome. The latter collected all of the letters which they had received, had them printed with Monsignor O'Connell's assistance, and submitted them to the Propaganda before the January meeting of that congregation. Back in Baltimore the Cardinal took the occasion of the dedication of the new St. Wenceslaus Church for Bohemian Catholics to give a public pronouncement on the contested nationality question. He told the people that they had come from the shores of the Danube and Moldau to the shores of the Chesapeake where they would find a new climate, government, customs, and language, but not a new religion. He urged fidelity to the Church and their pastors, and then added:

> You have not only a duty of religion to discharge, but also of loyalty to your adopted country and to this city, in which you have cast your lot. Strive to be law-abiding citizens. Study and obey the laws of the country. Be always in harmony with the spirit of its institutions.[45]

Besides concern over the Abbelen memorial, Bishops Ireland and Keane were also advancing other causes during their Roman visit. These included the establishment of the Catholic University of America and toleration of the Knights of Labor in the United States. Further complications occupied them in the case of Reverend Edward McGlynn, pastor of St. Stephen's Church in New York, and the possibility of a condemnation of the most important work of Henry George, *Progress and Poverty,* whose doctrines McGlynn was espousing. Archbishop Corrigan had delated McGlynn to the Holy See, and Rome had summoned the New York priest to answer charges against him. In 1887 McGlynn was excommunicated because he refused to answer a summons to Rome. Corrigan also desired Rome to condemn George's book, but Ireland, Keane, Gibbons, and several others looked upon such a move as unnecessary. They feared it would arouse opposi-

[44] *AANY,* Corrigan to Simeoni, New York, Dec. 17, 1886.

[45] *Catholic Mirror,* Dec. 25, 1886. Alfred J. Adams, of Chicago, wrote to Gibbons after he had read this speech in the papers, and expressed his admiration and respect as an American citizen for the advice he had given to the immigrants. Adams stated that this speech could be given with profit from every pulpit, both Catholic and Protestant, in the country, and before every assembly of citizens. "It is only to be deplored that such wise counsel could not be addressed to congregations in cities where the apostles of disorder are more aggressive and dupes more numerous" (*AAB,* 82-I-8, Adams to Gibbons, Chicago, Dec. 27, 1886).

tion to the Church and associate the Church with the cause of the rich.[46] The differences over the University, toleration of the Knights of Labor, and the case of Henry George's book divided the hierarchy with Corrigan and McQuaid, supported by the German bishops, on one side, over against Gibbons, Ireland, Keane, O'Connell, and Moore, on the other. All who had originally stood out against the Abbelen petition, however, remained united in an exhibition of common agreement which was rare during those years. Cardinal Gibbons departed for Rome at that time to receive his red hat at the consistory of March 17, 1887. It was felt by his friends that he could also personally accomplish much, while in Rome, through conversations with Curia officials in expediting decisions on all of these items then pressing for decisions.

The rumor likewise was abroad that the Holy See was considering appointing a nuncio to the United States. Gilmour had spoken to Leo XIII against such a move as early as 1882, and Gibbons had replied in 1885 to a similar query from Cardinal Simeoni that he felt it would be an inopportune move. But by early 1887, because of the serious rifts and differences among Catholics in the United States, it appeared to the leaders of the American Church that Rome desired to see and understand these problems through its own eyes rather than through a multitude of conflicting reports. Rumor also had it that Bishop Dwenger, of Fort Wayne, would be named as the first nuncio, a development which was both favored by German Catholics and strongly opposed by most of the English-speaking party. Bishop Gilmour told Archbishop Corrigan:

> My view is — "no Nuncio" — I will not discuss the *man*. That would be to concede the principle, which at present is gravely inopportune. 2. "No Abbelen postulate" — that would be fatable harmony and would be the forerunner of a race war, and ruin wide spread.
>
> We have enough in the III Council for a good while. Save us from over loading, which Rome seems determined to do. I see a connection between Abbelen and this Nuncio — We rise up against the Germans and the Nuncio is proposed hoping that fear of the Germans will facilitate the Nuncio.
>
> May God direct all for the best.[47]

Bishop McCloskey also felt that the German bishops of the West were giving active encouragement to the appointment of a nuncio. In view of what had already happened, and especially of the clean-cut

[46] For treatment of these subjects, cf. Browne, *op. cit., passim.*
[47] *AANY,* Gilmour to Corrigan, Cleveland, Jan. 23, 1887.

indications of what was soon to follow, it would seem, however, that the coming of a papal delegate would have offered a solution to some of these vexing problems. With the Germans slowly forming an autonomous party and petitioning Rome for settlement of grievances or appointment of a cardinal protector for themselves; with many of the English-speaking bishops unable to understand the position of the Germans and distrustful for the most part of their demands; with other nationalities beginning in the same way as the German Catholics to demand special rights — it would seem, indeed, that such developments pointed to the necessity of an objective judgment on these burning questions which an apostolic delegation might possibly have afforded.

But Cardinal Gibbons felt that the appointment of a nuncio would harm the Church in the eyes of the non-Catholic American public and brand Catholics even more as a foreign body. His personal influence and valued judgment delayed the action for the time being, but the question would arise again in 1892, and this time it would be successful. Meanwhile, news trickled from Rome to the effect that the Abbelen memorial would not be accepted. Bishop McQuaid told his friend, Bishop Gilmour, that he had learned the Propaganda had not the least idea of granting what the Germans demanded and that the bishops had taken the Abbelen petition too seriously. Archbishop Jacobini, he said, had informed Abbelen that it was impossible for the petition to come before the congregation because, since the bishops saw no difficulty in granting parishes of respective language groups, it was not to be thought that all the restrictions and obligations the Germans requested could be admitted. McQuaid then concluded:

> The above shows that the dirty, mean, underhand business of these schemers has come to naught. They have had things too much in their own way in the past. They have found us asleep or indifferent while they were awake and on the warpath. After this rebuff, they will remain quiet for some time.[48]

Yet Monsignor O'Connell reported to Gilmour in a somewhat different vein. Ireland and Keane had talked a great deal, he said, but they had been unable to make an impression on the Propaganda which was entirely in Abbelen's favor when he first arrived. What turned the tide was the large number of letters received from the American hierarchy and presented in book form at the Propaganda. These letters astonished the cardinals and consultors, said O'Connell,

[48] *ADC,* McQuaid to Gilmour, Rochester, Feb. 4, 1887.

and altered the trend in such a way that Abbelen had already started for home on Jacobini's advice that it was impossible to comply with the German demands. However, something would probably be done, O'Connell added, about German parishes according to several "proposals" which Bishop Flasch, of La Crosse, had sent on for examination, and Abbelen had stated that if this were done the Germans would be content.[49]

There was much rejoicing for those who had successfully opposed the Abbelen effort. Letters of congratulation poured in upon Ireland and Keane with messages of appreciation for their vigor and success. Nor did Cardinal Gibbons fail to receive the thanks of those who felt it was his influence which had tipped the scales in their favor. Gilmour, however, was not entirely quieted; he feared that they had not seen the end of German demands and also that it was evident that Rome was determined to curb the American bishops.[50] The Bishop of Cleveland was right in both surmises, as he was personally to learn in a short time.

After all of the contestants in the struggle of 1886 had once more returned home to their respective dioceses, Cardinal Simeoni, on June 8, 1887, sent the decision of the congregation on Abbelen's memorial and similar petitions received by the Propaganda to Cardinal Gibbons with the request that he communicate the information to the archbishops of the country. The archbishops were, in turn, to transmit the decision to their suffragan bishops. Gibbons had an engagement to speak at the conferring of the pallium on Archbishop William H. Gross, C.Ss.R., in Oregon City, and was forced to leave Baltimore before the decision could be printed and distributed. He assigned this task to Very Reverend Alphonse L. Magnien, S.S., who mailed Simeoni's message to the archbishops as directed. At this point an unfortunate series of events again intensified national feelings. For a clear understanding of the fresh controversy that ensued, Simeoni's document must be detailed. The prefect listed nine *dubia* which he had received from Abbelen and others and then handed down decisions on these questions as follows:

> 1. Whether in the same territory, several parishes for people of diverse tongues can be erected that enjoy, in every way, independence of each other?

[49] *ADC,* O'Connell to Gilmour, Rome, Feb. 6, 1887. O'Connell wrote again on Sept. 4, 1887, to Archbishop Ireland that Cardinal Simeoni thought at that time that the German move was "from the beginning the work of a few partisans" (*AASP,* O'Connell to Ireland, Rome, n.d.).

[50] *ADC,* Gilmour to Elder, Cleveland, Mar. 25, 1887.

Response: Affirmative, as often as the erection of such parishes seems to the Ordinary opportune for the salvation of souls.

2. Whether a Bishop offends against the mind and laws of the Church, if he decrees that sons and daughters of families belonging to a certain parish and while living in their parents' home, remain bound to the same parish until they shall have been freed of paternal power, unless, because of peculiar circumstances, something else should seem more salutary for the salvation of souls to the Bishop?

Response: Affirmative as in number one.

3. Whether the quasi-parishes of diverse nationalities can be declared irremovable, provided the conditions prescribed by the Third Plenary Council of Baltimore, Title II, Chapter V, concur?

Response: Affirmative as above, the parents' right to send children to any Catholic school whatsoever being safeguarded.

To the petitions listed by Abbelen in his memorial, as numbers four to nine, the congregation made no reply, and it was explicitly stated that they should not be brought before that tribunal again as long as immigration continued, and when immigration to the United States ended, it was stated, it was the responsibility of the local ordinaries to decide whether the German or English language was to be used in parishes.[51]

[51] *AAB,* 82-S-5, Simeoni to Gibbons, Rome, June 8, 1887. Father McGlynn, to further his own cause against his superiors, wrote an article "The New Know-Nothingism and the Old," in the *North American Review,* CCCXXIX (Aug., 1887), pp. 193–205. There he asserted the growing army of foreign-born voters was a real danger to the country, because the growth of ecclesiastical power in the Catholic Church was harmful to the situation in the United States in regard to liberty and unity. He opened the whole question of the Abbelen memorial again and charged the German Catholics of the West with attempting to Germanize the Church in the Northwest, chiefly in Wisconsin and the northern Mississippi Valley, through their German parochial schools, parishes, and German-speaking bishops appointed through the aid of German cardinals in Rome. He claimed they had already captured Milwaukee and were now aiming at St. Louis and Cincinnati. The Boston *Pilot,* of August 6, 1887, carried a stinging rebuttal of McGlynn's charges, and prophesied that the American public, confident in the strength of its institutions, would refuse to take fright again as they did in the days of Know-Nothingism. The New York *Sun,* of August 4, 1887, declared that there was no true education without religion, and that McGlynn was taking a position against which Protestant as well as Catholic sentiment was arrayed. The Chicago *Inter-Ocean,* of August 3, 1887, reminded McGlynn that a few years ago the bugaboo was Irish influence with consequent injustice done to the Irish. This paper believed that the Germans were justified in clinging to their language because they were liberty-loving people. Their motives in coming to the United States were as good as the Irish, and German influence would not count for more than Irish influence, the paper declared, and "not even Dr. McGlynn will admit that there is much danger of the Americans of Irish antecedents becoming Germanized." But Edwin Cowles, of the Cleveland *Leader,* on August 4, 1887, applauded McGlynn's article on the grounds that his position was identical with what that paper had held

As he prepared the document for the printer, Abbé Magnien observed that it seemed as though the responses to the second and third *dubia* had been transposed, and that the answer to the second doubt should have been negative. Nonetheless, he forwarded the decision as originally received from the Propaganda, but he also wrote to O'Connell, asking him to inquire about this matter. The Rector of the American College proceeded to do this and discovered that a scribe at the Propaganda had made a mistake. O'Connell was then given a letter to the effect that the second and third responses should be exchanged. When Gibbons returned from the West and learned what had happened he regretted that Magnien had written to O'Connell, and the Cardinal himself informed O'Connell that he wished nothing changed since he felt "the least breaking down or weakening of the decision would only make the Germans more insolent & aggressive." O'Connell agreed with Gibbons that for the Propaganda to acknowledge publicly that it had been in error, especially when minds were so excited and when the demand had been made by none of the Germans but by Gibbons himself, would be a yet greater mistake. He, therefore, conferred with the Propaganda officials and suggested it would be better to hold the answer until a demand from the Germans would call it forth. Monsignor Donato Sbarretti, a consultor at the Propaganda, agreed with O'Connell and told him they would leave the publication of the reply to Cardinal Gibbon's prudence to make it known when necessary. But before O'Connell's letter could reach Gibbons the reversal of the second and third responses had been communicated to all of the archbishops, and Gibbons cabled O'Connell that the reversal was satisfactory. By this time O'Connell was really in a quandary. The Propaganda, however, decided that the document should stand as corrected and confirmed, and that no further action need be taken.[52]

It was the *Pastoral Blatt* which again picked up the question of interpretation of a document, and Reverend Bede Maler, O.S.B., of the Church of St. Mary of Victory in St. Louis, asked Gibbons, in the absence of Father Färber, concerning the obvious difficulties in the document. The Cardinal stated in reply that the copy of the letter which had been published was a faithful transcript. By a clerical

---

for twenty years, and that now he stood upon ground so long occupied by the American Union.

[52] Cf. *ADR,* Gibbons to O'Connell, Baltimore, Aug. 14, 1887; Sept. 19, 1887, cablegram; *AAB,* 83-J-4, Andro di Tiro to O'Connell, Rome, Aug. 29, 1887; 83-K-8, O'Connell to Gibbons, Rome, Sept. 4, 1887; Sept. 18, 1887; *AASP,* O'Connell to Ireland, Rome, Sept. 1, 1887.

error, however, the second and third responses were transposed and should be considered as such. Gibbons immediately went on to state that this did not at all affect the merits of the answer, and he added:

> The meaning of the answer of which you enquire, as I understand it, is that while the Holy See disapproves of Episcopal legislation binding the children, e.g., of German parents to the parental parish, it has no disposition to sanction or encourage any undue or improper tampering with the children by which they would be alienated from the parish of their parents. In other words, the aim of the decision is to protect the personal freedom of the children & their parents against undue coercion.[53]

Gibbons warned Maler that his letter was personal and should not be published. The *Pastoral Blatt* respected the Cardinal's wish, but it proceeded to publish the Propaganda decision with an "authentic interpretation" of it according to Gibbons' information.[54] It was at this point that Bishop Gilmour's active watch for a "German plot" brought him to an embarrassing juncture. In the December 22, 1887, issue of his diocesan weekly, the *Catholic Universe,* he publicly challenged the *Pastoral Blatt* to explain their substitution and transferral of the responses. Archbishop Elder had failed to pass on to his suffragans the announcement of the transposition of answers, and Gilmour was accordingly left in the dark. Reverend Nicholas Moes, pastor of St. Mary's German Church, Sandusky, Ohio, had forwarded his bishop a copy of the *Pastoral Blatt* containing their "authentic interpretation" to which Gilmour had replied: "I have to say that this German question is not going to be improved by the mad men of the Abbelen and Chicago stamp," and he termed the article their third gravest of faults.[55] Färber was not slow to respond to this attack. He informed Gilmour that the blame of falsification of Roman documents was utterly undeserved, and he said that since the editors did not wish to come out in public against a bishop they left it to his discretion and judgment to find a proper form of exonerating the *Pastoral Blatt* of what he called "a terrible reproach."[56] Gilmour now turned to Gibbons for exact information, and the Cardinal substantiated the position of the *Pastoral Blatt* while regretting the embarrassing position in which it left Gilmour.[57] The Bishop of Cleve-

[53] *AAB,* 83-G-11, Gibbons to Maler, Baltimore, Aug. 16, 1887, copy.
[54] *Pastoral Blatt,* X (Oct., 1887), pp. 109–110.
[55] *ADC,* Gilmour to Moes, Cleveland, Dec. 16, 1887, copy.
[56] *ADC,* Färber to Gilmour, St. Louis, Dec. 29, 1887.
[57] *ADC,* Gibbons to Gilmour, Baltimore, Jan. 4, 1888. Corrigan also told Gibbons

land then proceeded to exonerate the St. Louis magazine, but at the same time he insisted that both decisions had been correct. In a letter to Färber he said he had long advocated the decisions as corrected and had urged Rome to formulate them. He remarked:

> I am opposed to any attempt to foreignize American youth and do not shrink to say so. But I am, and my whole administration has been to carefully guide and deal with the foreign feeling and sympathies, asking them in turn to be as tolerant to American sympathies as they ask American sympathies to be to them. I do, and did, consider Abbelen's mission a blunder, and his petition a grave fault, also the offensive articles in the *Pastoral Blatt* some years ago on the German Churches and German Schools. I have no hesitancy in saying, all such moves are not wise.[58]

Gibbons had also sent a copy of the decision of the Propaganda to Abbelen himself, who, in turn, was grateful for this new proof of the Cardinal's kindness toward him. He stated:

> Your proved wisdom, justice, and charity, together with your eminent dignity, make it very painful for me to differ with Your Eminence on the matter in question. You speak of "special privileges." It was never my intention, nor can or will it ever be, to ask for more than equal rights, co-ordinated with and independent from English-speaking Parishes and Rectors. This was the substance of our petition; its details were considered partly as logical consequences from, and partly as proper means for preserving such equality.[59]

---

that the *Pastoral Blatt* was the "very publication which began the unseemly controversy regarding German and other Catholics, and that the German priests of St. Louis pushed the question till it reached the Holy See." He recommended that the case be referred to Rome so that, as he said, the "unjust deductions of the ultra-Germans would be clearly, wisely, and satisfactorily removed. The Holy See says one thing; it does not warrant wholesale deductions and inferences not contained in the instructions" (*AAB,* 83-G-10, New York, Aug. 15, 1887).

[58] *Catholic Universe,* Jan. 12, 1888; *ADC,* Gilmour to Färber, Cleveland, Jan. 4, 1888, copy. To O'Connell in Rome Gilmour expressed himself in no uncertain terms: "I have been a good deal puzzled to understand the instability of the Propaganda on the German document. 1st the bungling way it was sent out. 2nd the bungling way the correction was made, and 3rd the bungling way it was reset in its original form, and 4th the bungling way we were notified in our Province" (*ADR,* Gilmour to O'Connell, Cleveland, Mar. 4, 1888).

[59] *AAB,* 82-W-8, Abbelen to Gibbons, Milwaukee, June 30, 1887. O'Connell informed Gibbons that the German agitation did not help their cause in Rome, for in the recent episcopal appointments there were Germans on all the *ternae* except one, and no German was chosen. He also claimed that the Germans were carrying on a close correspondence with Cardinal Melchers, who had asked O'Connell for information. O'Connell said he informed the Cardinal that it was the work of discontented priests and not of the bishops (*AAB,* 83-D-12, O'Connell to Gibbons, Grottaferrata, July 31, 1887).

Abbelen said that the Cardinal's letter was the first intimation he had received of a decision by the Holy See. He characterized the decision as one of delay, since in the very nature of things he felt it could not be considered as final. His prophecy on this point was certainly correct. He also stated that he had resolved not to be induced into entering any unbecoming, passionate agitation of the matter despite the attacks on him which were weekly emanating from St. Paul. Abbelen was here referring to the fact that Bishop Ireland, when he had returned to his see, had given a copy of the memorial to Reverend John Conway, editor of his diocesan newspaper, the *Northwestern Chronicle,* who had published only parts of it and had gone on to characterize the movement as a demand for "special rights."

Then, too, Reverend John Gmeiner, editor of the German weekly *Der Seebote,* and professor at St. Francis Seminary in Milwaukee, but soon to transfer from the Archdiocese of Milwaukee to the Diocese of St. Paul, came forth in 1887 with the first pamphlet on the German question; the first in a long line of pamphlets which contributed nothing but excitement and misunderstanding in both camps. Gmeiner entitled his pamphlet: *The Church and the Various Nationalities in the United States. Are German Catholics Unfairly Treated?* He characterized the Abbelen memorial as secret and asserted it was high time to put an end to such mysterious murmurings which he claimed were sowing seeds of distrust and of disrespect for the hierarchy, and of ill-feelings among the priests of German and other nationalities. His first premise was that it was impossible to perpetuate German language, customs, and patriotism on American soil for many generations to come. He claimed he was not personally burdened by any views which he had imported from Germany, and he firmly believed that German Catholics should accept thankfully from Divine Providence the surroundings in which they found themselves, that they should conform themselves as far as prudence and conscience dictated, and not expect the mission of the Church to obstruct forcibly the natural course of events in favor of any particular nationality, although this might happen to be one's own. He then stated:

> The Catholic Church is no literary club to foster peculiar linguistic tastes, nor any ethnological society to advance any particular national cause, but a divinely instituted organization to bring men of "all nations, and tribes, and peoples, and tongues," to eternal salvation. She, indeed, encourages the study of languages, as she uses other tem-

poral means, in their relation to her God-given mission — not for the sake of the languages themselves.[60]

Father Gmeiner quoted the Third Plenary Council of Baltimore to the effect that aspirants to the priesthood should learn the language of the country, as well as some other language spoken in the United States which the bishops might consider advisable, and among these languages German was mentioned first. He claimed that Germans were better represented in the hierarchy than they were in both national and state legislatures. Undoubtedly some Germans who had adopted English had also given up their religion, Gmeiner admitted, but he claimed that souls were also lost even when German was retained, as could be proved from statistics in what he termed the "German Northwest," especially in and around Milwaukee. He even went so far as to suggest that the Germans consider how the Irish had lost their original language and adopted the English foreign language imposed upon them, while still remaining as faithful as ever to their religion. Besides, the author maintained, modern English was substantially Germanic and akin to the language yet spoken by Angles and Saxons living along the Elbe in Germany. "Let our German infidels who ignore the One True God, worship their idol 'Deutschtum,' " he declared. "To us as Catholics our German language is not an object of religious veneration."

The author next answered the charges of the two *Pastoral Blatt* articles of 1884, and he then went on to analyze Abbelen's petition. He asked why these postulates had not been submitted to the recent council at Baltimore or to diocesan synods. Furthermore, he wanted to know if immigrants, no matter how far they lived from a national church, were to be required to attend such churches just because of accidental circumstances of birth; he asked for a definition of "German customs, usages, and ways," and he inquired whether peculiar dialects, customs, and petty prejudices were to be respected in reference to Plattdeutsche, Bayern, Hessen, Schwaben, Luxemburger, Elsässer, Sachsen, Deutsch-Böhmen, Trierer, Kölnische, Hundsrücker, Nassauer, Vorder, and Hinter Pommerer? Gmeiner contended that it was quite right for priests born and educated in Germany to cling to the habits, views, and ways to which they had become accustomed from youth, but any attempt to force these habits and views on others in the United States would be a trespassing of personal rights. Besides, he concluded, there was an increasing number of priests of German

[60] John Gmeiner, *The Church and the Various Nationalities in the United States. Are German Catholics Unfairly Treated?* (Milwaukee, 1887), pp. 6–7.

parentage who knew nothing of Germany from personal experience or observation. To them the United States alone was their country both in reality and in affection. Of these he said:

> They do not claim to be Germans, but Americans of German descent. They feel quite at home in our American surroundings, and have no prejudice in favor of exclusively German customs, views, or ways; and no sympathy for any movement tending to perpetuate here any permanent nationality besides the American.
>
> And the number of priests of this class goes on increasing, as the years roll on.[61]

The Gmeiner pamphlet raised a great storm, and newspapers defended and attacked it for several weeks until Father Abbelen felt obliged to break his resolve not to be drawn into controversy. He entered the fray through the columns of the *Columbia* with a letter and article of defense. The *Columbia* of August 25, 1887, had supported Abbelen and had answered the harsh attacks against him as the "delegate" whom Conway had been attacking in the *Northwestern Chronicle*. Abbelen now stated that others had requested him to publish his memorial earlier, but he had refused to yield to this pressure after the decision of the Propaganda had become known. He had actually had the manuscript placed in the mailbox addressed to the *Pastoral Blatt*, but when the decision arrived he had considered the matter as settled and had withdrawn the letter. But then Bishop Ireland had allowed his memorial to be published. Abbelen insisted that he still clung to his resolve not to enter into controversy despite, as he said, "such mouthings, which seem to attack my personal honor and love of truth. The good opinion of those who know me best as also the testimony of my conscience are sufficient answer to such an attack." But nonetheless he proceeded to answer the attack.

On his word as a man and his honor as a priest Abbelen declared that the Germans had not sought special privileges. "We are not so wanting in modesty," he said. "Equal rights for all — that was our watchword." He did not believe that anyone could prove in fact that they had demanded special privileges. As for the decision itself, Abbelen avowed that Rome had granted their first three and chief postulates, and, accordingly, there could be question only of the other six points. He then proceeded to answer charges in reference to each point. He asked how it could be understood as a special privilege to request that the pastor's permission or approval of the bishop be given before descendants of Germans be transferred to English-speak-

[61] *Ibid.*, pp. 39–40.

ing parishes? Personal freedom was assured while a check was placed on arbitrary running from one parish to another. If they had asked that descendants of German parents always remain with the German church or that the German church should always continue, then that would have been asking for a special privilege.

In requesting that German language, manners, customs, usages, and form of worship be preserved, Abbelen stated that he and his companions had based their petition on the following points:

> Every people and every man especially in religious matters clings to his language, his manners, and his traditions; it is dangerous to offend him in these even though the offense comes from no bad intention. And under the aforesaid limitations it is absolutely not necessary. Why then should it come? Why then is not the assimilation of the Germans in language and manners left to the process of time to unfold it? But if we ask this, where then is the "special privilege?"[62]

As for priests knowing both languages in a mixed congregation, Abbelen stated that here they had not asked that the priest be German or Irish, but only that the German language be known. In requesting a German vicar-general or one who could speak German for a diocese with a mixed population, he did not understand how this could be interpreted as demanding special privileges, since their request was for this over and above an English vicar-general. He then concluded:

> It is superfluous to say that we would have been glad had they been accepted. But on this account we are not absolutely dissatisfied with the decision given by Rome. We are too loyal for that and moreover we believe that Rome had good reasons to disregard these points. Rome would with pleasure see, I am thoroughly convinced, the arrangements which we aimed at in these four points and which exist in some Dioceses, effected everywhere where they exist in fact. There it will occur to no one to hold them as "special privileges."
>
> Why, therefore, did Rome reject these points? Certainly not because she saw in them special privileges, but certainly because she did not wish with a general decision to pronounce on circumstances which, if indeed unfortunately not too separated, are nevertheless not altogether too generally imminent. These points do not enclose so much the relations of right in which our congregation should stand one with another, as the relations which regard the care of souls. It is certainly conceivable that Rome should leave the ruling of particular affairs to the Bishops without pronouncing herself upon them.

[62] *Columbia,* Sept. 1, 1887.

> Regarded from this aspect I grant that it would have been better not to have proposed these points. But that through these, special privileges were aimed at, I will emphatically as respectfully deny.[63]

Defenses of both positions advanced by Gmeiner and Abbelen were not slow in coming. Gmeiner himself published a rebuttal to Abbelen entitled, *Calm Reason and Furor Teutonicus,* while Nicholas Gonner, Sr., editor of the *Katholischer Westen,* answered Gmeiner in his *Goliath, der Bastardphilister und David, der ehrliche Israelite, oder Der Kampf des "katholischen" Anglo-Amerika mit dem katholischen Deutschtum* (Dubuque, 1887). This latter pamphlet was particularly intemperate, and evidenced the extremes to which the protagonists were drawn in the heat of controversy.[64] Reverend Karl Algermissen published *Der deutsch-amerikanische Katholik;* Monsignor Joseph Jessing, founder of the Pontifical College Josephinum, came forth with *Katholisch und deutsch-amerikanisch;* Charles F. St. Laurent entered the fray on the side of the Germans, while espousing the position of the French

[63] *Ibid.*

[64] Gonner divided his brochure into five sections. In the first he berated the English language on a philological basis, claiming it resembled the barking of dogs, and said every European language was superior to it, and especially the German language. It was providential that several languages existed in the United States, since it was a divine means of educating the people to live in different sections and on the land, thus avoiding the misery of big cities. To every attempt of children to speak English, the parents should respond with the rod. In the family, parish school, and religious exercises German must prevail. German bishops should go to Germany to obtain their priests, and young men of German extraction should be sent to Germany to study in seminaries there.

In the second section the author extolled the immigrant stock as superior both physically and morally to the consumptive Yankees. What the United States had accomplished in military achievement had been done by immigrants. German language and customs were what made them superior physically and spiritually, and he advocated the moderate use of healthful beer and natural wine.

Third, he stressed that Germans lived close to God on farms while the majority of the Anglo-Americans plied commerce, trade, and manufacturing. Americanization would mean the loss of their healthy outlook and conservative tendencies.

In the fourth place, Gonner stated, the German, and especially the German Catholic, should not consider himself as a guest of the Anglo-Americans. He used his heavenly Father's possessions according to His will, and besides Catholic Germany under Charles V owned the land of America before any Anglo-American did. Only by robbery, thievery, and might did the Puritan supplant the Catholic German, Spaniard, and Frenchman. He also prophesied that under the hegemony of the Catholic Hapsburgs Germany would dominate Europe and America.

In the final section he pointed out that with the loss of Gaelic customs and language the Irish had been weakened in their religion. The same would happen to German Catholics if they were considered as second-class Catholics. German priests, he said, learned the language of other nationalities in their parishes easily, and they practiced, not just talked about, love of neighbor.

Gonner's pamphlet was among the most extreme statements made at this time and cannot be regarded as typical of the German position.

Canadian minority, in *Language and Nationality*. A brochure, *Audiatur et altera pars,* by Dr. Anton Heiter, editor of the *Christliche Woche,* and Wilhelm Keilmann, editor of the *Täglicher Volksfreund,* which they published under the names of *Tacitus* and *Germanicus,* was a rejoinder to Bishops Gilmour and Moore's memorial of 1885. This latter brochure stressed the point that the Catholic Church embraced all nations but was of no nation. Catholics, they wrote, can render the Church a real service by working to unite all nationalities into one harmonious whole so that the immigrants could be Catholics and American at the same time. To do this the languages of the immigrants must be continued at least in church exercises. A far greater obstacle to them was the growing "Americanism" evidenced in certain sections of the Church, a nationalism which would do it harm. The line of attack pursued by Heiter and Keilmann would become more pronounced in the succeeding conflict.

The most characteristic German answer to Gmeiner, however, was given by Reverend Anton H. Walburg, pastor of St. Augustine's Church, Cincinnati, in his brochure *The Question of Nationality in Its Relation to the Catholic Church in the United States.* Because he had written in English as Gmeiner had done, the audience was much larger. Published in 1889 and dedicated to his fellow priests in the German American Priests' Society, which will be discussed in the following chapter, Walburg's effort left no doubts as to the existing rift between the Americanizers and the national groups in the Church.

Walburg began by declaring that differences of nationality and religion were on the same level, and that there was no more distinction between an Irish or German American and an Anglo- or native American than there was between a Catholic and a Protestant American. He attacked the thesis of Gmeiner and Shea, who asserted that the Church should not give the impression of being a foreign body and that different national groups should give up their foreign associations, habits, and usages, by asserting himself that a new Nativism was creeping into the Church by such Americanization efforts.

The author proceeded to examine the characteristics of the three leading national groups in the United States: the Irish, German, and Anglo-Saxon peoples. Of the Irish he had many complimentary things to say, the most important of which was that they were the pioneers of the faith in this country who had firmly planted the cross in the United States. But his point was that they were able to do this only because they kept their Irish nationality and did not enter at once into the spirit of American life and character. The second national group, the Germans, he wrote, were a naturally religious people who belonged among the best Catholics of the world. As proof of this statement he traced the influence of the Holy Roman Empire on Christianity and then stressed the resistance which German Catholics had been making for the past seventeen years to Bismarck's regime. Walburg, as the first native of German descent to be ordained to the priesthood in Cincinnati, denied that Americanism consisted in speaking the English language. He adduced statistics to show how large a number of the vocations to the priesthood and sisterhood had come from German areas where English was not spoken or spoken imperfectly. He also pointed out that Methodists, who were Anglo-Saxons, did not compel their brethren to speak English, but rather established separate, exclusive German Methodist congregations for which they imported preachers from Germany. By these arguments he arrived at his main thesis that,

> . . . here, where the people are sovereign, they can change the official language as well as they can change political parties, and could, if they so desired, make German or French the language of the country. Therefore, as a Republican does not consider himself a better American than a Democrat because his party predominates, or vice versa, so one who speaks English cannot consider himself a better American than one who speaks another language, simply because his language predominates.[65]

In fact, Walburg was convinced that America would have a richer culture if two or more languages were learned by its citizens, rather than one tongue, which limited their educational horizons and contact possibilities with the rest of the world. He went on to defend, with dubious logic, the value of military discipline, as practiced in Germany, in developing the moral and physical health of a nation, and he advocated a similar program for the United States as a means of approaching the standard of learning which Germany upheld in modern society as foremost in the ranks of civilized nations. His conclusion was that as the Irish had laid the foundation of the Church, so the Germans had contributed the principal share in beautifying and decorating it through music, painting, sculpture, and architecture.

When speaking of the Anglo-Americans, Walburg displayed an intemperate outlook which such "Americanizers" as Sarah Peter, Isaac Hecker, Orestes Brownson had earlier deplored, and which was now so strongly opposed by John Gilmary Shea and prelates, such as Ireland,

[65] Pp. 28–29.

Gibbons, and Keane. Walburg characterized the Anglo Saxon as a boaster, arrogant, pharisaical, worshiper of gold and material quantities, hypocritical in morals especially in regard to temperance, vain, lacking in nobility and eminent worth, intolerant and puffed up with spiritual pride. He asked:

> And now we are asked to assimilate with this element, to adopt its usages, customs, feelings, and manners? That cannot but prove detrimental to the Church. Are we going to lead our simple, straight-forward, honest Germans and Irish into this whirlpool of American life, this element wedded to this world, bent upon riches, upon political distinction, where their consciences will be stifled, their better sentiments trampled under foot?
>
> But it will be said, religion will keep them from rushing to this end, will sustain them in the path of virtue and rectitude. Nonsense! Denationalization is demoralization. It degrades and debases human nature. A foreigner who loses his nationality is in danger of losing his faith and character. When the German immigrant, on arriving in this country, seeks to throw aside his nationality and to become "quite English, you know," the first word he learns is generally a curse, and the rowdy element is his preference to the sterling qualities of the Puritans. A German aping American customs and manners is, in his walk, talk, and appearance, in most cases, an object of ridicule and contempt. Like as the Indians in coming in contact with the whites adopted the vices rather than the virtues of the latter, so the effort to Americanize the foreigner will prove deteriorating.[66]

In view of the above, Walburg's conclusion surprised everyone. He stated at the end of his pamphlet that it was doubtful whether the supporters of the movement to strengthen and perpetuate German nationality in the Church in the United States would be successful. He felt that no foreign nationality could permanently maintain itself in this country, because it was natural for immigrants to wish to find their fatherland in the land of their adoption: "They will Americanize in spite of themselves. The American nationality will finally prevail. It assimilates the children of foreigners, and is strengthened by contributions from foreign sources. Foreign nationalities will be absorbed by it and flow in the current of American life." His advice, then, was that the transition from one nationality to another should not be hastened or forced, and he begged:

> For the present we should remember that the American nationality counts for little or nothing in the American Church, and if it is ever

[66] *Ibid.*, pp. 44–45.

to be converted, it must be done by the clergy and population already Catholics. The most efficient portion of our Catholic body are of foreign birth and training, and will be for some time to come. However we may work for non-Catholics, we must carry with us the sympathies and affections of the Catholic body. This body is composed of various nationalities with peculiarities of languages, habits, and prejudices. If these are opposed, and the national sensitiveness wounded, they may become irritated and indifferent, and lose their affection for the Church. We cannot move much in advance of the public sentiment of our own body. We must hold a tight rein, check the impatience to Americanize, and though there may be some wrangling among conflicting nationalities, if we move slowly we will finally land in the American nationality with the Catholic body under full control and faithful to the Church.[67]

Walburg would be heard from on this question in the future, and then again he would come forward with surprising leadership. Meanwhile his advice to Americanize slowly became the rallying cry among German leaders, and the principal accusation they would make against those whom they considered their opponents was that the Americanizing process was being pushed much too precipitously.

[67] *Ibid.*, pp. 61–62. Reverend William Stang, of the Cathedral of Saints Peter and Paul, Providence, Rhode Island, presented a milder thesis than Walburg in a pamphlet entitled: *Germany's Debt to Ireland* (New York, 1889). This brochure was issued on the anniversary of the twelfth centenary of the introduction of Christianity into Franconia by Irish missionaries. Stang stated: "Germans, who are by nature grateful, have always acknowledged their religious and literary indebtedness to Ireland. . . . A thousand years of strange and sad changes have not cooled the warmth of gratitude in German hearts toward Ireland."

Chapter III

Union and Disunion

During the years of mounting tension over the German question in the West, the infant American branch of the St. Raphaelsverein was also faced with serious difficulties. When the cause of this society at the port of New York became associated with the aims of German Catholic leaders in the West, through a national campaign to build an immigrant house for the St. Raphaelsverein, the stage was set for one of the most unfortunate incidents in the history of the Church in the United States. It was then that the unpleasant charges associated with so-called "Cahenslyism" came to the fore.

Before his return to Europe after his first tour of the United States, Peter Paul Cahensly met, on October 18, 1883, with the members of the German Roman Catholic Central Immigrant Committee of New York and several prominent German Catholics of the New York region. At this meeting the New York committee recognized the St. Raphaelsverein as working with it in the care of the German immigrant.[1] Bishop Wigger of Newark accepted the presidency of the new society, and Archbishop Corrigan, coadjutor to Cardinal McCloskey, gave official endorsement and recognition to the work. He also agreed to serve as honorary president.[2] Joseph Kölble was retained as agent to meet incoming German Catholics at the port of New York. Since 1848 all ships with immigrants landed at Castle Garden, located on the tip of Manhattan Island, where the New York State Board of Commissioners of Immigration, established in 1847, directed screen-

[1] First members of the directorate of the St. Raphaelsverein in the United States included Bishop Wigger, president; Wilhelm von Sachs, first vice-president; Louis Benziger, second vice-president; Henry Amy, treasurer; and Reverend Anthony B. Schwenniger, Messrs. Wilhelm Schickel, Bernard Amend, Henry Ridder, and Augustus Rölker, trustees.

[2] *ALH,* Wilhelm von Sachs to Corrigan, New York, Aug. 1, 1883, copy; Nov. 12, 1883, copy. Cf. also New York *Katholisches Volksblatt,* Jan. 14, 1884.

ing and registration processes. At Castle Garden the St. Raphaelsverein hoped to offer the same services free of charge to Catholic immigrants as its agents had supplied in the European ports of departure.

The St. Raphaelsverein also began at this time an extensive correspondence with bishops and abbots throughout the country, enlisting their support, asking them to spread information of this endeavor and to promote the cause wherever possible. German newspapers, both Catholic and secular, were contacted and requested to print publicity of the society. Leaders of member societies of the Central Verein were asked to supply information on suitable places for homesteads in settlements where churches and schools were already established, and in areas where a German or German-speaking priest could be found. In all of this activity the American St. Raphaelsverein discovered from the beginning that their labors would not be hampered or restricted in the new world as they were then being limited in Germany. Cahensly, after he returned to Limburg, supplied directives as to procedure, suggested that people whom he had met on his trip be contacted, asked information on suitable colonization localities, and generally participated actively in the endeavor. Since his experiences had proved to be most effective in European ports, the American society copied the techniques which he recommended.[3]

The same personal charity was exercised toward all immigrants at the port of debarkation as they had experienced from St. Raphaelsverein agents before setting sail. Kölble met the boats, and was recognized on the docks by the St. Raphael cross and anchor emblem which he wore on his coat. He conducted families through registration and customs, helped them with language difficulties, directed them to low-priced lodging houses, and placed them on trains that would carry them to the West. Money was exchanged or banked for distracted immigrants, baggage claimed or recovered, names and addresses checked, and lost persons traced. Petitions for housekeepers, laborers, farm hands, and the like, were presented to immigrants who had no plans for their future. In the year 1883–1885, from a total of $2,712.90 taken

[3] *ALH,* Wilhelm von Sachs to the following: "Rt. Rev. Bishop," New York, Nov. 16, 1883; Friedrich Lederer, New York, Nov. 16, 1883; Innocent Wolf, O.S.B., New York, Nov. 18, 1883; Brucker Ludloff and Co., New York, Nov. 18, 1883; Nicholas Gonner, New York, Dec. 4, 1883; B. Herder and Co., Dec. 4, 1883; *Wahrheitsfreund,* New York, Dec. 5, 1883; Martin Marty, O.S.B., New York, Dec. 10, 1883; Francis X. Krautbauer, Dec. 15, 1883; Bernhardt Katz, New York, Nov. 12, 1883. Von Sachs was a well-known New York banker who took a deep interest in the work of the St. Raphaelsverein and who later served as its vice-president.

in by the St. Raphaelsverein in the United States, $1,745.32 was distributed for this work.[4]

Rumbles of dissatisfaction with the society began to be heard, however. The editors of the Baltimore *Katholische Volkszeitung* asked a series of pointed questions of the St. Raphaelsverein in their issue of August 2, 1884. They wanted to know why the society was limiting its activity solely to New York, since Cahensly had come primarily to establish branches in the West where most of the immigrants ultimately settled. Newspapers were not receiving publicity releases from the St. Raphaelsverein, whereas, the Baltimore editors insisted, each German Catholic paper should run a whole page of such information each week. The editors had told Cahensly that as soon as he left the United States the movement would disappear unless it was spread across the whole country. The *Katholische Volkszeitung* suggested that Cardinal McCloskey be approached to release a German priest, one who could help with the work and be free to travel throughout the country and create interest in the cause. If this plan were followed, they believed that within a year the German Catholics of the United States would be supporting the work.

These suggestions were excellent and to the point. While Kölble worked hard, yet he was only one agent faced with thousands of cases. Furthermore, a priest was badly needed to meet the spiritual needs of the immigrants, to establish a permanent mission with a chapel, and to prevent proselytizing on the part of Protestant ministers. On June 13, 1884, the St. Raphaelsverein decided to release Kölble from his position as its agent and made plans to have a priest appointed to Castle Garden. Kölble continued as agent for the New York Immigration Committee of the Central Verein, however, and insisted that he was official representative for German Catholic immigrants.

It was first agreed to appoint Reverend John A. Weber, a priest of German birth and pastor of St. Boniface Church, Westphalia, Iowa, to the position. However, because of ill-health, Weber refused. Cahensly then approached the chancery office of the Diocese of Luxembourg for a priest to act as agent of the New York St. Raphaelsverein, and he was given Reverend John Reuland, of Ettelbrück.[5] When Father Reuland

[4] *Mitglieder des St. Raphaelsverein in den Vereinigten Staaten zum Schutze der Ein- und Auswanderer* (New York, 1886). Cf. also *Der Ansiedler,* July 8, 1885. Early contributors included: Bishop Wigger, $500; Henry Amy, $500; St. Raphaelsverein in Limburg, $100; Peter Paul Cahensly, $50; Benziger Brothers, $250; Pustet Company, $100. In the New York *Katholisches Volksblatt* of May 22, 1884, seventy-five single contributors of from $10 to $1 were also listed.

[5] *ALH,* Cahensly to Chancery Office of Luxembourg, Limburg, May 11, 1885. Reu-

agreed to do the work, Cahensly proceeded to pay his first year's salary of $500 as well as his transportation to the United States. "It will be difficult the first year," he told Reuland, "and you must make sacrifices and have good will. But almighty God will take care of you."[6] Cahensly also sent Reuland to Bremen, Hamburg, Rotterdam, Antwerp, and to Father Rethmann at Le Havre to study the work of the missions there before he set out for New York.

It would have been better if a German American priest had been appointed to the position, since Reuland was unacquainted with the American scene and was temperamentally deficient in the art of winning people to the cause. He was a conscientious and zealous priest, a firm rock upon which to build, but as the New York *Monatszeitung* declared, "people were more afraid of him than close to him."[7] Old friends of Kölble on the New York Immigration Committee, such as the Amend family and Hermann Ritter, editor of the *Katholisches Volksblatt,* rallied to Kölble's side and viewed Reuland as an intruder. Consequently, not long after his arrival aboard the *Canada,* Reuland found himself in a charged situation.[8]

Upon making application before the New York State Board of Commissioners of Immigration for a license to act as a Catholic agent for work among the immigrants, Reuland was informed that Kölble was already caring for the Germans, and that there was already a priest stationed at Castle Garden for such activity. The Commissioners were referring to Reverend John J. Riordan, formerly of St. Bernard's Church in New York, who had established the Mission of Our Lady of the Rosary for Irish Immigrants at 7 State Street, on January 1, 1884. The Irish Catholic Colonization Society had at its meeting in

---

land had been chaplain at Heisdorf from 1877–1881, and assistant pastor at Ettelbrück from 1881 until he left for New York. He served as agent for the St. Raphaelsverein in New York from July 27, 1885, until November 7, 1891, when he resigned to become pastor of Holy Trinity Church in Syracuse.

6 *ALH,* Cahensly to Reuland, Limburg, June 4, 1885, copy. Reverend Peter Schlösser, St. Raphaelsverein agent at Bremen, visited the United States in 1884 with the view of possibly remaining as agent. But because he was not accepted at Castle Garden, and also because he knew no English, he returned to Germany. There he reported that it was difficult to interest people in the United States in the St. Raphaelsverein, and he recommended that a priest be sent to head the movement.

7 November 9, 1891.

8 Reuland drew up a documented chronicle of his administration and forwarded it to Reverend Urban Nageleisen on May 27, 1905, from Syracuse where he was then doing parish work. This important document is preserved in *ALH,* "Material zur Geschichte des 'Leo Haus' aus der Mappe von Rev. J. Reuland während seiner Amtsthätigkeit in der Einwanderer-Mission in New York vom 27 July 1885 bis zum 7 Nov. 1891."

Chicago in May, 1883, voted for the establishment of such a mission, a move which had been actively sponsored by Bishops Ireland, Spalding, and Stephen V. Ryan, C.M., of Buffalo. Cardinal McCloskey had approved the suggestion and had given one of his priests for the work.[9] Despite the fact that there were fourteen Protestant ministers and agents at the landing docks, both Kölble and Riordan viewed Reuland's entrance into the field with misgivings. Kölble insisted that he had never been informed officially by the St. Raphaelsverein that he was no longer their agent; moreover, he was still acting as agent for the New York Immigration Committee, a branch society of the Central Verein. Riordan claimed that since one priest was already at work no other was needed, and this despite the fact that he could not speak German. Cahensly himself appealed to the immigration board for recognition of his agent, but they once again refused.

The internal dissension dragged on for seven months before it ultimately reached the press of the country. Both Kölble and Reuland carried their cause before the public with resulting confusion and misunderstanding. Reuland intemperately charged that Kölble had not collected money for the cause, had not built up the St. Raphaelsverein, but had only acted for himself and was now being supported by his friends.[10] Kölble defended his sixteen years of service, while Riordan insisted that priests should not enter the work on a nationality basis, apparently at the same time forgetting that he himself was there professedly for the service of one nationality. Upon being questioned by the Board of Commissioners if he was there to serve more than Germans, Reuland replied, in the tradition of the St. Raphaelsverein which had from its very beginning cared for immigrants of all nations and religions who appealed for aid: "From the Catholic point of view and from the standpoint of charity there is no nationality. I always try to do good." To Reuland the difficulty was all the more vexing because Cardinal Simeoni had only recently again informed Prince Isenburg-Birstein, president of the St. Raphaelsverein:

> I am happy at the news I have received from Herr Cahensly con-

[9] Cf. John J. Riordan, "The Priest at Castle Garden," *CW,* XLII (Jan., 1886), pp. 563–570. Cahensly, in *SRB,* II (Oct., 1887), pp. 58–59, praised this new Catholic Immigration Bureau and stated that although the Irish were twenty years behind the St. Raphaelsverein, yet they had already made strong attacks against those misleading the immigrants. Cf. also "Sketch and History of the Irish Catholic Benevolent Union of the United States and Canada," *Proceedings* (New York, 1892), pp. 3–8.

[10] *ALH,* Reuland to George Weber, New York, Dec. 9, 1885. Cf. *Herold des Glaubens,* Dec. 23, 1885, for discussion of the controversy, by Rev. John N. Enzelberger, who stated that Kölble was being attacked because he took commissions from railroad companies on tickets which he sold to immigrants.

cerning the care and energy he devoted to this noble work of helping emigrants who leave their country. This work has always been dear to me, and I have done my best to help him. At the last Council of Baltimore the Bishops were invited to take heartfelt interest in immigration work, and what they decided there was very encouraging. You may tell the Secretary of the St. Raphaelsverein that he can be sure that I will do all I can sincerely do to interest the American Bishops in the noble work for the future of all immigrants, in both an earthly and a spiritual way.[11]

The German Catholic newspapers in the United States soon backed Reuland in his effort for recognition. Cahensly wrote an open letter in the papers asking for support of Reuland and entreating that, after his first year's salary had been paid, it would be a great loss to have him return to Germany.[12] The *Glaubensbote,* of Louisville, accused the German Catholics in New York of not being interested enough in the work, and asked them to come forth and accept Reuland. The Cincinnati *Wahrheitsfreund* advised that the New York Immigration Committee and the St. Raphaelsverein should merge their efforts for the common good, while both the Baltimore *Katholische Volkszeitung* and the Milwaukee *Columbia* believed that Riordan had enough to do with Irish immigrants. Since a priest could do more than a layman, both Riordan and Kölble should accept Reuland. The Baltimore *Volksbote* asked if in this case again, as so often in the past, work for the German immigrant would be neglected. They termed the incident a disgrace for German Catholics in the United States, and insisted that no privileges were being asked for Reuland, only that he receive equal justice with the Irish priest. Reverend A. J. Decker, pastor of St. Anthony's Church, Milwaukee, forwarded a long letter to Gonner's *Luxemburger Gazette,* accusing the Irish of playing politics to keep Reuland out and describing in detail the activity of Protestant missionaries among Catholics on the New York docks. He wanted both a German and a Polish missionary at Castle Garden to save the immigrant from proselytizers. He claimed that one priest of the English tongue was not enough, just as it was not enough in parish life:

This idea is current, but it cannot be carried through because people are not so green anymore, as the poor immigrants are in New York. Our German Bishops should show interest in this affair. We see evidences of German customs and spirit in both the East and the West;

[11] *ALH,* Simeoni to Isenburg-Birstein, Rome, Apr. 24, 1885.
[12] *Columbia,* Aug. 5, 1885.

that the German Bishops and Priests are out in front in regard to schools; that German parishes do great work. Why should the German priest Father Reuland be the fifth wheel on the wagon, or less than that? Should this agent, our German brother, take an assistantship, he who is not used to a lazy life, because he won't be allowed to work in Castle Garden? That would be a disgrace for the German tongue.[13]

Such attacks as Decker's accomplished little good for those concerned. The problem was rather resolved in a quiet way by a German Catholic layman from Brooklyn, a plumber by the name of Joseph Zoll, who visited Reuland and inquired from him what was happening. After Reuland explained the situation to him he replied: "Father, you will soon be in Castle Garden." Reuland could not believe that this simple workingman could help him where Catholic leaders had failed. But Zoll went directly to Senator James Wirth, a non-Catholic Republican, who had friends on the board of commissioners, and the very next day a new plea by Reuland was approved and he was received at Castle Garden on March 5, 1886, by what he described as "Ein Wirken des politischen pulls."[14]

Riordan went over to South Orange to Bishop Wigger when he heard of Reuland's acceptance and requested that Reuland be withdrawn, and that a German priest should be appointed as Riordan's assistant to care for the incoming Germans. But Wigger refused Riordan on the grounds that the Germans had founded their mission and wanted to retain it. He furthermore did not believe experience showed that the Irish and Germans worked well together. Father Anthony B. Schwenniger, editor of the *Wahrheitsfreund,* and also of the New York Central Immigration Committee, had approached Archbishop Corrigan with a like proposal of a German assistant for Riordan as the solution to the problem. Corrigan, however, had just received another letter from Simeoni in which Reuland and his work were recommended, and he, therefore, informed Reuland: "You are there and you are to stay there."[15] Riordan then sent a friendly message to Reuland in which he stated: "I was fighting for a principle. It was not against you personally." The difficulty was further terminated at the Thirty-First General Assembly of the

[13] *Luxemburger Gazette,* Oct. 20, 1885. Cf. also *Glaubensbote,* Oct. 6, 20, 27, and Nov. 1, 1885; *Wahrheitsfreund,* Aug. 5 and Oct. 7, 1885; *Columbia,* Oct. 8, 29, 1885; *Glaubensbote,* Aug. 4, 12, and Oct. 20, 1885; *Katholischer Hausfreund,* Oct. 20, 1885; *Katholisches Wochenblatt,* Nov. 8, 1885; *Sonntagsblatt für katholische Christen,* XLIX (Dec. 6, 1885), p. 777.

[14] *ALH,* John Reuland, "Ein ungedrucktes Blatt von hinter den Coulisen."

[15] *Ibid.* Cf. also *AANY,* Simeoni to Corrigan, Rome, Feb. 25, 1886.

Central Verein at Toledo, on September 7, 1886, when the New York Immigration Committee was disbanded and it was recommended that all immigrants be sent to the St. Raphaelsverein. This move was instigated by Reverend William H. Tappert, pastor of St. John's Church, Covington, Kentucky, who was to be one of the strongest defenders of the St. Raphaelsverein in the United States. Reports had been sent to Rome that the Central Verein had not been interested in the St. Raphaelsverein, and Tappert both refuted these charges and moved that the Central Verein support their endeavors wholeheartedly, a move which was passed and publicly affirmed by a special statement of co-operation.[16]

The St. Raphaelsverein was now in a position to carry through its program in earnest. A statement was issued by the board of directors, announcing that Reuland was its agent and that he was already at work in his office on the third floor at 15 State Street. Immigrants were directed to him for assistance and protection.[17] Then the German Catholic newspapers swung into line behind Reuland and he was supported strongly in over twenty-five weeklies and dailies across the country. The St. Raphaelsverein received favorable publicity, especially in the columns of the *Katholische Volkszeitung* in Baltimore, *Nord-Amerika* in Philadelphia, *Aurora und Buffalo Volksfreund, Stimme der Wahrheit* in Detroit, *Katholisches Wochenblatt* in Chicago, *Luxemburger Gazette* in Dubuque, *Nordstern* in St. Cloud, *Wanderer* in St. Paul, *Amerika* and *Herold des Glaubens* in St. Louis, *Wahrheitsfreund* in Cincinnati, *Katholischer Glaubensbote* in Louisville, *Beobachter* in Pittsburgh, *Californischer Volksfreund,* Ohio *Waisenfreund, Excelsior,* and *Columbia* in Milwaukee.[18]

Reuland's recognition coincided with the appearance of Cahensly's first publication, a quarterly magazine entitled *Der St. Raphaels Blatt.* Published at Limburg, this journal was devoted to furthering the cause of immigrant care, and was the fulfillment of one of Cahensly's

[16] *ALH,* Reuland to Spaunhorst, New York, Aug. 10, Oct. 22, Dec. 13, 27, 28, 1885; Reuland to Menges, New York, Nov. 27, 1885.

[17] *ALH,* "Statement of Policy," Mar. 8, 1886. This release was signed by Bishop Wigger, president; William von Sachs, first vice-president; Louis Benziger, second vice-president; Henry Amy, treasurer; and John Reuland, secretary. Local member societies of the Central Verein, such as St. Pius Verein in New York, Der Hl. Familien Verein in Union Hill, New Jersey, and St. Ludgerus Verein, Baltimore, the oldest member of the Central Verein, issued public statements of recognition of Reuland even before this meeting was held.

[18] *Festschrift zum silbernen Jubiläum des Leo-Hauses* (New York, 1914), p. 29. Cf. also *Volkszeitung,* Nov. 7 and Dec. 26, 1885; *Katholisches Volksblatt,* Dec. 31, 1885, and Jan. 3, 1886; *Nord-Amerika,* Dec. 12, 1885.

fondest dreams. In its first issue he laid down the editorial policy as follows:

> We wish, by honest reports of social and ecclesiastical conditions in several countries across the ocean, to place our emigrants in a position to decide for themselves where they can best care for their material and spiritual needs, where they may find a parish, church, and school to fulfill their religious obligations, and give to their children a Christian, Catholic upbringing. That is our program. . . .[19]

In the magazine emigrants could find the latest reports from St. Raphael agents, ship news, notices of available land and colonies, addresses of churches, people to contact in the new world, prices of travel by ship and rail, statistics of emigrants to each country, and warnings against dishonest agents they would meet en route. The German government was fearlessly attacked for its restrictions on emigrant work as early as the second issue, and Bismarck and his colleagues were reminded that Catholics were leaving Germany primarily because of his *Kulturkampf* program. Cahensly stated that the Church desired peace for her children, but when she cannot secure it and her children begin to wander away, then that same Church, which is international in character, must help and protect those who go in search of a better homeland. Grace, advice, and warning must be with Catholic emigrants at all times.[20]

In that same second issue the courage and independence of the St. Raphaelsverein were further manifested by an open attack on the Commissioners of Immigration in New York.[21] The *St. Raphaels Blatt* asserted that possible immigration restrictions contemplated by the United States Congress would not be a wise solution to the growing problem of the influx of paupers and poor from Europe. A program of more equitable distribution of funds by the commission would, in Cahensly's opinion, be a better approach, along with the establishment of a new commission for closer examination and screening. But as long as such control resided in the power of the New York State commissioners, who were appointees of the New York State legislature and like it were members of the same majority Republican party,

[19] *SRB,* I (Jan., 1886), p. 2.

[20] *SRB,* I (Apr., 1886), pp. 17–21.

[21] *SRB,* I (July, 1886), pp. 40–43; II (Jan., 1887), pp. 6–7. In April, 1890, Ellis Island was chosen as the landing place for all immigrants coming into New York Harbor. Authority was placed in the hands of the United States Congress which appointed a new commission to replace the New York State Board of Commissioners of Immigration.

not much could be hoped for. Not only political appointees were attacked, but also conditions at Castle Garden itself: the high prices charged unsuspecting immigrants for simple services, taxes on food and other necessities, as well as commissions on railroad tickets. Emigrants were warned not to buy anything at Castle Garden, but rather to go to Father Reuland who would assist them.

Meanwhile Reuland began to work unmolestedly among the new arrivals who were weekly coming in greater numbers. He quickly edited and had published in New York and Limburg small booklets containing basic and necessary information which he could place in the hands of immigrants.[22] He then turned to a program of directing immigrants to Catholic colonies already established in the West for Germans. In this way the American St. Raphael branch hoped to prevent German Catholics from settling in large metropolitan areas. German Catholic newspapers again co-operated wholeheartedly in this project, a program which they had been advocating for many years. The *Katholisches Volksblatt* encouraged the St. Raphaelsverein to organize this effort by starting other St. Raphael societies in the West, which would collect money from German Catholics already settled there. This money would then be used to build churches and schools in regions where good wooded lands were available and suitable for immigrant colonies of forty or fifty families who could be directed there through the St. Raphaelsverein both in Germany and in the United States.[23] It was an ambitious program, but the board of directors in New York did not hesitate. Early in January of 1886 they issued a newspaper release, asking priests and people to interest themselves in forming local branches of the society. Pastors in the larger cities where German Catholics were strongest were asked to be especially active, since Reuland was too busy to travel throughout the country for the cause.[24] Cahensly also joined in the campaign through the columns of his new magazine. There he insisted that German Catholic colonies in the United States were an absolute necessity: "Where the German Catholics live among German neighbors, they

[22] John Reuland, *St. Raphael Confraternity for the Protection of Immigrants and Emigrants* (New York, 1888); *Der Luxemburger in der neuen Welt* (Limburg, 1888); *Ein Erstes Wort in der neuen Welt dem katholischen Einwanderer* (New York, 1891); *Führer für deutsche katholische Auswanderer nach den Vereinigten Staaten von Nord-Amerika* (Limburg, 1893).

[23] September 23, 1885.

[24] *Der Wanderer,* Jan. 4, 1886. Cf. also *Wahrheitsfreund,* Jan. 4, 1886. Here the St. Raphaelsverein in New York for the first time spoke of losses suffered by the Church in the United States, and established the total losses at seven million.

not only can preserve their language and national peculiarities, but what is more important for them and their neighbors, their faith can be maintained." He asserted that millions of Catholic emigrants to North America along with their families had lost their faith because they lacked an opportunity to associate with their own people and companions in the faith, surrounded as they had been by an "a-Catholic and mixed national environment." He fixed losses to the Church in the United States at six million, based on his calculation of a total of twelve to thirteen million Catholic emigrants combined with natural growth. The official Catholic directory at the same time listed a total of only seven million Catholics.[25]

The *St. Raphaels Blatt* began to describe and to recommend regions most suitable for settlement by the emigrants. These suggestions had a real influence on immigration settlement, since the magazine was not only placed in the hands of every departing emigrant, but it was also distributed throughout the parishes and societies of Germany. As new branch societies were formed in other countries this influence on other nationalities became even greater than on the Germans, because the society was then better organized and had more contacts. In the period from 1886 to 1891 Cahensly recommended especially Lincoln and Boyle Counties in Kentucky and the area around Louisville because there were German parishes in those regions; Olpe in Lyons County and Westphalia in Anderson County, Kansas; Fostoria in Seneca County, Ohio; Roundout in Ulster County, New York; Templeton in Carroll County and Westphalia in Shelby County, Iowa; St. Kilian in Taylor County, Wisconsin; and any place in Stearns County, Minnesota. In the Dakotas he suggested the Fargo region because Cass County was traversed by both the Red River and the Northern Pacific Railroad. Also favorably mentioned were the Dakota counties of Grand Forks, Walsh, Pembina, and Devils Lake; Minnehaha, Moody, and Lake. In Oregon the Benedictine settlement around Mount Angel Abbey in Marion County was praised because of its good land and the flourishing church and school established there. The St. Raphaelsverein never encouraged German Catholics to settle in the southern section of the United States, because too many Catholics had lost their faith in the South and the climate was too hot for Germanic peoples. Cahensly wrote that his travels in the southern states had convinced him that no German Catholic should consider going there before he had first consulted a St. Raphael agent and learned of conditions in the West and the Northwest. German Catholic

[25] *SRB,* I (Apr., 1886), p. 22.

newspapers in the United States generally agreed entirely with Cahensly on this point.[26]

Bishops who had joined with Cahensly in his project in 1883 now also seconded his efforts to direct the immigrants to Catholic settlements. Bishop Fink, O.S.B., of Leavenworth, encouraged German Catholics to consider Kansas as their future home. If they did not come as a group, he claimed, they could not afford the high-priced land in the West. It would be better for them to stay in the East rather than to emigrate individually, because so many had previously gone off alone into regions far from churches and schools. But if they would consider Kansas, there they would find cheap land near the Missouri and Pacific Railroad in Anderson County, Catholic land agents, and a region that was "ganz Deutsch." If a number came, they would find a pastor awaiting them in Westphalia, Reverend Bernard Fresenborg, who had already built St. Teresa's Church.[27]

One of the unfortunate developments in the history of the Church in the United States during these years was the inability of the St. Raphaelsverein to continue and perfect this support of settling work which it had only begun. The need for a mission station in New York was a more urgent demand at the outset, and by the time the society had become associated with a newly formed national association of German priests in a campaign to build this mission station, misunderstandings and complications had quickly developed. In 1891 these misunderstandings combined to produce the so-called "Cahenslyism" battle, an event which branded the future work of the St. Raphaelsverein for many years. Support of existing colonization projects and plans for German immigrants were abandoned. Much more serious was the effect that this limitation of activity had on St. Raphael work among Italian and Slavic immigrants after the turn of the century. If the society had been able to set up a working program of directing immigrants to various Catholic colonies, and had fully organized this program by the time southern and central European immigration began in earnest, the history of the Church in reference to these peoples might possibly have been different.

In 1887, however, the directors of the St. Raphaelsverein had no idea of the storms ahead. They were primarily interested at that time in expanding their activities at the New York docks through a

[26] *SRB,* I (July, 1886), p. 48; II (Oct., 1887), pp. 41–42; III (Jan., 1888), pp. 7–8; III (Apr., 1888), pp. 26–30; III (July, 1888), p. 44. Cf. also Berlin *Deutsche Kolonialzeitung,* Nov. 19, 1888; *Amerika,* Sept. 23, 1888; Milwaukee *Herald,* Oct. 26, 1887; *Der Ansiedler,* Feb. 11, 1884, and Dec. 1, 1888.

[27] *Katholische Volkszeitung,* Apr. 16, 1886.

mission station which would have a chapel for spiritual exercises as well as board and lodging accommodations. In all of the European ports where the society was established such missions were operating. Reuland, in his one-room office, could not perform the services which Cahensly felt basic to their endeavor. Members began to join the society throughout the country, but the small yearly dues they submitted could never defray expenses for a project of such proportion as a mission station. German newspapers carried articles pointing up the need for the establishment of this mission,[28] but it was not until the German American priests of the United States became interested in it that the project became an actuality.

The active support of these churchmen was pledged on February 16, 1887, at St. Peter's Church in Chicago. At that time Vicar-General Mühlsiepen, of St. Louis, called to order the first conference of the *Deutsch-Amerikaner Priester-Verein.* Sixty-five German priests from all sections of the country attended this general council, to make preliminary plans for organizing national meetings of German priests and general assemblies of German Catholics, clerical and lay, both to be modeled on the famed *Katholikentage* of Catholics in Germany. For many years this idea had been discussed among German leaders in the United States as a means of uniting German Catholics in public manifestations of their faith and common interests. Mühlsiepen declared that organization was now available to introduce "the German procedure in the United States." Chicago was chosen as the site of the first general assembly and it was decided to hold the priests' meeting and the public congress in conjunction with the annual Central Verein sessions beginning on September 6 of that year. It was determined that discussion would center on all questions pertaining to the interests of the German American Catholic body, the reformation of the German Catholic press, improvement of church and school music, establishment of a training college for American school teachers of both sexes, and, most of all, the erection of an immigrant house for the St. Raphaelsverein in New York. Father Färber had been advocating such a move for a number of years in the *Pastoral Blatt.* Now it was suggested that it would be appropriate, in view of the approaching golden jubilee of the priesthood of Leo XIII in 1888, to collect money from German Catholics in the United States and to petition the Holy See for permission to use it for the construction of this gift memorial in honor of the Holy Father. A central committee was organized, with Reverend Francis Goller, pastor of SS. Peter and

[28] *Glaubensbote,* Mar. 10, 1887.

Paul Church in St. Louis, as chairman,[29] and Reverends Peter Fischer, pastor of St. Anthony's Church, Chicago, and William Robbers, of St. John the Evangelist, Covington, as members. This committee was to send collection lists to all German priests in the country and make its first report at Chicago in September.[30]

But, unfortunately, individual German priests began at once to make intemperate statements in the public press. A reporter of the New York *Herald* and Chicago *Times* released an interview to the Associated Press which he had with "a prominent Catholic rector of a German Catholic Church in New York," in which this priest was reported as saying that the coming convention of German priests in Chicago had been called to advance German priests and to retard the advancement of Irish priests to the episcopacy.[31] Father Tappert,

[29] Like Monsignor Joseph Jessing, Goller came from Westphalia. Together with Mühlsiepen and Färber he led the campaign for preserving the German language among immigrants. His parish, SS. Peter and Paul in St. Louis, was a model, and his high school, staffed by the Marianist Brothers from Dayton, Ohio, was not only one of the first in the nation, but also one of the finest. He was active as well in the establishment of the German priests' society.

[30] *Bericht über die Verhandlungen der amerikanisch-deutschen Priester-Versammlung in Chicago am 16. Februar 1887* (Chicago, 1887). Cf. also the Pittsburgh *Catholic,* Mar. 19, 1887. Catholics of Polish nationality also organized a Polish National Alliance in 1880 for the same reasons that the Germans were organizing. The aims of the Polish society were the moral and material betterment of the Polish element, guardianship over Polish immigrants, strengthening of the political status of Polish immigrants, national press, commemoration of Polish national holidays, and the establishment of a sinking fund.

The editors of the Milwaukee *Catholic Citizen,* in their May 7 and August 13, 1887, issues, became very worried over growing national differences in the Catholic body. In several editorials they insisted that envies and bickerings were wasted energy in the United States, where all forces were at work blending races and unifying languages. Nationalities which continued to strive against such forces were weakening themselves because the manifest destiny of the different nationalities was amalgamation and assimilation. They stated: "Americanism has the future. Nothing can prevent the inevitable. It is an instinct of birth and nativity to prefer the home way of doing things to any foreign method. It is an element of patriotism. The children of foreign parents in this country always prefer the American way. Their ideals are American institutions, American customs, and American tastes. Granted, for the sake of argument, that some of the foreign customs and tastes are better. Nevertheless the general tendency and drift is toward the American style, and the good as well as the evil is apt to be appropriated.

"It is with the children of the foreign parent, and not with the foreign born population, that the Catholic Church in America is now chiefly concerned. Not more than one-fourth of the Catholics of America are of foreign birth. The Church must, therefore, put itself *en rapport,* so to speak, with the spirit and thoughts and tendencies of American life. Not submitting to them, but understanding them, sympathizing with them where they are good and efficacious, and checking them by a thorough familiarity with the grounds where they are not good."

[31] New York *Herald,* Aug. 3, 1887. At the thirty-first annual convention of the

who had been elected chairman of the committee on arrangements for the convention, denied the truth of this dispatch, and explained that the German priests intended only to declare to the world "the humble, steadfast faith of the German American Catholics and their devotion to the Holy See and the episcopacy of the Church in America." The meeting, he explained, was to be like similar conventions, in Germany, Switzerland, France, Belgium, and Italy, the benefits of which, Tappert declared, "have long been known and felt, not alone by the Church in general, but by Catholics of those countries." What Tappert failed to mention, however, was the fact that these assemblies he referred to were of all Catholics in each country, and not of one national group. He concluded by saying:

> It will be the aim of the convention to plant deeper the tenets of our holy faith in America, and from an observance of the manly love, good will can come to all men. We will not forget we are Catholics. Neither will we, while acknowledging our German descent, forget another thing — that we are American citizens.[32]

This interview, along with Dr. McGlynn's article in the *North American Review* which had appeared during the same month, brought prompt response from the *Northwestern Chronicle* in St. Paul. Bishop Ireland and his editor, Father Conway, were disturbed over the approaching Chicago convention, and they determined to ask the leading German ecclesiastics of the Northwest whether they felt there was growing discontent among the Germans there, and whether or not the assembly was likely to assume an anti-Irish character. Bishop Marty, O.S.B., responded that the Irish were among the most valuable members of his vicariate in the Dakotas, while Abbot Alexius Edelbrock, O.S.B., of St. John's Abbey, answered straightforwardly:

> Though a German by birth I have lived in this country since a child and admire and love its institutions. The question of nationality should not enter into God's Church. Unquestionably Catholics should have every opportunity to practice their religion in their own language, and in mixed congregations no matter how small any particular nationality may be, those who are best acquainted with a foreign tongue should have the advantage of hearing the Gospel read and sermons preached

---

Catholic Central Verein in Toledo on September 7, 1886, it was voted to combine a general Catholic assembly with their next convention. The committee set up to make arrangements for the first *Katholikentag,* and to co-operate with the committee of the Priests' Society, included Friedrich Arendes, St. Louis, Wilhelm Caspar, Milwaukee, and Tappert of the Priests' Society.

[32] Milwaukee *Catholic Citizen,* Aug. 13, 1887.

to them, in their own language. I always instruct our Fathers [the Benedictines] to carry out this idea. Unfortunately it is not always done in congregations where the German-speaking portions of the congregation are in a minority and hence some dissatisfaction and grumbling. But there is no widespread ill feeling between Catholics on account of national differences and priests and religious are respected by all irrespective of where they were born. The Chicago convention does not propose to touch upon this national issue at all. I have been several times invited to attend it, but I do not know if I will be able to attend it.[33]

Four pastors of the Diocese of St. Paul, Reverends John Stariha, of St. Francis de Sales Church; Charles Kögerl, of Sacred Heart Church; and Edward Ginther, O.S.B., of Assumption Church, all of St. Paul; and James Trobec, of St. Felix Church, Wabasha, were unanimous in the opinion that the Germans were not discontented in the Northwest, and that all children must be given an education in both the German and English languages. Archbishop Heiss stated that he had nothing to do with calling the convention, nor had any bishop made arrangements for the gathering. He knew nothing about anti-Irish declarations, doubted that such moves were contemplated, and believed that the assembly would be solely for educational and benevolent purposes.[34]

On the same day that this statement of the Archbishop of Milwaukee was published in the *Northwestern Chronicle,* another interview which he gave to a reporter of the Milwaukee *Sentinel* appeared in the columns of that paper. Here the Archbishop was quoted to the effect that he had canvassed the provinces of the United States with the reporter and pointed out that he was the only German archbishop, and that there were only eleven German bishops in the entire American hierarchy. In reference to the projected congress, Heiss was quoted as believing they would probably discuss the need for more German bishops as well as lay the plans for a St. Raphaelsverein immigrant house at New York. When asked if the Chicago congress would discuss perpetuation of the German language in the United States, he declared:

The congress will undoubtedly consider this subject, which is of such vital importance to the Germans of America, but what will be done I am unable to say. For my part, I can say that the church desires to keep up the German language or any other language for the spiritual

[33] *Northwestern Chronicle,* Aug. 18, 1887.
[34] *Ibid.*

> welfare of its children, and for no other purpose. It will do this so long as it is found to be necessary. If the Germans prefer the English or the French language, the Church will interpose no objections, but it will also protect them if their conscience dictates that they must receive the sacraments in their mother tongue. With the great majority any other language would be meaningless and would fail to reach the heart. It remains with the Germans to do for themselves what they may. I have been forty-five years in America and the demand for the German language has been growing right along, although it was at first supposed, and I believed it myself, that it would disappear with the older immigrants.[35]

When Archbishop Gross, of Oregon City, who had been born in Baltimore of German English ancestry, read this interview he sent a copy of it to Cardinal Gibbons, protesting that it enkindled among the clergy and laity of the United States what he called "that horrible curse of national feeling," with resulting dissensions and dislikes based on national animosity. Gross believed rather that

> anyone acquainted with the American people knows, that they believe and trust that the various nations pouring into our country's bosom will become amalgamated into the one great American Nation. That these peoples coming here will leave behind gradually at least, their German, French, Dutch, Irish, and other national European customs and adopt the American ideas, habits, and politics. But Archbp. Heiss here makes no secret of his determination to perpetuate German habits on American soil and tries to make the Catholic Church an advocate of the same un-American views. He does not [from this statement] acknowledge an American nationality as even existing. For according to him Bp. Spalding is an Englishman; Archbp. Elder is a Briton; His Grace of N. Y. an Irishman — and as for poor me — well, I have no nationality at all! . . . All know that the enemies of the Church from the days of the Roman emperors down to the leaders of Know-Nothingism have endeavored to bring the reproach that the Catholic Church is a foreign establishment. And Archbp. Heiss makes every Bishop and Archbishop in the United States to be an Englishman, Frenchman, Irishman, German, or Belgian — there is not an American among us. Your Eminence knows so well our country — knows that just now there are great exertions making to have another political crusade against Holy Church and this document of Archbp. Heiss will do more than anything else to hound on the attack.[36]

Gross wanted Gibbons to inform the Holy See of this interview,

[35] Milwaukee *Sentinel,* Aug. 18. 1887.
[36] *AAB,* 83-J-6, Gross to Gibbons, Portland, Aug. 30, 1887.

and three days later Archbishop Elder requested the same action by the Cardinal on the grounds that grievances and complaints had been aired in a public paper with resulting injury to discipline and authority. Elder pointed out that the Holy Father had strongly admonished Catholic journalists not to comment on episcopal administration, that the recent council in Baltimore had likewise imposed penalties on priests who offended in this way, and yet an archbishop was now communicating complaints against the hierarchy to the press.[37] If all concerned in this question had followed Elder's warnings, many misunderstandings which lay ahead might have been averted. After consulting with several of the archbishops, Gibbons determined to take no personal action in the matter, although he informed the Archbishop of Cincinnati that he thought it better if Elder himself wrote to Rome. In the final analysis, Elder concluded that the Archbishops did not desire such a move and decided to take no step at that time.[38]

The *Wahrheitsfreund* attempted to restore calm, especially since many German papers had republished the interview of Archbishop Heiss and the *Northwestern Chronicle* had made editorial criticism of the opinions expressed. The *Wahrheitsfreund* declared that the *Sentinel* reporter had misquoted and exaggerated the statements of Heiss. But, as in the past, the earlier questions of succursal parishes in St. Louis and the Abbelen petition were joined to the discussion, and the *Wahrheitsfreund* itself joined other German papers in defending the action taken by German Catholics in 1884 and 1886. The Cincinnati paper also reminded the *Northwestern Chronicle* that it was incorrect to assert that German grievances were localized in St. Louis. The same situation continued to exist in Albany and New Orleans, they claimed, and had existed in Baltimore, until Cardinal Gibbons had ended the distinctions between English-speaking and national parishes.[39] William Hesing, German Catholic publisher in Illinois, also added to the strained situation by declaring that the Germans were not represented in the hierarchy in proportion to their numerical strength, and he stated that the Irish were "irrepressible office seekers and office getters." The Pittsburgh *Catholic* felt that Hesing was ventilating his opinions with a zeal worthy of a better cause, and reminded him that the Irish "with all their proclivities for place and preferment . . . never yet held a convention representative of the

[37] *AAB,* 83-K-1, Elder to Gibbons, Cincinnati, Sept. 2, 1887.

[38] *AANY,* Corrigan to Elder, New York, Sept. 10, 1887, copy; *AAB,* 83-N-12, Elder to Gibbons, Cincinnati, Sept. 24, 1887.

[39] *Wahrheitsfreund,* Sept. 15, 1887.

Irish Catholic millions that are in America, to boost them into the episcopacy or vicar-generalship."[40]

These discords, even before the German Catholics assembled in Chicago on September 6, presaged little hope that the aims of the first *Katholikentag* in the United States would be understood.[41] At the congress there were three sessions for the German Catholic delegates who came from all parts of the United States. The first session was the Thirty-Second Annual Meeting of the German Roman Catholic Central Verein held in St. Michael's Parish Hall. Lieutenant-General Henry J. Spaunhorst, president of the Central Verein, stated in his response to the address of welcome given by Major John A. Roche, of Chicago, that they had assembled to consult and deliberate as to their best interests as a body. They had no intention to create national rivalry or strife, and all allusions which had been made, sometimes hastily, about a fight between different nationalities in the faith were erroneous and out of order in any of the meetings to be held during that week. Bishops Wigger of Newark, and John Vertin, of Marquette, attended the meetings along with a large number of German clerical and lay leaders.[42] There was some discussion in the press after Wigger had preached at the opening solemn Mass on the necessity of parochial schools. He was accused of discouraging the teaching of the English language in such schools, whereas actually he had rather advocated the use of both German and English as long as it was deemed necessary to retain the German language.[43]

Much more serious was a resolution which George Mitsch, a dele-

[40] Pittsburgh *Catholic,* Aug. 20, 1887.

[41] Cardinal Gibbons wrote to Bishop Ireland the day after the convention had opened: "I hope the convention in Chicago will pass away without doing much harm. It is not likely to do much good. After it is over, I look for a reaction in the right direction" (*AASP,* Gibbons to Ireland, Baltimore, Sept. 7, 1887).

[42] These representatives included several well-known persons, such as Vicar-General Anthony Scheideler, of Vincennes; Monsignori Peter Abbelen, Joseph Salzmann, Joseph Rainer, Michael Lochemes, and Reverend Anthony Decker, of Milwaukee; Monsignor J. S. Münich, of Racine, Wisconsin; Reverends A. Heiter and P. Hölscher, of Buffalo; Monsignori John Rothensteiner, Francis Goller, Francis G. Holweck, Francis Willmes, and Reverend Innocent Wapelhorst, O.F.M., of St. Louis; Monsignori George Bornemann, of Reading, Pennsylvania, John Enzlberger, of Piopolis, Illinois, Joseph Jessing, of the Pontifical College Josephinum, Worthington, Ohio, A. J. Thiele, of Chicago; Max Wurst and John Meier and Reverend Charles Köberl, of St. Paul; Monsignor William Cluse, of Belleville; Monsignori George Heer, Francis Xavier Böding, and Reverends F. J. Brune and Joseph Kümper, of Dubuque.

Lay representatives included Dr. Augustus Kaiser, of Detroit; Dr. Rudolph Seifferth and Michael Schwissthal, of Chicago; Clement Kelorlege, of Freeport, Illinois; Henry Mühlberger, of St. Louis; Henry Brockhagen, of St. Charles, Missouri; Henry Mehring, of Jonesboro, Illinois, and Edward Weber, of St. Paul.

[43] The *Oregonian,* Sept. 15, 1887; Portland *Sentinel,* Sept. 22, 1887.

gate from St. Paul, placed on the floor for adoption. Mitsch asked for a condemnation of the Knights of Labor on the grounds that this labor union had a demoralizing influence on German workingmen, because its head, Terence V. Powderly, was a prohibitionist and an enemy of the Germans and had petitioned Congress to restrict German immigration. Furthermore, Mitsch asserted, the entire union was governed by Irishmen, and, he added, "the Germans ought to consider it a disgrace to be ruled by Irish ignoramuses." This heated speech of Mitsch's created great excitement and a number of cries of approval. Powderly rushed a telegram to the convention in which he insisted that the attack was unkind, unjust, and based on misrepresentation. He refuted the charges made against him and the Knights, wished the convention Godspeed, and expressed the hope that the deliberations of their body would be for the good of all men, whether German or not. The leaders of the Central Verein were able to bury the resolution in committee, and the unfortunate incident ended when Mitsch rose in the afternoon session and declared that he had not intended to attack the Knights of Labor but was condemning only anarchists and socialists. But opposition newspapers did not forget the incident for a long time.[44] Reverend John S. Meier, pastor of St. Joseph's Church, Winona, Minnesota, warned the delegates not to act on such matters as the Knights of Labor, since, as he stated, following a popular though erroneous opinion of the times, the Holy See had already approved this labor union. He also warned that the walls themselves were listening to this convention. The delegates had already been charged with activities in the English press, he said, which would make one's hair stand on end.[45]

The Central Verein meeting was but a three-day preparation for the First American German Catholic General Assembly, or *Katholikentag,* which was held in Battery D Hall on Tuesday, September 9. Over 2500 people listened to speeches on the accomplishments of Leo XIII and several defenses of Catholic thought and practice, especially with reference to parochial schools, the Christian home, necessity of organization, and social justice. Modeled on the Catholic General Assemblies of Germany, the assembly was a striking manifestation of

[44] Portland *Sentinel,* Sept. 15, 1887; *Northwestern Chronicle,* Sept. 8, 1887. Cf. also Henry J. Browne, *The Catholic Church and the Knights of Labor* (Washington, 1949), p. 291.

[45] An example of this coverage was a report in the Chicago *Tribune,* Sept. 8, 1887, which read: "The crowd began to assemble early, and by the time the delegates began to arrive at the school house, about 8 o'clock, all the adjacent saloons began a boom, which lasted without intermission until the close of the church services."

co-operation between German clergy and laity in the cause of their common Catholic faith. Leo XIII sent his blessing to the assembly through Mariano Cardinal Rampolla, and the stage was set for the First Assembly of the German American Priests' Society, which was called to order on Wednesday, September 10, at Uhlich Hall. Over 300 German American priests devoted themselves to carrying out the resolutions of the General Assembly and to advancing the material, intellectual, and official interests of its members. Mühlsiepen was elected president, Tappert, vice-president, Färber, first secretary, Enzlberger, second secretary, and Joseph Fischer, pastor of St. Joseph's Church, Wayland, New York, treasurer. Resolutions passed by the delegates included devotion to the Holy Father, adherence to the Catholic school system, respect for the priesthood, support of the German press, social influence of the laity, and social organizations for Catholics. Then the committee for the proposed immigrant house, to be named after Leo XIII, made its first report. Monsignor Mühlsiepen, who was treasurer of the committee, reported that $20,000 had been collected since the previous February, that the German Catholic press had been co-operative, and that the campaign would be pushed in earnest during the autumn months ahead.

The convention ended on this happy note. Press dispatches to the effect that Archbishop Feehan had refused to attend the sessions of the Priests' Society proved to be false and exaggerated. The local ordinary could not preside at the meetings because, according to the rules of the Society, the German language was required in all discourse, and the Archbishop of Chicago did not speak that language.[46] But those members of the hierarchy who had been mistrustful of the convention from the very beginning were still of the same opinion, and they determined to watch carefully over the activities of its members who had voted to meet the following year in Cincinnati. Monsignor O'Connell proceeded to interpret what he considered to be the mind of the Holy See on the assembly for Bishop Gilmour's benefit. He said:

> The nature of the German question is better understood in Rome now than ever before. And some of the Cardinals looked on the late convention as an attempt to influence the Cong. of Prop., and they do not look with favor on appeals of such kind to people and priests.[47]

Unmindful of such accusations, the German priests pushed ahead through their national organization to achieve the end of building a St. Raphaelsverein mission in New York. Episcopal approval and

[46] *Freeman's Journal,* Sept. 24, 1887; Pittsburgh *Catholic,* Sept. 24, 1887.
[47] *ADC,* O'Connell to Gilmour, Rome, Oct. 1, 1887.

support were received from Chicago, Philadelphia, San Francisco, St. Louis, Davenport, Green Bay, Nashville, Omaha, Peoria, and Rochester. Bishop Wigger informed his priests that they had his permission to take up collections anywhere for the proposed Leo House. The response was excellent and Reuland believed this was so because everyone was interested as soon as the name of the Holy Father was mentioned. "Little stone by little stone it comes in," he announced. Larger donations from such individuals as Vicar-General Michael May, of Brooklyn, who gave $1,000, or Archbishop Corrigan, who gave $500, were for the most part exceptions. The mission was built by the multitude of German Catholics who knew by personal experience, or from their relatives, the importance of spiritual and material care while en route to their new homes. The *Herold des Glaubens* in St. Louis featured the story of a German family in Illinois whose three sons, Henrich, Joseph, and Karl, years twelve, ten, and eight respectively, brought the proceeds of their summer berry picking to their pastor for the Leo House.[48] Father Goller was most active in advancing the cause, both through letters and personal contacts across the country. He reminded Reverend Ignatius F. Horstmann, editor of the *American Catholic Quarterly Review,* not to forget his promise of a donation for the project, because a gift from a person of his position would enable Goller to persuade others to be liberal. He also asked Horstmann to approach the Drexel family in Philadelphia for financial assistance, and he then stated: "Rt. Rev. Keane makes you believe that all Christian civilization is the work of the Celtic race. *Nolumus gloriari verbis, sed facta loquantur.*"[49]

Donations were particularly numerous from the areas around St. Louis, Cincinnati, Milwaukee, Cleveland, Covington, Alton, Detroit, Erie, Leavenworth, Buffalo, New York, St. Paul, Philadelphia, Pittsburg, Scranton, St. Cloud, and Vincennes. The Central Verein, through President Spaunhorst and Reverend Henry Brockhagen, pastor of the Church of the Assumption at O'Fallon, Missouri, sponsored a drive among its member societies, which was also satisfactory in returns obtained.[50] By the spring of 1888 the committee had collected $52,000 of their $75,000 goal and were ready to choose the spot for their

[48] *Herold des Glaubens,* Oct. 26, 1887.

[49] *ADC,* Goller to Horstmann, St. Louis, Dec. 1, 1888.

[50] ALH, "Report of the Rt. Rev. Henry Mühlsiepen of the Leo House Committee," Feb. 25, 1888. Mühlsiepen by himself collected $45,000 in the West for the Leo House. In the East, which fell behind the West in totals, Vicar-General May of Brooklyn and Reverend Adam Tonner, pastor of St. Mary Magdalen Church, New York, were the leaders in the Leo House drive.

immigrant house. It was determined by the board of directors that a building at 6 State Street in Castle Garden Park should be purchased. The building which they purchased had a frontage of twenty-eight feet and a depth of eighty-six feet. Its four floors were easily divided into office space, chapel, and sleeping accommodations. On October 31 the directors held their first meeting in the new building and proceeded to form their corporation of the Leo House and to petition the state of New York for incorporation. Membership in the corporation was limited to fifteen, both clerical and lay, to be elected for life, with the Archbishop of New York as honorary president.[51] Monsignor Peter Gratzfeld, secretary to Paulus Cardinal Melchers, Archbishop of Cologne, informed Reuland that Melchers had obtained a portrait painting from Leo XIII, and that it was being forwarded to the new mission as a token of the Holy Father's warm interest in their work.[52] German newspapers, publishers, priests, and societies made special gifts of an altar for the chapel, religious articles, furniture, and other necessities. Bishop Wigger was very anxious to obtain a community of nuns to manage the establishment, and after being refused by several religious superiors in the East, he at last obtained the services of the Sisters of St. Agnes, of Fond du Lac, Wisconsin, who continue to the present to serve at the Leo House. On December 7, 1889, Bishop Wigger had the joy of blessing the mission which was already caring for immigrants at full capacity according to the system which Cahensly and his followers had developed.

[51] *Bylaws of the Leo House for German Roman Catholic Emigrants in the City of New York* (New York, 1889). The original incorporators included Archbishop Michael A. Corrigan, Bishop Winand N. Wigger, Vicars-General Michael May, Brooklyn, and Henry Mühlsiepen, St. Louis; Reverends Francis Goller, St. Louis, Adam F. Tonner, New York, A. Arnold, Brooklyn, and William Tappert, Covington; and Messrs. William Schickel, Henry Amy, James R. Wigger, Peter Klein, Henry Hübner, Joseph Schäfer, all of New York.

The first board of directors of the newly incorporated Leo House were Archbishop Corrigan as honorary president; Bishop Wigger as vice-president; William Schickel, treasurer; Joseph Schäfer, secretary; Peter Klein and Henry Hübner as members.

Cf. also Joseph Schäfer and Charles G. Hebermann, "The Society of St. Raphael and the Leo House," *HRS,* I (Jan., 1900), pp. 110–129; Charles G. Herbermann, "Right Rev. Winand Michael Wigger, D.D., Third Bishop of Newark (with illustrations)," *HRS,* II (Jan., 1901), pp. 292–321; J. M. O'Reilly, "The Leo House for Immigrants," *RACH,* XVI (1905), pp. 445–451; *Golden Jubilee Celebration of the Leo House, St. Raphael Society, 1889–1939* (New York, 1939); A. B. Schwenniger, *Katholikentag, Central-Verein, Raphaels Verein, Leo Haus* (New York, 1890).

[52] *ALH,* Gratzfeld to Reuland, Rome, Aug. 4, 1888. Monsignor John A. Nageleisen, late rector of the Leo House, declared in an interview with the writer that Leo XIII gave this painting of himself to the New York branch of the St. Raphaelsverein as a testimony of his interest in the aims which Cahensly was endeavoring to achieve.

Thus it came about through the support of the German American priests, joined by Catholics of several national origins across the land, that the St. Raphaelsverein was firmly established in the United States within the short period of six years. The Catholics of Germany had found wholehearted co-operation and unity of purpose especially from their German Catholic brethren in the United States. At the new Leo House the board of directors was able to report at the end of its first year of service a total of spiritual and material services which was very encouraging: 3970 immigrants were received at the mission along with 241 other guests, while 2493 free meals and 845 free lodgings were given to needy persons; $1,290.83 was taken in and $976.80 was distributed by Reuland and his assistants; $7,311.75 was deposited for new arrivals who did not understand American banking procedure; 1416 letters were written; $734.45 given for cases of need, and eighty marriages had been performed in the house chapel.[53] Not only had a suitable memorial been established in honor of Leo XIII, but the results accomplished in one year were beyond the expectations of all who had entered upon this important venture. (See Table III, on the following page, analyzing social services of the Leo House during the period 1889–1901.)

Meanwhile the German American Priests' Society was completing preparations for their second convention and general assembly of German American Catholics in Cincinnati on September 3–4, 1888. John Ireland in St. Paul, who had just been elevated to the rank of metropolitan of the new ecclesiastical Province of St. Paul, informed Monsignor O'Connell in Rome: "The German question is reviving, in view of the approaching convention in Cincinnati, but reviving with the cough of death in its throat."[54] This prediction was ques-

[53] *Jahres Bericht des New York St. Raphaelsvereins vom 1. Oktober 1888 zum 1. Oktober 1889* (New York, 1889). The German Lutherans of the United States also had a mission house near Castle Garden. A Lutheran Emigrant Association had been established on April 12, 1871, and in 1873 a mission house was purchased at 26 State Street. Later the location was changed to 4 State Street and a house prepared for $78,000, which was enlarged in 1885 and also served as home for the General Council of the Lutheran Church of North America. On October 31, 1898, this Deutsches Emigrantenhaus celebrated its silver jubilee, and its missionary pastor, Wilhelm J. Berkemeier, published the record of the previous twenty-five years. A total of 20,270 free meals, 33,048 lodgings, and 227,035 guests were cared for, while DM 7,140,000 ($1,785,000) was banked for immigrants. Cf. New York *Staatszeitung*, Nov. 1, 1898. In *Der Ansiedler* of December 1, 1888, the activity of the St. Raphaelsverein, German Lutherans, and private agents was compared. The Missouri Synod German Lutherans also had a Lutherisches Pilgerhaus at 8 State Street, erected in 1885 at a cost of $45,000. In its first twenty years of operation 79,843 German and 5342 Scandinavian immigrants were cared for.

[54] *ADR,* Ireland to O'Connell, St. Paul, July 11, 1888.

TABLE III: AN ANALYSIS OF SOCIAL SERVICES OF THE LEO HOUSE (1889–1901)

	Immigrants	*Other Guests*	*Free Meals*	*Free Lodgings*
1889–1890	3970	241	2493	845
1890–1891	8290	477	3746	1265
1891–1892	5330	610	5672	1785
1892–1893	4400	765	4203	1195
1893–1894	2084	1290	3746	1276
1894–1895	2460	1250	3350	1069
1895–1896	2276	1155	2425	826
1896–1897	1941	1136	1792	605
1897–1898	1249	801	824	287
1898–1899	1877	1206	1066	355
1899–1900	1978	1366	852	320
1900–1901	2274	1718	1363	470
Total	38,129	10,975	31,532	10,238

tionable, especially in view of the part Archbishop Ireland himself was to play in keeping the question alive.

On July 31 Vicar-General Mühlsiepen requested from the Propaganda that the blessing of Leo XIII be sent to the Cincinnati convention as it had been bestowed the previous year on the Chicago gathering. Bishop Camillus P. Maes, Ordinary of Father Tappert in Covington, then informed the Propaganda that he felt the conditions which Cardinal Simeoni had imposed upon the blessing previously given to the Chicago gathering had not been fulfilled. Simeoni had told Tappert on July 1, 1887, that the papal blessing was coming to the convention through his bishop, Maes provided that the convention was "under the leadership and approval of those bishops concerned." Tappert had informed Maes that both Feehan and Wigger had approved the assembly, but Maes had stated in return that he did not feel this fact fulfilled the requirements of the Propaganda, since he himself did not look with approval on the aims of the Priests' Society. When the papal blessing had been announced to the Chicago convention this stipulation was not mentioned, nor the fact that the blessing had come through Maes. Father Tappert had, moreover, demanded publicly that Bishop Wigger testify that the blessing had been obtained in conformity with the rules of the Church. Maes had then informed the Cardinal Prefect of Propaganda:

> Since, then, many Archbishops and Bishops of the United States have complained that this assembly and the one following, which will be in Cincinnati at the beginning of September, are all simply organized by

> a clique of German priests, and their prevailing spirit is dangerous; that its purpose is to counteract the wise efforts of the bishops to create gradually a single homogeneous Catholic people in the United States, without at the same time encroaching on the rights of Germans, French, Poles, etc. One thing is certain, the spirit which previously marked the actions of the two most ardent propagators of German ideas in opposition to purely American Catholic ideas, has been something less than a spirit of submission to the authority of their bishop. It is true that some approvals of bishops have been obtained in response to the first circular, but I know no bishop who has approved the idea which is said prevails in all their actions: namely, that of uniting the Germans in order to make a breach in the American Catholic idea, and to perpetuate German, cost what it may, even to making second the best interest of the Church in the United States.[55]

Maes, himself of Belgian origin, felt that the Germans were a good, solid, active, and practical people, but they did not adjust to the formation of an American people in the United States because they were generally strange to the language, customs, and spirit of the country. For the sake of patriotism it was necessary, he believed, that the Church as an institution be as American as the Protestant churches were. The Church always adjusts herself to the customs of a country to bring all to Jesus Christ, rather than acting with a domineering and critical spirit such as the German Priests' Society had evidenced. Force and courage would be found through the union of all nationalities in firmness and charity. The American Church should be, he felt, united and indivisible; it was this that non-Catholics admired. In conclusion, he stated that he was not referring either to the Central Verein or to the St. Raphaelsverein and their Leo House project, but to the Priests' Society specifically.

A letter of this nature from Bishop Maes, who was known for his particular interest in the foreign groups in his diocese, necessarily was given careful consideration. Maes sent a copy of his letter to Archbishop Ireland, who immediately proceeded to send off instructions to O'Connell in Rome. Ireland urged O'Connell to "have a conversation with the Powers that be in Propaganda. . . . It is vital that no blessings be sent to the coming Cincinnati convention. Rome sheds around blessings rather profusely. In America they are looked upon as positive 'approvals'; and a blessing sent to Cincinnati will be taken as the approving seal of infallibility upon German tricks. I view this as a very vital matter, and beg that you attend to it."[56] Ireland also proceeded to ex-

[55] *AASP,* Maes to Simeoni, Covington, July 10, 1888, copy.
[56] *ADR,* Ireland to O'Connell, St. Paul, Aug. 18, 1888.

pose the whole background of the Chicago blessing in the columns of his *Northwestern Chronicle.*

Cardinal Simeoni, however, had already presented Mühlsiepen's letter to the Holy Father, and on August 9 a papal blessing for the approaching convention was sent from Rome. Maes' letter arrived soon afterward, and O'Connell informed Ireland that Simeoni had decided to recall the blessing, had prepared a cablegram to that effect, but then discovered that the convention had already been held, so the matter was dropped for a few days. The Prefect of Propaganda was not satisfied, however, and he sent a cable to Mühlsiepen, recalling the blessing after the convention was over. "I had a presentiment," he told O'Connell, "when we sent the blessing that it would create trouble."[57]

At the convention itself events moved smoothly and with general satisfaction to all concerned. After the meeting of the Central Verein had been completed, the second *Katholikentag* of German Catholics in the United States was held in Holy Trinity Church and School in Cincinnati. Bishops Marty, Wigger, Flasch, Joseph Rademacher, of Nashville, and John Janssen, of Belleville, were in attendance, along with Archabbot Andrew Hintenach, O.S.B., of St. Vincent's Abbey, and Abbot Fintan Mundwiler, O.S.B., of St. Meinrad's Abbey, Indiana. Archbishop Elder reported to Denis O'Connell on the happenings of these days. He praised the Central Verein as the old and meritorious mutual-aid union of German Catholics which all had grown to respect. He had authorized his name to be used in asking for the customary papal blessing for the Central Verein, which had been received through Cardinal Rampolla, secretary of state to His Holiness. As to the *Katholikentag* and the assembly of German priests, Elder was less complimentary. He told O'Connell:

> Its objects have not been so clear, and its method of proceeding not so satisfactory. Some of the members have the German national spirit. Many however are free from it. I declined giving positive approbation by my presence. But I gave a cordial welcome to the Bishops who proposed coming: and I was glad of their presence because all of

[57] *AASP,* O'Connell to Ireland, Rome, Sept. 19, 1888. Turning again to the *Northwestern Chronicle* as a handy instrument of action, Ireland published this intelligence which he had received from Rome through O'Connell. In the October 12, 1888, issue, under the title of "Nationalism in Religion," he wrote: "Father Mühlsiepen, we understand, is quite disconcerted at this recent action of Rome; but its meaning to the Catholic body at large cannot be misunderstood. The meaning is that Rome will not tolerate any movement among Catholics in America that breaks up among them unity, and that separates from the general body, sections or divisions of Catholics, resulting from distinctions of foreign nationalism. The revocation of that blessing is an act most significant that all Catholics will do well to note."

> them who were here, are *opposed* to that nationalizing spirit: & I believe they came chiefly to give their influence & direction towards a good result. They tell me today they have succeeded: & they expect it will take a good course towards a General Congress of all Catholics.[58]

Elder described exactly what had happened at the meeting of the Priests' Society. Bishop Marty rose at the second closed session of the Priests' Society on September 3 and recommended that the group consider broadening the *Katholikentag* so that eventually it would embrace assemblies of other Catholic societies in the United States. He admitted that the German Catholics were one of the strongest elements in the Church in the United States, but he also warned the assembly that, as St. Benedict had taught his followers, the virtue of humility demanded that a Christian should seek the lowest place and not strive to exalt himself. It was no new idea that he was presenting, he stated; Bishop Spalding had advocated a general yearly assembly of Catholic societies for some time. Marty asked the Priests' Society to extend their hands to all the Catholic clergy and laity of the country. It was a suggestion that evoked much discussion. Father Goller was on his feet in a minute to warn that the whole is only as strong as its parts, and thus the German assembly should be first strengthened and perfected, and the mother tongue preserved in their sessions. "Advance slowly," he warned. Others, such as Tappert, Reverends Ferdinand Hundt, of St. Peter's, Indiana, Henry Meissner, of St. Charles Borromeo Church, Peru, Indiana, and Anton Röslein, of St. Louis, joined in the discussion. It was pointed out that a yearly assembly such as Marty had suggested was being held in both Silesia, for German and Polish societies, and Switzerland, for German, French, and Italian societies. In these cases several languages were used at separate sessions. It was voted that the matter be entrusted to a committee for further investigation. This committee was composed of Marty, Tappert, Meissner, Röslein, and Augustus Kaiser, of Detroit. The resolution, as finally accepted, read as follows:

> Mindful of the American saying "United we stand, divided we fall," and mindful likewise of the High Priest our Lord and Saviour, in which He besought unity for His Church, we shall do all in our power to arrive at a complete understanding with our brethren of the same faith, yet of different tongues and nationalities:
>
> *Resolved:*
>
> 1. That we hold yearly Catholic assemblies.

[58] *ADR*, Elder to O'Connell, Cincinnati, Aug. 31, 1888.

2. That in the future, ways and means be found of arriving at an understanding with other Catholic societies both regarding time and place of convening, and the religious questions of the day which thus will be thoroughly sifted from all standpoints.
3. That for the present the meetings of the Catholic societies be held separately, according as they differ in language.[59]

This resolution was a major achievement and opened the way for mutual co-operation of all nationality groups in the Church. But events moved too fast and crowded too closely upon this decision, so that within two years' time such a development proved impossible. Both the intransigence of members of the German American Priests' Society and the lack of understanding evidenced by their opponents prevented union in annual public manifestations of Catholic faith and purpose. Just as the St. Raphaelsverein's program of fostering existing colonies was destined never to accomplish the goals which were set for it, so the same conflict made it impossible that annual public assemblies of clergy and laity in the United States develop from this promising beginning. Nor has such a development come about since that time.

The Cincinnati assembly was closed on a high note with a speech by Dr. Ernst Lieber, associate of Windthorst and Cahensly in the Center Party, who had come from Germany to address the gathering and to bring the greetings of German Catholics to their brethren across the ocean. Cardinal Melchers likewise sent personal greetings by cablegram from Rome, and the delegates disbanded to meet the following year in Cleveland. It was only after the meetings were over that Cardinal Simeoni's revocation of the papal blessing was sent to Mühlsiepen. Archbishop Ireland expressed his satisfaction to Bishop Richard Gilmour when he wrote:

> So you see, our vigorous American policy is in the ascendancy. I trust I shall be able to keep you in the front ranks. Providence wills that you meet the foe on your own ground. They adjourned in Cincinnati to meet next year in Cleveland. I have thanked God for this. Of all places in America, where I would wish them to meet, Cleveland is my choice.[60]

Cardinal Gibbons also congratulated Ireland on his stand concerning

[59] *Verhandlungen der zweiten allgemeinen deutsch-amerikanischen Katholiken-Versammlung in Cincinnati, O., am 3 und 4 September, 1888* (St. Louis, 1888), p. 88.

[60] *ADC,* Ireland to Gilmour, St. Paul, Oct. 12, 1888. To Cardinal Gibbons, Ireland also rejoiced: "I consider the revocation a great triumph of our American policy. Next year the German convention will meet in Cleveland, & will receive its *coup de grace* from gentle Richard" (*AAB,* 85-F-13, Ireland to Gibbons, St. Paul, Oct. 12, 1888).

the German convention, and he added: "They have received such a set back that I think they will be less aggressive & more modest & submissive in the future." Gibbons told Ireland that he would do nothing on this matter without consulting him, while Monsignor O'Connell from Rome stated: "You may count on me every time in every circumstance. I could stay in Rome contentedly forever, if everyone were as firm as you."[61] O'Connell also informed his American friends that he was awaiting the arrival of Maes in Rome, who was coming, among other reasons, to inform the Propaganda on Tappert's activities and attitude, and to talk with Melchers so that the Cardinal would know more of the nature of the German movement in the United States.

Archbishop Ireland did not have long to wait until what he considered another challenge to "our vigorous American policy" presented itself. Reverend Casimir Hüppe, O.S.F., pastor of Guardian Angels Church, Chaska, Minnesota, had written to him on July 31, 1888, requesting him to approve a program and to procure a papal blessing for a Minnesota *Katholikentag* to be held at Chaska on October 16. At the annual assembly of the Catholic Aid Association of Minnesota in Mankato in 1887, the convention had voted to follow the procedure laid down by the national *Katholikentag* held in Chicago that year, and to make arrangements for a state meeting modeled on it. The program at this Catholic Day was to include religious services, parade,

[61] *AASP,* O'Connell to Ireland, Rome, Oct. 31, 1888. In the *Northwestern Chronicle,* Dec. 7, 1888, a Roman letter was published, obviously information obtained from O'Connell, in which it was stated that French journals were reporting that Tappert was at the head of a movement to Germanize the United States and to start a German Catholic Church. It was also affirmed that the convention in Cincinnati had been held without the consent of the American bishops, and that the Pope had revoked his blessing to that gathering.

In its December 14, 1888, issue Father Conway ran a letter to the *Northwestern Chronicle* from "N.C.L.," of St. Paul, who insisted in strong language that the Cincinnati convention had been held for the protection of the German language and not to Germanize the United States or to start a German Catholic Church. This writer insisted that, since five bishops were present, it was untrue to say that the American bishops did not approve the gathering; also, not a word was spoken at the assembly about Germanizing the United States. The letter then ended as follows: "You say that the Germans are most always for a German Catholic church, or a German convention, instead of having an American Catholic church, and so on. I say that the Irish do the same and to a greater extent, as, for an example, the *Northwestern Chronicle* publishes every week an Irish letter. I don't see nothing Irish about it, because I can read it, and therefore it must be English. Now don't the Irish do the same as the Germans, and still worse?

"Now for the last. I would ask is there any person in the U. S. that can prove that the Germans try to Germanize America? I would like him to come out and prove it, or should the Germans put a Mac or a Pat before their name, and become Irish?" To which Conway added an editor's note: "The letter printed above hardly needs comment."

and addresses on the Papacy, education of youth, organizations, and the social question. Hüppe was chairman of a committee on arrangements which included Reverend John Meier, pastor of St. Joseph's Church, Winona, Matthias Meyers, and the same George Mitsch who had attacked the Knights of Labor at the Chicago convention. Ireland replied on August 6, 1888, and refused to approve the projected assembly, to appear himself, or to petition the Holy See for a blessing because, to his mind, certain parts of the program were indicative of what he called a "spirit of ultra-nationalism, hardly consistent with the fullness of Catholic unity which should characterize the life of the Church in America."[62] The Archbishop believed that this projected Minnesota *Katholikentag* was instigated by the German American Priests' Society which had voted in Chicago to hold subsidiary conventions in several states of the union. He pointed out that the Chicago General Assembly had not received the general approbation of the hierarchy and that the papal blessing was given without mention of its important qualification. On the Priests' Society itself, Ireland had very definite opinions:

> What does the formation of associations of this nature mean, but the institution of new and self-authorized bodies to serve as tribunals to discuss and pass judgment upon Catholic morals and Catholic discipline? Catholics are taught that religious matters are in the keeping of each Bishop of his diocese, whatever the race or the language of the people concerned, and from him they know there is an appeal, should he neglect his duty, to the Supreme Head of the Church or his representatives. A new order of things is now proposed — organizations of priests and laymen are formed in each State, apart from diocesan limitations, notice of the existence of which, after they have been formed, may or may not be given to the bishops. The real controlling power to which these State Conventions or Societies are subject is not the Bishop, or the Bishops, within each State, but national conventions or assemblies, whose decisions are the laws of subaltern societies. To the minds of the leaders in this new order of things the hierarchical organization in the Church must have appeared quite insufficient or so neglectful of its duties as to need to be supplemented by self-constituted "citizens' committees."[63]

This was a new attack upon the Priests' Society, and in view of the number of bishops, abbots, monsignori, vicars-general, and worthy priests listed among its 900 members, Archbishop Ireland's accusation

[62] The whole subject of the Chaska *Katholikentag* is covered exhaustively, including letters and speeches, in the *Northwestern Chronicle*, Aug. 10 and 17, 1888.

[63] *Northwestern Chronicle*, Aug. 10 and 17, 1888.

of a leveling or antihierarchical character cannot be viewed seriously. However, his concluding sentences got to the heart of the problem:

> These conventions and clerical societies are based upon lines of foreign races and languages, a most dangerous omen for the peace and oneness of the Church in America. For the same reason we may have one day Polish, Bohemian, Irish, French conventions and clerical societies for the furtherance of the religious interests of those several nationalities. Already certain ones among them have given unmistakable signs of strong tendencies in this direction. Episcopal approval of the German movement will compel the approval of other national movements as they may arise. And, then, what chaos in the Church? That in practical dealings with our Catholic populations special considerations have to be given to race and to language, no one will deny. But, again, those considerations must in the Church be sought for through the duly constituted authority of each diocese, before which Catholics are all alike in the obedience they owe and in the care they are to receive, whatever be the accidental differences of race distinguishing them from one another.
>
> I am not afraid that priests or laymen of German origin will misunderstand my remarks. German-American Catholics are most loyal and devoted children of the Church. The instigators of this movement are not the representatives of them. It does them a serious injustice by placing them in a false position before Church and country, and I am confident that they will be careful not to encourage it.[64]

After this letter, the Priests' Society could have no doubts as to the position of the Archbishop of St. Paul, and throughout all future controversies he was consistently painted as opposition leader to the Germanizing movement, and as the exponent of a kind of "ultra-Americanism."

Hüppe's committee assured the Archbishop that the proposed *Katholikentag* had originated with the Central Verein and had been advocated for several years in German Catholic papers. Ireland had never applied his strictures to the Central Verein, which he considered deserving of all praise, and after he had stipulated that the assembly be termed a "dramatic and musical entertainment," he permitted it to be held at Holy Angels Parish in Chaska according to schedule. Moreover, he came himself and delivered a lengthy address which he characterized as a frank sketch of his convictions and principles of action in regard to Catholics of foreign races and languages under his jurisdiction. It was a clear and important statement of policy and should have removed all misinterpretation of his stand. But animosities had been so aroused

[64] *Ibid.*

by this time that Ireland was forced repeatedly in these years, as often as opportunity presented itself, to reiterate the same sentiments he had first expressed at Chaska that autumn day of 1888. In fact it could, perhaps, be stated that the lines of battle were drawn and remained unbroken for a decade after the full import of this speech became apparent.

Ireland began by assuring his audience that he in no way opposed the German language and practice of it by their children. He extolled the German language for its literary richness, and asserted it was a stringent duty upon him to provide priests for Catholics of foreign tongues who would understand them and who would be understood by them. More than that, the people had a right to demand from the hierarchy an opportunity, as far as it was possible to afford it, to practice their religion in the language through which their religion could be made most easily accessible to them. The same could be said of their children, and he then added: "Yes, speak the German language and teach it to your children. But permit me to add in very earnest words, whatever be your conclusions as to your own selves, see that your children learn well, and speak well, the English language."

He then approached the core of his message. He pointed out how business and law were conducted in English, and he warned that he who did not speak English would be relegated to the lower levels of the political and business life of the nation by saying:

> Through an exaggerated love of old habits and of trans-Atlantic lands are you to forget the present and the future, and reduce to social inferiority your sons and daughters? Think you, if you follow this course, will they afterwards deem your affection in this regard reasonable and salutary, and will they thank you for services rendered? Your children are Americans; their field for the display of all their activities is America; their hopes and prospects are bound up in the folds of her flag. They would be neither loyal to her, nor to themselves, did they not seek to know well her language; and if one language is to be known by them better than another, give to the English the first and honored place. It might be, perhaps, that by speaking differently to you I would evoke from you, in the name of the German fatherland, louder applause. But I have no right before God and men to address you except to tell you what is for your good, and I appeal to your reason, rather than to your sentiments. . . . Your duty, it seems to me, is plain: your schools must give your children an English education, as good, as complete, as is given in the land, and teachers not capable of imparting this education should not be placed in your schools. It is too true that so far in America our Catholics of German origin or

descent have not made in public life the mark which their energy and the high order of their natural talents call for, and the reason, you will agree with me yourselves, has been their imperfect knowledge of the language of the country. It is time that plain facts be brought to your notice, in order that better things be done in the future.[65]

Ireland warned the audience that, despite their efforts to preserve the German language and German habits for their children and grandchildren, as time passed their children and grandchildren would become Americans both in language and manners. The very air they breathed, he insisted, carried with it the principles of Americanization, the whole current of influence was in that direction, and one might as well try to arrest the Niagara in its precipitous race as change this current. He further claimed that the reason so many German Catholics lost the faith when they Americanized came from a neglect to teach them their religion in English. He then proceeded to explain what he meant by Americanization, since he was aware it was a word of alarm to some. He claimed he did not advocate hasty, overactive Americanization; there would be a danger in such an experiment. Nor did he advocate the forgetting of old lands and precious traditions, but he declared:

> What I do mean by Americanization is the filling up of the heart with love for America and for her institutions. It is the harmonizing of ourselves with our surroundings, so that we will be as to the manner born, and not as strangers in a strange land, caring apparently but slightly for it, and entitled to receive from it but meagre favors. It is the knowing of the language of the land and failing in nothing to prove our attachment to our laws, and our willingness to adopt, as dutiful citizens, all that is good and laudable in its social life and civilizations. . . . I am sure I speak in the name of the children of the Church in America, and I tell their truest thoughts, when I proclaim that they are to the core Americans in love and loyalty, and that they deem it highest honor to be and to be called Americans. And why not? Has it not been to their gain that Catholics have passed from other lands to America? Have they not here, as nowhere else, rewards for thrift and industry? Have they not here as nowhere else, liberty? Is not the Church in America free, as nowhere else, to work, and to grow, and to shed around her the benign influence of truth and grace? He who does not feel all this, and does not thank God that he is an American, should in simple consistency betake his foreign soul to foreign shores, and crouch in misery and abjection beneath tyranny's sceptre.[66]

Ireland left no doubts that he was referring to German Catholic

[65] *Ibid.*
[66] *Ibid.*

newspapermen, the German American Priests' Society, and the leaders of the General Assemblies in Chicago and Cincinnati. All of these he branded as pursuing harmful aims which were not approved in Rome and which presented the Church to the American public as an aggression of foreign nationalities camped upon her plains. In conclusion he stated:

> To me all Catholics, whencesoever they have come, are Catholics and nothing else. I know, in my ministrations, no race. The motto of the Diocese, chosen by its first bishop, is "All to All," and I pray that my tongue be stilled, and my arm fall nerveless, if ever I am not true to it. Catholic I shall be in faith, and American in nationality, and thus I shall be one with all, who whatever their origins, are Catholics and Americans.[67]

Within two short years Archbishop Ireland would again use a like figure of speech when he warned that "withered be the hand" which would rise against the public schools in the United States. Then opposition leaders among the Germans would have no doubts that "Americanization" had gone too far and their treasured parochial school system was in real danger.

A further spark was added to the spreading fire of national discord when the Cincinnati *Volksfreund,* a secular paper edited by a Catholic, published an obviously untruthful accusation against several bishops who had gathered on August 15, 1888, for the golden jubilee of Very Reverend Edward Sorin, C.S.C., founder of the University of Notre Dame. The *Volksfreund* charged that at that time several archbishops and bishops present had signed a petition circulated by Archbishop Ireland which was to be carried to Rome by either Bishop Dwenger or Bishop Maes, to the effect that all Catholics should first be nationalistic Americans in the hope of converting the many millions of non-Catholic Americans to the faith. Religious instruction was to be in English in all parochial schools, and where German had been preached before, now English was to be used. All celebrations held according to German customs were to be suppressed and only "oyster suppers" or "strawberry festivals" were to be held in the future.[68] It was further alleged that these measures had been originated at the Third Plenary Council of Baltimore and were being pushed at this time. Elder immediately denied the tale, as did both Ireland and Gilmour. Benziger's *Wahrheitsfreund,* the German Catholic paper of the area, came to the defense of the bishops, and Heinrich Wohlgemuth de-

[67] *Ibid.*

[68] Cincinnati *Volksfreund,* Nov. 8, 1888.

nounced the whole affair as notoriously untruthful.[69] But the *Volksfreund* refused to publish a retraction.

Such excitement in the Province of Cincinnati was a poor preparation for the third General Assembly of German Catholics and the German American Priests' meeting which was to be held in Cleveland in September of 1889. But Bishop Gilmour exercised particular care in preparing for the convention, as he informed Archbishop Elder, and no conflicts emerged during or as a result of the meeting. Gilmour insisted that the word "German" be dropped as an adjective for the General Assembly, a dubious accomplishment, since all who attended were of German origin. He strove to keep the Priests' Society meeting separated from the *Katholikentag* by directing the German priests to meet at St. Peter's Church and hall, and by seeing to it that the convention was held at St. John's Cathedral. The Bishop of Cleveland then stated to Elder:

[69] *Wahrheitsfreund,* Nov. 15, 1888. The *Northwestern Chronicle* at this time also entered into editorial controversy with *Der Wanderer,* published in St. Paul and edited by Hugo Klapproth. Conway, on October 5, 1888, protested against *Der Wanderer's* reference to Archbishop Ireland as having administered the sacrament of confirmation in both the "Irish" church and the "German" church at Shakopee on the same morning. He declared that this persistent habit of the German Catholic newspapers of classing, in general, Catholic churches in the States under two headings — German and Irish — was bringing positive injury to the Church, of which this pernicious custom was the efficacious cause. He stated: "The Church in America suffers incalculable injury when it is made to seem to be — as the German Catholic journals, in their fatuous policy, try to prove it is — divided into two national divisions, neither of them belonging to this country. There are a large number of Catholics born in this country, not belonging to the two races mentioned, who resent the improper appellations applied to the churches which they attend as strongly, and indeed with as much reason, as we all resent the epithet, 'Romanist,' which Protestants so frequently apply to us. Here in America the Church has a special mission. While ministering with mother-like love and care to those who have the happiness to be within her household she had to extend her benign solicitude to the 'others that are not of this Fold.' Them also must she bring, into the fullness of the Faith; and in her earnest efforts towards this end, she is being continually thwarted and harassed by the pointless agitation, the sterile discussions, the constant bickerings, and the uncatholic acerbities, which the course pursued by the German Catholic press in this matter of foreign nationalism tends to perpetuate. . . . We put it frankly to our German contemporaries: Is it not high time that you dropped the policy of offensive foreignism, and fell into line with the rest of the Catholics of the country?"

For the *Northwestern Chronicle* to condemn agitation, discussions, and bickerings was strange in view of its own policy. *Der Wanderer* answered this attack on October 10, 1888, and accused the *Northwestern Chronicle* of attacking German Catholics. To this Conway replied on October 12, 1888, that *Der Wanderer* had "cynical bad faith" by disingenuously ignoring the point of his article, and he again charged German Catholic editors with thwarting the Church in her action in this country. Cf. *Northwestern Chronicle,* Mar. 1, 1889, for further differences between that paper and *Der Wanderer* over the German language.

> My fear only is the priests & their beer — as they were elsewhere — but I have got much to have the "German" taken from the call for the Congress, & to get the meetings separate & in separate halls.
>
> If I can now keep Rome out, something may be done with it yet.
>
> I am more than proud of your recent vigor, and as the Scotch sometimes say — "weel din."[70]

By "keeping Rome out" the Bishop of Cleveland was undoubtedly referring to the possibility of a papal blessing being sent to the gathering. O'Connell had informed Ireland that one of the American bishops had written to the Propaganda for a blessing for the Cleveland assembly, but in their reply they had told him that such a blessing would have to be asked through the Ordinary of the place.[71] Much to the surprise of all concerned, however, Bishop Wigger communicated the blessing of the Holy Father to the convention when the delegates assembled in Cleveland. O'Connell informed Gilmour that when Wigger had been in Rome during the summer of 1889, "anticipating, no doubt, some difficulty in Cleveland," he had asked personally for a blessing for the convention. Ireland told Gilmour that he considered this act to be one "of gross impertinence on the part of Bp. Wigger," since he had acted in a spiritual capacity within the limits of another bishop's jurisdiction without the knowledge of the latter.[72] Later, however, Archbishop Ireland did not hesitate to enter into the controversy over the Bennett Law in Wisconsin, in Archbishop Katzer's jurisdiction, and in the 1894 political campaign and the school question in New York, actions which Archbishop Corrigan felt were exactly the same type of interference as Ireland now accused Bishop Wigger of performing. More important than these considerations, however, was the fact that apparently the Holy See did not look with the same misgivings on the annual assemblies of German Catholics as did several of the American bishops. This fact was borne out with emphasis when not only was Wigger commissioned to impart the papal blessing at Cleveland, but the following year when the assembly was held in Pittsburgh, Vicar-General Mühlsiepen announced to the convention that the Holy Father had commissioned him to inform them that he sent his blessing and wished the best results for their labors.[73]

[70] *ADC,* Gilmour to Elder, Cleveland, Aug. 3, 1889, copy.

[71] *AASP,* O'Connell to Ireland, Rome, July 17, 1889.

[72] *ADC,* Ireland to Gilmour, St. Paul, Jan. 9, 1890.

[73] *Verhandlungen der vierten allgemeinen Versammlung der Katholiken deutscher Zunge der Vereinigten Staaten von Nord-Amerika in Pittsburgh, Pa., Am 22, 23, 24 und 25 September, 1890* (Pittsburgh, 1890), p. 114. At Pittsburgh the Priester Verein

The Pittsburgh *Katholikentag* in 1890 aroused much more attention than did the Cleveland convention of 1889, for it was there that a new figure, who was to play a major role in the "Cahenslyism" battle of the following years, made his appearance on the national stage. He was Monsignor Joseph Schröder, professor of dogmatic theology in the recently opened Catholic University of America in Washington.[74] Schröder came to the front with his address at the Pittsburgh Convention and established himself as the theological adviser and intellectual defender of the German position during the following years. Schröder did not hesitate to plunge directly to the core of the question of the moment as he rose to speak on "The Church and the Republic." It cannot be said that he spoke disparagingly of the American republican form of government, for he attested that a democracy was the best form of government for the United States, and he had no doubts that American Catholics would be good citizens and loyal subjects. He stated: "I say and pronounce from my heart: *Vivat, floreat, crescat republica.*" He also denied that the Pope had any right to rule over the United States, that any Pope ever had or would have such an intention, nor had any bishop, priest, or layman in the Church in the United States attributed such a right to the Holy Father. The State alone had the right to makes laws for all its citizens in civil and worldly affairs.

But the professor then made other observations that were somewhat at variance with the theories being advocated by the so-called Americanizers. He asserted unequivocally that no form of government, monarchy, aristocracy, or democracy, was by its nature Catholic; that no Catholic as such could consider one form of government as superior to the others. However, a Catholic could be a true, warm, and loyal democrat. This traditional position was not the warm advocacy of

---

joined its meeting to the general assembly and the whole convention was extended to four days.

[74] Schröder was invited by Bishop Keane to accept the chair of dogmatic theology at the newly founded Catholic University of America when the latter was in Europe in 1889 in search of professors. Schröder had won his doctor's degree with distinction at the German College in Rome, but because of the *Kulturkampf* he could not return to his native Germany. He first taught at St. Trond Seminary, Liége, Belgium, and when he was able to return to Germany in 1887, he succeeded Matthias Joseph Scheeben as professor of dogma in the archdiocesan seminary of Cologne. It was from here that he came to Washington at Keane's invitation. Cf. Ahern, *The Catholic University of America, 1887–1896. The Rectorship of John J. Keane* (Washington, 1948), pp. 20–21. Schröder's career at the university is discussed in Ahern and also in Hogan, *The Catholic University of America, 1896–1903. The Rectorship of Thomas J. Conaty* (Washington, 1949), *passim.*

American political forms that Cardinal Gibbons, Archbishop Ireland, Bishop Keane, and Monsignor O'Connell were supporting. Furthermore, Schröder encouraged the assembled German priests and lay people to remain German in language and attachment to their fatherland. He did not mean that they should not become Americans, since he considered that such a process was inevitable and that it was taking place rapidly. He advocated rather that German Catholics follow Carl Schurz in this one principle which he had advocated in a speech in Hamburg: "I love Germany as my mother, America as my bride." Schröder also stated that his friends in Germany looked upon him, when he returned for a visit there after less than a year in the United States, as already Americanized. So quickly, he believed, had the process taken place.[75] There would be others who would believe that Schröder never assimilated any American outlooks, but these people could at the same time in no way be considered his friends.

Doctor Ernst Lieber returned again to the Pittsburgh *Katholikentag* with greetings for the convention from Catholic Germany and the Center Party. Lieber, whose home was in Kamberg near Limburg, also brought greetings from his neighbor and fellow party member, Peter Paul Cahensly, who was overjoyed at the support which the American Germans had given to the St. Raphaelsverein. While his address, which ended the convention, was received with great enthusiasm, yet the presence of a German Catholic politician who did not hesitate to give advice on how the German Catholics should proceed in the United States, did little to lessen the approaching storm. Especially disturbing to the opposition was his final admonition, in which he counseled:

> Remain united as Catholics and as Germans. The world knows that you attack no one when you assert your right to remain American citizens and Germans. And when all prejudice disappears as mist before the sun, then also will opposition fade away. I, a Christopher, have seen this by comparing the second with the fourth *Katholikentag*. And may it with God's help continue in the future. Go slowly, it will be good if you irritate no one, but also suffer no injustice in the consciousness of your rights. Thus let me close with a phrase that has been proved so often as a battle cry and which has always inspired us in great battles:
>
> For God and the Catholic folk.[76]

Lieber's prophecy that opposition was about to fade away as mist

[75] *Verhandlungen . . .*, pp. 68–79.

[76] *Ibid.*, p. 150. Lieber delivered a lecture while visiting the United States and donated the entire proceeds. $1,100, to the Leo House fund.

before the sun was a singularly uninspired prediction. For during the very month that the fourth *Katholikentag* was being held in Pittsburgh, an international conference of Catholics at Liége, Belgium, was igniting the fuse which would set off the explosion at Lucerne, Switzerland, the following December. It was then that so-called "Cahenslyism" became the center of truly grave discord among American Catholics.

But before this came about there was one more development in Wisconsin which, in a sense, was a preparation for succeeding events. This Wisconsin affair was twofold, but each of its aspects was closely related. Early in 1891 an American Catholic Clerical Union was organized in Milwaukee by priests who were largely of Irish ancestry and who stood in opposition to the aims, as they judged them, of the German American Priests' Society. John Talbot Smith spoke out, in the *Catholic Review* of New York, against these societies of priests:

> Priests . . . ought not to be allowed to organize, as priests, into national bodies. There is here a very grave danger. . . . What a check, embarrassment, almost insuperable obstacle those Unions may be to the administration of a bishop! . . . This is America and . . . within the American Church there must be no nationalism.[77]

Reverend Sebastian G. Messmer, professor of canon law in the Catholic University of America, answered this charge with a long letter to the *Catholic Review,* in which he defended especially the aims and purposes of the *Priester Verein,* accused the *Review* of calculated prejudice, and admonished the magazine that there were other appointed watchmen upon the walls of Jerusalem besides the public prints.[78]

The *Northwestern Chronicle* picked up this item immediately and accused Messmer of a verbose and ill-tempered criticism, and then went on to attack the *Priester Verein* as a divisive influence in the Church which was hindering Americanization. They admitted the distinction which Messmer had made in his article between nationalism and nationality, but they insisted that the German priests were fostering nationalism, not nationality, by their union, and they expressed astonishment that Messmer should belong to the *Priester Verein.*[79] At this same time Archbishop Ireland expressed his own approval of the new American Catholic Clerical Union in Wisconsin when he informed O'Connell:

[77] Mar. 7, 1891.
[78] Mar. 21, 1891. Cf. also a letter of C. Shaus to the editor in the Mar. 28, 1891, issue.
[79] *Northwestern Chronicle,* Mar. 20, 1891.

The "American Clerical Union" in Wisconsin is doing a splendid work. It has frightened the Germans, & driven them to their lairs. The "Union" is managed with great prudence. It professes a great admiration for the zeal & success of the German "Verein," and professes to walk in the footsteps of the latter.[80]

Messmer answered the *Northwestern Chronicle* by a letter in its April 3, 1891, issue in which he said in part:

The time will come (we hope before another century is passed) when the American nation will embrace but one nationality, not, indeed, through force and violent measures, but as you rightly say, "that will come of itself, and cannot be kept back indefinitely." Hence, we all must become Americanized. But meanwhile, under the present conditions, with the different nationalities of our Catholic population, clerical unions may do a great deal in strengthening and furthering Catholic faith and life among them. And as our different national sections live peaceably together in church and state, so may and ought clerical unions to work side by side in peace and harmony.

For the rest, everyone will agree with you, that if ever these unions should impair the spirit of unity, or injure the interests of the Catholic people; if they should lose the spirit of the church or disobey her authority, let them be suppressed at once.

In the future, Rev. Sir., I shall follow your kind advice, and, remaining on the rostrum, leave you the floor.[81]

To this Father Conway rejoined in a postscript, congratulating Messmer on his resolve to keep to his rostrum, rather than to join three or four professors at the University who had announced themselves as Germans. These professors, said Conway, should rather be reflecting Catholic thought for the country:

If Dr. Messmer wants to see some of the evil results of these clerical unions let him look at Wisconsin. The *Deutscher Verein* occasioned the formation of a union of English-speaking clergy. The church in Wisconsin presents the sorry spectacle of certain sections of the church and people arrayed in hostile camps, and encouraged in their hostility by the secular press . . . clerical unions are an obstacle to the natural and gradual Americanization so desirable for the best interests of Christianity in America. These unions do not help to greater efficiency in the work of religion, nor do they assist our people to harmonize with their surroundings. They hamper the spiritual usefulness of the bishops and clergy; they foster a bad spirit; they are a standing mis-

[80] *ADR,* Ireland to O'Connell, St. Paul, Mar. 8, 1891.
[81] Apr. 3, 1891.

representation of our Catholic people before their fellow citizens of the United States.[82]

Conway also accused the *Priester Verein* of sending Abbelen to Rome where he had maligned the hierarchy. This attack then brought Abbelen himself into the fray. The Milwaukee Vicar-General denied this accusation in the May 1, 1891, issue of the *Chronicle,* maintained that the German Priests' Society did not exist at that time, denied he had maligned the hierarchy, and invited anyone to read his memorial calmly and dispassionately while comparing it with those of Bishops Gilmour, Moore, Keane, and Ireland. Conway also had an answer for Abbelen. He denied that Archbishop Heiss had sent Abbelen, asserted that Heiss himself stated he had signed the document on trust, and that the plot had come rather from St. Louis and Milwaukee priests. But Conway passed over in silence Abbelen's invitation to compare his memorial with those of his opponents.

Reverend Hermann J. Heuser, editor of the *American Ecclesiastical Review,* at this point invited Messmer to prepare an article for his journal which would examine exhaustively the whole question of clerical unions. At first Messmer thought of accepting, but after seeing how Conway had treated his first effort along these lines, the professor informed Heuser:

> I am exceedingly sorry that I cannot furnish you with the desired article on "Clerical Unions." Archbishop Ireland's organ, the "Northwestern Chronicle," has attacked me shamefully on account of my reply in the "Catholic Review" & to a short rejoinder that I sent to it, it has subjoined this week a stronger attack yet, especially on the ground that no professor of our University had a right to take part in public in this discussion. I have since also been told by Bp. Keane, our rector, that he is positively opposed to my continuing the controversy. Nay it was more or less contemplated to bring the matter before the University Board when they met about 3 or 4 days ago. You see, therefore, I could not without giving great offense to several parties, engage any further in this particular discussion. They are the very men who have their mouths full with "American liberty & fair play!" . . .
>
> I greatly regret that things have turned the way they did. For I earnestly believe the Clerical Unions, keeping within the proper limits, would do much good. Archbp. Ireland's main objection, that they keep up the spirit of nationalism, is nonsense. It is not in the nature of these "Unions," and if some extremists, as they are found everywhere, wish to drag nationalism into these Unions, they must be restrained.[83]

[82] *Ibid.*
[83] *ACHSP,* Messmer to Heuser, Washington, Apr. 12, 1891.

Perhaps it was for the good of all concerned that the discussion was thus ended, as there was obviously no meeting of minds. Besides, the vacancy which occurred at this time in the archiepiscopal see of Milwaukee, and the resulting division over the succession to that see now fully occupied parties on both sides of the controversy.

After the death of Archbishop Heiss, on March 26, 1890, the consultors and the suffragan bishops of the Province of Milwaukee prepared their separate *ternae* of names thought worthy to be appointed by the Holy See to the vacant bishopric. According to the precepts of the Third Plenary Council of Baltimore, the archbishops of the United States also had a right to submit their opinions to the Holy See on the *terna* of the suffragan bishops when an archiepiscopal see was vacant. The bishops of the Province of Milwaukee proposed as candidates: Bishops Katzer, of Green Bay, Flasch, of La Crosse, and Richter, of Grand Rapids, in that order, and informed the other American archbishops of their decision on April 18. The consultors of the Archdiocese of Milwaukee also chose Katzer in first place.[84] Before taking any action, Cardinal Gibbons decided to await the annual meeting of the archbishops, which was scheduled to open in Boston on July 23. In this manner the choice of the suffragan bishops could be made the subject of a joint discussion by the American Metropolitans. Just as in 1880, when Heiss had succeeded Henni, so now there was great interest and activity in regard to Heiss's successor. Archbishop Ireland had a voice in the proceedings now, however, due to the fact that the Province of St. Paul had been erected on May 15, 1888, and he was serving as its first archbishop. As in 1880, the English-speaking priests of Milwaukee again addressed the archbishops individually and requested them to use their influence to have an English-speaking Ordinary appointed. When Ireland heard that Katzer had been chosen *dignissimus* by both the suffragan bishops and the consultors, he told Gibbons that he felt Katzer was "a man thoroughly German & thoroughly unfit to be an archbishop. The Milwaukee question," he continued, "is a most important one for the American Church & I will rely on your enlightened co-operation in solving it."[85] Archbishop Ryan also informed Abbot Smith in Rome: "The national feeling runs quite high in the Milwaukee case. I do not know what the Abps. will agree upon, but I have sometimes thought that Bishop Marty would suit the place. He is German but quite enough American to fit the posi-

[84] *AAB,* 87-J-2, Katzer to Gibbons, Green Bay, Apr. 18, 1890.
[85] *AAB,* 87-J-5, Ireland to Gibbons, St. Paul, Apr. 21, 1890.

tion."[86] When the archbishops assembled in Boston they decided, as they had done in 1880, that Bishop John Lancaster Spalding, of Peoria, would be their recommendation to the Holy See as the most suitable man to govern the Church in Milwaukee. The archbishops arrived at this conclusion "for the sake of peace and the advancement of religion," as Gibbons informed Simeoni.[87] As the second and third choices, the archbishops sent on the names of Bishops Marty and Richter.

Throughout the summer and autumn of 1890 all awaited an announcement from the Holy See, and individual letters from members of both parties were sent to Rome on behalf of their nominations. O'Connell informed Ireland in August that Bishop Richter, whose name had been submitted on all three lists, appeared to be gaining in the councils of Rome, since, as he said, "they don't trust Spalding and . . . Katzer goes very probably as the recognized head of a party."[88] But O'Connell, it would seem, was interpreting events, as he often did, in terms of his own hopes. In december the Holy See announced that Bishop Francis Xavier Katzer had been transferred from Green Bay to become the third Archbishop of Milwaukee. Gibbons transmitted the news of his appointment to Katzer, who, in turn, replied: "As regards the information, I feel like a dwarf succeeding a giant. I have not sought the position. I have most reluctantly allowed my name to be put on the list and I have prayed to God to be spared the great responsibility — it comes to pass against my will. Please, remember me in your prayers."[89]

Naturally the Germans interpreted the appointment of Katzer as an important recognition of their position. Many of the other archbishops and bishops had not favored the advancement of Katzer, because it had been consistently reported that while bishop of Green Bay he had worked to have a German bishop appointed to Detroit. Gibbons, Elder, Maes, Gilmour, Ireland, Keane, and O'Connell has been, on the other hand, advancing successfully the name of Reverend John S. Foley, pastor of St. Martin's Church in Baltimore, to that position. Katzer was likewise known to be a strong proponent of the German claims to language rights, customs, and usages, and he had made a trip to Rome in 1888 for the purpose of defending attacks there on the German Catholics of the United States.[90]

[86] *AASPOW,* Ryan to Smith, Philadelphia, July 16, 1890.

[87] *AAB,* 87-R-5, Gibbons to Simeoni, Boston, July 25, 1890, copy.

[88] *AASP,* O'Connell to Ireland, Rome, Aug. 18, 1890.

[89] *AAB,* 88-F-3, Katzer to Gibbons, Green Bay, Dec. 24, 1890.

[90] Cf. *ADC,* Gilmour to Elder, Cleveland, Nov. 1, 1887; *AAB,* 84-S-9, Elder to Gibbons, Cincinnati, July 18, 1888; *ADR,* Ireland to O'Connell, St. Paul, Apr. 12, 1888.

After the decision had been announced, O'Connell furnished Ireland with the reasons which he considered to be behind the appointment:

> About Milwaukee I inquired how it was done in spite of the letter of the archbs. The answer was: "The Archbps have a right if they wish to send us their views on the candidates, they have no right to send us another list." That recalled what Card. Mazzella, the *ponente,* had said to me a short time previous: "For me there are only two lists — the consultors' and the Suffragans'." This is founded on a deep determination on the part of the Cardinals to put the American Bps. a little more in their place. On my way over here, Vaughan told me in Manchester that he noticed a growing disposition on our part to get away from the Holy See. I really believe they fear it here. . . . This sounds strange in view of the fact that in Europe every power except Italy names its own Bps., the Queen of Spain, King of Portugal, King of Bavaria, send only one name and that to be confirmed. The same is practically true of Franz Joseph of Austria, Wm. of Germany, who likewise has a veto on every parish priest, and of the Republic of France. And in the treaty lately made about Malta, they bound themselves to name no Bp. to Malta and the adjoining See that was not acceptable to Queen Victoria. . . . Germans wrote here that there were no Catholics in America but themselves and that the others would have nothing from Rome but dogma. Indeed the prospect is not cheerful.[91]

These comparisons of the practice followed by Rome in relation to the American Church over against the Church in the countries of Europe would grow sharper in the succeeding years, especially when the issue of "Cahenslyism" focused these differences directly upon the question of nationality rights in the Church of the United States.

[91] *AASP,* O'Connell to Ireland, Rome, Dec. 31, 1890.

CHAPTER IV

The Cahenslyism Turmoil of 1891

AFTER Peter Paul Cahensly had successfully established his first daughter branch of the St. Raphaelsverein at New York in 1883, he turned to other countries in Europe for further expansion. The society was operating in the main European ports of departure, as well as in the United States, but in lands like Italy, France, Austria, Switzerland, and Belgium national organizations, it was hoped, could implement their St. Raphael aims for the spiritual and material support of departing emigrants. In this way Cahensly likewise hoped to bring about that international co-operation in Catholic emigrant care which Leo XIII had advised him to develop in 1882.

At the Second International Social Congress in Liége, Belgium, on September 4–7, 1887, Cahensly was able to prepare the way for the organization of the second national branch of his society. Count Waldbott-Bossenheim invited Cahensly to attend the congress and to explain the activity and goals of the St. Raphaelsverein. The reception to his speech was so favorable that the Belgian society was constituted, with Senator Leon von Ockerhout as president and Waldbott-Bossenheim as secretary. Thus Germans, Austrians, Belgians, Italians, Poles, and other Slavic groups began immediately to pass through the mission at Antwerp. There William Würden served as agent, and the priests at St. Ignatius Church were delegated to supply the necessary spiritual care.[1]

[1] *Rechenschafts-Bericht St. Raphaels-Vereins zum Schutze katholischen deutscher Auswanderer für das Jahr 1891.*

At the 1890 International Social Congress in Liége, Reverend Alphonse Villeneuve, a French Canadian priest who was then pastor of St. Paul's Church in Sandy Hill, New York, claimed that twenty-five million Catholics had emigrated to the United States and that the Catholic population of the country as of 1890 was slightly over five million. From this Villeneuve concluded that the other twenty million Catholics had either turned Protestant or become indifferent. Villeneuve also presented a resolution to be sent to the Holy Father thanking him for his interest in the emigrants of all nations, and asking that in North and South America the emigrants have,

Cahensly also attended the second Austrian *Katholikentag* at Vienna in 1889, and there explained the purpose of the St. Raphaelsverein. He was able to obtain support among Austrian Catholics, especially from the nobility, and from Emperor Franz Josef who personally donated 2000 kronen ($400) for the establishment of an Austrian branch of the society. The Austrian hierarchy enthusiastically supported Cahensly's proposal, because they realized the importance of care for their Catholic members who were beginning to emigrate in large numbers to North and South America. Cahensly often declared that in his entire career he received more understanding support from the Austrian and Hungarian bishops than he did from any other hierarchy. Prince Johann zu Schwarzenberg accepted the presidency of this Austrian St. Raphael Society, and distinguished Catholics from the different crown lands of the empire agreed to serve on its board of directors.[2]

In Italy Cahensly also was successful. In 1882 Leo XIII had encouraged him to organize his society in Italy, and in succeeding years the Limburg merchant made many trips to Italy for this purpose. He first contacted Don Giovanni Bosco, but the founder of the Salesians and future saint could not assume leadership in the movement because of a lack of priests and too many previous commitments. Cahensly was

---

wherever possible, priests and parish schools of their own nationality. Unquestionably he influenced Cahensly of the St. Raphaelsverein who was present at this conference and who reprinted the priest's statistics and comments in the *SRB,* V (Oct., 1890), pp. 54–58.

[2] Cahensly, *Der St. Raphaelsverein,* p. 32. The Austrian branch began organized efforts to preserve the faith of Austrian emigrants. A monthly publication of this society, *Der Auswanderer,* was pointed toward serving the material and spiritual needs of their countrymen, which in the case of the Austrians was often a more difficult accomplishment. Protests appeared in the columns of *Der Auswanderer* that the Austrians did not attend church in the United States, that they read liberal papers, did not know prayers when they brought their children to be baptized, and were unaccustomed to supporting the Church since in Austria it was State subsidized. In the columns of this magazine appeared also for the first time a recognition that the Catholic emigrants had not received in their homeland adequate instruction in their faith, along with schooling and capacity to meet the new conditions of American life. But at the same time the Austrian branch was also critical of American insistence on the English language, and articles appeared in which exaggerated estimates of losses were traced to this cause. Cf. "Jahresrundschau und Tätigkeitsbericht," *Beiträge zur Auswandererfrage und Rechenschaftsbericht des österreichischen St. Raphael Vereins zum Schutze katholischer Auswanderer* (Vienna, 1911), p. 42; an article by the secretary of the society and imperial treasurer of the empire, Franz Josef Fischer, "Die Auswandererfrage," *Beiträge* (Vienna, 1907), pp. 5–29. Following Tardivel, Fischer estimated that the Church had lost one half, perhaps three fourths, of her children in the United States, and he attributed this loss to the secular state, moral atmosphere, public schools, secret societies, mixed marriages, lack of priests, weakness of the Church outside the large metropolitan centers, and the spirit of religious freedom, indifference, and materialism.

then introduced to Bishop Giovanni Battista Scalabrini, of Piacenza, and a friendship was established between the two men which ultimately resulted in the establishment of the Italian St. Raphael Society.[3] Scalabrini was deeply interested in the problem of caring for Italians who were emigrating from their homeland without protection and direction. He had labored hard and with success to establish a mission seminary, first in Genoa and later in Piacenza itself, in which priests were trained to follow the Italians to North and South America. These priests were trained to assist Italian emigrants in practicing their faith in their native language, and holding to their religious beliefs in a new environment. By 1887 Scalabrini had laid the groundwork for the *Istituto Christoforo Columbo,* the mother house of the Congregation of St. Charles Borromeo, a society of priests devoted to Italian emigrants. Along with his mission congregation, he now supported the establishment of a St. Raphael Society as an auxiliary force which would incorporate the laity in this important work. With the approval of the Holy See he set up a *Comitata Centrale Associazione di Patronato per l'Emigrazione Italiana* in 1889, with Marchese Giovanni Battista Volpe-Landi, a lawyer from Piacenza, as president, and himself as honorary president. Scalabrini, Volpe-Landi, and Cahensly traveled about Italy creating local units of the St. Raphael Society in major cities, such as Rome, Florence, Turin, Genoa, and Milan. In February of 1890 Scalabrini held a conference in the Church of Sant' Andrea della Valle in Rome, which was attended by a large gathering of prelates, diplomats, senators, and deputies of the Italian parliament. Prince Luigi Buoncompagni was named president of the Roman branch, and Count Eduardo Soderini assumed the office of secretary. In Genoa, Marchese Vittorio del Caretto di Balestrino accepted the presidency of the local society, and Volpe-Landi, with Cahensly's assistance and companionship, went to work at once to ameliorate conditions aboard ships of the Lavarello and La Veloce companies sailing from that port. Reverend Peter Bandini headed a committee in New York for the reception of Italian immigrants and acted as agent for that work.[4]

[3] Scalabrini was born in Fino di Coma on July 8, 1839. After teaching literature and serving as rector of the archdiocesan seminary in Milan he was appointed Bishop of Piacenza in 1867. In 1900 he came to the United States and established a house of his institute in New York; in 1904 he sailed for Brazil to create a similar new house there for the training of Italian priests in immigrant work. He was to have been created a cardinal in recognition of his pioneer efforts in behalf of the Italian emigrant, but he died on March 31, 1905, before he could be appointed.

[4] Nathem, S.A.C., *Peter Paul Cahensly. Ein Gedenkblatt zu seinem 100. Geburtstag. 1838* 28. October *1938* (Hamburg, 1939), p. 21; Cahensly, *Der St. Raphaelsverein,* pp. 32–33; *LfThK,* VIII, p. 631.

Thus, by 1890 St. Raphael societies were established in Germany, Belgium, Austria, and Italy, the countries which at that time led in total numbers of Catholic emigrants leaving for the Americas. In the United States, as well, there was a branch of the society. These branch societies had never assembled to discuss common problems, and their only contact was with the mother society in Germany. Accordingly, it was determined that the boards of directors of the European St. Raphael societies should assemble in Lucerne, Switzerland, on December 9–10, 1890, so that they might profit from a mutual exchange of ideas. In this way the less experienced branches in this specialized work could also learn from the older societies. Little did the St. Raphael leaders who journeyed to Lucerne in that winter of 1890 realize the powder keg that was about to explode as a result of their conferences.

Cahensly himself represented the German St. Raphaelsverein, while Marchese Volpe-Landi and Very Reverend Francesco Zaboglio, vicar-general of the new Congregation of St. Charles Borromeo, came from the Italian St. Raphael Society. The Austrian and Belgian societies had excused themselves from attending, but both later acceded to the resolutions of the conference. There were several observers in attendance who were active in the work, including three priests, but who were not official delegates in so far as they were not members of the boards of directors of the established national societies. The assembly was held in Lucerne because a Swiss St. Raphael Society was just then in the process of formation, and a delegate of the Swiss unit was accepted at the meeting in the person of Baron Rudolph von Reding-Biberegg. Charles Plista, of Paris, represented in the same way a French St. Raphael Society still in the making.

It is apparent from this enumeration of directors in attendance that the majority of St. Raphael leaders were from the nobility, since at this time lay leadership of the Church in Europe was almost entirely drawn from aristocratic and professional circles. Striking also was the obvious absence of delegates from the American branch of the society, an absence which was destined to prove very regrettable and which was never explained by any members of the St. Raphaelsverein. Perhaps, the meeting was called too suddenly, funds were lacking, or the season of the year was difficult for ocean travel. But if Archbishop Corrigan, Bishop Wigger, or Father Reuland had been present they could in all likelihood have tempered the judgments of those whose acquaintance with the United States betrayed a lack of knowledge based on firsthand evidence.

Bishop Scalabrini informed Cahensly that he could not personally attend because of pressing business, but that Volpe-Landi and Zaboglio, whom he was sending, would interpret his thoughts, hopes, and views. "You have undertaken a great task, my dear Cahensly," he wrote, "and I wish for you and your confreres of the different nations of Europe united at Lucerne the blessing of God on your work."[5] On the first day the delegates deliberated concerning protective measures for the emigrants before they left their homes, at the port of departure, during the ocean voyage, and after their arrival in the new world. On the second day Volpe-Landi presented a document to the congress which Scalabrini had read before they had left Italy, and which Zaboglio had checked with him. The object of this memorandum was to suggest means of safeguarding emigrants of the various nationalities in the practice of their faith after their arrival and settlement in the United States. After some changes the document was accepted by all delegates present, and Cahensly and Volpe-Landi were voted as delegates to bear this memorial to the Pope as expressing the wishes of the congress.

After the assembly was adjourned this memorandum was submitted to all St. Raphael boards of directors in Germany, Belgium, Austria-Hungary, and Italy. It was signed by them to a man, and the Swiss and French representatives to the congress likewise signed it. At that time Premier Henri Mercier, of Quebec, along with his Minister of Finance, Joseph Shehyn, and thirteen other Canadian Catholics were in Europe. A separate copy of the memorial was prepared for them and attached to the original document of Lucerne, as a testimony of the interest in this question of the numerous French-Canadian Catholics living in the United States. This second copy was then signed by Mercier, Shehyn, and their thirteen companions. Such activity consumed some time, and it was not until April that Cahensly and Volpe-Landi were able to meet in Piacenza and to proceed together to Rome to present the memorial to Leo XIII. The two delegates arrived in Rome on April 6, 1891, and petitioned the maestro di camera to His Holiness for a private audience. While waiting for this privilege, Volpe-Landi, on April 14, was called back to Piacenza due to a sudden illness in his family. The next day the bigletto for an audience on April 16 arrived, and Cahensly felt compelled to present the memorial alone at the time appointed. Leo XIII received him kindly, accepted the document, and promised to give it careful examination.[6]

Because of its central importance in all succeeding developments, the Lucerne Memorial, as it was called, along with the names of its

[5] *ADCV,* Scalabrini to Cahensly, Piacenza, Dec. 7, 1890.

[6] Cahensly, *Der St. Raphaelsverein,* pp. 32–34; *SRB,* VI (July, 1891), pp. 33–41.

signers, has been included in Appendix IV (pp. 313–315). The document was signed by ten members of the German branch of the society, nine directors from Austria, seven from Belgium, eight from Italy, and one representative each from Switzerland and France. The duplicate copy, representing the French-Canadians, was signed by fifteen gentlemen. Therefore, in all, fifty-one Catholics from seven nations joined in presenting this memorial, drawn up in the French language, to Leo XIII. But from the very first public knowledge of the document, fifty of the signers were forgotten, and one, Peter Paul Cahensly, was charged with its authorship.

In the memorial eight recommendations stand forth as the aims which the delegates at Lucerne judged necessary for holding the immigrant Catholics within the Church after they reached the United States. These included the establishment of separate churches for each nationality, and the appointment to these churches of "priests of the same nationality as the faithful." If immigrants settled in an area where they were not numerous enough to create special national parishes, then, it was further stated, it would be desirable to have a priest in such parishes who understood the respective languages of these immigrants. Such a priest would be strictly bound to give catechetical instruction to each group in their mother tongue. Parochial schools should be set up everywhere and should be separated, as far as possible, for each nationality, with the language of their country of origin included in the curriculum of each school as well as the language and history of their adopted country. Priests of every nationality should have equal rights with native priests, and Catholics should be organized into societies and mutual aid unions to prevent them from joining the Freemasons and related organizations. The seventh recommendation, which proved to be the most provocative, read as follows:

> It seems very desirable that the Catholics of each nationality, wherever it is deemed possible, have in the episcopate of the country where they immigrate, several bishops who are of the same origin. It seems that in this way the organization of the Church would be perfect, for in the assemblies of the bishops, every immigrant race would be represented, and its interests and needs would be protected.[7]

Finally, the delegates asked the Holy See to sponsor mission seminaries in which priests could be trained for the United States, as Scala-

[7] Cahensly, *Der St. Raphaelsverein,* pp. 34–39. The New York *Herald,* May 28, 1891, carried an English translation of the Lucerne Memorial with mistranslations and inaccuracies. The fifty-one signatures attached to the document were not listed.

brini was already doing. They also requested that St. Raphael societies be established through the recommendation of the Holy See in those countries from which emigrants moved, if they were not yet established, and that these societies be placed under a cardinal-protector.

On May 4, 1891, a telegram went out from the Wolff Continental Telegraph Bureau in Rome, a German news agency, in which a report of the memorial was first announced. In this telegram the origin of the Lucerne petition was attributed exclusively to the German St. Raphaelsverein. Other releases from the Associated Press in Rome, Brussels, and Berlin, on May 8, 26, and 27 respectively, elaborated on the original telegram and the text of the memorial itself which had been obtained by the *Moniteur de Rome* and published in its columns on May 8. First news of the memorial, which was growing in reputation each day, reached the American public on May 9, 1891, when the New York *Herald* published a cable from Rome. In this cable Cahensly was misquoted and accused of submitting a document to the Pope asking for the appointment of American bishops representative of the nationalities of the immigrants because, as it read, "the Irish bishops in the United States only nominate Irish priests, who do not know the languages spoken by the immigrants."

The *Catholic Review* in New York and the *Northwestern Chronicle* in St. Paul editorialized on these cables in their first issues after the news was released. The explosive cables had stated that Cahensly had asked for national bishops, schools, and priests, that the Propaganda was interested in giving an international character to these activities, that Dr. Ernst Lieber, deputy in the Reichstag, was connected with the project and that he had made journeys to the United States for that purpose. Moreover, it was stated that Cahensly had had long conferences with Simeoni and Rampolla before he left Rome, and it was believed that the plan was first elaborated, or at least inspired, by a group of German priests and laity in the United States. The *Catholic Review* declared that it was an insult to the American Church to term as Irish all Catholics who had not come from Germany, Switzerland, Belgium, Austria, or Italy; that the memorial treated the United States as a mere camping ground, ignoring the existence of millions of native-born Americans, and that it was an effort to alienate the rising generation more and more from the faith. The *Northwestern Chronicle* began rather mildly; its wrath would come later. Here it was stated that the effort would not succeed, but it indicated the extreme foreign national spirit which was sedulously at work, of which Cahensly and Lieber were named as the figureheads. To the St. Paul paper it was rather the members of the *Priester Verein* who were behind the memorial and who spent their time foreignizing the American Church. It was said that the German priests had obtained this idea from a number of Polish Catholics, led by a few Polish priests of Chicago, who had demanded that Polish bishops be specially appointed to look after their countrymen in the United States.[8]

The cables of that first week in May were only a faint foreshadowing of what was to follow. On May 27 the Associated Press released a story, date-lined from Berlin, in which the whole "conspiracy" was unveiled as follows:

> It is learned here that Herr Cahensly has been the principal mover in the efforts of the European Catholic emigration societies to induce the Pope to follow distinct national lines in fostering the Church work among Catholic immigrants in America. The dispatches from Rome will already have given American readers some information touching this movement. Herr Cahensly only recently returned from the Eternal City, where he had gone to lay before Leo XIII, the memorial formulated last December at Lucerne by the conference of representatives of Catholic emigration societies of different countries. It was Herr Cahensly who called that conference, as he had previously, in September, called a similar conference in Liege. Cahensly is a member of the Prussian diet, where he has long shown special interest in the question of Catholic emigration. He is also the general secretary and controlling spirit of the Society of St. Raphael. His championship of the interests of German Catholics in America has borne fruits in frequent instructions to Herr von Schlözer, the German representative at the Vatican, to use his influence in their behalf whenever occasion arose. The Lucerne conference, which was made up of the presidents of the national emigration committees, commissioned Herr Cahensly to bear the memorial to the Vatican.
>
> On his way thither he stopped at Genoa for conference with the Italian emigration committees, and from there he was accompanied to Rome by the president of the Italian association, Sgr. Valpilandi [*sic*]. Herr Cahensly was also armed with letters from many influential

[8] *Northwestern Chronicle,* May 15, 1891; *Catholic Review,* May 16, 1891. John Talbot Smith, in succeeding issues of this journal, concentrated on the issue of double episcopal jurisdiction which had been wrongly deduced from the recommendations of the Lucerne memorialists that several bishops of the different nationalities be included in the hierarchy. The *Catholic Review* of May 30 printed Leo XIII's brief *Studio et vigilante* of August 26, 1884, condemning double jurisdiction in India under the headline: "Official Opinion of Pope Leo XIII on the System Which the Conspirators of Luzerne Would Fasten upon the United States." In the following issue of June 6 a letter of Cardinal Jacobini on the same subject was printed under a similar headline.

Catholic leaders expressing approval of the movement he represented. Among these was a letter from the late Dr. Windhorst [*sic*], and documents showing that he had the support of Cardinals Schönborn, of Prague, the archbishop of Vienna, the chiefs of the Catholic party and the princes of the Austrian aristocracy, the Belgian cardinals, and the representatives of the Catholic movement at Rome and in Italy. There were also expressions of approval from influential Catholics of Quebec, such as Premier Mercier and Messrs. Joseph Sheyn [*sic*] and Robert Ness. At Rome Herr Cahensly put himself in communication not only with the Propaganda and the Vatican, but also Cardinals Mazella, Ledochowski, and Melchers, who approved of the project and the memorial submitted to the Holy See. Herr Cahensly visited Herr von Schlözer and solicited his support. The latter, who had already received information and instruction from Berlin, promised intervention. Speaking of the nomination of Mgr. Katzer as archbishop in America, Herr von Schlözer said to Herr Cahensly: "This is an important act that will interest all Prussia, whether Catholic or Lutheran." He added that he would warmly congratulate and thank the cardinal secretary of state for his choice, so favorable to German interests.

Herr Cahensly then visited the Austro-Hungarian ambassador to the Vatican, who promised his support, adding: "I am all the more disposed to support your mission to Rome as my government has already sent me instructions in regard to this subject. You may count upon me. . . ." It is a significant fact that the whole movement has been conducted so far without the knowledge or advice of the American hierarchy. The campaign has been directed solely by the committee in Germany, which, by its activity, has secured the support and approbation of other European countries. The American bishops have probably no information about it except what they have gained from the press dispatches. There will be great curiosity to know their view of the matter. The plan proposed in the memorial would, if adopted, seem to be peculiarly well adapted for the preservation in America of the languages and race distinctions of the immigrants.[9]

The St. Paul agent of the Associated Press immediately approached Archbishop Ireland for his opinions on this cable, and the reporter received an interview, the text of which swept across the country after

[9] St. Paul *Daily Globe,* May 28, 1891. In this release Prime Minister Mercier was also quoted as having said to the Pope at an interview: "When I assisted at the Baltimore centenary I felt an acute regret on finding that there were no Canadians among the American bishops, notwithstanding that there are more than a million Canadians in the United States. As the diocese of Ogdensburg is about to become vacant, I shall pray the Holy See to nominate a Canadian to the vacancy." In December of that year Henry Gabriels, a Belgian-born priest, was named second Bishop of Ogdensburg. On May 26 a Brussels dispatch also associated Spain with the memorial.

it was released. Ireland began by saying that he had no objection to talking on the proceedings of the Lucerne convention, and he laid down at the outset his fundamental thesis, namely, that Cahensly and his colaborers were working with might and main, as he said, to harness the Church in America into the service of the recently arrived immigrants from Germany. Other Catholic interests in the country were apparently looked upon as quite secondary. Then he stated:

> What is the most strange feature in this whole Lucerne movement is the impudence of the men in undertaking to meddle under any pretext in the Catholic affairs of America. This is simply unpardonable and all American Catholics will treasure up the affront for future action. We acknowledge the Pope of Rome as our chieftain in spiritual matters and we are glad to receive directions from him, but men in Germany or Switzerland or Ireland must mind their own business and be still as to ours.
>
> Nor is this the most irritating fact in this movement. The inspiration of the work in Europe comes, the dispatch tells us, from a clique in America. The great mass of German-speaking Catholics, laymen and priests, are totally opposed to all plots and intrigues to retain foreign ascendancy and are most heartily in sympathy with everything that is American. As a body there is no more loyal element than they in the population, and in religious matters they are thoroughly in accord with their bishops. I have under my care a very large German-speaking population and never could I have found ground for the smallest complaint.[10]

Ireland believed that there was not the slightest possibility of any result coming from the Lucerne Memorial except the utter extinction of all foreign influence. He felt that the American bishops were fully capable of warding off foreign invasions and of maintaining the Church on thorough American lines. If they did not themselves have the courage and common sense to do so, then the Catholic people, whatever their race or origin, would compel them to do their duty. Nor would the authorities in Rome listen to Cahensly and his friends, since the well-known policy of Rome was to trust the hierarchy of each country and to encourage in each nation Catholics to the manner born. The Archbishop of St. Paul then concluded:

> Speaking of the several classes of immigrants coming to America, Leo XIII said to myself: "The bishops should see that all can practice their religion in the language they understand, but when this much is done, let the work be toward amalgamation and union."

[10] New York *Herald,* May 31, 1891.

Our bishops will be chosen for their offices without regard to their race or their birth place. The condition for their elevation being their fitness, and for this fitness two things will be required: that they be strong in Catholicity and strong in Americanism. . . .

Indeed, Mr. Cahensly and his supporters are somewhat excusable when they see in Americans naught else, or little else, than foreigners or foreign dominations. This is largely, they perceive, the case in politics. Why should it not be, they ask, in religion? When we will be more American in civil and political matters, there will be fewer petitions from vereins in America and from conferences in Lucerne for the foreignizing of Catholics in America.[11]

The words of the forceful Archbishop of St. Paul on this occasion, as on so many others, evoked warm support from non-Catholic America. The editors of the Philadelphia *Press* felt that the American people would be generally reassured by the archbishop's words, and they then went on to state that the program of Cahensly compromised "about all the elements of antagonism to foreign supremacy in this country which found a place in the platform of the Native American party and the Constitution of the Know-Nothing order." To the *Press* the chief point of Ireland's interview — and the point that he would have desired them to grasp — was:

. . . the assurance that the executive and administrative branches of the Government have in so distinguished and representative a prelate a strong ally (if good citizenship, which is the duty of all, may be called alliance) in the struggle which will shortly engage the best of their abilities — the struggle to assimilate the desirable and reject the undesirable elements of the immigration which is now pouring into the country.[12]

An interesting correspondence at this time between Archbishop Ireland and Monsignor O'Connell in Rome supplied revealing indications of the origin and dissemination of these manufactured news cables of 1891. These cables spread abroad misinformation, exaggeration, and unjust innuendoes concerning Cahensly and, perhaps, did more to impair the unity and harmony of the Church than any single development of these troubled times. On May 21, after the first dispatches reached the United States, Ireland thanked O'Connell. He said:

[11] *Ibid.*

[12] Philadelphia *Press,* June 3, 1891. Ireland's interview was also published with comment in the Catholic press across the land. Cf. "The Would-Be Swiss Pope," Louisville *Catholic Advocate,* June 4, 1891.

Well, God bless Böglin & the Associated Press, & the friends associated with him in the writing of the dispatches. They are so cleverly put, and always hit the nail on the head. Of course to me the guiding hand is clear. They are creating a tremendous sensation, & affecting more than ought else could have done Catholic public opinion. Those on the School question were capital—provided of course that future pronouncements of Pope or Prop. sustain them. The revelations of the tricks of Cahensly & his American backers have frightened our Germans, and aroused our bishops. The Germans will be afraid to interfere at Rome, lest their machinations be found out. They are dreadful, and mean absolute subjugation of the American Church.

Goodbye for today. Look out for a series of letters.[13]

To this O'Connell replied:

I wanted to know your opinion about those Roman telegrams. Most of the Catholic papers showed great dulness regarding them. The one on the schools contained the sentiments of Mons. Jacobini.

You have no idea of the extent and perfection of the German scheme. They have all the most notable men in Europe involved in it. Rome is in their favor and I found no intention here of consulting the Amer. episcopate. The opposition of the "Irish" in America was assumed and disregarded. Nothing I said made much impression until I mentioned the probability that the Amer. government would present opposition. Then they sent back M. Cahensly's Mss. from the Vatican Press. I expect to give more news on the point and it seems a better way of exploding the scheme than endeavoring to arouse individual Bps. by correspondence. Conde Pallen wrote the correspondent here of the Cath. Associated Press to say nothing on the subject of nationality. The Germans here are not in the least disconcerted. When I have a good expression of American opinion I hope to put it into the Vatican.[14]

Ireland rushed two cables to O'Connell on June 9 in which he said: "SEND MORE. SEND ALL. MIRACLES OF GOOD DONE," and "GREAT DISTURBANCE, DANGER OF SCHISM AND PERSECUTION UNLESS ROME DENOUNCE CAHENSLY, AND DENOUNCE ONCE FOR ALL, AND FOR TIME BEING NAME

[13] *ADR,* Ireland to O'Connell, St. Paul, May 21, 1891. Monsignor Eugene Böglin, referred to here by Ireland, was a priest from Alsace Lorraine, resident in Rome, whom O'Connell had recommended to the Propaganda as suitable for preparing news releases emanating from Vatican offices. He was retained by O'Connell, Ireland, Keane, and Gibbons as press agent in their controversies of these years to prepare and place copy on such topics as Cahenslyism, the school and social questions, and the American Philippine occupation. On January 9, 1901, Ireland, in a letter to O'Connell, referred to Böglin's "Cacoethes scribendi." Cardinal Gibbons did not enjoy this transaction, but Bishop Keane informed him that it was necessary that they have someone to present their position through the international news agencies.

[14] *AASP,* O'Connell to Ireland, Rome, June 5, 1891.

NO GERMAN BISHOPS." O'Connell acknowledged these messages and assured his friend: "You will have then another shock. I know it will shatter this movement for at least ten years to come, but I was afraid it might excite public opinion too much. Anyhow, considering the suspicious attitude public opinion lately assumed in America toward the Church, I deemed a conflict of some kind or other sooner or later inevitable, and a more favorable moment than the present I cannot imagine when the evils that Americans feared are all bound up with one small foreign party and when all English-speaking Catholics can stand shoulder to shoulder with their fellow citizens to put these evils down." O'Connell felt that if they properly utilized this occasion they could overcome this new attitude of the Propaganda; namely, that the Germans had represented the Americanizers as a dangerous set of liberals, Ireland the worst of them, and the Propaganda had become convinced that they must be tempered. The Germans, O'Connell warned, had been represented as the only reliable Catholics in the States, and they were to be patronized. Furthermore, the Irish bishops in America had the influence of no government to back them up since the American government would always remain indifferent, while the Germans had the patronage of a strong government and the value of German governmental influence in Rome was incalculable. The Monsignor then outlined his plan of attack, a blueprint which was pursued consistently by the so-called Americanizers throughout the remaining scenes of this drama. He stated:

> Now the apprehension of the American government must be your protection. When I spoke to Cardinal Rampolla of the indignation the Amer. Bps. would feel if the Cahensly plan were approved, I made no impression on him. They were Irish, they were interested and their opposition and indignation were only a matter of course. But when I said that the American Government would settle the matter for itself without Mr. Cahensly, the Cardinal changed his manner. It was an idea they never contemplated, and I said a Culturkamp [*sic*] was as possible in America as in Germany. So I verily believe this is the only grounds on which to settle the question. They thought they had it all their own way, to settle according to their views or interests between "German and Irish" without even being required to take into account the feelings of the American people. This element must figure in all future considerations of the question and then the solution will be easy and practical. The indignation of the "Irish" counts for nothing. They are after all like the Irish in Ireland, they will obey anyhow and the influence of the Government in Germany need not be sacrificed for their sakes.

> The present embarrassment will of course be pushed aside by the Germans in America disowning the action of Cahensly and the Holy See declaring that it never intended to entertain the project, but enough should be saved from the commotion to convince the Holy See that Catholics cannot do as they please in America on the school question.[15]

Both secular and Catholic papers in the United States, with few exceptions, gullibly accepted the cables and reached their editorial conclusions from this source alone without making any further checks.[16] Several of the earlier opponents of the Germanizing process also made haste to grant interviews on the Lucerne Memorial. Phelan, of the *Western Watchman,* was quoted in the New York *Times* on May 31 as tracing the origin of the memorial either to the Center Party or to the German American Priests' Society, and of asserting that it

[15] *AASP,* O'Connell to Ireland, Rome, June 11, 1891. Ireland told O'Connell: "The last message of the Associated Press which appeared in our Sunday papers was a daisy. It has made a sensation. Notice my comments on it in the *Chronicle.* It is well to bring in the lies which Cahensly keeps on telling about the Bishops of America. Then it was advisable to set Cahensly against New York. La Signora [Miss Ella B. Edes, Archbishop Corrigan's Roman agent] will receive instructions to down foreigners.

"I am still at work on the Cardinal to have him call a meeting of the archbishops, so as to send out a fierce protest. This I deem most important. He is waiting to hear from you. I hope you have by this time cable [*sic*] him to move forward.

"Abp. Katzer is fearfully annoyed. Everyone in Wisconsin looks upon him as von Schlözer's prelate. The English-speaking laity are preparing to organize in Milwaukee a monster anti-Cahensly meeting. They are under control and will go far, without danger of exceeding. . . .

"I wish you would tell me what might be done. I have been thinking of writing a letter direct to the Pope. What do you think of it? If this were advisable, & should be done at once, cable me 'Do'—If time does not press, write to me at length" (*ADR,* Ireland to O'Connell, St. Paul, June 16, 1891).

[16] Cf. St. Paul *Pioneer Press,* May 31, 1891; Chicago *Daily Inter-Ocean,* June 5; Chicago *Daily News,* May 29; Baltimore *American,* June 1; Denver *News,* May 29; Spokane *Review,* May 29. *Public Opinion* in its June 6, 1891, issue found the large majority of newspapers strongly opposed to the "Cahensly conspiracy." The opinion of the St. Louis *Republican* of May 31 was typical: "The fact that the Roman Catholic Christians alone of the denominations in this country acknowledge a spiritual allegiance to a head whose seat is located in Europe makes that church an object of peculiar jealousy in the United States—so much so that it is often hard for American democrats to maintain religious liberty against the attacks of prejudice. The present Pope is one of the most sensible men alive, and, while it is certain that he will not interfere with American politics, least of all against a national policy on which all Americans are agreed, he may find American Catholics much embarrassed by Herr Cahensly's attempts to found a religious and political Prussia in the United States. American Catholics are certainly in favor of nothing of the kind and they should not hesitate or delay in making manifest their disapproval of the plan for preventing the Americanization of immigrants by dividing the Catholic church in America up into little foreign kingdoms with Herr Cahensly of the Prussian diet operating through the Prussian division."

was likely that they all had a hand in it. Reverend George Zurcher of Buffalo, fervent temperance advocate but a man of proved intemperance both in word and idea, stated to a reporter of the Buffalo *Sunday News* that Cahensly of the Prussian Diet had been inspired by the German Priests' Society which feared that the country was tending toward the prohibitionist camp at an alarming speed. So they determined to secure a majority of bishops, he said, "saturated with German customs. They are ashamed to go and whine in Rome about their drink privileges being curtailed."[17] Archbishop Ireland followed up his earlier interview with a reporter of the New York *Herald* with an address at Fulda, Minnesota, in which he voiced his ideas in no uncertain terms. This speech also was carried in papers throughout the nation. He accused Cahensly of meddling in American affairs, the Priests' Society of being behind the memorial, and Herr von Schlözer of sponsoring it at the Vatican.[18] One of the few tempered judgments came from a quarter where it could be expected, namely, from John Gilmary Shea, an outstanding Catholic lay editor of the day, who disregarded the cables and said of Cahensly:

> He is not the agent of the German archbishops, bishops, and priests of the United States; he is not the delegate of the great German societies. He represents no one in this country, and what he does is not only unauthorized, but is sure to produce evil results by arousing public opinion against the Catholic Church in this country. His mischievous conduct is repudiated by all prominent Catholics in the United States.[19]

It was unfortunate that Shea did not investigate the matter further and get to the true source and character of the Lucerne Conference.

The German Catholic press, on its side, did little to clarify the issues and to ward off the gathering storm. A frontal attack was made all down the line: the charges against Cahensly were "wicked and false"; the truth of the Lucerne Memorial was bound to prevail over the existing arbitrariness in ecclesiastical rule which resulted in serious losses to the faith; Catholic prelates and papers were dishonoring themselves by inconsiderate and unjust language, and were making

[17] Buffalo *Sunday News,* June 7, 1891.

[18] New York *Sun,* June 5, 1891.

[19] *Catholic News,* May 31, 1891. For other less moderate opinions, cf. Wheeling *Intelligencer,* June 3, 1891, in which the memorial was termed "a piece of sublime impudence"; Louisville *Catholic Advocate,* June 11, 18, 25, and July 16, in which Cahensly was pictured as at the head of a great conspiracy and employing malignant arts to carry out his ends; Boston *Advertiser,* June 4, in which insurmountable obstacles were pictured as arising in diocesan administration if the memorial were accepted.

the Church a laughingstock before the country; pharisaical zealots were striving to rob Catholic emigrants of the necessary means of preserving their faith; press gypsies were setting the representatives of Church and State against each other; German priests were superior to Irish priests because they could speak more than one language; a nativistic storm was being created by publishers who would not admit they had made a mistake. Thus the charges and recriminations went on until the Lucerne Memorial became the burning question of the day. Only one German Catholic editor, Victor Dworzak of the New York *Katholisches Volksblatt,* stood forth against Cahensly. When asked his opinion about the latter's rumored visit to the United States where he was supposed to implement his program, Dworzak replied that the New York Germans would have nothing to do with him, that the American Catholics were well able to take care of their own spiritual matters, and that they would not tolerate foreign interference.[20]

While these charges and countercharges were being exchanged, both the German priests and Cahensly replied to their attackers. Father Färber, in his capacity as secretary of the German American Priests' Society, issued a formal statement to the Associated Press on June 3, declaring that the Society was neither directly nor indirectly connected with the so-called Lucerne Memorial. In the June 13 issue of *Church Progress* he followed up that original denial by openly attacking Archbishop Ireland as having totally misrepresented the true situation. He went back over old ground and declared that the Priests' Society could not have been behind Abbelen, since they were founded as an organization after his mission to Rome, but neglecting to add, of course, that the same priests who sponsored Abbelen were the ones who organized the Priests' Society. As for similarities between the Lucerne Memorial and the petition of Abbelen, Färber explained that

[20] Illinois *Staatszeitung,* July 10, 1891; Rochester *Katholische Volkszeitung,* July 24; California *Volksblatt,* July 18; Pittsburgh *Katholisches Familienblatt,* July 26; St. Louis *Amerika,* June 15; *Luxemburger Gazette,* June 9 and 30; New York *Katholisches Volksblatt,* May 31.

The *St. Raphaels Blatt* published letters received from German Americans in favor of the Lucerne Memorial. A workman from Milwaukee spoke of the great losses among immigrants and then said: "We respect our bishops, but generally all nationalities except the Irish are neglected. Our good Archbishop is doing everything to get priests in his diocese for the immigrants. All our children should learn English, but they must receive instruction in their mother tongue." On the same day, July 27, 1891, an Irish Catholic from Texas wrote that he knew much about American conditions and understood what was lacking: "I believe the steps you have taken have been guided by Divine Providence and will bring boundless blessings" (*SRB,* VI [Aug.-Oct., 1891], pp. 70–71).

away by observing that Cahensly could have obtained his ideas from the printed copies of Abbelen's text which had appeared in many papers, or from the pamphlet containing the documents which Abbelen himself had issued. The dispatches from Rome were completely discredited, and with good reason, Färber said, because the country had grown used to these manufactured cables which the Vatican had only recently repudiated. "One cable not many months ago," he said, "stated that the Holy Father was dissatisfied with the latest nominations of American bishops. Soon after, this dispatch was shown to one of the highest authorities at Rome who exclaimed: *'C'e niente di vero'* — there is no truth in it." In conclusion, Färber indignantly repudiated Ireland's charge against the German priests to the effect that they were an exotic organization as well as hyphenated Americans:

> I am as good an American as the most blue-blooded Yankee can be, although not by birth but by naturalization. If the accident of being born on American soil alone constitutes an American — then let us turn over all our States to the aboriginal Indians, for in this way, they were and are the only legitimate Americans, and if they had no rights themselves, they could not transmit it to their descendents. . . .
>
> There are neither Germans nor Irish in this country. This is true: Polanders, Frenchmen, Spaniards, Germans, Irish, Britons, are all united by the bond of one grand and glorious American Republic. But is it possible to give up individualities? To shape all citizens in one mould?
>
> Is it a crime to love the dear country of our fathers and ancestors and perhaps of our own birth? . . .
>
> No, this can be no reason to brand the Priests' Association as an exotic. Nay, it is American above all, and it is the American air, that is most congenial to it. It would have only to be brought forth in the atmosphere of our glorious American constitution, which guarantees liberty to all — liberty of thought, and liberty of form of expressing thought, i.e., language, liberty of association, liberty of religious worship — to make it really and truly American.
>
> Any attempt to infringe this liberty is truly un-American as is the futile attempt to lay the Cahensly Memorial at the door or within the walls of the Priests' Association.[21]

This approach of Färber's was a careful application of the same

[21] *Church Progress,* June 13, 1891. On June 17 the American Catholic Clerical Union of Milwaukee drafted a set of resolutions denouncing the Lucerne Memorial as unwarranted, inaccurate foreign interference, and praising the American hierarchy for its care of the immigrants. These resolutions first appeared in the Milwaukee *Sentinel* on June 20, 1891, and were carried in practically every Catholic paper across the land.

"American" line of thought which the Americanizers were using against the German leaders, but it came too late to be effective. Cahensly sent a denial of Phelan's charges to the St. Louis *Westliche Post,* in which he also denied that the memorial had originated in St. Louis, or that the Center Party was sponsoring it. He further wrote that he would be forced, unless Phelan repudiated his charges, to accuse him of slander and untruth.[22]

But, sadly enough, these denials were not to halt the public disturbance. When Cahensly had first presented the memorial agreed to by the delegates to the conference at Lucerne, he had been requested by Cardinal Rampolla, in an interview which the Secretary of State had granted Cahensly, to present further particulars and statistics on the important matter of emigration. In accordance with this wish, Cahensly and Volpe-Landi drew up a second memorial for the papal Secretary of State, which, they were careful to state, was presented by themselves personally, and was in no way associated with the St. Raphael societies of Europe. After outlining statistical background, the two St. Raphael leaders listed six reasons why, in their opinion, the losses to the Church had been so heavy. These causes were: the lack of sufficient protection for Catholic emigrants en route to the new world; lack of priests and parishes of their own for different nationalities; lack of Catholic societies for the protection of the working classes; lack of representation in the episcopacy of various immigrant nationalities; exaggerated demands for money contributions from the faithful; and the existence of public schools.[23]

If the original memorial had proved explosive, this second memorial contained material for even more violent repercussions. There was a strong possibility that the agitation in the United States would have died down if this subsequent document had not been made public. Monsignor O'Connell secured a copy of the text of this second memorial and forwarded it to Archbishop Ireland. The latter wrote an introduction for one of his biggest scoops before releasing it to the Associated Press on June 30. The next day he cabled O'Connell: "PRINTED. THANK BOEGLIN," and on July 2 he informed his Roman friend:

> Well, I gave to the Associated Press the Second Memorial. We are in war, & we must use all our powder. Neff of London had sent on

[22] June 21, 1891. Cahensly also most imprudently granted an Associated Press interview in Berlin on June 13, 1891, in which he said: "It is a well-known fact that the Irish in America try to obtain all the bishoprics possible for themselves." He thus played directly into the hands of his opponents. For a politician he evidenced in this case little political acumen.

[23] See Appendix V (page 316) for the text of this second memorial.

word that the document was in my hands, and telegrams poured in on the St. Paul agent to obtain it from me. I wrote the introduction, which, I think, was good.

We are under many obligations to Mgr. Boeglin. He has co-operated well with you. I think we have the country well worked up now, & we will be able to begin reaping our harvest. Your telegram that the Pope is writing to Card. Gibbons, appears today, & following the publication of the memorial the country takes it as the sequence of this. I am glad we got the memorial in before it appeared.

I sent an "alarming" cable to you yesterday. You may be able, I thought, to show it around. As a matter of fact, Americans are most angry — & I am sure that in the next Congress Cahensly will get an airing. If I were not afraid to injure Blaine's presidential campaign, I would secure at once from him an expression. . . . I am most anxious to have a meeting of some at least of the archbishops. I will go East this month to see them. I intend — while cautious — to strike hard the hot iron. I am so glad that Cahensly paid his compliments to New York. That will force the little man over to our side. . . .

Your letter, of course, interested me much. I will certainly spend next winter in Rome. Meanwhile, it is well that I am here, so as to work up our prelates, and alarm the country so as to go to Rome in the name of the country.

The Associated Press did not care for the French copy of the Memorial.

May God bless you & preserve you. We were lost without you.[24]

Not only Ireland, but a large number of the American bishops, thoroughly aroused by this time, were encouraging Cardinal Gibbons to assemble at least the archbishops so that a formal and official answer might be made to the Lucerne memorialists. Throughout the gradual build-up of this situation letters poured in to 408 North Charles Street in Baltimore requesting action from the Cardinal.

[24] *ADR,* Ireland to O'Connell, St. Paul, July 2, 1891. On June 27 O'Connell had informed Ireland that the news of the American agitation had been officially communicated to Leo XIII, and that he had reserved settlement of the matter to himself through a letter which he was preparing for Cardinal Gibbons. Cardinal Simeoni felt that the Pope would refuse to comply with the request for national bishops, but that national parishes would be granted. Then O'Connell continued: "One little telegram in our Roman papers of an interview with Mr. Blaine to the effect that any attempt to carry out the Cahensly Memorial would meet with the opposition of the American government would settle the whole matter. The memorial presents nothing here of the political aspect that it is seen to bear in America, and the reason of so much fuss does not appear. Or if its political bearing is understood, it causes no alarm. It may be that its political effect in Europe is more prominent; and that can be hardly considered as harmful to the Holy See. In America religion is always free, but in Europe it is bound up with the State and the State with it" (*AASP,* O'Connell to Ireland, Rome, June 27, 1891).

Bishop John S. Foley, of Detroit, expressed the typical reaction of these prelates when he requested:

> To your Eminence must we look for salvation from the wicked wretch, Cahensly, who is striving to undo the work of the Church in our country. Will not the Archbishops take some united action to show Rome the feeling of the Bishops and people of this republic. You can scarcely imagine the feeling among our Western Americans by the outrage of Lucerne. The Americans are indignant at it. The Poles especially are looking forward to "national Bishops." Some decided, and at the same time respectful, action is demanded. It will not be sufficient to rest upon newspaper protests. There ought to be united, archiepiscopal, and provincial action taken at once to allay public feeling and to enlighten the Holy Father.[25]

But Gibbons, to his credit, and with his usual prudential direction of affairs, moved slowly and carefully in this charged situation. It was not that he disagreed with Ireland, Gross, and the other prelates who were urging him to assemble the metropolitans or to write to the Holy Father himself. In this matter their position was his, and he felt very deeply that something must be done. In fact, his first biographer, who spoke long hours with the Cardinal on the problems of his life, wrote that the so-called Cahenslyism turmoil was "his

[25] *AAB,* 88-Q-1, Foley to Gibbons, Detroit, June 2, 1891. Bishop John Kain, of Wheeling, in an interview to the Wheeling *Intelligencer* of June 3, 1891, considered the memorial doubly impertinent because it came from laymen, and stated: "A large number of foreigners coming to this country have no intention of making our country their permanent home. Some Huns in Pocahontas county do not want their children to learn English, as they expect to return to Hungary when they have made enough money. Father Annavazzi, the Italian priest who was here on Trinity Sunday, informed me that there were 5000 Italians in Pittsburgh, that only five hundred attended church, and that these did not contribute enough to support him and his assistant. There are many such cases. And these are the Catholics whose interests are neglected, and who should have separate bishops to attend to their interests. I would say to Mr. Cahensly and his friends: 'Instead of interfering with the American hierarchy, look to your own bishops and see if there cannot be introduced in Europe some means of making better Catholics of the immigrants you send to our shores.' "

Archbishop Gross was equally as forceful in his protest to Gibbons: "I hope that Your Eminence will devise some means to destroy utterly the horrible move initiated by Herr Cahensly and the Lucerne Conference. In my humble opinion, Satan himself could not invent a means more capable of rendering the Church in our country odious to Americans; and rife with fearful discord for Catholics, than would be the adoption of such a measure by the Holy Father. It would hopelessly blight the prosperity of the Catholic Church in America. And yet I know from what one of the Cardinals said to me when last in Rome, that just such a foolish and most iniquitous measure finds his [the cardinal's] support. That disgusting and diabolical nationalism hatched in Milwaukee has already done grievous mischief. I grow weary of the intense Germanism of that nationality from which for many years I have much to endure" (*AAB,* 88-R-8, Gross to Gibbons, Portland, June 28, 1891).

greatest battle."[26] To Gibbons the recommendations of the Lucerne Conference that nationalist bishops be appointed for the United States appeared to threaten the possibility of antagonistic groups in the hierarchy with resulting discord and arrested growth of the Church. Such a plan was in open conflict with Gibbons' cherished program of American assimilation of foreigners. He desired that the United States should settle its own problems through internal development; he deprecated the introduction of foreign nationalism and class voting into national politics; he worked for understanding and love of American institutions by Catholic immigrants who, he felt, should abandon their foreign political theories when they embarked upon life in a democratic nation. The Cardinal of Baltimore was then determined, as his biographer clearly stated:

> . . . that the Church in this country should continue homogeneous like the nation. If the discord of rival nationalist aims were definitely introduced, his work would go down in wreck. He was firmly convinced that nationalist groups in the Church would tend to become political elements. Factions would entangle her in whatever direction she might turn. The defeated side in a contest over a bishopric for a foreign constituency would be resentful and might resort to reprisals, perhaps by combinations with a different group. The American Bishops would thus be beset with pleas and harassed by pressure to align themselves with one group or another, and complications all but insoluble might ensue. . . .
>
> It would have crushed Gibbons if, while the Church was advancing so fast in America, she had been diverted into side paths from her journey on the main road. Harmony was essential to her, and never more so than at that period; Cahenslyism meant a direct assault on that harmony. The constant rivalries which it invited would beget new ones.[27]

Ireland, Keane, Williams, Ryan, Elder, McCloskey, Gross, Foley,

[26] Allen Sinclair Will, *Life of Cardinal Gibbons,* 2 vols. (New York: E. P. Dutton and Co., 1922), II, p. 497.

[27] *Ibid.,* II, pp. 507–550. John Gilmary Shea regretted the dissension in the *Catholic News,* June 28, 1891: "A year ago the Catholic body of the United States . . . was made up of devout men of every nation under heaven. Now dissension, jealousy, a spirit of bickering has been aroused which will not easily be banished or allayed. Archbishops, bishops, priests, as associated in societies or individually, disclaim any part or responsibility in the Lucerne action, but the evil has been accomplished. . . . The *Herold des Glaubens* says there are American priests in this country who would rather see several million Germans go to hell than forego the opportunity to convert a few hundred Yankees." Cf. also New York *Herald,* June 14, 18, 28, 1891; New York *Evening Post,* June 28; New York *Times* and New York *Tribune,* June 14; *Catholic Review,* July 25.

and O'Connell were of one mind with Gibbons on this important matter. It was only on the mode of action that they did not sometimes proceed together, and in this case Gibbons preferred a constructive program of preserving peace and biding time for the right moment to administer a strong protest against this sword of division. Certainly Williams of Boston was with him in this *festina lente* plan, but Ireland, Keane, and O'Connell were far out ahead, giving a glow to the fire which only deepened the recriminations and animosities.

Conversely, it was in regard to this outlook on the American nation that the German group was in fundamental error. It was apparent in both memorials that the European Catholic leaders of the St. Raphael societies did not view the United States as a nation with its own characteristic homogeneity. They were not cognizant of or did not understand the strong current of national feeling that was then surging through American thought and action. They were conscious only of the parts which composed the whole, and these parts, either Italian, Belgian, Austrian, French, or German, were viewed from their own frame of reference, not in terms of the new world. Several German Catholics in the United States revealed the same attitude, and certainly there was evidence enough in foreign-language Catholic newspapers of this group consciousness rather than an American consciousness.[28] To a degree this was a natural phenomenon, and the assimilation would have to be slow, but it also would have to be consistent. To have followed such suggestions as those that came forth from Lucerne in 1891 would have cemented national consciousness in European national grooves and branded the Church as a foreign institution.

Gibbons and his friends, especially Ireland, Keane, and O'Connell, appeared to understand what German Catholic leaders were slower to grasp, namely, that national consciousness had taken over the center of the stage in American life. People in the United States were becoming conscious since the 1880's of what they considered to be their

[28] The *Catholic Record* of Indianapolis on August 2, 1891, maintained that Americanism was pharisaical: "What has America that has not been brought and planted from Europe?" Population, religion, language, cities, customs, art, economics, law, population, all came, the editor stated, and accordingly it was pure imagination to fear European influence. America was rather a mixing of Europe. *L'Observateur,* of New Orleans, on August 6, 1892, advised French Catholics that only a political bond had been broken with the fatherland, but not their bond of love, blood, morals, soul, mother tongue; and that their children must preserve these traits. *L'Travailleur,* of Worcester, on July 11, 1892, blamed fanatics for wanting to wash away from the soul of the immigrant all remembrance of his fatherland, and introduce an Anglo-American system which would quickly lead to apostasy.

heritage and their destiny. They were turning their eyes outward in a new policy of securing freedom abroad while the United States at the same time acquired colonies, naval stations, and a powerful navy. The Americanizers in the Church were in sympathy with American aspirations, while the immigrant groups, like the Germans, who were still arriving in the country in large numbers, did not participate at once and so readily in this growing vision of the so-called "inevitable destiny" of the American people. They did not have the advantage of those, like the Irish, who had immigrated earlier in the century and who had more time to become attached to American institutions. The new expansive nationalism was based, as Denis O'Connell's close friend Senator Albert Beveridge, of Indiana, declared in the Senate, on a special choice by God of the "American people as His chosen nation to finally lead in the regeneration of the world."[29] Samoa, Hawaii, the War with Spain in 1898, seizure of the Philippine Islands, acquiring of the Panama Canal, and the big-stick diplomacy of Theodore Roosevelt were the culmination of this new American determinism and national destiny.

In Germany a similar movement of imperialism and nationalism was under way. The union of the Hohenzollern Williams with the dominating force of Bismarck, as well as the impetuous policy of William II in foreign affairs after 1890, were a disturbing force in the world, particularly in the United States. Germany's opposition to America's War with Spain, Bismarck's labeling of the Monroe doctrine as "a species of arrogance peculiarly American," the Reich's colonial and naval expansion, particularly into what Americans considered to be their own sphere of influence, the Pacific Ocean, all created the definite impression in the American mind that Germany was at the forefront of powers unfriendly to the nation. Romantic nationalism had seized the imagination of many Germans at this time as well, and the Lucerne suggestions, painted in German hues through press releases, convinced many Americans that a colonial thrust had been made at the country through the Catholic Church. The fact that such German Center Party members who did sign the memorial were ultramontanes in foreign policy and federalists in domestic policy was entirely unknown in the States. The Church could have been placed in an unfortunate position if her leaders in the country had not spoken forth in denial of what was popularly conceived to be a consciously formulated German plan of securing influence within the United States.

[29] *Congressional Record,* 56 Cong., I sess. (Jan. 9, 1900), p. 71.

Gibbons took advantage of his presence at the dedication of St. Mary's Church for Germans in Washington on June 28, 1891, to make his first public statement on the subject. He remarked that the vast number of churches throughout the country for the spiritual benefit of the various European nationalities reminded everyone that the Church was a family of many peoples. He defended the bishops of a nation where almost every Sunday of the year witnessed the dedication of a church for the use of Poles, Lithuanians, Bohemians, Italians, or Germans. He ventured to assert that the hierarchy of no country in the world was paying more attention to the spiritual wants of foreign-born Catholics than the prelates of the United States. He referred to instances of large foreign colonies in Paris, Vienna, Berlin, and Rio de Janeiro where little or no provision was made for the foreign Catholic populations of those cities. The Cardinal then concluded:

> With these facts before us we cannot view without astonishment and indignation a number of self-constituted critics and officious gentlemen in Europe complaining of the alleged inattention which is paid to the spiritual wants of the foreign population and to the means of redress which they have thought proper to submit to the Holy See.[30]

The very Sunday that Gibbons was making these statements, Cardinal Rampolla, under orders from Leo XIII, addressed a letter to the

[30] Washington *Post,* June 29, 1891; *Catholic Review,* July 5 and 11; New York *Herald,* June 29, 1891.

Bishop Gilmour died on April 13, 1891, before the Cahensly controversy broke, and an animated issue was brought to the front at this time concerning succession to the see of Cleveland. Differences, in the same pattern as at Milwaukee a few months previously, divided the members of the hierarchy in the United States. Cardinal Gibbons wrote to Archbishop Elder: "I regard your meeting as exceedingly important as the first to take place since the revelation of the Americo-European conspiracy, which has inflicted so deep an insult on the Episcopate and the Catholics of the United States, & seems to regard the sees of America as fit to be filled by the first greedy ecclesiastical adventurer that comes to our country. An American bishop, in view of the important position he holds as a property holder and as a citizen, should be a man possessed of deep love not only for his Church but also for this country, & a thorough acquaintance & sympathy with our political institutions" (*AAB,* 88-Q-2, Gibbons to Elder, Baltimore, June 2, 1891, copy). The Cleveland consultors, with a German majority, nominated Bishops Rademacher, Richter, and Zardetti, while the suffragan bishops recommended Reverends Thomas Byrne, of Cincinnati, Ignatius F. Horstmann, of Philadelphia, and John Schönhoeft, of Cincinnati. This appointment was also discussed at great length in the newspapers. On December 14 the Holy See appointed Horstmann, who was then editor of the *American Catholic Quarterly Review,* as successor to Gilmour. Archbishop Ireland considered Horstmann's Americanism as resting "on a very thick German foundation" (*ADR,* Ireland to O'Connell, St. Paul, May 21, 1891).

American cardinal, the first official recognition by the Holy See of the controversy. The Secretary of State wrote:

> The Holy Father can only be pleased to see that societies are organized in your country to render assistance for the material and especially the spiritual welfare of the great number of Catholic emigrants. Information has reached us, however, that some of these societies, the German St. Raphael Society for example, are advocating among means expedient to achieve these goals, a proposal to give to each group of emigrants according to their nationality their own representatives in the American episcopate. Reports from America indicate strong opposition to such a plan and that the hierarchy is considering occupying itself with this matter in special meetings.
>
> The Apostolic See, however, after careful examination, finds that plan neither opportune nor necessary. It furthermore does not believe that a change should be made in the practice heretofore observed in supplying the numerous American dioceses with saintly pastors, but will, in justice, act according to the proposals of the episcopate.
>
> Therefore the Holy Father has instructed me to address Your Eminence not only to dissuade you from encouraging or assisting this movement, caused by unfounded fear, but also to beg you to labor, in union with your brother bishops, for the restoration of peace, being assured that the Sovereign Head of the Church is not inclined to accept any of the proposals which could provoke even the slightest misgivings, while the pastoral care of the Catholic emigrants from different countries may be entrusted to national parish priests as is already the customary practice.
>
> In delivering myself of this instruction conveyed to me by His Holiness, I have the honor to renew the assurance of my deep esteem. . . .[31]

The day before the Secretary of State wrote this letter to Gibbons, Cardinal Simeoni apprised Corrigan that he had personally informed Cahensly in an interview that such a proposal was impossible, and Archbishop Ignazio Persico added a postscript to the effect that the Holy Father was occupied with the matter and would shortly express himself on the subject.[32] This turn of events at Rome was ample vindi-

[31] *AAB,* Rampolla to Gibbons, Rome, June 28, 1891, copy. Gibbons forwarded a copy of this letter to the archbishops who, in turn, communicated it to their suffragans. Gibbons informed Corrigan: "All fears regarding the Cahensly affair are groundless as far as the appointment of bishops is concerned" (*AANY,* Gibbons to Corrigan, Cape May, New Jersey, July 16, 1891).

[32] *AAB,* 88-T-1, Corrigan to Gibbons, New York, July 13, 1891. Here the Archbishop of New York thanked Gibbons for his communications and went on to say: "The Church in this country owes Your Eminence a great debt of gratitude, for we all feel that the outspoken expression of your views has had deservedly great

cation of Gibbons' temperate leadership of the previous weeks. The Holy See was now asking him to pursue a course exactly as he had been doing, and it was much better to have a rejection of the Lucerne proposals come from the Holy Father, to whom they had been directed, rather than from the American bishops, who felt they were under attack. The letters of protest which had poured in on the Vatican from American bishops had made an impression. This was surely the proper medium for lodging remonstrances, not through the public press. A meeting of the archbishops would have aroused further speculation and excitement with possible subsequent division in the ranks. A decision was now in hand which avoided these difficulties, and Leo XIII had indicated that he was about to send a personal message.

Cardinal Gibbons was vacationing at Cape May, New Jersey, as the guest of the Philadelphia merchant, Cockcroft Thomas, when he received Rampolla's message. On July 11, a few days after the letter arrived and as he was walking with his secretary and confidant, Very Reverend Alphonse L. Magnien, superior of the Sulpicians, Gibbons met President Benjamin Harrison, who also happened to be vacationing at the time at Cape May and who was just then returning along the boardwalk to his cottage. He greeted the Cardinal cordially and invited him to walk with him. They walked along together for some time chatting pleasantly, until they approached Harrison's residence and, as Gibbons was about to say farewell, the President invited him into the house. There Harrison himself introduced the subject of the Cahensly memorials and the agitation they were then causing in the country. He remarked to Gibbons:

> I have followed the question with profound interest, and I regard it as a subject of deep importance to our country at large, one in which the American people are much concerned. I have also conversed on this subject with Mr. Tracy, a member of my cabinet. Foreign and unauthorized interference with American affairs cannot be viewed with indifference.
>
> I was very much pleased with the opinion that you expressed publicly in the matter. I had thought several times of writing to you, and offering you my congratulations on the remarks that you had made, but I refrained from doing so lest I should be interfering with church matters. But I am glad to have the opportunity of expressing my satisfaction at the words you have spoken and of opening my mind. This is no longer a missionary country like others which need missionaries from

weight in Rome. Such opinion was needed to offset that of the European governments and foreign dignitaries."

> abroad. It has an authorized Hierarchy and well-established congregations. Of all men, the Bishops of the Church should be in full harmony with the political institutions and sentiments of the country.[33]

Harrison told Gibbons that the Cardinal had his authority to make any use he thought proper of these remarks. Gibbons, in turn, was happy to inform the President of his recent letter from Rampolla, the contents of which pleased Harrison.

The Archbishop of Baltimore fully realized the implications of this chance meeting, and the advantages to which it could be turned. Gibbons not only released information of the interview to the papers, but in his acknowledgment to Cardinal Rampolla for the opinion of the Holy Father on the Lucerne Memorial, he did not neglect to detail the events of that July 11 at Cape May. He also told Rampolla that Harrison had been "greatly satisfied and manifested his pleasure" when he was informed of the Secretary of State's letter.[34]

In the meantime newspaper agitation continued in the United States at the same tempo,[35] while the first comments on the memorials began to appear in both public and Catholic papers in Germany. In the *Kölnische Volkzeitung,* organ of Cahensly's personal friends and fellow Center Workers, the Bachem family, it was maintained that

[33] *ADR,* Gibbons to O'Connell, Cape May, July 12, 1891. President Harrison was referring here to Benjamin F. Tracy, of New York, Secretary of the Navy in his cabinet.

[34] *AAB,* 88-11-3, Gibbons to Rampolla, Baltimore, July 29, 1891, copy. Cf. Baltimore *Sun,* July 23, 1891. Gibbons stated to Elder: "The remarks of the President are very significant, coming as they do spontaneously from the leader of the nation" (*AAB,* 88-4-9, Gibbons to Elder, Cape May, July 16, 1891, copy); to Bishop Keane he exclaimed: "I was delighted with his words" (*ACUA,* Gibbons to Keane, Cape May, July 21, 1891).

[35] Cf. Buffalo *Catholic Union and Times,* July 16, 1891, in which the free condition of the Church in the United States was extolled over against concordat-hampered Catholicism in Europe, and Gibbons was praised for his wise, public-spirited patriotism; "Herr Cahensly's Scheme Smacks of Politics," in New York *Herald,* July 12, 1891; the interview of Reverend Thomas O'Gorman in the *Catholic Review,* Aug. 8 and 15, 1891, on Roman views concerning Cahenslyism, along with comments on the views of Cardinals Persico and Simeoni. Martin I. J. Griffin's characteristic views on the whole question appeared in his *Irish Catholic Benevolent Union Journal,* July 13, 1891, in which he wrote: "Wouldn't it be a Catholic Unity state of affairs to have a German, Polish, and all the other nationalities having office seeking clerics, to have each with an Archbishop in Philadelphia along side of Archbishop Ryan? Wouldn't the angels rejoice and the devils sigh at such a spectacle?

"Then to think how humbly and submissively the other Catholics would bow to the order of the Pope. Yes we would! Wouldn't we! Well, there would be such a time as there wasn't since the Deluge." Reverend John Gmeiner, of the St. Paul Seminary, again stepped into the fray with a pamphlet, *The Church and Foreignism* (St. Paul, 1891), addressed to "the humble subjects of trans-Atlantic feudal masters," which did little to clarify the atmosphere.

the excitement and confusion was based on reports from the Irish side, and it was said:

> It is well-known that Irish laymen and some priests often do not allow German Catholics to have their own priests. It is still to be proved whether the excitement is justified or not. Neither Katzer nor any other bishop coming from German parents has caused any excitement. This cannot be said of the well-known Archbishop Ireland who reveals a certain extreme attitude.[36]

The *Kreuzzeitung*, a Junker paper in Berlin, observed that never before had Rampolla and the Pope been so much beloved by the Yankees as now. The *Germania*, of that same city and official organ of the Center Party, upheld the aims of the Lucerne Memorial as both necessary and self-evident for fruitful mission work, and asked how Catholics could protest against such demands. The *St. Raphaels Blatt* actively entered the lists and ran summaries of American statements and newspaper articles with its own postscripts attached to each attack from across the ocean. The Baltimore *Sun*, of July 24, particularly disturbed the German St. Raphaelsverein by editorializing to the effect that Cahensly, von Loë, and von Schorlemer were only determined to increase their own reputations, and that their narrow-minded opinions did not extend beyond the little villages in which they were born. To this the *St. Raphaels Blatt* replied: "This is a masterpiece of Yankee impudence."[37] But the most significant develop-

[36] July 31, 1891. In their July 28 issue the editors described, by quoting from a Pennsylvania German American priest, what conditions were supposed to be like as far as the Germans in the United States were concerned. This German American priest was assisting in an industrial Pennsylvania town where the English-speaking pastor did not understand a word of German, Italian, or Hungarian, while these peoples were members of his parish in large numbers. When asked if the poor immigrants had an opportunity to receive the sacraments some time during the year, he was quoted as saying: " 'The Dutchmen should be glad if they have a German-speaking priest at Easter. I cannot give them a German priest every year. Let them learn English.'

"I replied that it is too much to expect poor workers to sit down in the evening and learn English grammar. A priest should learn the languages; his duty is to learn to speak the language of his flock instead of the flock learning the language of the shepherd. 'What can I do? I do not desire to learn their boring language. I didn't call them here. As far as I am concerned they may go wherever they like, or better they may return to their own country. I don't want them here.'

"What a tragic lot for these quite abandoned souls, and even more, what a tragic death after losing peace of heart and perhaps their faith."

[37] *SRB*, VI (Aug.-Oct., 1891), p. 69. To show "how much the Yankees rejoice" the *SRB* quoted the Baltimore *Sun* of July 24, 1891, in which a birthday dinner party for Cardinal Gibbons by Cockcroft Thomas was described. Archbishop Ireland was present and was congratulated on all sides for his attitude in regard to the Lucerne petition, to which the *SRB* replied: "Archbishop Ireland lives in St. Paul, Minnesota, which is very far away from Baltimore."

ment of this entire German newspaper uproar came about as a result of editorials in the *National-Zeitung* and the *Magdeburger-Zeitung.* Both of these public papers accused Leo XIII of being opposed to Germany and particularly to the Triple Alliance because of the unfavorable decision which Rampolla sent to Gibbons. Cahensly immediately responded to this attempted association of the memorials with German political aspirations by stating unequivocally: "We strongly protest against this arbitrary interpretation of Cardinal Rampolla's letter, which was written from ecclesiastical and not from political motives."[38] This was a significant development, for here Cahensly was repudiating precisely what he was being accused of by his American critics.

More than this, Cahensly and Volpe-Landi wrote to their own Ordinaries, Bishops Klein, of Limburg, and Scalabrini, of Piacenza, detailing the whole controversy, maintaining that they had no intention of interfering with American affairs or of giving offense to the American bishops, and explaining that their only desire had been to protect European emigrants and to keep them faithful to the Church.[39] A copy of this letter, along with a reproduction of the Lucerne Memorial in French, was sent to all members of the hierarchy in the United States. Beyond this Cahensly released a public letter repudiating all charges made against him personally, a letter which was countersigned by all officials of the German, Austrian, Italian, Belgian, and Swiss branches of the society. Once more Cahensly spoke up bravely when he said:

> I am a German and I am engaged in no secret politics. As I appear, I am, and as I prove myself and act, I am. Abuse, even from Catholic pens, leaves me cold, and hate finds no response in my breast.[40]

He and the other leaders were not only sending out mail on the question of the memorials at this time, but they were also receiving numerous communications concerning their action. Those from the United States could not in any way be said to have lent support, and

[38] *Ibid.*, p. 71.

[39] *ADL,* Cahensly and Volpe-Landi to Klein, Limburg, and Piacenza, July 6, 1891. Isenburg-Birstein and Cahensly also sent a printed letter to all members of the German hierarchy, explaining their side of the question, along with a copy of the *SRB* which included "many of the false accusations coming from America" (*ADL,* Isenburg-Birstein and Cahensly to Klein, Schloss Birstein, Sept. 1, 1891). Bishop Klein replied; assuring the gentlemen of his support and praising their work for the emigrant (*ADL,* Klein to Isenburg-Birstein and Cahensly, Limburg, Sept. 16, 1891, copy).

[40] *ADCV,* Open Letter of Peter Paul Cahensly to Member Societies of St. Raphael, Limburg, June 16, 1891.

even Cahensly's friends and colaborers felt constrained to criticize and to censure the action at Lucerne. Bishop Wigger and the directors of the St. Raphaelsverein at the Leo House penned a joint letter to Cahensly in which they recognized the good intentions of the Lucerne petitioners, but regretted the action taken in no uncertain terms: "Why has the St. Raphaelsverein not addressed its wishes and desires first in a proper manner to the American Bishops? . . . The demands or requests of the Memorial are altogether too far reaching. . . . Why . . . should you ask . . . for ordinances which might be suitable for colonial endeavors in South America or Africa, but will not suit at all for conditions as they exist here?" The American directors admitted that the interpretation of the memorials in the United States had been in a number of cases malicious. But they also reminded Cahensly that there was probability for such propaganda, because the memorial had been an insult to the national pride of Americans as well as detrimental to foreign-born citizens and to new immigrants.[41]

Archbishop Corrigan, in his position as honorary president of the society, had also been preparing a letter. He delayed his communication, however, until he had Cahensly and Volpe-Landi's second memorial in hand as well as the Holy Father's message through Rampolla. Then, after showing his letter to Gibbons, who felt it was firm and yet sufficiently respectful, Corrigan dispatched his long remonstrance to Limburg. He expressed his profound grief at the memorial, charged Cahensly with "a total misconception" of American institutions, and explained that if these proposals were adopted it would result in incalculable harm to religion. Corrigan endeavored to explain to the German leader the traditional American prejudice against the Church as a *"foreign institution,"* and he remarked: "You can conceive then with what grief we would see this prejudice confirmed and strengthened by one of our own friends." He went on to apply the Lucerne proposals to his own archdiocese, and then by statistics he effectively disposed of the plan as impractical. He concluded:

> It is no wonder that . . . Cardinal Simeoni has written to me that he himself from his knowledge of this country felt bound to declare openly to you that your request was impossible of realization. . . . Permit me to express the hope that in future you and your zealous colleagues, before presenting to the Holy See any important project regarding the welfare of souls intrusted to our charge, will have the kindness to consult with the Bishops who are their legitimate Pastors.[42]

[41] *AANY,* Directors of the American St. Raphael Society to Cahensly, New York, July 1, 1891, copy.

[42] *Ibid.,* Corrigan to Cahensly, New York, July 22, 1891, copy.

At this time Bishop Katzer was preparing to transfer from the Diocese of Green Bay to Milwaukee. As a farewell message to the clergy of Green Bay and also as a first pronouncement to his new flock, he composed two pastoral letters, the greater parts of which were devoted to the nationality question. Since his name had been dragged into the Cahensly affair, the Archbishop-elect desired to make his position clear in a public manner before the whole country. He declared that he never sought or desired to leave Green Bay, praised his clergy for the valiant, united defense of the parochial school system in Wisconsin, and encouraged them to continue to labor even more zealously to elevate genuine Catholic education as the best basis for a firm and truly Christian republic and social life. He attributed the success achieved in the Diocese of Green Bay to the fact that the great majority of the faithful, priests, and bishop, were of one heart and one mind. He pleaded that the same condition be allowed to continue under the new bishop:

> Let no discord, no selfishness, no spirit of nationality arise among you. Let us never forget that we all are children of the *ONE* father who is in Heaven, children of the *ONE* holy apostolic Roman-Catholic Church, the redeemed and brethren of the Son of God, cleansed and sanctified in the *ONE* Baptism, and called by the *ONE* Faith and its works, to be *ONE* with God by an incomprehensible union, and to form the *ONE* triumphant Church in the beatific Vision and fruition of the *ONE* infinite God. . . .[43]

Katzer also declared that he was coming to Milwaukee in the spirit of his motto: *"Soli Deo honor et gloria,"* as the spiritual father of all without regard to language, birth, or nationality. He asked for co-operation and obedience, and stated that he had no grounds for fear that Milwaukee would not supply these qualities, because that archdiocese had understood how to preserve the singular spirit of sacrifice of its pioneers. Where that spirit reigned, Katzer declared, "animating both clergy and laity, there is true Christianity, there is Catholic life."[44]

The Archbishop of Milwaukee sent copies of these pastorals to Gibbons in order that they might shed some light upon his true views and position. At the same time he stated unequivocally that he knew absolutely nothing about "the deplorable Cahensly affair," and he requested that the Cardinal come to Milwaukee on August 20 to

[43] *AAM, Archbishop-elect Katzer to Clergy and Laity of Green Bay, Apr. 5, 1891.*
[44] *Ibid., Archbishop-elect Katzer to Clergy and Laity of Milwaukee, May 17, 1891.*

confer his pallium upon him.[45] Gibbons accepted this invitation and very carefully prepared the address which he was to deliver at that ceremony. Throughout his lifetime the Cardinal showed an innate sense of the strategic importance of occasions that presented themselves to him, and now, fortified as he was by the message from the Holy Father and the opinion of the President, he felt that the time had arrived for him to come out clearly and directly on the nationality question. Here the dean of the American hierarchy was to confer the symbol of authority, received from Rome, upon the acknowledged leader of the German group in the Church of that time. On his way into the German triangle of the West with Bishop Foley, the Cardinal stopped at Chicago, and the interview he gave to reporters there was an intimation of what was to follow. He said: "The efforts of foreigners to change the existing condition of affairs will meet with strenuous opposition and, I am satisfied, will prove utterly futile."[46] When he arrived in Milwaukee on August 19 he was so exhausted and weak from the heat and the journey that he was forced to abandon the idea of celebrating the pontifical Mass on the following day. But he was able to preside at the ceremony in St. John's Cathedral and, as he ascended the pulpit to begin his discourse, he faced over seven hundred prelates and priests who represented every nationality included in the Church.

Gibbons began his sermon by commenting on the streams of immigrants which had flowed into Wisconsin and the solicitude which the Church had shown for their welfare. He stated that the scene of that morning was a proof to all that the Catholic Church of the United States was a family derived from many nations, a heterogeneous group like the multitude which assembled on Pentecost to hear, each in his own tongue, the wonderful works of God proclaimed by the Apostles. In fact, he asserted, the pentecostal company was not so varied as the peoples who knelt at altars in the United States and commingled together in prayer with the great American Catholic body that held out to them the right hand of fellowship. While differing in language, habits, and tastes, yet, as the Cardinal insisted, these peoples were united not only by the bonds of a common religion but, thanks to God, by a more precious union, the bond of Christian brotherhood. He continued to speak of the harmony existing in the hierarchy as a preparation for what was to follow, the heart of his message, that

[45] *AAB,* 88-S-4, Katzer to Gibbons, Milwaukee, June 5, 1891.
[46] Washington *Church News,* Aug. 23, 1891.

national rivalries must not be allowed to break the existing unity of the Church. He said:

> Woe to him, my brethren, who would destroy or impair this blessed harmony that reigns among us! Woe to him who would sow tares of discord in the fair fields of the Church in America! Woe to him who would breed dissension among the leaders of Israel by introducing a spirit of nationalism into the camps of the Lord! Brothers we are, whatever may be our nationality, and brothers we shall remain. We will prove to our countrymen that the ties formed by grace and faith are stronger than flesh and blood. God and our country! — this our watchword. Loyalty to God's Church and to our country! — this our religious and political faith.
>
> Let us unite hand in hand in laboring for the Church of our fathers. The more we extend the influence of the Christian religion, the more we will contribute to the stability of our political and social fabric. . . .
>
> Next to love for God, should be our love for our country. The Author of our being has stamped in the human breast a love for one's country, and therefore patriotism is a sentiment commended by almighty God Himself. . . .
>
> The Catholic community in the United States has been conspicuous for its loyalty in the century that has passed away; and we, I am sure, will emulate the patriotism of our fathers in the faith.
>
> Let us glory in the title of American citizen. We owe our allegiance to one country, and that country is America. We must be in harmony with our political institutions. It matters not whether this is the land of our birth or the land of our adoption. It is the land of our destiny. . . .
>
> When our brethren across the Atlantic resolve to come to our shores, may they be animated by the sentiments of Ruth, when she determined to join her husband's kindred in the land of Israel, and may they say to you as she said to their relations: "Whither thou hast gone, I also shall go — where thou dwellest, I also shall dwell; thy people shall be my people, and thy God my God. The land that shall receive thee dying, in the same will I die, and there will I be buried."[47]

Twenty-two years later Gibbons reminisced on this address and he declared at that time: "It was one of the most audacious things I ever did, but it had to be done. When I finished they were aghast, but I think the lesson had its effect. It was a question upon which there could be no compromise or hesitation."[48]

The American press acclaimed the speech in glowing terms. The

[47] James Cardinal Gibbons, *A Retrospect of Fifty Years* (New York, 1916), II, pp. 148–155.

[48] Will, *op. cit.*, II, p. 530.

Chicago *Tribune,* of August 21, called it "patriotic in every sense," and the next day editorialized on the appropriateness of a Wisconsin city as the site for the admonition. The *Tribune* went on to state that, although there were Americans who feared the Catholic Church, and the silly utterances of Cahensly made that fear grow, yet the majority of Americans knew that Gibbons was the real representative of American Catholicism, and consequently they could not become alarmed over the un-American talk of European sympathizers. The Washington *Post,* of August 24, in writing of Gibbons' Americanism, likewise termed his words wise and patriotic, and pointed up their significance because Katzer's appointment had been regarded by some "as a distinct triumph for the German-American element in the Catholic Church of America." Gibbons received many personal notes of congratulation and praise, but none was more appreciative than that from his close friend and Roman agent, Denis O'Connell, who declared: "You converted your dangerous position at Milwaukee into a very pedestal of glory. It was truly masterly, your bearing there, and I was delighted at it. Only extremists could make any objections to it."[49] Archbishop Ireland also was pleased, and he begged the Cardinal to guard against overtaxing his strength because of the need which the American Church had for him. Ireland then went on to state that he had received word from Milwaukee that Archbishop Katzer had submitted his plans to the Cardinal and that they had merited the latter's approval. If these plans did not include the appointment of English-speaking bishops for both the Dioceses of La Crosse and Green Bay, then Ireland felt that all concessions would be futile and would not bring peace, because the exclusiveness of German supremacy in Wisconsin would be maintained. Bishop Vertin had promised Ireland that he would co-operate in such appointments, and if they should not come about, then Ireland felt the fault must lie entirely with Archbishop Katzer.[50]

If Cardinal Gibbons had agreed to Katzer's nominations for the vacant Sees of La Crosse and Green Bay, it was obvious when the announcement of these appointments was made that he had returned in practice to his *festina lente* program after his dramatic stand in Milwaukee. It was also obvious that the Holy See likewise favored a cautious policy and recognition of the dominant group in a region. On December 14, 1891, the appointment was made known of Reverend James Schwebach, administrator of La Crosse after the death of

[49] *AAB,* 89-E-7, O'Connell to Gibbons, Rome, Aug. 29, 1891.
[50] *AAB,* 89-K-3, Ireland to Gibbons, St. Paul, Aug. 24, 1891.

Bishop Flasch, as Bishop of La Crosse, and Reverend Sebastian G. Messmer, of the Catholic University of America, as Bishop of Green Bay to succeed Katzer. Schwebach was a native of Luxembourg; Messmer, of Switzerland. Especially in the case of the latter, a man of outstanding qualities had been advanced to the hierarchy, regardless of his national background. In 1903 he succeeded Katzer as Archbishop of Milwaukee, and remained throughout his lifetime an advocate of slow yet consistent assimilation, and an open defender of the Church from what he considered to be a dangerous spirit of liberal nationalism. Messmer would be heard from often in succeeding years, and he would remain a strong force opposing outside interference in the affairs of the Province of Milwaukee, especially the efforts of Archbishop Ireland to influence policy in Wisconsin, as he had done in the ecclesiastical division and direction of Minnesota.

There were further indications at this time that everyone was not solidly behind the assimilation program, or at least was not in accord with the tempo at which it was being encouraged. The Roman agent of Archbishop Corrigan, Ella B. Edes, in commenting to Abbot Smith on an interview which she had with Cardinal Simeoni, described their conversation on Cahenslyism as follows:

> I could not help remarking to the Cardinal the inconsistency of the American Hierarchy — that is the members of the "Baltimore-Ireland clique" in raising such a row over the idea of Foreign Bishops, whilst they are the very ones to insist and to compass — *in barba alla Ppgda.* — the appointment of a Frenchman to a Metropolitan See in America, simply because he is one of *their* clique, and will run *their* game. H. E. answered with one of his grim smiles — Yes, they are the first to propose foreigners on the ternae. . . . O'Gorman is in Rome, a follower of Duchesne in his teaching of *modern ecclesiastical* history in the Catholic University of Washington, & he wrote to Ireland's organ the *Northwestern Chronicle* on August 19, 1891, that the Cahensly movement was by no means dead in Rome, that its supporters are merely awaiting and watching their opportunity. This, to try to keep up a stupid and lying excitement, raised and furthered, I do not doubt, in the least, wholly by themselves, for their own ends. *Usquequo Domine, usquequo?* No wonder God sends woes upon the Church. I heard it said, long since, that it would be the aim of Cardinal Gibbons to endeavor to fill up, as they became vacant, the various metropolitan sees of the United States, with his own creatures. The prophecy appears attaining verification.[51]

[51] *AASPOW,* Edes to Smith, Rome, Sept. 7, 1891. Miss Edes was referring here to Reverend Placide L. Chapelle, native of France and pastor of St. Matthew's Church, Washington, who had been appointed coadjutor of Santa Fe on August 21, 1891,

Martin I. J. Griffin, in his *Irish Catholic Benevolent Union Journal,* also noted at this time that Bishop James McGolrick, of Duluth, who had been recommended to that see by Archbishop Ireland, was in Ireland in search of ecclesiastical students for the American mission. While claiming that such practices by American Irish tended to turn native vocations into other fields, he stated:

> So these Irish students come here, and getting priested before they get Irish-priest ruling notions knocked out of them, start out often with the idea that they can govern Catholics here as they were "at home."
>
> Oh yes, plenty of students can be had from Ireland. Numbers are ready to be priests as industrial and professional careers are accessible to but few.
>
> There's an *Irish* Cahenslyism but you mustn't say so.[52]

Apropos of this seeming neglect of the American stock, Right Reverend Robert Seton, pastor of St. Joseph's Church, Jersey City Heights, observed to his friend, Abbot Smith, in Rome:

> Every "element" is recognized in episcopal appointments: German & French and Irish & Spanish and from every nationality, almost, in Europe; and the so-called Irish-American and German-American, etc., but the "plain American" element of old stock seems to many to be seriously neglected. One or two bishops, or two or three here & there & one or two converts — all in unimportant Sees, astonishes alike the Protestants and Catholics of a more ancient American status in the country. I keep quiet & prudent and have never opened myself before, as I am now doing to you: but these things are being thought about and have been written about & printed in this country. It would not be tolerated in any other country in the world.[53]

But the most significant comment of all on the Lucerne Memorial came from one who was of an unquestionable American background and sympathy. Bishop John Lancaster Spalding was quoted by the *St. Raphaels Blatt* as saying at this time:

> It is simply laughable to see a kind of treason in this memorial against American liberty, and to accuse them of the intention of introducing foreign practices into the country. Actually Cahensly's plan

after O'Connell and Magnien had encouraged Gibbons to recommend him, and after a long delay and discussion of his promotion by the Propaganda. Miss Edes also told Smith on August 11, 1891, that Archbishop Corrigan was going ahead with his plans for an Italian St. Raphael Society in New York. When she informed Cardinal Simeoni of this fact the Prefect of Propaganda was quoted as having remarked: "He will probably have all the other Irish Bishops down on him in consequence."

[52] Nov. 1, 1891.

[53] *AASPOW,* Seton to Smith, Jersey City Heights, New Jersey, n.d.

does not entail any principal changes in America. It is certainly a prudent proposal to place the care of souls in the hands of priests of their own nationality, acquainted as they are with the language and national peculiarities. This does not by any means bring the Church into opposition with American institutions. Catholics emigrate to improve their living conditions, and this improvement makes them appreciate the value of American citizenship. Anything which makes immigrants more satisfied also makes them better citizens.[54]

While these opinions on the danger or worth of the St. Raphael memorials were being exchanged, a ludicrous event occurred which served only to intensify feelings already aroused. The golden jubilee of Archbishop Kenrick's consecration was approaching in November of 1891, and the clergy and laity of St. Louis prepared to celebrate the occasion with fitting solemnities. Father Goller hit upon the plan of asking Monsignor Paul Maria Baumgarten, of Rome, to come to St. Louis at the expense of a number of American German priests, bearing with him an appropriate testimony from the Holy Father for Kenrick. Then Baumgarten could also tour the country in order to acquaint himself better with conditions. Baumgarten was a German historian of some repute who resided in Rome and who was at that time studying theology in preparation for ordination.[55] He looked upon himself as a Roman agent for Catholics in Germany, and he had also become interested in the cause of German Catholics in the United States through contacts which he had made in Rome with numerous American Germans who had come to Rome during previous controversies.[56] Reverend J. B. Diepenbrock, pastor of St. Joseph's Church, Cairo, Illinois, and Goller worked out the plans for this American tour. They felt that the Americanizers would not become suspicious if Baumgarten came with an official message from the Vatican. They presented the proposal to Vicar-General Mühlsiepen who, in turn, informed Baumgarten that he could better serve in the future if the reasons for his visit were not known. A storm would certainly arise, he stated, if it were learned he was coming to study

[54] *SRB,* VI (Aug.-Oct., 1891), p. 63.

[55] Monsignor Paul Maria Baumgarten was born on July 25, 1860, at Elberfeld; ordained February 17, 1894; resided in Rome 1887–1899, 1902–1904, 1918–1925; died at Neuötting a. Inn, Germany, on December 29, 1928. His published works included seven volumes on archaeological, biblical, canonical, and personal topics. *DGH,* II, p. 70. For further reference to his activities in Rome, cf. Wilhelm Wühr, *Ludwig Freiherr von Pastor, 1854–1928* (Heidelberg, 1950), pp. 593, 772, 777, 780, 887, 889.

[56] Baumgarten discussed his career, his journeys to different parts of the world, and the whole background of this American incident in *Wanderfahrten. Europäische und Americanische Erinnerungen* (Traunstein, 1928), pp. 69–171.

the conditions of German Catholics in the States. Mühlsiepen felt it would be valuable for him to view the United States at firsthand, but he then went on to give Baumgarten some wise counsel which he could have used to good advantage:

> To obtain a clear idea of our conditions, I would advise you to be slow to judge, and to make a judgment only at the end of your journey. Unfortunately we have several German priests who are too extreme, who demand too much, or express themselves in an unsuitable way, from which the greatest harm arises, to the extent that their . . . methods will encumber all of us.[57]

But Baumgarten at once committed the first of several *faux pas*. In conversation with the Countess Marianne Kinsky in Rome he spoke of his approaching trip to the United States. She asked him questions about his connections there, the names of those sponsoring him, and the like. All of these enquiries were put to him, Baumgarten later decided, under the direction of Monsignor O'Connell who was also a friend of the Countess. O'Connell then proceeded to employ the cablegram technique which he had used earlier in the year. The information was forwarded from the Associated Press in Rome to its Berlin office along with the name of the ship and landing date of Baumgarten in New York. Accordingly, when the young ecclesiastic, for he was then only in his thirty-first year, came down the gangplank in New York, Diepenbrock was there with a copy of that morning's New York *Herald*, containing a dispatch from Berlin to the effect that he had come to advance the Cahensly scheme, that he had acted as Cahensly's *cicerone* in Rome, that he was to contact members of the German American Priests' Society, and to spy on the Church in the United States. All Baumgarten could exclaim when he saw this article was: "Denis O'Connell."[58] Diepenbrock and Baumgarten immediately went to the offices of the *Herald* and demanded a retraction, which was forthcoming in the issue of the following day. But the harm had already been done, and newspaper reports and rumor trailed him throughout his entire visit.

Fortunately for all concerned, Archbishop Mario Mocenni, Undersecretary of State, had naturally refused Baumgarten's proposal of himself as bearer of official greetings to Kenrick on the grounds that he was only a theological student and that the Holy See would communicate its greetings through more proper channels. Baumgarten then moved on to St. Louis as a private tourist with Diepenbrock, at

[57] *Ibid.*, p. 81, Mühlsiepen to Baumgarten, St. Louis, June 2, 1891.
[58] *Ibid.*, pp. 83–84.

which place he met many German pastors and viewed their parochial organizations. After several speeches at Goller's instigation, he departed for Buffalo where, on September 21, the fifth annual *Katholikentag* was about to open. The leaders of both the general assembly and the *Priester Verein* were determined to keep all aggressions and accusations from appearing in any of the public proceedings, especially in view of the widespread misunderstandings concerning the Lucerne Memorial. Archbishop Katzer opened the congress with a pontifical Mass, and Bishop Otto J. Zardetti, of St. Cloud, delivered an address in which he likened Germany to a mother and America to a bride. Immigrants, he stated, had left their mother Germany and were wedded to America where they should learn the English language, but where they were also bound in gratitude to remember and to love the language of their mother.[59] Resolutions concerning the temporal power of the Pope, parochial schools, secret societies, and fidelity to the American bishops were passed at the meetings. The convention would have ended on these happy notes except for two unfortunate incidents. The first concerned Father Zurcher, of Buffalo, who forced his way into the secret meetings of the Priests' Society and demanded proof that the delegates were not plotting. In recording his own account of this unnecessary action, he said:

> Four priests — one Buffalonian and three from elsewhere — guarded the entrance. At the beginning of the proceedings the Buffalo guard absented himself from his post of duty for a few seconds. Father Zurcher, who was watching from a short distance for just such an opportunity, walked briskly towards the door, scolding, as he approached the three strange guards in German, about so many being late, and entered. They were considering a system of organizing the German lay Catholics, so that the German Catholics of this country would be like a disciplined army backing the German Clerical Union. The proceedings were stopped. The chairman — Father Meissner, of Peru, Ind. — stated that their constitution allowed no layman, no reporter at these meetings; and that it allowed none but members to be present. Angry

[59] *Northwestern Chronicle,* Sept. 28, 1891. The *Chronicle* also chided Zardetti on his figure of speech, and insisted that he neglected the bride in his sermon: "No wonder she should grow somewhat jealous, and complain of the cold treatment accorded her. Bishop Zardetti's appreciation of Scripture is too great not to have noticed how the spirit of the following text was violated: 'Wherefore a man shall leave father and mother and shall cleave to his wife.' No wonder the bride should utter complaint through the press that she was subordinated to the mother-in-law. The blushing beauty was neglected." Zardetti replied on October 30 to this remark, accused Conway of quoting the entire passage incorrectly, and stated that he did not speak of German immigrants alone, but of all not born on American soil, which included himself and the editor of the *Chronicle.*

speeches at the intruder and a vote of the assemblage emphatically endorsed their chairman and constitution. One spokesman was wrathy and boisterous enough to tempt the reporters outside to push the door a little ajar, and peep in. The chairman repeatedly yelled to the guards to shut the door tight, or he would appoint another set of guards. When quiet was restored, and the vote announced, Father Zurcher withdrew.[60]

The second incident concerned Paul Maria Baumgarten, who had been originally scheduled to address the general assembly on the subject of Windthorst's contribution to the solution of modern problems. Reporters discovered him there and, although it had been decided for the sake of prudence that Baumgarten would not deliver his scheduled speech, they made much of his attendance at the convention. More than that, reporters of the Buffalo *Courier* were able to get into Baumgarten's hotel room, open his valise, and escape with the copy of his address. The next morning, September 25, as he came down to breakfast with Bishop Zardetti and other delegates, they handed him a copy of the *Courier* with his speech printed in full, along with an article bearing the title "Paul Baumgarten. Is He or Is He Not an Apostle and Envoy of Cahensly?" Baumgarten rushed up to his room, discovered that the speech had been lifted from his bag, and returned indignant to the table, determined to take the whole matter to the police. But Zardetti advised him to forget the affair since it would take much money and time to prosecute and, besides, most Americans looked upon such a trick as a press scoop. To Baumgarten the incident was a further evidence that, as he expressed it, "in the United States a double morality existed."[61]

Baumgarten did, however, give an interview to newsmen, and he

[60] George Zurcher, *Foreign Ideas in the Church of the United States* (Buffalo, 1896). This intemperate pamphlet was written as an exposé of the Germans and their supposed efforts to divide the Church in the United States.

[61] Baumgarten, *op. cit.,* pp. 123–125. Archbishop Ireland contacted the Associated Press at this time and asked them to "keep an eye on this congress. Little of its doings, I presume, will be found out — but its general un-American character may be pointed out." He warned the AP to call attention to the closed meetings of the Priests' Society, to Baumgarten's presence as a representative of Cahensly, and to call on Father Zurcher for assistance and information. Ireland himself wrote to Zurcher, and requested that the AP keep his connection with the affair strictly confidential. After the AP reporters discovered Baumgarten and issued dispatches on his address, Ireland congratulated William Henry Smith, declared that the AP had accomplished "some specially clever work," and stated that a signal service to America and American institutions had been rendered. "None are more grateful than the Catholics who loyally love their country as well as their Church." Cf. Archives of the Ohio Archeological and Historical Society in Columbus, William Henry Smith Collection, Ireland to B. S. Cowan, St. Paul, Sept. 1, 1891; Ireland to Smith, Sept. 25, 1891, and July 17, 1892; Smith to Ireland, July 23, 1892, copy.

was not slow to repudiate all the insinuations made against him, especially the dispatch from Berlin. He said:

> Yes, I know the article by heart. It was sent from Berlin, but was doubtless concocted in Rome. I laughed heartily when I first read it. It is all false, all bosh, and you may say that the rest of that dispatch is bosh also. It is true I am an LL.D. I am privy chamberlain of His Holiness and am in training in the academy of noble ecclesiastics at Rome.[62]

The German visitor stated that he had met Cahensly only once in his life, and that at a dinner in Rome, and he denied that he was in sympathy with Cahensly's supposed ideas. With this interview and the ending of the Buffalo convention, Baumgarten fortunately passed from public notice. He traveled throughout the country before returning to Rome, and after his arrival there he wrote a letter to Archbishop Domenico Jacobini, former secretary of Propaganda and at the time nuncio to Spain, in which he registered his protest against the treatment he had received in the United States. He also protested the favorable decision rendered on the Faribault-Stillwater school plan of Archbishop Ireland which had just then been handed down by the Holy See. The Archbishop replied with advice that Baumgarten published in his book; it was counsel which he might well have had before setting out on this visit of 1891. Jacobini said:

> I do not like to mingle in affairs for which I have not a right. I am inimical to intrigue.
>
> The question is grave because under the appearance of a discussion about instruction in schools there is a struggle of nationality. If we do not go to Rome with much caution in defending a cause, we will have much trouble. What has happened to you, the advice I give you, and which you should not state publicly, is to conduct yourself as you have said you have done, according to which I praise you. You are young and can withstand violence or intrigue. Monsignor Ireland is better in this matter than you perhaps think, but he is of an Irish nature, fervent and ardent, and this affair must be handled quietly. He is my friend and I desire to have his advice. But it would be better that he were outside all of these affairs. Yes, my dear Baumgarten, for your sake I would pray you to think in these years only of pursuing a good course of

[62] Buffalo *Courier*, Sept. 26, 1891. Baumgarten praised Windthorst's program against godless schools and called on German Americans to clasp hands across his grave while promising the dead that they would not sleep or rest until they had succeeded through Christian education in freeing youth from immorality and unbelief. This was an obvious reference to Archbishop Ireland's school plan. Baumgarten said: "Whoever in the din of a fight has the courage to announce a new fight must win the first fight and is bound in conscience to fight the second fight."

ecclesiastical science for the service of God in that way which will please Him. Believe me that in these great questions of the Church it would not be good for you now to disturb yourself. Today, perhaps as in all other times, exaggerated ardor is part of all great questions, and I do not approve especially the erratic excitement of the principal nationals.[63]

Archbishop Kenrick's jubilee celebration on November 30 was held according to schedule. There was no reference to the tension existing in the country at that time concerning the St. Raphael memorials until the banquet at the Hotel Lindell in the afternoon. There the address of welcome to Cardinal Gibbons, the visiting prelates, and clergy was given by Father Goller, the recognized intellectual leader of the German American priests of the Archdiocese of St. Louis and, in fact, of many priests outside the archdiocese. Goller had always been a very close friend of Archbishop Kenrick and, as the historian of St. Louis stated, since the jubilee year was the high tide of "Americanism," Goller "saw his opportunity of setting his compatriots right in the matter by holding up the object of his and the noble assembly's veneration, Archbishop Kenrick, as a true shepherd of his entire flock, who knew his German Catholic people and his German priests, and who entertained no suspicion in regard to their ecclesiastical or civic loyalty."

Goller began by praising Kenrick's treatment of all immigrants who had come into the lower Mississippi Valley. Then he went on to extol the peoples who had come to the United States and had proved themselves worthy of being ranked among the most loyal and active defenders of the American Republic. He stated:

If you rejoice in the fact that America is great and glorious and free today, that the United States forms the most prosperous, and most enlightened, the most powerful empire of the world, then you owe heartfelt thanks and praise to the adopted sons and daughters of America. Do not call them foreigners, for they are true Americans. Learn to abstract the essentials from the accidental, the primal duties of citizenship from the customs and manners of private life. They are loyal Americans, for they love liberty and independence above all earthly goods, above the gaudy pomps of royalty, above imperial splendor. They have demonstrated on many fields of battle how they love their country — America.

They may still retain a fond regard for the land of their birth; they may still treasure in their hearts the sweet memories of childhood; for only the renegade can forget the mother that bore him — but far dearer to them than the memories of childhood is the strong and

[63] Baumgarten, *op. cit.,* p. 132.

beautiful bride, Columbia, who taught them to walk erect on God's earth in the proud consciousness of manhood. . . .

We have a country, but we are not as yet a nation in the full sense of the term: we are, as it were, "the rudis indigestaque moles" of a nation in the state of formation. All Europe, not England alone, is our mother, and we disdain to become a mere second edition of John Bull. A grander destiny awaits us. From the "disjecta membra" of many tribes and peoples we are gradually forming a new national type: we are absorbing the noble traits of various foreign nationalities. A hundred, perhaps more, years must roll on ere the typical American will be produced, embodying in himself the common sense and business capacity of the Anglo-Saxon, the patient research of the German, the keen wit of the Celt, the brilliant dash of the children of France, the childlike piety of Catholic Italy: but when he does make his appearance, all the world will recognize in him the ideal man.

Archbishop Kenrick discovered in Catholic immigration, not a danger to the Republic, but a priceless acquisition. Mindful of the word of Sacred Scripture: "Do you, therefore, love strangers, because you also were strangers in the land of Egypt," our noble prelate welcomed all the children of the Church, unconcerned about their disparity in language and manner. For he based his hopes of a bright future upon the unifying bond of faith. . . .

"In necessariis unitas, in dubiis libertas, in omnibus caritas." This is the noble principle from which he never deviated in his intercourse with his priests and his people. He was firm in exacting what was just, yet ever ready to grant freedom of action in all matters not defined by Divine or human law.[64]

The address of Father Goller caused a sensation, and was recognized on all sides as a challenge to the Americanizers. While he was undoubtedly correct in the general principles he enunciated, yet he revealed the fundamental lack of contact which many German leaders had with the strong spirit of nationalism sweeping the country at that time when he again pointed up their belief that the United States was a country but not yet a nation. At the conclusion of his address there were loud and prolonged calls for Archbishop Ireland from those

[64] Rothensteiner, *History of the Archdiocese of St. Louis* (St. Louis, 1928), III, pp. 572–573. The *ICBU Journal,* Jan. 1, 1892, termed Goller's address an insolence to Gibbons and the prelates of the land. Archbishop Corrigan had also made careful preparations for his address at this banquet. He was asked to give the toast: "The Catholic Church in America." He asked for statistics and advice from John Gilmary Shea and prepared a speech to refute the Lucerne charges of large-scale defections from the Church in this country (*ACHSP,* Corrigan to Shea, New York, Nov. 2, 1891). Corrigan then proceeded to vindicate the honor of the American Church and to emphasize that since the days of Bishop John England there had been misconceptions on losses to the Faith.

in the audience who did not agree with Goller, and the Archbishop of St. Paul rose majestically in his place to deliver an eloquent, if brief, response. In conclusion he asserted: "We recognize in civil matters no other power than the authorities at Washington, and in religious matters no other power than the Pontiff of the Vatican," thus making what would seem reference to the supposed tie-up of the Lucerne Memorial with the German Government.[65]

This public clash in St. Louis was the final act in the drama of 1891, but it was not to be the end of misunderstandings and differences over "Cahenslyism." Archbishop Ireland, upon the advice of Monsignor O'Connell, was waiting for the next session of Congress to carry the question before the people through the American Government, and to show Europe that, as he said, "we have a government in back of us."[66] O'Connell had convinced Ireland of the necessity of this action when he told him:

[65] At this time Father William Färber, rector of Our Lady of Victory Church in St. Louis, and the editor of the *Pastoral Blatt,* petitioned Propaganda, because he could obtain no satisfaction from Archbishop Kenrick, to build a new German church. Vicar-General Mühlsiepen supported Färber in this move to erect a national parish within the territorial confines of St. Vincent's Parish, operated by the Vincentian Fathers, and attended by both German and English. Simeoni asked Gibbons to investigate the matter. Reverend Thomas J. Smith, C.M., visitator of the Vincentians from Perryville, Missouri, maintained that the Germans were perfectly satisfied at St. Vincent's before the interference of the "verein" which he claimed did not consider the Vincentians German enough. Vicar-General Philip P. Brady, of St. Louis, informed Gibbons in the same vein as Smith that, as the chancellor of the archdiocese, Reverend Henry Van der Sanden, had stated: "The entire movement is for no other purpose, on the part of a few radical German Priests, than to destroy St. Vincent's Parish as a German and English Parish, and to force the Lazarists to have an exclusively English Parish." Gibbons, in turn, informed Simeoni that, in his opinion, Kenrick's action in withdrawing the permission was fully justified, and the Propaganda decided the case in favor of the Archbishop of St. Louis and the *status quo* (*AAB,* 89-D-7, Simeoni to Gibbons, Rome, Nov. 30, 1891; 89-F-7, Smith, C.M., to Gibbons, Perryville, Dec. 23, 1891; 89-G-6, Gibbons to Simeoni, Baltimore, Dec. 29, 1891, copy; 89-H-6, Gibbons to Simeoni, Baltimore, Jan. 8, 1892, copy).

[66] *ADR,* Ireland to O'Connell, St. Paul, July 14, 1891. Ireland also enclosed a letter which he instructed O'Connell could be shown in proper quarters. In this letter the Archbishop spoke out strongly against the Lucerne memorialists. O'Connell reported to Gibbons on August 3, 1891, that he had left copies of a letter which Gibbons had also written on this subject with members of the Roman Curia, but their reaction had not been favorable. O'Connell detailed his interview with Persico at the Propaganda: "He then began: I cannot understand the reason of all this excitement. It seems to me that some agitators have seized this occasion for their own purposes. I have just shown him [Simeoni] Mgr. Ireland's letter which he looked at and laughed. You have your own legislation in America which will not be interfered with and it seems to me that that is all you can desire or ask for. The Pope has written you and the Holy See can do no more. That is all I can say and I have spoken with the Pope on the subject one hour yesterday" (*AAB,* 88-U-2, O'Connell to Gibbons, Rome, Aug. 3, 1891). O'Connell also advised Gibbons not

The impression that all this anti-German agitation was unreal and worked by a few persons for their own purposes has pretty well taken hold here. You are the man that made all this hollow thunder, using false telegrams of the Assoc. Press for that purpose. Nobody here sees all the reasoning for preoccupation that you see. It was simply an effort to frighten the H. See and the Germans and to keep them from their share of the places. So they write. So they print. Ireland is opposed to the Germans on account of his Total Abstinence and his favor of the Public Schools. So it goes. Of course the Authorities have never read nor thought of reading the tide of indignation that flowed through the Associated Press. They only heard of it by little odds and ends, and it was all pretty well explained away. Ireland is about the only man that has made himself prominent in having this agitation, and we all know Ireland goes too far, etc., etc. That is the situation. I send you an article in the German review of Munich on the subject. Now it is my opinion that the only way to convince officials here, once for all, that all this excitement was not false thunder, is if the government were to speak. Then no doubt would remain about the mind of Americans. Card. Rampolla says they are bound to hear Cahensly and his companions in position when they come to speak of the religious interests of their compatriots in America, and that the Holy See cannot take into account the susceptibilities of Americans in the preservation of German nationality in America, and Mgr. Persico said that as long as the canonical legislation of the Country was not altered he saw no reason for complaint from the Amer. Bps.[67]

The year of turmoil drew to a close as these plans were taking shape. In retrospect, several characteristics of the two St. Raphael memorials stand forth, both in their favor and to their disparagement. From the very beginning it was obvious that the timing and presentation of these petitions were a serious mistake. A group of European Catholics had clearly placed themselves in the position of reporting to the Holy See on the hierarchy and clergy of the United States concerning matters of internal administration which more properly should first have been respectfully submitted to those who were charged with neglect of immigrants. No representatives of the American St. Raphael Society were present at Lucerne or were consulted on

---

to expose himself further on the matter, but to let it go before Congress "and then they will be happy to have your influence to quiet public feeling after all their doubts of the reality or gravity of this question, which is a purely spiritual one for us, and which is a political one for them, and which forms a part of their policy in dealing with the Central powers."

[67] *AASP,* O'Connell to Ireland, Grottaferrata, Oct. 21, 1891. O'Connell also warned that in Rome Ella B. Edes was exposing the cablegrams on Cahensly.

either memorial. The European colonial attitude was clearly evident in the tenor of the documents. The lack of knowledge of American conditions, revealed in the recommendations advanced, also played directly into the hands of the American Protective Association which was then beginning its attacks on the Church with several arguments that could be traced to these Lucerne recommendations. More than that, a number of the requests from Lucerne were strikingly similar to earlier requests emanating from St. Louis and from Abbelen's mission of 1886, a fact which left the memorialists open to charges of collusion with American German demands. Peter Paul Cahensly further, by his interview of June 13, 1891, in which he set Irish Catholics against German Catholics and accused his opponents of an "Irish Plot," made a serious blunder and only contributed further to misunderstanding and bitterness of feeling. Reverend Friedrich Fröhling, present director of the St. Raphaelsverein, stated in an interview in Hamburg that Cahensly was a very sincere man, but that he never realized the implications which might arise from his words in other nations. Nor did he realize the danger of his aims and statements being politically interpreted.

On the reverse side of the ledger several facts stand forth in exoneration of the "Cahenslyites." The very term was inaccurate, since fifty-one signers and not merely Cahensly had taken responsibility for the first memorial. No one could rightly challenge the good will of all involved in this move, nor could anyone justly trace the origin of this memorial to the German branch of the society alone. The St. Raphael societies have insisted to this day that the Lucerne Memorial had been presented to the convention by Volpe-Landi, had been previously seen by Bishop Scalabrini, and had been checked by three priests in attendance at the meetings. Thus the accusation that the move was entirely lay in origin would also appear to be unfounded. Moreover, the St. Raphael societies have maintained that the recommendations were intended primarily to apply to Italian and Slavic immigrants, who were leaving for the United States in ever larger numbers. They had no special reference to German Catholic immigrants, who were beginning to decline in numbers because of improved economic conditions in their homeland. Nor was the first memorial directed at conditions in the United States alone, but rather toward a solution of immigrant problems in all the missionary countries of the new world to which European Catholics were then moving, such as South America and Canada. Since all of these countries were still under the ecclesiastical jurisdiction of the Propaganda, and were still in a missionary status, the memorial was presented to the Holy See. Several points in the memorials had also been advanced previously in the nineteenth century by the Ludwig Missionsverein and the Leopoldine Foundation. The validity of such recommendations as equal rights, the right to their native tongue, priests of each nationality for that nationality when possible, parochial schools and mutual aid societies — all of these points could scarcely be questioned. Nor had national bishops been advocated at Lucerne, but only that several bishops of the same origin as the immigrants should be included in the episcopate of countries where they settled.

But it is, above all, to Peter Paul Cahensly personally that history owes in simple justice an acquittal. To attack Cahensly without checking or at least giving an ear to his clear denials of having arranged a plot; to release manufactured cables in which his name was associated with a conspiracy; to coin a phrase, playing upon the name of a man who had struck out, under hierarchical direction, as a pioneer in social work for emigrants in Europe, on the ocean, and at American shores before any American bishops or societies had inaugurated such activity; to associate political intrigue of a Pan-German character with a man who had been at odds since 1871 with his own government over emigrant care — all this was both precipitous and unjust.

Two speeches of Cahensly, delivered shortly before the troubles of 1891 broke, reveal his true position. In an address at the Freiburg im Breisgau *Katholikentag,* in September, 1888, he reported on the state of the Leo House in New York. He noted that Germans, particularly in the larger cities of the East, had given proportionately little to the project, and he went on to explain the reasons for this fact. To Cahensly it was the desire of the Germans themselves to become Americanized. He did not criticize the American hierarchy or the Americanizers, but rather the Germans themselves, when he stated:

> In many dioceses where a large Catholic population exists, the dominating influence is for all to Americanize, no matter if souls thereby fall away. The leading advocates of this tendency can be found among the Germans themselves, who, whether born in America or just recently emigrated, are ashamed of their German origin. Unfortunately also, many German priests secular and religious, know nothing more of their nationality. This group recommends the banning of German language from Church and school, and the establishment of English. The outcome of this is that the children, with the loss of their German

mother tongue, lose good morals and the Catholic faith. . . . The bond between parents and children is broken, for they can no longer understand each other.[68]

In the Prussian House of Representatives, of which Cahensly was a member at that time, and not of the Reichstag as he was accused, a lengthy discussion ensued on January 28, 1890, over the "epidemic" of emigration, especially to Brazil and the United States. Cahensly took the floor, and there also in a lengthy speech he reviewed his twenty years of work in the St. Raphaelsverein. He pointed out that care had been offered to all who came to their missions regardless of their religion, that no charges had been made to the immigrants, although the Society had entailed an expense of over four million marks up to that time; that the Society was not associated in any commercial venture nor had it accepted compensation from either the state or from shipping companies. He asked the German Government to take measures to keep emigrants at home, reviewed the hostile treatment which had been given to the St. Raphaelsverein by the imperial regime, and again asked the Reich to take the initiative in international emigration legislation with the seafaring nations of Europe and of North and South America. Once more he entreated the Minister of Interior to draw up an emigration law in Germany itself, rather than continue the Bismarckian policy that any person who left the fatherland was no concern of the German Empire.[69]

A detailed examination of Cahensly's activities and speeches while he was in the Prussian House of Representatives revealed this same pattern, namely, a consistent opposition to the regime's emigration policy. As a member of the Center Party, he spoke and voted against the liberal, anti-Catholic measures of Bismarck's government. Cahensly was not a parliamentary leader of the Center, but in the proceedings his voice was always registered for social betterment legislation. He favored improvement of conditions for domestic servants, pensions for

[68] *Verhandlungen der 35 General-Versammlung der katholischen Vereine Deutschlands in Freiburg im Breisgau, 2–6. September 1885* (Freiburg, 1885), p. 172. Cahensly, however, praised the German priests in the United States who, he said, "in spite of all enmity hold to German language in Church and school. They, the German Catholic priests, are the true pioneers of *Deutschtum* in North America." He also emphasized that Lieber was in Cincinnati at the American *Katholikentag* where he would "without doubt substantially fortify, through his fiery words, the efforts of our German brothers in the faith" (p. 173). It was utterances such as these which left Cahensly's words open to misunderstanding, and which associated him with the aims and movements of the German Priests' Society in the United States.

[69] *Stenographische Berichte über die Verhandlungen des Hauses der Abgeordneten* (Berlin, 1890), I, pp. 516–517.

railroad workers, and rights of Catholic state-aid schools. He concerned himself particularly with trade and communication regulations, railroads, taxes, warehouses, a progressive income tax, associations for consumers, mineral control, Sunday rest for workers, pensions for private school teachers, and amelioration of conditions among vine dressers.[70] In the two legislative periods of the Reichstag, which Cahensly attended from 1898–1903 as a member from the fourth Wiesbaden district, his speaking and voting record centered around industrial regulations, erection of a bureau for foreign languages, trade and banking control, budget enactments, drug laws, broadening of pensions, and defense of workers' rights.[71] In both houses his social interest was primarily centered on emigration, and in the discussions on Germany's serious leakage through emigration, Cahensly's was a prominent voice. In these sessions he defended the rights of private societies in emigrant work, encouraged the erection of an emigration bureau of information, and condemned the regime for a century of almost total neglect of emigrants. Cahensly's political record, then,

[70] In seventy-five volumes of proceedings of the Prussian Landtag from 1885 until 1900, covering the fifteenth through the nineteenth legislative periods, Cahensly was found speaking eighty-nine times. There was no evidence of his advocating government colonial policies, no tie-up between his emigrant activities and state direction, but rather an open and courageous criticism of the regime's lack of interest in emigrant care.

[71] Cahensly's record in the Reichstag during the tenth legislative period of that body from 1898–1903 was more striking. He spoke more frequently, and he appeared to be accepted as an experienced and respected legislator of the Center. Cf. *Stenographische Berichte über die Verhandlungen des Reichstags. X Legislatur. I Session:* 1898–1900 (15 vols.); *II Session:* 1900–1903 (18 vols.) (Berlin, 1898–1903). His thirty-five speeches and reports, especially on emigration, indicate that he was accepted as an authority on emigration care. Cf. "Auswanderungswesen," Bd.II, 38. Sitz.v.31.1. 1901S. 1041D, 1042B, 8076C; "Reichsamt des Innern-Auswanderungswesen," Bd.V, 132.Sitz.v.1.2. 1902S. 3825C; "Auswärtiges Amt.Auskunftsstelle für Auswanderer-zuschutz an die deutsche Kolnialgesellschaft für die Shaffung einer solchen," Bd.V, 157.Sitz.v.4.3. 1902S. 4585D; 158.Sitz.v.5.3. 1902S. 4595A; 4597A; "Zur Geschäftsordung," S.4590B, 4675D; "Dienstgebäude der Kolonial-Zentralverwaltung," Bd.V, 148.Sitz.v.5.3. 1902S. 4603B; "Staatssekretär-Frage der Errichtung deutscher Handelskammern im Auslande," Bd.V, 161.Sitz.v.10.3. 1902S. 4669D; "Verwaltung im allgemeinen: Missionen," Bd.X, 289.Sitz.v.21.3. 1903S. 8804B; "Schiffsleute, Stellenvermittlung für dieselben. Entwurf eines Gesetzes, zweite Berathung-Strafbestimmungen," Bd.VI, 169.Sitz.v.19.4. 1902S. 4930C; "Seemannsordnung. Entwurf einer solchen: Disziplinargewalt des Kapitäns," Bd.V, 167.Sitz.v.17.4. 1902S. 4863B; "Heuervertrag," Bd.IV, 99.Sitz.v.28.11. 1901S. 2820B; "Seemannsämter," Bd.IV, 97. Sitz.v.26.11. 1901S. 2766C; 99.Sitz.v.28.11. 1901S. 2804C; "Sonntagsfrage-Ausreise betreffend," Bd.IV, 100.Sitz.v.29.11. 1901S. 2844A, 2849B; "Sonntagsruhe und Sonntagsandacht," S.2851D; "Strafbestimmungen — leichtere Verfehlungen des Kapitäns," Bd.V. 168.Sitz.v.18.4. 1902S. 4890C; "Verpflegung und Heilbehandlung," Bd.IV, 101.Sitz.v.30.11. 1901S. 2876B. "Arbeitszeit des Schiffsmanns-Sonntagsfrage," Bd.VI, 174.Sitz.v.25.4 1902S. 5077D.

revealed him as ahead of his time, a man recognized by his colleagues as a pathfinder in emigrant work, and in no sense a tool of the imperial government.

An excellent case in point occurred in 1902. In a session of the Reichstag the budget committee was reporting on the floor as to the advisability of granting 30,000 DM ($7,500) to a central emigration agency, or of voting subsidies to private emigrant societies as assistance and support so that their agents could supply information on favorable locations for emigrant settlement abroad. Cahensly spoke out against granting state money to private emigrant societies. He said:

> Colleague Dasbach has just remarked that the existing societies [for emigrants] should be given State support. I, who am the president of the St. Raphaelsverein, would be thankful for State money. But we would rather preserve our independence and not assume further commitments than we now have. Although we have placed our agents in the main ports of Europe, North and South America, they would not be in a position to supply information on all questions which pertain to emigration in the different lands across the sea. It is impossible for an agent, who resides in Buenos Aires, to give information on conditions in a certain province of Argentina. The Consul who lives in that province can better advise on land suitable to corn, cattle, or other purposes.[72]

He was challenged from the floor on his motives for not accepting state money when his society had experience and position in the work. To this challenge Cahensly replied:

> Colleague Heim has evidenced wonder that the St. Raphaelsverein has rejected State support. If colleague Heim had been present at the entire previous discussion he would come nearer to understanding my reasons. I have expressly stated that the St. Raphaelsverein, although it cares for 30,000 emigrants yearly, and helps all emigrants without differentiating religion, is at the same time primarily directed toward Catholics. It is for religious considerations not in a position to accept these 30,000 DM for fear that they would not be equally distributed. We cannot fulfill the task nor accept the grant that the Reich offers.[73]

When he had finished, a fellow member of the Reichstag, by the name of Raab, declared: "Representative Cahensly has acquired merit in the field of emigration care for which one can find the correct expression only with difficulty."[74]

[72] *Ibid.,* Bd.V. 157.Sitz.v.4.3. 1902S. 4595.
[73] *Ibid.,* S. 4596.
[74] *Ibid.,* S. 4597.

Likewise to accuse Cahensly of co-operation with Baron Kurd von Schlözer, the first Prussian minister to the Vatican, following the resumption of diplomatic relations after the *Kulturkampf,* showed on the part of his American critics a surprising lack of understanding of German conditions at that time.[75] For a member of the Center Party, with a record such as that of Cahensly, to approach the Prussian minister to the Vatican for intercession on the part of the regime in Catholic matters with which the Center was supposed to be concerned was, to say the least, improbable. Moreover, an examination of all of Schlözer's published correspondence during his diplomatic career revealed not only that Cahensly's name was unmentioned, but that there existed an open antagonism on Schlözer's part to Windthorst, Lieber, Bachem, Porsch, Ledochowski, Kopp, and other ecclesiastical and political Catholic leaders from Germany who were close friends of Cahensly.[76] Schlözer's various diplomatic appointments took him from Rome to Copenhagen and St. Petersburg, where he served under Bismarck himself, then to Mexico as minister, to the United States as minister, and then, at the height of his career, to the important post of Prussian minister to the Vatican. During his residence in Washington, from 1871–1882, Schlözer was on the scene when Cahensly and Isenburg-Birstein first petitioned President Grant to work for international care of emigrants. This letter of the St. Raphaelsverein leaders did not pass through von Schlözer's hands at that time, nor is there any evidence that the Lucerne Memorial to Rome of 1891 went through his office.[77] While in Rome Schlözer's main preoccupation was that of binding the Vatican in a new central European alliance with Prussia over against the traditional Franco-Vatican

[75] Baron Kurd von Schlözer was born on January 5, 1822, at Lübeck, served as undersecretary of German embassies in Italy, Denmark, and Russia, as resident minister in Mexico, 1869–1871; as minister in the United States, 1871–1882; as minister to the Vatican, 1882–1892. He died in Berlin on May 13, 1894. His published letters include: *Jugendbriefe. 1841–1856* (ed. Leopold von Schlözer; Stuttgart and Berlin, 1920); *Petersburger Briefe. 1857–1862. Briefe aus Berlin-Kopenhagen. 1862–1864.* (Stuttgart and Berlin, 1921); *Römische Briefe. 1864–1869* (Stuttgart and Berlin, 1913); *Mexikanische Briefe. 1869–1871* (Stuttgart and Berlin, 1913); *Amerikanische Briefe. 1871–1882* (Stuttgart and Berlin, 1923); *Letzte römische Briefe. 1882–1894* (Stuttgart and Berlin, 1924). His brother-in-law, Paulus Curtius, wrote a short biography, *Kurd von Schlözer* (Berlin, 1912), from a strongly nationalistic viewpoint. Cf. *DGH,* X, p. 1041.

[76] Cf. *Letzte römische Briefe, 1882–1894,* pp. 8, 30, 32, 68, 88, 91 f., 95 f., 100 f., 123, 139, 146, 160, 167.

[77] Curtius states that von Schlözer had a favorable impression of American Catholicism and its growing influence, which his friend and fellow liberal, Senator Carl Schurz of Missouri, assured him was a growing factor in United States life. Cf. *op. cit.,* pp. 110–112.

friendship. He had made some headway in this effort with the support of a party in the Roman Curia friendly to Germany which included Cardinals Carlo Laurenzi, Serafino and Vincenzo Vannutelli, Domenico Jacobini, Girolamo Gotti, Monsignori Giovanni Montel, auditor of the Rota, Gabriele Boccali, auditor of Leo XIII, Nazereno Marzolini, papal chamberlain, and especially the future nuncio to Bavaria and cardinal, Antonio Agliardi. But by 1887, with the advent of Cardinal Rampolla as Secretary of State, the traditional friendship of the Vatican with France was reaffirmed with the support of Cardinals Charles Lavigerie, Raffaele La Valletta, and Lucido Parocchi. It was then that von Schlözer lost the greatest diplomatic prize of his career. Under the direction of Bismarck, the alliance had continuously aimed at the subjection of Center Party activities and direct Vatican co-operation with the Bismarck regime. In view of this background, it would have been a real *faux pas* for von Schlözer to have sponsored Cahensly or the Lucerne memorialists who were in opposition to his program of rapprochement. By 1891 von Schlözer's influence was not only on the wane, but regardless of this fact, it would have been a contradiction for him to sponsor German Catholics who had united with Catholics from seven nations, including one from France, in proposing care for emigrants to the new world, a policy to which his government was opposed.

The lack of judgment and understanding of American conditions on the part of the Lucerne memorialists cannot be excused, nor can they be exonerated from an obvious and unwarranted interference in ecclesiastical administration of the Church in the United States without reference to its leaders. But in simple justice, history must protest against the accusations of 1891, and the myth which has been handed down from that time that Peter Paul Cahensly, merchant of Limburg, a sort of Frederic Ozanam of the high seas in emigrant care, had conceived and executed a plot of Pan-German proportions which aimed at nationalizing the American Church on foreign or European lines.

Of Cahensly's traducers it might be said, as Lord Acton remarked in his inaugural lecture at the University of Cambridge in 1895, that it is the duty of the historian "to suffer no man and no cause to escape the undying penalty which history has the power to inflict on wrong."[78]

[78] Lord Acton, *A Lecture in the Study of History* (London, 1895), p. 63.

CHAPTER V

Liberals vs. Conservatives

> Liberal doctrines are becoming more and more popular in this country, and some even of the higher Ecclesiastical Dignitaries think their diffusion is the high road to American favor, and a passport for the claims of the Catholic Church.[1]

THESE words of Archbishop Corrigan clearly expressed the broader underlying differences which racked the Church in the United States during the years that marked the transition from the nineteenth to the twentieth century. The question of German nationality was an important phase of the issue, but it was not dominant or conclusive. It served rather to draw exponents of the German standpoint into a position, over against the Americanizers, where they found themselves grouped with a number of non-German Catholics of the country in defense of a conservative approach to administrative, procedural, and racial problems. This party preferred a careful application of tried and universal methods of advancing the life of the Church. To the left, in viewpoint, stood other American Catholics intrigued with more adventuresome methods of bringing the Church into harmony with the spirit of the times, specifically with the peculiar character and destiny of the new world. Each group called the other conservative and liberal respectively. The conservative ranks numbered for the most part the German American bishops, priests, news editors, and their accepted spokesman, Monsignor Joseph Schröder, of the Catholic University of America; Archbishop Corrigan, of New York, and his outspoken

[1] *AASPOW,* Corrigan to Smith, New York, Apr. 2, 1891. O'Connell had informed Ireland that there was a growing feeling in Rome also that among the American archbishops there were eight who were liberals, with Ireland at their head, and three "very obedient to the Holy See as we call them Intransigenti." O'Connell indicated two of the "intransigenti" archbishops as Corrigan and Katzer, and he added: "If the narrow policy of the 'three intransigenti' Abps. is to govern America in the future, I can see nothing before it in the long run but the lot that befell the Church here" (*AASP,* O'Connell to Ireland, Rome, Dec. 31, 1890).

suffragan, Bishop McQuaid, of Rochester; and a number of the intellectual leaders of the Society of Jesus both in the United States and at Rome. Among the liberals or Americanizers were Cardinal Gibbons and Monsignor O'Connell at the American College in Rome; Archbishop Riordan in San Francisco; Archbishop Ireland and his favorite religious society, the Paulists; and Bishop Keane and the great majority of the faculty of the newly erected Catholic University of America. Taking a middle course, but always a little left of center, were such prelates as Archbishops Williams, of Boston, Elder, of Cincinnati, and Bishop Spalding, of Peoria, but their numbers were few and they never became the stabilizing or compromising force which could have drawn the ends closer together. These divisions within the leadership of the American Church were not absolute, and the so-called liberals or conservatives were not infrequently found united on issues. Nor was there ever a question of dogmatic error among any of these men, although this charge was sometimes made intemperately in the heat of controversy. Unlike American Protestants of the period, the Catholics of the country remained united in love and devotion to their common faith and traditions as they had been handed down.[2] But on issues of national importance, such as the school question, the assimilation of immigrants, temperance, secret societies, and Americanization, differences stood forth in marked relief.

It was the school question, coming to the front in 1890, which united the cause of the "Cahenslyites" with other non-Germans, and extended the life of the nationality question long beyond what at first seemed to be a final decision in the matter, when Cardinal Rampolla conveyed the opinion of Leo XIII to Cardinal Gibbons on June 28, 1891. One of the principal scenes of conflict centered itself in the state of Wisconsin where, upon investigation, it was discovered that in several German schools, both Catholic and Lutheran, the English language was not being taught, and in a number of grades it was only a secondary branch. As a consequence the Bennett Law was introduced into the Wisconsin legislature in 1890, which required that English be taught in all schools of the state for at least sixteen weeks during the year. Archbishop Heiss and his two Wisconsin suffragans, Bishops Katzer and Flasch, united on March 12, 1890, in a joint protest against the Bennett Law on the grounds of undue state interference,

[2] The terms "liberal" and "conservative" as used here have no relation to "realistic" or "fundamental" divisions in American Protestantism after the War between the States. Cf. Andrew L. Drummond, "Theological Emancipation and Re-Statement," *Story of American Protestantism* (Boston, 1950), pp. 340–357.

through regulatory clauses of the law which governed qualifications and attendance, not on the grounds of the language question.[3] Archbishop Ireland in turn, gave public support to the Bennett legislation because he was sincerely convinced of its need, as he explained to Cardinal Ledochowski, Prefect of the Propaganda. He made his reasons clear when he said:

> In America among the Germans whether Catholic or Lutheran, there is little difficulty in establishing schools for primary education because it is the only means of perpetuating their language. Among the Catholics, the children are retained in these schools until they have been grounded well in the use of the German language. After that they are permitted by all the pastors of the German churches to frequent without prohibition the public schools. The period of departure from their parochial schools is when the child has made his first Communion which with them takes place about the age of ten or twelve years. I can safely assert that in all the United States the schools for advanced German children do not count more than one-half dozen if they arrive at that number. After that, all over America, the German children are allowed to go to school where they please, and no further danger seems to be entertained for their faith. Hence, they look with the utmost suspicion and apprehension on anything that would imperil the predominance of their language in the primary school, or on any measure of protection from the State that would fail to recognize the supremacy of the German language.[4]

But the excitement over the Bennett Law was nothing compared to the repercussions that followed Archbishop Ireland's famous address to the National Education Association at St. Paul in July, 1890. Speaking on "State Schools and Parish Schools," the Archbishop eloquently investigated the possibility of union between the two educational systems. He granted to the state the right to establish schools and to enforce attendance at some school, and he then gave free rein to his oratorical talents as he proclaimed: "The Free School of America! Withered be the hand raised in sign of its destruction." He expressed his regret that there was a necessity for the existence of the parochial school because the state schools tended to eliminate religion from the minds and hearts of youth. His suggestions for a solution of the problem were that the religion of the majority, "be

[3] Cf. "A Historical Pronouncement: Wisconsin Bishops Protest the Bennett Law," *Social Justice Review,* XXXIII (Dec., 1940), pp. 282–284, 318–320. The Bennett Law was repealed when Lutherans joined forces with Catholics to sweep Democrats into office.

[4] Daniel F. Reilly, O.P., *The School Controversy* (*1891–1893*) (Washington, 1943), p. 257.

this religion as Protestant as Protestantism can be," should permeate the state schools, while denominational schools for minorities, should receive tax funds equal to the cost of tuition for a pupil in the state schools. Second, he advocated a plan such as the one then operating in Poughkeepsie, New York, where the parish school building was rented by the state and religion was taught outside the regular hours. Following his address, Ireland explained to the Propaganda that he had thus spoken because he wanted to admit all he could in favor of the state schools in order to gain co-operation for the schools of the Church. He did not fail to advocate the claims of religious education, but he deplored the burden it placed upon Catholic parents in supporting parochial schools as they existed while they received no part of the tax monies they contributed for education.[5]

The proposal of the Archbishop of St. Paul was courageous and farsighted. But Ireland was attacked by shocked Catholic editors, especially in German Catholic papers, for what they considered his lighthearted abandonment of the parish school, built up so laboriously and commanded by the Third Council of Baltimore, for his friendship and advocacy of state schools which had long been branded as "godless" by a number of bishops and priests, and for advocating compulsory education.[6] More than that, he was delated to Rome for opposing the decrees of the late council. Monsignor O'Connell, who was actively defending Ireland's cause, warned him of the protests against him that were reaching Rome. One official at the Propaganda had informed O'Connell that a basket of papers arrived every day on the subject, while an accusation in German had gone so far as to assert that Ireland was a Mason. "My how hard those Germans are," Monsignor Mesczynski, secretary to Cardinal Ledochowski, had exclaimed. However, Cardinal Ledochowski, Prefect of Propaganda, recognized and respected Ireland's position in the United States and stood by him in the controversy.[7]

Firm in his policy of Americanization, the Archbishop of St. Paul

[5] *Ibid.*, pp. 46–49, 251. In Reilly's work the details of the school question have been treated from the viewpoint of Archbishop Ireland and his party. Their position is given only in summary here, while the outlook of the opposition is developed somewhat more completely both because it was the position of the Germans and also because it still awaits adequate treatment.

[6] Bishop Spalding published an article of scholarly clearness in the *Educational Review* a year later in which he advocated substantially the same educational principles, while not employing the same glowing praise for state schools that Ireland had used, namely, that denominational schools were best for the state. Cf. *Educational Review,* II (July, 1871), pp. 105–122. This journal was the official organ of the National Education Association.

[7] *AASP,* O'Connell to Ireland, Rome, Aug. 18, 1890; Aug. 30, 1890; June 4, 1891.

went on in August, 1891, to negotiate an arrangement whereby the school boards of the towns of Faribault and Stillwater were permitted to take over control of two parochial schools in those communities.[8] It was not a revolutionary move, as similar plans had been in operation for some years in Boston, Savannah, Newark, Hartford, Cleveland, and one was still operating in Poughkeepsie, New York. More than that, the Jesuit Fathers had, both in Missouri and Pennsylvania, sponsored similar arrangements. The concerted opposition of Archbishop Corrigan and of the Jesuits to the Faribault-Stillwater Plan was strange in view of this background. Because of the differing opinions among Catholics, Cardinal Gibbons asked Reverend Thomas Bouquillon, professor of moral theology in the Catholic University of America, to prepare a pamphlet summarizing the pertinent principles on education. This work, *Education: To Whom Does It Belong?*, upheld the right of the state to control education and to make it compulsory. Many of Ireland's opponents viewed Bouquillon's pamphlet as a defense of the Faribault-Stillwater Plan, but in reality the Archbishop had not sponsored Bouquillon's treatise. Answers were forthcoming in papers and magazines, especially from Reverend René I. Holaind, S.J., in his pamphlet: *The Parent First,* in which the primary authority of the state in educational matters was flatly denied. Newspapers had a holiday with the controversy, and Ireland while he was in New York granted an interview to the New York *Herald,* which was the most explosive statement of the case to date. Bluntly and unequivocally the Archbishop declared that Holaind's pamphlet was "quite unfair," that Holaind was stationary while the world moved, and that the German Catholic papers were attacking his plan with motives that one could apprehend without much difficulty.[9] Corrigan, who had clashed with Ireland before and who would do so again, was highly displeased at this interview given within his own ecclesiastical jurisdiction, nor did he agree with the Faribault-Stillwater Plan. Ireland, on his side, felt that Holaind's pamphlet had been instigated by Corrigan, and he obviously intended his interview to be

[8] Cf. William Watts Folwell, *A History of Minnesota* (St. Paul, 1921–1930), IV, pp. 174–183.

[9] New York *Herald,* Dec. 14, 1891. When Bouquillon's pamphlet came out, Schröder considered it "the weakest and most arrogant thing" he had ever given out. Then he continued to Heuser: "I would have written at once an article under my name to a German paper if Messmer had not stopped me. Some time ago I wrote openly to German papers: 'You are going too far. Don't be unjust in your attacks.' But now I feel like saying 'Take your hammer and hit without hesitation.' Bouquillon deserves it because of his presumption. O quam difficile mihi non scribere" (*ACHSP,* Schröder to Heuser, Washington, n.d.).

an answer to both gentlemen.[10] At the November meeting of the archbishops in St. Louis, Ireland had explained his Minnesota experiment to the assembled metropolitans and had apparently satisfied them, but now the whole controversy had been greatly intensified.

Opposition crystallized at this time in a new and effective public forum. A monthly magazine for the American clergy was begun in 1889, with Reverend Herman J. Heuser, professor of Sacred Scripture at St. Charles Borromeo Seminary in Philadelphia, as editor. For the first two years of its existence the publication was nonpartisan, although conservative in spirit. But with the advent of the school question an interesting alliance formed around the person of Dr. Heuser. It was made up of those groups in the Church who felt obliged to speak forth against what they considered to be a nascent and strident American liberalism. This conservative group was composed of Archbishop Corrigan, Bishops McQuaid and Chatard; the Jesuit Fathers, Alphonse J. Maes, professor of Sacred Scripture, and Aloysius Sabetti, professor of moral theology in Woodstock College, Maryland, along with René Holaind, of St. Francis Xavier College, New York, James Conway, of Canisius College, Buffalo, and Salvatore M. Brandi, of the *Civiltà Cattolica,* Jesuit biweekly journal published in Rome; Archbishop Katzer, Bishops Wigger, Messmer, and Zardetti; and Arthur Preuss, of St. Louis, who was organizing a German Catholic publication, the *Fortnightly Review,* to appear in English as an exponent of the German position. The correspondence of Heuser revealed the strong convictions of these leaders that something had to be done to curb a tendency which they feared would implant European liberal ideas in the American Church.[11] Dominant in this group and controlling mind and spirit of the countermovement was Monsignor Schröder, of the Catholic University of America. Schröder emerged as the continental-trained scholar who saw European liberal implications in American Catholic theories and practices. He feared and distrusted the modern state both from personal experience as a result of his exile at the hands of Bismarck's regime, and from his

[10] For indications of the Corrigan-Holaind co-operation, cf. *ACHSP,* Holaind to Heuser, New York, June 21, July 1, 11, 27, 28, Oct. 25, Dec. 3, 1891. On June 29, 1891, Holaind had sent proofs of his article to Corrigan and added: "I must say that he is satisfied that I am a thorough Catholic."

[11] Heuser's papers, intact for the most part, are preserved in the manuscript collections of the American Catholic Historical Society of Philadelphia at St. Charles Seminary, Overbrook, Pennsylvania. As yet they have remained largely untouched as a source for all the questions of this period. They contain a rich store of materials worthy of independent treatment as representing the position of those who opposed the Americanizers.

theoretical studies of developments in Europe since the Protestant Revolt. He was, furthermore, determined to crush what he believed to be an American theological minimism.

The Archbishop of New York, in advising Heuser to propagate sound views on the social question in his journal, stated:

> The question of Liberalism is most important. Mgr. Schröder has done a great deal; but so much more will remain to be done! . . . This is a burning question, & if not solved properly & quickly, will do vast harm to souls in this country.[12]

In reply to Heuser's request that he contribute an article on the school questions, Bishop McQuaid stated that he did not wish to take public part in the controversy, since his views were already well known and could be found in several speeches if they were desired. He went on to observe:

> What leads some of our bishops in the U.S. to fall down before the State in abject slavery for the possible gain of a few dollars, & at the same time sacrifice of the best spiritual interests of our children is to me more than a mystery.
>
> However, I am so much at variance with the new liberalism that has of late sprung up among some of our bishops, under the leadership of Card. Gibbons, with regard to secret societies, & parochial schools that I prefer to stand to one side & safeguard my own diocese.
>
> When Rome comes to understand the extent of the mischief already brought about she will be amazed.[13]

Later McQuaid continued in the same vein, after he had asserted that it was impudence for Bouquillon to lecture on the school question in the United States, and that the country would not go to the archdiocese of St. Paul for instruction. He said:

> Some of our false liberalism proceeds from ignorance. These wrong ideas are given out by high dignitaries in utter unconsciousness of the harm they are doing to the laity. These innocent people accept everything that drops from the lips of a cardinal or bishops as gospel truth.

[12] *ACHSP,* Corrigan to Heuser, New York, Mar. 24, 1891. Bishop Messmer spoke in a like vein to the editor: "While you keep fully abreast with the needs & demands of new conditions, you show that conservative spirit which alone, under God's providence, can save the children of Holy Church from the disastrous consequences in this *fin de siecle* rush of the human mind. This moderation & conservative attitude in regard to ecclesiastical doctrine & discipline I consider to be a most important and praiseworthy feature of your *Review,* the more that a very large portion of our clergy, not to speak of the laity, know very little, if anything at all, of the true principles determining the extent of liberty in theological matters" (*ACHSP,* Messmer to Heuser, Green Bay, Aug. 9, 1897).

[13] *ACHSP,* McQuaid to Heuser, Rochester, n.d.

> You are applauded when you are called an advanced thinker, a great liberal, a true American, etc. I pride myself on my Americanism, but always inside the teaching of the Catholic Church.[14]

Meanwhile, Heuser carefully prepared a symposium on education to appear in the February, 1892, issue of the *American Ecclesiastical Review.* The editor contributed an article, and he likewise secured contributions from Bishops Messmer and Chatard as well as from Reverend James F. Loughlin, chancellor of the Archdiocese of Philadelphia. Here Bouquillon was attacked and any compromise repudiated which would endanger the faith of Catholic children in a nonsectarian school.[15] Heuser, Messmer, and Reverend Denis T. O'Sullivan, S.J., of Woodstock, continued the attack in the April issue, and in the May number Schröder wrote on "American Catholics and European School Legislation." The latter article was an analysis of the condition of church schools in European lands and a reaffirmation of the rights of the Church in the school over against the encroach-

[14] *Ibid.,* Jan. 28, 1892. McQuaid's position was that "nothing will win the day for our Catholic Schools but Catholic schools, large & well equipped, under the control of competent teachers, & giving good results, as necessarily they must" (*ibid.,* Mar. 16, 1892).

[15] *AER,* VI (Feb., 1892), pp. 89–127. An article by Reverend James Murphy also indicated the unfavorable results of Catholic schools being placed under state control in Britain (pp. 127–131), which Heuser termed "an important lesson to Catholics in the United States." Loughlin labeled the controversy in a fashion typical of many conservative American Catholics when he wrote: "To me the whole discussion looks like a raging tempest in a very diminutive tea-pot. To be sure, we have heard some hard words bandied on either side. We have been informed that two antagonistic schools are forming amongst us, the one 'progressive' with its headquarters, I believe, in the far Northwest and its literary center in Washington, the other 'foggy, and stationary,' fossilizing about the Ordinary of New York or Milwaukee — I am not certain which nor does it matter much, since the Jesuits are at the bottom of it.

"I admit that in one direction, at least, there has been a 'new departure.' To those of the clergy who learned their notions of clerical and episcopal etiquette in the dignified school of a Kenrick or Wood or McCloskey (men who never appeared in public except in an official capacity), it certainly is novel and bewildering to be obliged at each instant to make distinctions between the eloquent utterances of Mr. Thomas Jones, American citizen, and the orthodox pastorals of the Right Rev. Thomas, Bishop of Jonesville. Now, mind, I am not finding fault at all. If any person in authority conceives it timely or necessary to doff his official robes and mount a stump, either in his shirt-sleeves or a swallow-tail coat, that is no business of mine: *Miror magis.* But whoever appeals to Caesar, to Caesar must go, and by Caesar's judgment abide. A great many soldiers are delighted when they see their commander brandish his shillalah and plunge into the thickest of the fight, giving and receiving black eyes. Many others might prefer that he should take his stand upon some vantage-ground from which he could quietly survey and direct the operations of his host, without making his person a receptacle for dust and bullets" (p. 120).

ments of the modern state which was to Schröder Masonic, liberal, and neutral.[16] Schröder's essay was by way of a rebuttal to a dispatch of December 23, 1891, from Berlin. This dispatch had again been prepared by O'Connell and Böglin, and had summarized educational conditions in France, Belgium, Italy, Austria, and Prussia. The Berlin dispatch listed examples of cases where the Church had not contested the right of the State over primary schools, especially in Germany, and where it had striven to give religious instruction in public schools by adapting itself to existing laws.[17]

The opposition of these gentlemen of conservative persuasion to the Faribault-Stillwater Plan was but a part of their determined mission, as Sabetti told Heuser, to curb liberalism in the American Church in favor of true and solid doctrine.[18] Sabetti contacted Bishops Zardetti,

[16] *AER,* VI (May, 1892), pp. 366–393. The Heuser Papers reveal the close contact and exchange of ideas between Heuser and Holaind during the school controversy. Holaind was firmly convinced that the cause of Catholic education was at stake, and he told the Philadelphia editor: "What in the world prompts Catholics to stab us in the back when we are fighting against state monopoly & for the liberty of Holy Mother Church? Is it *cussedness* or want of practical sense? Well, I am the last man to pick up a quarrel, in fact I hate controversy, but there is such a thing as driving a cat to the wall" (Dec. 3, 1891).

He rejoiced when bishops and other conservative leaders entered the field, because he did not want the Jesuits to be alone in the struggle (Jan. 10, 1893). Moreover, he expressed strong opinions against the liberal influence of the Catholic University of America: "If The University goes on giving the young priests who are *not posted at all* on philosophy a jumbling of lectures as diversified as the robe of Benjamin (I am told by respectable witnesses that one of the lecturers defended evolution, not only for the body but for the soul), of course this will be counteracted by such men as Dr. Pohle, & if these young men were thoroughly grounded on the scientific basis of biology & psychology, very little harm would be done; but to present to them a panorama of incoherent systems before they are capable of finding their way, is to a practical teacher a lamentable piece of absurdity. . . . I am much afraid that unless a different impulse is given to the University, it will do more harm than good. First class seminaries is [*sic*] what we need most, we have several but all are not up to the mark. . . . In the meantime keep B. lively but smiling, and kill mercilessly any plan which would surrender our boys in the future of the Catholic Church in this country to a pack of evolutionists and free-masons" (Jan. 23, 1893).

Heuser was very interested at this time in establishing a Catholic daily, to be named "The Tablet," which would refute growing liberalism in America. Holaind informed him that the Jesuits would contribute to it, as he had spoken to their provincial, and he was convinced it was a necessity to contribute. Heuser consulted many persons on this project, but it never materialized.

[17] Reilly, *op. cit.,* pp. 102–104. Cf. Reilly, *passim,* also for a discussion of further pamphlets of Bouquillon, Holaind, and other controversialists who took sides on the school issue.

[18] *ACHSP,* Sabetti to Heuser, Woodstock, Maryland, Jan. 11, 1891. In this letter Sabetti stated: "You have a great mission before you. Don't be afraid of being unpopular. A certain unpopularity is better than a great popularity." Cf. also Dec. 6, 1891; Jan. 15 and 21; Feb. 14; Mar. 28; June 8, 1892.

of St. Cloud, and James A. Healey, of Portland, and encouraged them to speak out for the cause. Meanwhile he also kept in close contact with Brandi on developments in Rome, convinced that it was a shame that the bishops maintained silence. Zardetti sent notes to Heuser to be used in the educational issues against the right of an indifferent state, and promised that he would write to Cardinal Ledochowski and others in Rome. He had high praise for Heuser's efforts, and he said: "This is the right way to make German influence and intellectual preponderance to be felt and acknowledged."[19] Brandi worked to secure some first class European writers for Heuser, wrote against liberalism in the *Civiltà Cattolica,* spoke to Camillo Cardinal Mazella, S.J., who had taught at Woodstock some years before, "of the noble work in which we are engaged," and all the while kept Heuser informed of his Roman activities in exposing Ireland, Bouquillon, and company.[20] Bishop Chatard prepared an article for the August, 1892, number of the *American Ecclesiastical Review* on the correct approach to the problem of total abstinence, to preserve it from its erring friends and to foster it within the bonds of discretion and practice. Archbishop Katzer also, four months before, discussed secret societies for readers of the journal, denied that Freemasons were the only forbidden group, and advocated a careful watch by the American bishops over doubtfully dangerous secret societies.[21]

[19] *ACHSP,* Zardetti to Heuser, St. Cloud, Jan. 2, 1889. Cf. also Jan. 16 and Mar. 5, 1892. Maes, Conway, and Messmer likewise had carried on a spirited correspondence with Heuser. At one point, after Bouquillon had answered Brandi's article in the *Civiltà Cattolica,* Messmer again revealed his balanced approach. He told Heuser: "Dr. Bouquillon's rejoinder to the *Civiltà Cattolica* was distributed last evening. There is no doubt that it deals hard knocks, some of which will hit the spot. It is the fault of those who went for the Dr. *blindly,* as so many of our German Catholic papers did. But there is one ugly note in it (p. 32, note 1) which I have no doubt comes from other quarters than Dr. Bouquillon's brains. It explains the whole fierce attack of German Catholic papers against Dr. B. merely on the ground that Germans are afraid they might be compelled to teach the English language in their parochial schools. This is simply an insult. How many Catholic schools in German parishes can the Dr. name us where English is not taught. The Germans ought to challenge him publicly to prove his ugly insinuation. The note, moreover, ignores the real cause of the onslaught, the fear that our parochial schools should be turned into State schools. This is the real cause" (Feb. 14, 1892).

[20] *ACHSP,* Brandi to Heuser, Rome, Jan. 12, 1892. Cf. also Dec. 26. On November 16, 1891, he stated: "The noisy Liberalism of certain American writers is well known in Rome. I need not tell you what our Fathers in the Church think of it."

[21] VII (Aug., 1892), pp. 101–106; VII (Sept., 1892), pp. 177–181; VII (Oct., 1892), pp. 254–258; VI (Apr., 1892), pp. 241–247. Both the questions of secret societies and temperance were divisive factors in the American Church at this time. For a treatment of the attitudes on secret societies, cf. Fergus McDonald, C.P., *The Catholic Church and the Secret Societies in the United States* (New York, 1946).

The temperance question was one of the most fundamental points of difference

But the leader and director of the campaign remained Monsignor Schröder. Not only was he speaking at German celebrations across the country, writing in numerous German Catholic newspapers, and penning his opinions to friends in Rome, but he also took the occasion of the publication at this time of a theological treatise, *I criteri theologici,* by the Italian Canon di Bartolo, to center his entire case around the errors of this book.[22] In a series of articles in the *American Ecclesiastical Review,* Schröder accused Bartolo of attenuating or minimizing Catholic doctrine, of being out of harmony with the spirit of the Church, injurious to her authority and opposed to filial obedience. He asserted that Bartolo was succumbing to the spirit of the times, which, as St. Augustine had said, was "like a river which often sweeps away the most eminent and most noble souls." He branded the Italian theologian as one who was attempting to reconcile the Church with the world in the spirit of the French and German liberal theological schools of the past two centuries. He further accused Bartolo of opposing the temporal power of the Pope as not being an infallible doctrine, and of having a direct kinship with Jansenism,

between Germans and Americanizers. Both Ireland and Keane were total abstainers, and many of the Irish American prelates fostered strong temperance campaigns. Such individuals as Griffin and Zurcher, with their wild defenses of abstinence from drink, did little to convince Catholics from the European continent of the validity of this campaign. Cf. *ICBU Journal,* July 1, 1891, and John T. Reilly, "Brewery of the St. Vincent's Archabbey. Celebrated St. Vincent Beer," *Collections in the Life and Times of J. Card. Gibbons* (McSherrytown and Martinsburg, 1890–1905), II, pp. 75–93, for examples of antagonism to the Germans because they adhered to their traditions in regard to beer and wine. For some ideas on the German position, cf. *Catholic Citizen,* Oct. 7, 1882, and Apr. 26, 1884. Chatard informed Heuser, in reference to his articles on temperance which were sound and practical, "You can hardly find a Catholic Temperance Society which is not more or less extreme. I do not want to offend them and I do not want to compromise myself" (Jan. 19, 1895). Archabbot Boniface Wimmer, O.S.B., expressed his sentiments to Abbot Benedict Braunmüller, O.S.B., of Metten Abbey, on the temperance campaign in the United States when he said: "What do you think of our temperance people? The Methodists, Baptists, also many Catholics, the Irish Bishops and Priests included, have set down, in their zeal against drunkenness and for the sanctification of the Sabbath, that from today on (3 July) no inn keeper, saloon keeper or wine dealer may sell wine, beer or schnapps, etc., etc., etc., to any person who does not belong to his family, or give it away, or drink with meals, under heavy fine or jail sentence?! *neque rure, neque in oppidis, neque in urbibus!* There was a Beer Revolution in Munich; but we must suffer it until the Prohibition Law will be abolished when the opposition wins the election. The misconduct of drunkards was to be sure bad enough, especially in the case of the Irish, while the Germans were not out of line when they drank their beer" (*AAM,* Wimmer to Braunmüller, St. Vincent Archabbey, July 3, 1887). For a thorough treatment of the temperance question, cf. Sister Joan Bland, S.N.D., *Hibernian Crusade* (Washington, 1951).

[22] Bartolo's work was first published at Torino in 1888; a French edition appeared in Paris in 1889.

Josephism, Febronianism, and Döllingerism in restricting the infallibility of the Church to revealed dogmas, and of turning theology into politics.[23] Likewise Schröder, with German scholarly thoroughness, but with an undue eagerness to associate European Catholic errors with the American Catholic climate, saw progressive and "scientific" theories taking root in the United States. He exclaimed to Heuser:

> Well, well, now you have a co-editor who will cause you plenty of trouble. Since you said A, you now have to say B. . . . How much on this side of the ocean do they indulge in this minimizing! In case they confront me with the statement: "We are Americans, this question is not for this country," in that case I ask St. Lawrence for a little patience. . . . I know that there are some in this country to whom charity and kindness of heart means more than theology. . . . There was a time in this country when a leader once warned me: "For our country only modern theology is fitting and the old heretics are all dead." Oh no, the heretics have a long life. And they are still sticking their heads out of the grave where they should have found rest in St. Peter, anno 1870. And there will not be wanting attempts to resurrect these theories in the future.[24]

The Washington professor proceeded very much in this vein, month after month, making war on liberalism, the while he inquired of Heuser if the latter was not reminded of the days in Germany before the Vatican Council. Cardinal Gibbons had given a hasty approval to the book of Bartolo upon the request of the author, and Ireland's organ, the *Northwestern Chronicle,* proceeded to attack Schröder's articles against the Italian canon as they appeared. Schröder informed Heuser:

> Inter Nos: Reverendissimus [Gibbons] told our Professor O'Gorman: He deplores my article because Bartolo is a book for our country! — Monsignor Ireland, as I am informed from a good source, has summoned up the powers to refute me (certainly in vain). That is strong pepper. Both gentlemen were here last week, but no one gave me the pleasure of expressing disproval of the critique. Enough: all this can only be a challenge to adhere more closely to the motto: no *Liberalism,* under any conditions, under no mask, and also not under that of Americanism. Archbishop Corrigan expressed his pleasure on this motto at our first meeting; his judgment is weightier in this matter than all the others.[25]

[23] *AER,* IV (Feb., 1891), pp. 115–132; IV (Mar., 1891), pp. 161–178; IV (Apr., 1891), pp. 286–305; V (July, 1891), pp. 51–65. Brandi continued the attack on liberalism with an article "Touchstone of Catholicity," VI (Feb., 1892), pp. 89–98.

[24] *ACHSP,* Schröder to Heuser, Washington, Jan. 12, 1891; Jan. 22, 1891.

[25] *Ibid.,* Feb. 7 and 9, 1891.

Letters poured in on Heuser, some favoring the series against Bartolo, others opposed to Schröder's effort, and convinced that the *Review* was pushing the interests of the Germans. On May 21, 1891, however, the Congregation of the Index condemned Bartolo's book and placed it on the *Index,* thus bringing the American comment to an end to the satisfaction of those who had written against the work. Schröder was exultant and informed Heuser that he was convinced the congregation and its prefect, Cardinal Mazella, S.J., would have condemned the book even without the demands he had made at Rome for that action.[26] Schröder now resolved to turn his attention to other aspects of the minimizing tendency and to the school question. He expressed his regret to Heuser:

> If I could only write English perfectly. Now I have to be content to write three or four articles in German every week for our German press which anyway is orthodox on the question.[27]

Reverend Thomas J. Shahan, professor of Church history in the Catholic University of America and future rector of that institution, indicated his displeasure at the *American Ecclesiastical Review* and its writers in a letter to O'Connell. He also expressed a point of view which unquestionably was shared by many others of the Americanizers. Shahan had sent two articles to O'Connell, one in defense of Archbishop Ireland and the other on the Pope and the World's Fair,[28] both of which he asked O'Connell to have translated into French and to have published in the *Moniteur de Rome* so that the Holy Father could see, as he said, that "we understand him, and appreciate his acts." Shahan then continued:

> My classes take up all of my time. I only wish I had more to take a

[26] *Ibid.,* Apr. 14, 1891.

[27] *Ibid.,* Jan. 27, 1892.

[28] At this same time Cardinal Gibbons likewise revealed his position in a letter to Ireland as to the procedure he should adopt in Rome: "Impress on Cardinal Ledochowski that we have a golden opportunity of bringing the sentiment of the country to the side of the Church — (and public sentiment is Emperor here, more powerful than the Kaiser). This will be done by showing that the Catholic religion and her people are in harmony with our political institutions. If on the contrary the German or any other foreign element is sustained in Rome, and some German Catholic papers are boasting that such is the fact, then the Church will be held back in her progress — the charge of our Protestant enemies that ours is a foreign church and dangerous to the country will be sustained, the true friends of religious progress will fall back discouraged, and then we will have peace, but it will be the peace of Warsaw. The saner part of the German priests and people see that the English language is fast becoming the language of the country. In this city several foreign priests have asked my permission to use English in their churches" (*AASP,* Gibbons to Ireland, Baltimore, Feb. 26, 1892).

hand in the controversies, such bad faith, secret tyranny, double-dealing, and distortion of the plain truth was seldom witnessed in the Church — never in our American Church history has there been such a spectacle. The motives of action on the part of our opponents are so clearly ambition, personal jealousy, & order-interests, that every non-Catholic sees it now.

I trust the right views will prevail at Rome, and the Church will not be saddled with a burden that a century of efforts will not rid her of.

The Catholics of the English-speaking race have toiled for three centuries to break down the accusations of disloyalty to government, intolerance, slavish submission to Rome in pure politics, and the like. Though a minority, we have worked wonders, and now here come the German mediaeval priest and members of an order, whose powers for harm are great, to upset the whole. May they reap confusion. My forthcoming article in the *American Ecclesiastical Review* "A Page from the Theology of the Catacombs" was sent in before this row began. You will not see my name again among the contributors to such a dangerous and stupid organ.[29]

Cardinal Gibbons was moved by similar sentiments when, after sending a long defense of Archbishop Ireland and his school plan directly to Leo XIII, he told Monsignor O'Connell:

Yesterday I prayed at Mass that the Lord might inspire him [the Holy Father], & that right & justice should prevail. It is not the Faribault school that is on trial, but the question to be decided is whether the Church is to be governed here by men or by children, — by justice & truth, or by diplomacy & intrigue, — whether the Church is to be honored as a bulwark of liberty & order, or to be despised & suspected as an enemy of our Institutions.[30]

Ireland had gone to Rome at this time to defend himself and his cause personally before the Holy Father and the Roman Curia. He had been encouraged to make the trip by O'Connell, who stated that a new movement was abroad in Rome to check the liberals and to patronize the conservatives in the United States. For it had been apparent for some years that there was a Roman division of opinion in regard to American relations between the cardinals of the Propaganda, on the one side, and the Pope and his secretary of state, on the other. Leo XIII and Rampolla were seemingly more sympathetic to the policies

[29] *ADR,* Shahan to O'Connell, Washington, Mar. 31, 1892.

[30] *ADR,* Gibbons to O'Connell, Baltimore, Mar. 1, 1892. Gibbons also expressed himself to Archbishop Ryan about Ireland, whom he never failed to support: "I am pained to see the abuse heaped on Archbishop Ireland. . . . I think Prelates of the American Church ought to stand by one another. . . . I am praying and sighing for peace" (*AAB,* 89-T-9, Gibbons to Ryan, Baltimore, Apr. 11, 1892, copy).

of the American "liberals," while the Propaganda stood fast by the American "conservatives." O'Connell had presented the whole case to Leo XIII, told the Pope that harmony had been broken in the United States, and that the feelings of the bishops had been wounded by what was termed the "obstinate course of the Propaganda." It was just such moves as these of O'Connell, however, that the opposite party back in the United States resented so deeply as being partisan and without authorization. Nonetheless, O'Connell continued to act in this capacity, and he reported that the Holy Father had been profoundly affected, had expressed his deep regret, and assured the rector of the American College that he desired relations with the American bishops to be intimate, cordial, and confiding. According to O'Connell, Leo XIII had proceeded to inform the cardinals at the Propaganda that he was *"dispiacentissimo,"* and that they had gone too fast. O'Connell felt that their leader had been Mazella, S.J., and he thus advised Ireland:

> Anyway, thank God, now it is ended and the tide is turning. Let the Bps. only be firm. But now it is *essential* that you *come to Rome after Easter.* Everybody expects it and the situation requires it. You must come on and confirm this new turn in events and pull the old up by the roots. The Holy Father is most anxious to see you and I told him you were coming. When he was speaking to me about your discourse and declaring his intention of studying it, I said you would be here soon to give light if necessary and it pleased and relieved him to hear it. You can do more in Rome in one week now than you can do in a year in America. The Prop. will be delighted to see you. . . . You have not treated your French friends well. . . . Catholic France is throbbing with your sentiments and they are hungering to hear from you. . . . So you must come. Do good like Manning for the toiling world and don't shrink into a simple Minnesotan. All Europe will echo your words and you can move the entire struggling mass.[31]

[31] *AASP,* O'Connell to Ireland, Rome, Nov. 10, 1891. Bishop McQuaid, who was always friendly to O'Connell, wrote to the rector concerning Ireland's trip to Rome: "The newspapers tell us that Ireland will soon leave for Rome. As it is not his *ad limina,* we wonder what takes him there. He is the head and front of the new liberalistic party in the American Church. If he would stay at home a little more, and mind his own diocese, the latter would be the gainer. He is away from his diocese only a little more than Cardinal Gibbons" (*ADR,* McQuaid to O'Connell, Rochester, n.d.).

Goller also warned Baumgarten in Rome that Ireland was coming: "I am afraid he will skillfully maneuver and deceive many, returning with still greater arrogance to place the purest Americanism on the throne. . . . We German Catholics would accomplish the greatest results if we had our definite rights. But thus we struggle, educate the people and then the Irish priests come and snatch them for themselves. Otherwise the Irish priests would starve. At last one arrives at the despairing

Too often extravagant and sensational messages of this kind were flashed by O'Connell to his friends across the ocean, but in this case Ireland's subsequent triumph across Europe more than bore out the rector's prophecy. He began in Rome. There the Archbishop of St. Paul presented his case to the Holy Father, the Propaganda, and to Cardinal Rampolla at the Secretariate of State. To Rampolla he especially stressed the importance of the Holy See continuing and cementing its friendship with France and the United States. Nor did he fail to bring Cahenslyism into the picture again, for, as he informed Gibbons: "Rampolla is all right. . . . He is the dead enemy of the 'Triplice alleanza' — the dark advance of which over America I pictured to him in Cahenslyism and its allies. I am all right with him, and he inspires the Pope."[32] The heated controversy that had arisen over Ireland's school plan was finally resolved on April 21, 1892, by a committee of five cardinals of the Propaganda in a decision which was approved by the Holy Father on the same day. The Faribault-Stillwater agreement was approved with the famous words *"tolerari potest,"* while at the same time the decrees of the Councils of Baltimore were declared to remain firmly in force. Nine days later Ledochowski penned a personal letter to Ireland, expressing the great pleasure that was felt by the Holy See at the filial respect and obedience he had evidenced. Thereupon the Archbishop of St. Paul moved north into France where, at the private suggestion of Leo XIII, he

---

thought: So long as we live we hold the cabin. Après nous le déluge" (Baumgarten, *Wanderfahrten, Europäische und Americanische Erinnerungen* [Traunstein, 1928], pp. 157–158). In the same letter Goller informed Baumgarten that he had asked both Katzer and Zardetti to send their Peter's Pence through him, and he also reported on his "biting allusion" to Archbishop Ireland at Kenrick's jubilee which was warmly applauded and understood by the majority. But Martin I. J. Griffin felt that: "it is plain that Archbishop Ireland left his country for his country's good. We hope he will be away until he knocks dead Cahenslyism and routs its abetters as he did the prize-fighters.

"America requires some one in Rome to prevent foreignism fingering our plums or managing us as they do the wilds of Africa. Some Italians haven't discovered America yet" (*ICBU Journal,* Feb. 3, 1892).

[32] *AAB,* 89-P-1, Ireland to Gibbons, Rome, Feb. 21, 1891. Bishop McGolrick informed Gibbons of his latest communication from Rome: "I just had a letter from Rome; — and the cleaning of the Augean stables was but play to the labor of going through the baskets of pamphlets, manuscripts, and letters sent against Archbishop Ireland and his co-laborers in the work of rooting out prejudice and customs grown grey in German and French backwoods and 12th Century parishes.

"Each nation grows up in this country with its own language and customs, even to beer and bolognas, and don't go near the Protestants — to touch them is defilement. Two hours will bring me into the centre of Germany in America — where children of the Irish have to speak German or go without instruction. *God help us"* (*AAB,* 89-Q-4, McGolrick to Gibbons, Duluth, Mar. 3, 1892).

delivered in Paris on June 13, 1892, his masterful plea for democracy, in support of the French Government against the conservative and monarchical elements in the French Church, and in defense of a rallying of the Church behind the Republic. It was, indeed, a significant triumph for all that he and his friends had stood for.[33]

In the United States the *"tolerari potest"* decision was interpreted as full approval, and a sweeping victory by both the Americanizers and the greater part of the press of the land. But the opposition viewed it as having given approval only to a local arrangement and nothing more. In this sense letters were sent to the Vatican by the bishops of the Provinces of New York and Cincinnati in defense of the parochial school system. In the case of the New York prelates, they firmly denied the reports made to the Holy Father by the Americanizers that there had been danger of a persecution of the Church in the United States if the conduct and views of Ireland had been condemned. Archbishop Ireland's letter to Reverend James C. Byrne, pastor of Immaculate Conception Church, Minneapolis, carried in the St. Paul *Dispatch* of May 10, 1892, also antagonized the German Catholics of the country because of the sweeping statement to the effect that "the so-called Faribault plan is now formally allowed in spite of Germans and Jesuits." In less than a month O'Connell warned Ireland that he should temper this statement and explain it as meaning only those Germans who had opposed him, because Germans in both Europe and America were deeply hurt at the slur and were writing vigorously to Rome.[34] Feelings ran high and the newspapers

[33] Cahensly wrote to Baumgarten, asking him to supply information on events transpiring in Rome, and he then commented on Ireland's success there: "According to information I have received Msgr. Ireland has won so much influence at Rome, and so charmed the Holy Father and the Cardinals, that it would be hard to shake that influence. Cardinal Ledochowski and his secretary Msgr. Mesczynski especially are entirely enthusiastic toward him. In the interest of the welfare of our Holy Church I am very upset, for the liberalizing ideas of Msgr. Ireland cannot be advantageous to the progress of the Church in America. Have you no advice, or is it not so bad" (Baumgarten, *op. cit.*, p. 167). Goller also commented to Baumgarten: "As I have said previously [Ireland] has led the Romans about by the nose and returns home triumphant" (*ibid.*, p. 158). Gibbons felt quite differently on the matter, for not only did he write a warm defense of the Minnesota school plan, but he also followed up this letter with another in which he recommended Ireland's name for the cardinalate on the grounds of personal merit and public reputation (*AAB*, 89-Q-1, Gibbons to Leo XIII, Baltimore, Mar. 1, 1892, copy; 89-T-14, Gibbons to Rampolla, Baltimore, Apr. 15, 1892, copy).

[34] *AASP*, O'Connell to Ireland, Rome, June 6, 1892. Ireland followed this advice, and in a sermon at St. Bernard's Church, St. Paul, he reiterated his position on Germans and other immigrants in the Church, as well as his policy of administration toward their parishes. As at Chaska in 1888, so now he declared it the duty of bishops and clergy to minister in foreign tongues to those who needed such care;

took sides with obvious delight, while Archbishops Corrigan and Ireland granted contradictory interviews to the press with surprising acrimony. The question was resolved soon thereafter on the practical level at Faribault and Stillwater, where the agreement had broken down, and where the American Protective Association had entered upon the scene in Minnesota with open opposition to the plan on the grounds that it was against their interpretation of the principle of separation of Church and State. Ireland annulled the lease of the Faribault parochial school on October 22, 1893, and the theoretical victory he had won at Rome was lost at home for other reasons. His farseeing project did not become general practice, intransigents both within and without the Church claimed a victory for the status quo, and a reasonable adjustment of the obvious injustice of Catholics paying educational taxes without sharing in those taxes failed to be realized.

Archbishop Ireland had himself associated Cahenslyism with the school question, and by so doing he had continued that subject as an issue in American Catholic circles. He likewise associated opposition to himself with a supposed German-Austrian-Italian political movement. But the evidence would indicate that his opponents were conservatives, both in Europe and America, who feared more his innovations than they did the nationality issue. Nationality was not the

---

no bishop in the United States had ever refused people this right. He defended his record in caring for all Catholics and insisted anew that he never had any intention of interfering with the teaching of German language in German parochial schools. But he wanted English spoken, desired that immigrants not isolate themselves from the community, but rather that they, no matter what their national origin, fit themselves for life, march in the front ranks, occupy the highest of offices and honor, and elevate the Church by honoring and elevating themselves. He then observed: "There are, of course, those suspicious and unreasoning spirits among Catholics of foreign tongues, whose password to cover every folly and every ambition is nationalism, or so-called patriotism, that will profit of the difficulties of times and places, of the occasional impossibilities for bishops to procure reliable priests of foreign tongues, to praddle aloud that foreign-speaking Catholics are neglected and despised. Such men do the bishops of America supreme injustice. . . .

"I am not — understand me well — urging anything approaching a total or partial neglect of the mother tongue. I merely recognize the fact that such neglect, voluntary or forced, does occur and will occur. We, who regard religion as paramount to all else, must act with an eye to this fact, and so provide that, whatever else passes away, religion shall not pass away. It were fatal to the religious faith of our descendants to bind it up in America with any foreign tongue. It were fatal to this faith to say of it that, a foreign tongue forgotten, faith is forgotten.

"Faith is independent and supreme above all tongues. Tongues are but its instruments, and its own life should be prominently brought out as being endowed with immortality, whatever be at one time or another its perishing instruments of form" (Memphis *Catholic Journal,* Sept. 24, 1892).

dominating factor with all the "intransigents," since some Irish American prelates and several Jesuit Fathers united with the German Americans in advancing their cause. Accordingly, when Ireland granted an interview in mid-March to the Roman correspondent of the Boston *Pilot,* his statements brought sharp response from the German Catholic press. He spoke of the multitude of letters which had been sent to Rome by opponents of his school plan and of the determination of the Holy See to maintain hierarchical unity in the Church of the United States. He then stated: "But strange to say, this . . . does not prevent constant renewal of efforts. There are people in America and in Europe who are under the positive belief that the country is a wild Congo, to be partitioned off into so many foreign colonies." And to this assertion the Archbishop added a further caustic reference to Cahensly's "lie in his famous memorial of last summer" concerning losses to the Catholic faith among immigrants.[35] Statements of this kind by Ireland, Bishop McGolrick, and Father Gmeiner, whose latest pamphlet was circulating at that time, brought the whole question out into the open again.[36] It was, however, the promised governmental intervention in the Cahenslyism quarrel which brought the controversy to a head. "Let the question go before Congress," O'Connell had advised Gibbons, and at the strategic moment when Ireland was in Rome awaiting the decision of the Propaganda in his favor the blow was struck.

[35] Boston *Pilot,* Mar. 19, 1892.

[36] In January Reverend Henry A. Brann, of St. Agnes Church, New York, had also attacked Cahenslyism, quoting figures to show that the Lucerne statistics on losses were exaggerated, and finishing up with words that could only antagonize with their insulting connotations: "We want no foreign bishops here, with the stamp of Kaiser Wilhelm or of Franz Joseph or of the Carbonaro Crispi on their mitres. We take European immigrants and we improve their condition, physically, mentally, and morally. Heaven knows many of them are poor specimens of European civilization and of European Christianity! We say to fault-finders from Austria, purify the corrupt capital of your half-infidel empire; you French Gascons, look to the beams in your own eyes; you Machiavellian intriguers at Rome, go preach the Gospel to the Camorra of Naples and to the Mafia of Sicily. We say to the Marchese Landi that until he and his countrymen free Leo XIII from the chains which they have permitted to be fastened around the feet of his authority, they are in no position to criticize the Catholicity of other nations" ("Mr. Cahensly and the Church in the United States," *CW,* LIV [Jan., 1892], pp. 568–581). Brann's statistics were furnished by John Gilmary Shea, who, at Archbishop Corrigan's suggestion, had prepared a series of articles refuting the accusation of serious Catholic losses which ran in the New York *Catholic News* from June 28–November 22, 1891. Gibbons and Corrigan planned on combining Brann and Shea's articles for foreign publication in rebuttal of the Lucerne Memorial. In these letters Corrigan speaks favorably of Brann's article. Cf. *AANY,* Shea to Corrigan, Elizabeth, Nov. 3, 1891; Gibbons to Corrigan, Baltimore, Nov. 18 and 19, 1891; *AAB,* 89-E-9, Corrigan to Gibbons, New York, Dec. 16, 1891; *AANY,* Corrigan to Gibbons, Dec. 22, 1891, copy.

Cushman Kellogg Davis, Republican United States Senator from Minnesota, had been preparing an attack on Cahensly and had been awaiting an opportune moment to deliver a speech on the floor of the Senate against foreign interference in American life. Professor Thomas O'Gorman, of the Catholic University of America, who had come to the University from Minnesota and who was later to be a suffragan bishop of Archbishop Ireland at Sioux Falls, South Dakota, reported to Ireland at this time that a senate speech was ready:

> I saw Davis a few nights ago. He is fully prepared and most anxious to launch out on the subject, the moment he sees the opportunity. He expects it soon. Two questions are soon to come up that will give occasion, the exclusion of the Chinese, and immigration. Anxious as he is — I assure you he thinks his re-election depends very much on you, now that Merriam very lately has announced he is out of the race for the Senatorship — he dare not drag this particular question in by hook or crook, without rhyme or reason; and he sees no way of making an opportunity, it must present itself.[37]

The opportunity came on April 22, 1892, when, in the course of an address on the Chinese Exclusion Act, Davis concluded with a presentation of the Cahensly question, during which he declared:

> There is more matter for profound concern in the attempts of Herr Cahensly made last year to denationalize American institutions and plant as many nations as there are people of foreign tongues in our midst than in all the Chinese questions which have arisen since 1858.
>
> He proposes to use the power of the Catholic hierarchy to bring about this great political result. I rejoice that I can speak upon this subject without the offense of bringing in religious matters, because it is infinitely to his renown that Leo XIII, the greatest statesman since Ganganelli who has sat in the Chair of St. Peter, repulsed the attempt

[37] *ADR,* O'Gorman to Ireland, New York, Apr. 15, 1892. Cushman K. Davis was elected to the United States Senate in 1887 by the Minnesota legislature, after he had been in retirement for eleven years following his service as Governor of Minnesota. He framed and championed the dependent pension act of 1890, as chairman of the Senate pension committee, which won him the support of veterans, including Archbishop Ireland. The re-election which O'Gorman speaks of here was that of 1893, which Davis won by a majority of one. William Watts Folwell, *op. cit.,* III, 204, states that it was "claimed by friends of Senator Davis that a conspiracy had been concocted to frustrate his election on the first ballot and to bring forward at an opportune moment thereafter the name of a prominent Republican on whom it was hoped all could unite." Folwell says Davis blamed Governor William Rush Merriam for this move. There is no direct evidence of Ireland's support of Davis for re-election except a *Northwestern Chronicle* editorial of October 28, 1892, in which it was stated that "Senator Davis has a claim on Minnesota which this state cannot afford to ignore. He has carefully guarded its interests and won fame for it in the councils of nations."

as soon as it was formally submitted to him. But this attempt was not instigated by the American hierarchy at all. I believe it met with the reprobation of Cardinal Gibbon [*sic*], and I have reason to know it met with the reprobation of Archbishop Ireland. . . .

It is perfectly amazing throughout this entire memorial how utterly oblivious this intruder is to the fact that there is an American nationality, an American people, destined to become throughout an American stock. We are to his mind a nation upon whom the political intriguers of the European world are to operate all their own theories at their own sweet will. . . .

There was never, Mr. President, a more infamous attempt to prostitute religious power to political purposes than the one proposed in that memorial. This man is no inconsiderable man. He moves with no inconsiderable allies. He is, or was, a member of the Prussian Diet [*sic*]. It is stated that Herr von Schlözer, the German representative at Rome, is in hearty accord with him and supported this memorial; that Austrian families of high rank, moving in noble and royal circles, were interested in the scheme. It is to the glory of the American Catholic hierarchy that they have fought this proposition and are fighting it to-day. With a man less wise than the present Pontiff very serious consequences might have ensued.[38]

Quite naturally, Cahensly was stung by these charges made by a United States Senator, and he replied with a statement to the press as well as an open letter to Davis in which he accused him of irresponsible, malicious, and systematic misrepresentation of the Lucerne petition. He denied unequivocally that there had been any nationalistic or political background to his endeavors, that Windthorst, von Schlözer, or any other statesmen or diplomats had sponsored the memorial. He detailed the aims and history of the St. Raphaelsverein and pointed out that the only country benefiting from these charitable activities had been the United States, since the great majority of German emigrants had settled there. Cahensly then attempted to

[38] *Congressional Record,* 52 Cong., 1 sess. (Apr. 22, 1892), pp. 3532–3533. Davis' comparison of Leo XIII with Ganganelli was in obvious bad taste. Lorenzo Cardinal Ganganelli was elected Pope as Clement XIV in 1769, and on July 21, 1773, forced by the Bourbon courts, he suppressed the Society of Jesus in his brief *Dominus et Redemptor*. The society was restored on August 17, 1814, by Pius VII. It would be remarkable knowledge for a man of Davis' background to know the full implication of this remark. Could it have been directed at the Jesuits who were then opposing Ireland's stand on education and Cahenslyism? Philip Des Marais, in his "John Ireland in American Politics, 1886–1906" (unpublished master's dissertation, Georgetown University, Washington, D. C., 1950), p. 58, asks: "Was this a thinly veiled suggestion that the Pope should in like manner yield to the demands of the U.S. Government? This was one of the 'bitter things' that Ireland had forewarned Rome of."

explain to Davis, and, of course, to his international reading public, the reasons why Catholics of European countries were interested in the welfare of their brethren across the seas:

> The preservation of religion is an imperative prerequisite of social, economic, and political order, in public and private life, on your side of the Atlantic as well as on ours. Religion has become an all-important public matter of all civilized countries and all governments, since the Socialist heresy has organized on an international scope and threatens the foundations of all nations and governments. American freedom, which I have always highly esteemed, permits every individual full participation in industry and commerce and in the political and social life of the nation. European countries and their governments cannot be indifferent to the danger that their emigrants to America, the far-reaching influence of whom on the Old World is growing rapidly, might succumb to the allurements of Socialism because of religious neglect. America, at least those Americans who cherish Christianity and wish to save the nation from the Socialist peril, ought to be grateful to European countries that try, as far as they can within their own jurisdiction, to save America from the Red Deluge. . . . It is self-understood, of course, that they cannot, shall not, and will not meddle in internal American affairs.[39]

Cahensly likewise advocated once more what he had been urging for years, namely, international co-operation in emigrant care, and he concluded with the following dignified and gentlemanly request:

> As a member of a legislative body of one of the foremost European States I request of a member of the highest legislative body of the North American Union compliance with a duty toward a colleague, namely, that the Senator avail himself of the first opportunity to announce at the Capitol in Washington my statement: "My efforts have no connection whatever with any political powers in Europe."[40]

When Davis was informed by the press of Cahensly's letter before he had himself received it, he merely remarked to a reporter: "It is not likely that there is anything in it which will change my views as to the enormity of Cahensly's offense against our institutions." The senator from Minnesota neither retracted his assertion, nor was his answer of June 7, 1892, to Cahensly anything more than a brief acknowledgment of receipt of the German representative's letter.[41]

Just before the Davis episode the boards of directors of the St. Raphael societies of Germany, Austria, Belgium, and Italy had drawn

[39] *Der Wanderer,* June 15, 1892.
[40] *Ibid.*
[41] *Der Wahrheitsfreund,* Dec. 7, 1892.

up and forwarded another letter to Cardinal Rampolla on the as yet unsolved problem of their original memorial of February, 1891, and the newspaper quotations of Rampolla's letter to Gibbons of April, 1891. They wrote:

April, 1892

YOUR EMINENCE:

Some time ago the Roman papers published a letter Your Eminence addressed to His Eminence Cardinal Gibbons, Archbishop of Baltimore, in reference to the memorandum submitted in April of last year to the Holy Father in the name of the European St. Raphael societies.

We have observed with great joy that the Holy Father approves of the societies which have been established for the temporal and spiritual protection of the many Catholic emigrants to America.

The newspapers further report a remark of Your Eminence to the effect that certain societies, for instance the German one, maintain that it is one of the most effective means for the attainment of their goal to secure a special representative in the American episcopate for each national group of emigrants. We do not know if this passage of the letter is rendered accurately. But since it gives rise, not only to criticism hardly in accord with Christian charity, but also to dangerous attacks on the work itself, we beg Your Eminence to permit us briefly to restate our position.

We have felt particularly hurt by the accusation that we intended to interfere in the internal administration of the Church; even more that we desired to overthrow the hierarchical order prevailing in the United States by asking for national bishops who would have jurisdiction over their compatriots. It will suffice to repeat the pertinent sentence of our Memorial to prove that this assumption is wrong and not in accord with our intentions nor with our Catholic sentiments. We declared:

"It seems very desirable that the Catholics of every nationality have in the episcopate of the country, wherever this is considered possible, several bishops of the same origin."

The meaning of this wish cannot surely be ambiguous when expressed in a document addressed to the Father of Christianity.

We set forth with Catholic frankness the dangers which we know from our experience in emigration matters, and we submitted to the sublime wisdom and inspired judgment of the Holy Father some means which seemed suitable to us for removing or reducing the spiritual perils associated with emigration. We confined ourselves, as was our duty, to expressing a wish, namely, the desire to know what the highest authority would think of the possibility, if circumstances permit, of granting to the different nationalities one or several bishops of their own nationality in the American episcopate.[42]

[42] Cahensly, *Der St. Raphaelsverein,* pp. 47–48.

Within a few days after receiving this communication the papal Secretary of State, on April 23, 1892, responded to Prince Isenburg-Birstein, president of the German society, as follows:

> YOUR HIGHNESS:
>
> I have received the address signed by Your Highness and many eminent persons who are not only members of your society but also of other societies devoting themselves in various countries to emigration of Catholics to the United States of America. Because of its importance this document deserved to be presented to the Holy Father and I have not failed to perform this duty. Therefore, I am now able to inform Your Highness that His Holiness has received with satisfaction the explanations contained in the address — explanations which confirm the purity of sentiments animating the signers, which, however, had never been doubted.
>
> Trusting that you will continue as good Catholics to protect your emigrating brethren in the faith and that you will always willingly submit to the decisions which the bishops and particularly the Holy See will make for the religious well-being of emigrants, His Holiness, from the fulness of his heart imparts to the different societies mentioned in the above address, as well as to each individual member, the Apostolic Blessing.
>
> In conveying this message to Your Highness, I have the honor of assuring you of my high esteem.[43]

In previous discussions on Cahenslyism this letter has not been given the attention or emphasis which it plainly deserves. It was not a noncommittal form letter from the Secretariate of State, but a clear recognition by the Holy Father, through his Secretary of State, of the good intentions of the Lucerne memorialists and a blessing on their continued efforts. The suggestions of the memorials were quietly rejected by a failure to mention them — of that there would be no further doubt — but the wild accusations and insinuations against the petitioners were repudiated by this papal blessing, bestowed on the leaders and members of the branch societies who were labeled as men of good will. The Apostolic Nuncio to Bavaria, Archbishop Antonio Agliardi, also sent a letter of reassurance to Cahensly in the same vein as that of Rampolla's, in which he further clearly indicated that the Holy See was far from viewing the Lucerne memorialists as conspirators. Agliardi stated:

> To be sure the St. Raphael Society has not escaped the fate of all work of God which, especially in the beginning, meets opposition of all

[43] *Ibid.*, pp. 48–49.

kinds. But I am convinced that the society will soon triumph over all misfortune. Your Excellency as well as the directors should take courage and double your efforts to serve with confidence the glory of God and the salvation of souls. As far as I am concerned, I have not failed to inform the Holy See on more than one occasion of the difficult situation encountered by the St. Raphael Society, to petition the Holy Father for fitting decisions, to remove difficulties, and to encourage the work of Christian love of neighbor and of religion.[44]

The final official letter on the Lucerne Memorial was sent in May, 1892, by Cardinal Ledochowski of the Propaganda through Cardinal Gibbons to the hierarchy of the United States. Like Rampolla a year previous, the prefect again reassured the American hierarchy that the Holy See desired bishops to be chosen only on the basis of procedures approved at the Third Council of Baltimore. There was no intention of infringing upon the bishops' proper jurisdiction. Then Ledochowski treated of a matter which was of long duration in the United States and which extended back to the days of the first American bishop. It concerned the divisive factions who were working for the appointment of bishops. He stated:

You are certainly aware that on the occasion of vacancies in episcopal sees in the United States diverse commotions very often arise among both clergy and people, which . . . are growing more serious and frequent as time goes on. The effects which usually result in such cases are neither trivial nor hidden, nor are they of such a nature that this Sacred Congregation can pass them over in silence. For we have now and again seen clergy and people active beyond their legitimate rights in the nominations of candidates for the episcopal office; contentions are diffused and are fomented through the press. But what particularly fosters these contentions is the violent zeal with which each faction endeavors to secure Bishops of its own nationality, as if private utility and not the Church's interest were the end to be looked for in the selection of a suitable pastor. . . . It is desirable, therefore, that in every diocese both clergy and people be warned of the deplorable results which come from contests of this kind; that they not only rend asunder the bond of harmony which should exist among souls, and relax the vigor of ecclesiastical discipline, but become a stumbling-block and scandal to non-Catholics as well.[45]

[44] *ADCV,* Agliardi to Cahensly, Munich, Mar. 27, 1893, copy. Cardinal Krementz, Archbishop of Cologne, also wrote a letter of sympathy in the name of the Fulda Conference of the German hierarchy to Prince Isenburg-Birstein on September 17, 1892. He expressed "the warmest interest in the efforts of the St. Raphaelsverein," and enclosed a personal donation of 1,000 marks ($250).

[45] *AAB,* 89-V-10, Ledochowski to Gibbons, Rome, May 15, 1892. Gibbons, in an earlier letter to Leo XIII, thanked him for his benevolence toward the Church

This was an obvious reference and rebuke to the recent disturbances over successions to sees where Germans and non-Germans had formed parties in favor of their respective candidates. But it cannot be held that the Germans were being reprimanded exclusively, for reports from Rome during the previous year had indicated the displeasure of the Propaganda at similar efforts emanating from non-German circles. True, the Lucerne petition in reference to the appointment of bishops was clearly denied by this letter but, too, a rebuke to all concerned in previous controversies was as clearly administered. If Rampolla, Simeoni, and Ledochowski gave assurances to the Americans that the petitions from Lucerne would be rejected, so did Rampolla and Agliardi make it evident in Germany, that the petitioners were in good standing. Moreover, their motives were understood in Rome, and far from being under a cloud, the St. Raphael Society through its branches was encouraged to continue its work among emigrants. Thus again it would appear that the whole Cahensly episode can in no way be pictured in stark hues of white and black, but that the area of gray must be blended over into each camp.

In the meantime, Monsignor Schröder journeyed to Mainz in the summer of 1892 for the thirty-ninth *Katholikentag* to give testimony to the general assembly of German Catholic societies that the American St. Raphael society and its leaders were not suspect among the group he represented in the United States. By moving from the journalistic forum into the public forum Schröder planned to indicate how liberal and minimizing theories had been at the basis of the attack on Cahensly. After Cahensly himself had again reviewed the whole affair and characterized the politico-nationalistic charges made against him as "a thoroughly laughable and silly insinuation," Schröder rose to speak. He began by stating that no defense of Cahensly was necessary, but he then proceeded to deliver a most ardent defense. He associated his own efforts with those of Corrigan, Katzer, Zardetti, and Messmer, and declared:

> But what is Cahenslyism? Although this question may be delicate, I stand here freely and will answer openly [bravo], not so much for you, my friends, as for certain Americans on the other side of the great

in the United States, and he included a paragraph on national bishops: "we did all in our power to dispel this idle apprehension, especially when we saw the matter bitterly discussed in the public press, and looked upon with disfavor by the government. Our works remained, however, of no avail, until the voice of Your Holiness was heard; that put an end to all discussion, and manifested to our government the wisdom and prudence with which Catholic affairs are handled by Your Holiness" (*AAB*, 89-W-8, Gibbons to Leo XIII, Jan. 14, 1892, copy).

> ocean, to whom, we speak directly, I shall convey testimony over this water to the truth concerning a most worthy man as well as the deeds he has so meritoriously realized [loud applause]. I have no hesitation in declaring clearly that the name Cahenslyite is already an honorable title, and that it ever more will be honorable [long bravo].
>
> We ask then: What really is Cahenslyism? Further: What is it as the war cry of the supposedly Catholic full-blooded American and personification of patriotism in North America?
>
> Without Cahensly, no Cahenslyism. Thus who is Cahensly? That we must understand above all in order to comprehend the entire comedy, as well as the great unfairness of this attack and accusation.
>
> Who is Cahensly? Beautiful Limburg answers us: he is our countryman, a true pearl of our land, the example of the true Catholic man . . . in one word: a nobleman in the truest sense of the word. I ask his constituents from dear Lahnthal and Westerwald, and they answer with joyful pride that Cahensly is a glorious phalanx of the Center, true and courageous. . . . The representatives of the Center say to me that the representative from Limburg occupies no ostracized place in their ranks; no, we cannot do without our true colleague and friend in the Center.[46]

This obvious effort of Schröder to point out that Cahensly was both an exemplary pioneer in emigrant care and a member of the Center Party was justifiable, but it was hardly prudent at a time when that precise relationship was being so hotly questioned in the United States. To emphasize the Center as Schröder did gave a handle to some Americans to continue their charges that Cahensly's efforts were political. Schröder then continued to praise his emigrant work and to declare that emigrants from Buenos Aires to Boston, from Quito to San Francisco, owed their care while emigrating to Cahensly. He proceeded to define Cahenslyism as a "restless endeavor of sacrificing charity, a true part of the resolution of the social question, so that, as an instrument of divine providence, it may improve and seek to alleviate, in all concerns of body and soul, the condition of poor and helpless emigrants." It was not the bone of discord nor the bugbear which Americanizers had thrown into the Church in the United States in order further to harmonize their own Catholicism in an inconceivable blend. Nor had Cahensly offended the American episcopate by interfering in American affairs. He had rather exercised a right which all Europeans possessed of being interested in their descendants in the new world so that they might gain the

[46] *Verhandlungen der 39. General-Versammlung der katholischen Vereine Deutschlands in Mainz, 28. August-1. September 1892* (Mainz, 1892), pp. 503–504. Schröder spoke on August 31 at the general session of the St. Raphaelsverein.

esteem of their new fellow citizens and might thus come to observe a true and sound American patriotism. Schröder derided in forceful language the charges that Cahensly had acted as a tool of the Prussian or Austrian Government for the appointment of foreign bishops. Every Catholic, he stated, had a right to send memorials to the Holy See, and with this principle the Monsignor arrived at the main point of his discourse, namely, that the Holy Father was Pope also in America, and these attacks on foreignism and foreign interference in the territory of the Monroe Doctrine did not apply to the Catholic Church. Accordingly, Schröder affirmed, the nativistic attacks were actually against the full and universal jurisdiction of the Papacy itself.[47]

Here, clearly, was Schröder's practical application of the thesis which he had first advanced in the columns of the *American Ecclesiastical Review,* and which he was now carrying into the open and applying against the Americanizers. To him the latter were modern minimizers who were attempting to lessen papal jurisdiction over the American Church and they were, turning their own arguments against them, nationalistic rather than Catholic. Schröder did not limit this attack to the meeting in Mainz, but as soon as he returned to the United States in the late fall he wrote to Archbishop Corrigan from Allentown, Pennsylvania, where he was staying with Reverend John B. Maus, pastor of Sacred Heart Church, and reported on his refutation of the "calumnies of which this model Catholic [Cahensly] has been the object." The yearly *Katholikentag* of German Catholics in the United States was approaching, and Schröder sketched the line of attack he planned to develop at the coming sessions in Newark. He asked for Corrigan's approval and advice on the points which he was going to make, "naturally without too direct allusions," against liberalism and hypernationalism among American Catholics. He informed the Archbishop that he was coming to New York to see him personally, as he did not trust himself on the frank position he had taken, and wished to maintain on questions agitating the Church. He also informed Corrigan that Rampolla had written to him through

[47] *Ibid.,* pp. 503–507. Dr. Joseph Pohle, of the Catholic University of America, accompanied Schröder to this gathering. After Schröder finished, Pohle confirmed in a short statement what his companion had said. Lieber then rose to praise both priests as "the two champions of Catholic Germanism in America." Lieber also asked the audience not to bring all they had heard into the general sessions of the convention because every word on the subject would be a further cause of calumny. Cahensly again took the floor and stated that he did not care about himself personally, but that the untruths were harming the work he represented (pp. 507–508).

Bishop Zardetti, and in the name of the Holy Father, that he approved entirely of what was termed his "courageous defense, notably in America." Schröder thought the time had arrived to deal openly and forcefully with this faction in the American Church.[48]

Not only did Monsignor Schröder again defend Cahensly and speak on the subject of liberalism and nationalism at the sixth annual *Katholikentag,* held in Newark under the sponsorship of Bishop Wigger on September 26–29, 1892, but Archbishop Corrigan celebrated the opening pontifical Mass and delivered a speech. This address was the clearest defense made up to that time by a non-German, of Cahensly, the St. Raphael Society, and the German Congresses. Corrigan began by declaring that he was in hearty sympathy with the objects of the convention. At that time, he continued, duty to God and the Church was displayed by two crucial tests: devotion

[48] *AANY,* Schröder to Corrigan, Allentown, Pennsylvania, n.d. John Conway, editor of the *Northwestern Chronicle,* entered the fray again with an article on "Cahenslyism Versus Americanism," *Review of Reviews,* VI (Aug., 1892), pp. 43–48, in which he expanded on the thesis that foreign powers were entering a wedge in the United States. Then he named three groups as encouraging foreignism in the country: editors of German Catholic newspapers, German priests, such as Abbelen, Tappert, Schröder, Bonneman, Walburg, Färber, Mühlsiepen, John B. Duffner, of St. Peter's Church, Pittsburgh, Paul Hölscher, of St. Louis' Church, Buffalo, and William Netsträter, of St. Joseph's Church, Wilmette, Illinois; bishops, among whom he listed Wigger, Zardetti, and Katzer. Concerning Katzer he said: "Among these Archbishop Katzer of Milwaukee holds a first place," while characterizing him as a protégé of Cahensly.

Katzer was deeply wounded at this new slander and protested vigorously to Gibbons: "Your Eminence will undoubtedly recollect what has transpired at our meeting in St. Louis, at which in the presence of all the Archbishops I have repudiated any and every knowledge of and connection with the Luzerne conference and its subsequent petition to the Propaganda and the Holy Father. I may add, that even the very name of Cahensly was unknown to me so much so, that when I read his name first in the Am. Papers, I did not know whether he was a Swiss or German or Slave [*sic*]. . . .

"I am an Austrian by birth, Cahensly is a member of the German Reichstag and Baron Schloetzer [*sic*] was Prussian Ambassador — whether they have expressed themselves concerning me or not, I cannot and I do not know, but suppose they have, is this to be laid at my door, will this justify any ecclesiastic to make accusations 'of even conspiring with foreign powers' and this against an Archbishop. . . .

"To my knowledge I have given not even a shadow of ground, which could justify those false and most hateful assertions.

"If I hold different opinions in the School question and with regard to societies is the [*sic*] a reason to belie me in a manner which is almost diabolical" (*AAB,* 90-B-4, Katzer to Gibbons, Milwaukee, Aug. 3, 1892). Gibbons replied that he had not read the article, but that he regretted very much this unjust and injurious attack. The Cardinal accepted Katzer's disavowal since, as he said, his word was sufficient, and he took pleasure in recording his sentiments (*AAB,* 90-B-9, Gibbons to Katzer, Baltimore, Aug. 14, 1892, copy).

to the Holy See and devotion to Christian education. On both of these touchstones of the Catholic faith the German Catholic congresses had given triumphant and conspicuous evidence. The Archbishop of New York discussed the temporal power of the pope and parochial education, emphasizing points he had advanced in previous years. He then arrived at the core of his message:

> I see further on your programme a discourse on the "Love of Our Country." Delicacy forbids entering into the merits of a question which has already elicited much controversy. I do not propose to discuss it, but yet, as we are all here as a band of brothers, may I not at least, putting aside controversy, quote certain *facts* that cannot be disputed. The first fact is this: When it was supposed that measures were in contemplation to foist foreign influences upon the United States, the St. Raphael Society for the Protection of German Immigrants, a society of which the venerable Bishop of this diocese is the zealous and efficient president, and of which all the officers, except the president himself, were born in Germany, at once in the clearest terms expressed their disapprobation of any such project.
>
> The second fact is this: that the Holy See, with its practical wisdom, no sooner learned of such a project than it quietly put it aside. The late Cardinal Prefect, Cardinal Simeoni, wrote that a scheme of this kind was of impossible realization.
>
> The third fact is, that when "Rome had spoken the case was decided." In a letter which came only last week, the zealous secretary of the St. Raphael Society in Germany, the Hon. Peter Paul Cahensly, writes that he heartily accepts the decision of the Sacred Congregation of the Propaganda, as intimated in the recent letter of his Eminence, Cardinal Ledochowski. Neither can there be a doubt, that the gentleman in Germany had *no political end in view, but only a religious one.*
>
> Consequently with such reiterated assurances from quarters which cannot be suspected, the minds of our fellow citizens may be perfectly at rest on this point. Indeed, to the reflecting mind, there could not have been at any time very serious fears in this regard. We who are born in this Land of the Free, regard our country, not only with love and affection, but as the dearest spot on all the earth. We thank God that our lot is cast under the Stars and Stripes, and we pray that His benediction may ever be upon it. And yet with all our love for our native country, we do not feel called upon to trumpet our patriotism in season and out of season, because in this world many things may well be taken for granted. An honest man does not proclaim, for instance, that there is no taint on his birth, nor does he feel bound to prove the legitimate marriage of his parents. Insinuate the contrary, and you offer a very grave insult. We feel the same way if our devotion to the land of our birth is called into question. Enough for us that we have

been born here, or that we have voluntarily made it our home, that our patriotism should not be challenged with good reason. I take it for granted that most of the members of the Young Men's Societies here present are Americans by birth. Those of you who have been born on the other side have a national characteristic that is gladly admitted by all observers. There are also other good Americans, people, not born in this country, and when we bring these Germans to the front, we may be convinced, that *they are always devoted to the country of their choice, their adopted fatherland, for devotion to home and country is peculiar to the Germans.*[49]

Not only did the leaders and members of the congress rejoice at this important endorsement, but they had several reasons for further satisfaction from their Newark gathering. The convention was by far the most successful held to date; attendance was estimated at 2000 delegates and 8000 laymen and members of societies. Civic leaders of New Jersey participated in the public parades and assemblies, and the number of bishops present, besides Wigger and Corrigan, included Messmer, Schwebach, Zardetti, Richter, Janssen, Charles E. McDonnell, of Brooklyn, Archabbot Leander Schnerr, of St. Vincent's and Abbot Hilary Pfrängle, of St. Mary's Abbey, Newark. Cardinal Rampolla cabled a papal blessing to the congress through Bishop Wigger, while expressing satisfaction at the obedience and love evidenced at the gathering. Fortified by these manifestations of strength, among its resolutions on the Holy Father, Christopher Columbus, parochial schools, secret societies, Catholic press, and the language question, the congress also unanimously passed a forthright repudiation of all attacks on Cahensly and the St. Raphael Society:

> We offer our sincere thanks and our most cordial approval to the St. Raphael's Society, because of the great good it has done and still does for the temporal and spiritual welfare of Catholic immigrants. We recommend this association most strongly to the active assistance and generosity of all Catholics, especially the Leo House in New York, the grand creation of the association. We deeply regret that completely ignoring the useful aims of the association vile attempts have been made to attribute political motives to its leaders and friends. We indignantly reject in particular the accusations in which the name of the most worthy Catholic and member of the German Center-Party, Mr. Cahensly, has been and still is abused in order to arouse prejudice

[49] *Verhandlungen der sechsten deutsch-amerikanischen katholiken Versammlung abgehalten in Newark, N. J., Am 26. 27. 28. und 29. September 1892* (New York, 1893), pp. 151–157. Schröder's speech is found on pp. 68–79. Pohle was again present and delivered a sermon at the Mass of Thanksgiving in St. Benedict's Church (cf. p. 146).

> against brethren of the same faith and to excite an unwholesome nationalism by ignoring plain facts, by misrepresenting them; or by misconstructing motives of action. The accusations and attacks hurled at prominent Catholic prelates, priests and laymen of this country, at the German-American Priesterverein, at the Catholic Congress, clearly condemn themselves by their evident absurdity and falseness, especially when they are hidden under the cover of patriotism or even of devotion to the Holy See.[50]

One of the most vitriolic agitations over Cahenslyism arose as a result of this Newark Congress. Reverend Patrick Corrigan, pastor of Our Lady of Grace Church, Hoboken, New Jersey, found the resolution passed in favor of Cahensly unacceptable. He proceeded to attack the Priests' Society in the New York *Sun,* October 29, 1892, to charge them with treason to Church and State, and of a conspiracy to Germanize the country by means of the Catholic Church. Reverend L. Hofschneider, pastor of SS. Peter and Paul Church, Hoboken,

[50] *Ibid.,* pp. 101–102. Comment of the secular press was generally unfavorable. The New York *Times,* Oct. 2, 1892, stated: "We do not recall any other body of American residents, and presumably of American citizens, which has shown itself so completely out of touch with American institutions. The European Ultramontanes, who have become nuisances in every European country that is at all progressive, are the models of these curious persons at Newark, who oppose all the distinctive institutions of their adopted country, not only because they are American, but because they are modern.

"It is no news to anybody that there are Catholics in this country, and men high in the councils of the Church, whose aim is to reconcile their obligations as Catholics with their obligations as Americans, and to persuade their countrymen of other Beliefs that a devout Catholic may be as good a citizen as if he were not a Catholic. These men are striving to win converts and friends to their Church by Americanizing it, and they are going about their work in a very enlightened and a very effective way. Among these men are Cardinal Gibbons and Archbishop Ireland. It is a very good augury for the Church in this country that they should have persuaded the authorities at the Vatican to favor, or to acquiesce in, the methods they have devised to reconcile the obligations of Roman Catholics and of American citizens. Yet these patriotic and devoted Churchmen are the objects of a peculiar animosity on the part of the men represented at Newark. . . .

"It would be most unfair to judge Catholicism in America by the ridiculous persons who assembled at Newark, and who represent comparatively few Catholics except themselves. They have kept themselves as clear of any taint of Americanism during their sojourn in this country as if they were so many Chinese laundrymen. They cannot do great harm, because the *zeit-geist* of which they are completely ignorant, is too strong for them. But it is not too much to say that, if the spirit of the Roman Catholic Church were that expressed in the proceedings of the Newark conference, that Church would be a public enemy. All that we are justified in saying is that the persons who took part in those proceedings are bad citizens, and dangerous in proportion as they are powerful." The Baltimore *American,* Oct. 18, 1892, spoke of narrow seventeenth-century methods and declared: "Cahenslyism dead! Well, it's a living corpse, and its shadow instead of diminishing, is getting larger every year. It was never killed — only scotched."

and one of the active workers for the Newark convention, rushed to the defense of the *Priester Verein,* classified Father Corrigan's remarks as false and unfounded, and denied anew that the German priests had been connected in any way with the Lucerne Memorial. He also at the same time defended Cahensly vigorously. Priests of the Diocese of Newark took sides, and secular papers in New York, the *Times* and *Sun* especially, as well as the Catholic *Freeman's Journal* entered the fray. Father Corrigan employed language that was intemperate and disrespectful to his ordinary and his metropolitan, Bishop Wigger and Archbishop Corrigan. He denounced Miss Edes, the Archbishop's Roman agent, and her activities at the Holy See, defended the public schools and questioned the statements of Wigger concerning the attendance of Catholic children at public schools. Wigger determined, owing to the widespread scandal resulting from this incident, that he must bring Corrigan before an ecclesiastical court on the charge of publishing false statements. But before the trial could be held on December 12, 1892, Father Corrigan apologized publicly for his language about both Archbishop Corrigan and Bishop Wigger, and the matter was dropped. Nonetheless, much harm and useless agitation had been stirred up and the names of the leaders of both groups in the Church had once more been dragged into public dispute, not only in New Jersey, but in practically every state in the union.[51]

While this episode was transpiring, the important annual meeting of the archbishops took place in New York during November, 1892. There Archbishop Corrigan was chosen to draft a formal protest, and to answer the charges made at Lucerne concerning losses suffered by the Church in the United States. At St. Louis in 1891 the archbishops had determined that a formal answer would have to be made to this charge, and Corrigan had entirely agreed on this point. With the assistance of John Gilmary Shea, the historian of the Church, who

[51] Cf. T. W. McGrath's compilation of all documents in this controversy, perhaps the most heated one in these years, *Father Corrigan and Bishop Wigger of New Jersey on America vs. Foreignism. Is It Cahenslyism?* (New York, 1892). Schröder explained to Corrigan what appeared to him to be the implications of Father Corrigan's controversy: "It seems to me that peace cannot return if in the question of Cahenslyism our motto is not *Roma locuta, ergo causa finita est.* For the adversaries are not susceptible to any argument. They do not want to see the truth which has been demonstrated a hundred times, and continue stubbornly to attack the good faith of Cahensly — in order to repel the Cahenslyites in America. I cannot but believe that there is some system in the unanimity with which the liberal Catholic press and the so-called neutral journals, *Herald, Sun,* etc., point up the movement provoked by a priest disobedient and disrespectful to his bishop" (*AANY,* Schröder to Corrigan, Washington, Dec. 4, 1892).

did research on the leakage suffered among American Catholics, he prepared a letter to Leo XIII.[52]

Here again was an excellent juncture for a cease-fire agreement among all participants in the German nationality question. The archbishops of the land had given a formal response and defense of the administration of the American Church; ample evidence had been adduced that the Lucerne Memorial had not been the public statement of conspirators in Europe and the United States; the Holy See had both assured the Americans that the suggestions in regard to proportional representation in the hierarchy would be rejected, and had acknowledged the good will and blessed the further effort of the St. Raphael Society. The unfortunate misunderstanding could thus have been terminated with unquestionable advantage to all concerned. But 1892 was not the year for a truce, because the question had now grown more complex and had become entangled with several other major issues of the times.

The New York meeting of the archbishops in November, 1892, again brought forth the conservative and liberal differences which had divided their councils for so long a time. Leo XIII had been deeply disturbed over the American reaction to Propaganda's decision on Ireland's school plan, and he determined to send a personal representative to this annual session of the metropolitans to try to effect peace. It was also a convenient occasion for the Pope to actualize a plan he had favored for a number of years, and which he felt would draw the American Church closer to the Holy See while putting an end to the acrimonious differences among its leaders. This was the establishment of an apostolic delegation in the United States. John W. Foster, Secretary of State, had informed Gibbons that President Harrison wished the Pope to know that a personal representative of His Holiness would be welcomed as the bearer of a number of valuable Vatican

[52] *AANY,* American Archbishops to Leo XIII, New York, Nov. 16, 1892, copy. This document, the official response of the American metropolitans to the Lucerne Memorial, is translated and included in Appendix VI (pp. 317–319). Corrigan sent a copy of this letter to Cahensly, who replied that their figure of sixteen million losses submitted in the Lucerne Memorial was "somewhat too high," although he asked Corrigan to consider that this figure included not only emigrants, but also their children and their children's children. Then he went on to praise Corrigan's care for emigrants, support of the Leo House, and his interest in the Italian St. Raphael Society founded in his archdiocese. He wrote: "The time will surely not be far off when in the archdiocese of New York one million at least of devout Catholics will contribute and help to finish and to maintain all your Grace's splendid institutions, such as e.g. your beautiful Cathedral, your grand Seminary, etc., and when your archdiocese will be at the head of all the dioceses of America" (*AANY,* Cahensly to Corrigan, Limburg, Dec. 31, 1892).

maps of the fourteenth and fifteenth centuries, at the forthcoming World's Columbian Exposition to be held in Chicago. Thus with the title of ablegate, Archbishop Francesco Satolli was sent to the United States in October both to attend the World's Fair in Chicago and the archbishops' meeting in New York.[53] Monsignor O'Connell accompanied him as secretary and succeeded in steering him successfully into the sphere of the liberal group, for after a brief call on Corrigan in New York, Satolli went on to Baltimore and then to St. Paul where he resided for a month before the New York meeting. At that gathering Satolli presented fourteen propositions to the archbishops which he stated represented the mind of the Holy Father on Catholic primary education. In these propositions the Faribault-Stillwater Plan was openly justified, parents were not to be forbidden the sacraments if they sent their children to public schools, and no repugnance to Catholic doctrine was declared to exist in children learning the elements of art and science in schools controlled by the state.[54] The assembled archbishops could not reach an agreement as to the propositions at that time, and the controversy over the schools was renewed soon thereafter with great vehemence. Archbishops Corrigan, Katzer, and Elder and the great majority of their suffragan bishops did not accept the propositions, and wrote their disagreement to the Holy See after Satolli had asked the American bishops to send their views to Rome.[55] This matter soon reached the press and violent statements

[53] Cahensly informed Baumgarten that the latter's suggestion, made on September 5, 1892, to the effect that a new memorial be presented to Satolli by Cahensly before the Archbishop departed on his mission to the United States, would be inopportune. Cahensly believed that enough material had been sent for an impartial judge, and an authoritative friend had assured him such a move would arouse the impression that the St. Raphael leaders were informers and intruders. Cahensly also stated that, according to the judgment of his friend, there could not be more unfortunate choices for this observation trip to the States than Satolli and O'Connell (Baumgarten, *op. cit.*, p. 167).

[54] The text of Satolli's propositions is found in Reilly, *op. cit.*, pp. 271–276.

[55] Archbishop Katzer's letter to Leo XIII on Satolli's propositions was indicative of the opposition point of view. He felt they should not be considered *de jure* until approved by the Holy Father, that they needed much explanation lest dangers for religion result, that enemies of the parochial schools and "liberal Catholics" looked upon the propositions as the approval of the Holy See of the public school system. To him the plan which was aimed at solving the school question in the United States scarcely approached a solution. The decrees of the Third Plenary Council of Baltimore contained the real solution, while Satolli's plan advised a compromise with civil authority. Various state constitutions would create many problems in regard to school regulations, and Catholics had evidenced that they could bear the double expense of their own parochial system. After refuting the Faribault-Stillwater Plan he concluded that the parochial system was the most satisfactory arrangement (*AAM*, Katzer to Leo XIII, Milwaukee, Jan. 14, 1893, copy).

were made, even to the extent of attacking and questioning Satolli's authority.

Cardinal Gibbons became worried. He feared that the entire legislation of the Third Plenary Council was endangered and, therefore, informed the Pope that only an encyclical letter could settle the matter. It was then that Leo XIII acted. Satolli had also informed the archbishops at New York that the Holy Father desired that the Church in the United States, like other countries, should have an apostolic delegate. But the metropolitans had side-stepped the issue by declaring that they would have to refer the matter to their suffragan bishops, thus abiding by an admonition the Pope himself had given them two years before because of the protests Rome had received that decisions were being made exclusively by the archbishops at their annual meetings. Leo XIII then took the matter into his own hands, and five weeks after the meeting, on January 24, 1893, he informed Satolli that he had been appointed as first Apostolic Delegate to the United States. Apparently the Holy Father had felt it was time to put an end to controversy and recrimination. On the day after Satolli's appointment O'Connell explained the move to Ireland, who had been the only archbishop to favor openly the establishment of a delegation with Satolli, who was then his friend, as delegate. He wrote:

> Well my dear friend it is accomplished. The delegation is created. Satolli named delegate and Sbarretti & Papi named his aides. The consequences you can see, and on the immediate controversy you know its effect, and under the circumstances, I do not see what better could be done, or what other way there was out of it. . . . You cannot imagine what an opposition I found here against Satolli and how well it was organized. All his, your, and the Pope's enemies united on the point determined to make the mission a failure, and then to proceed to make it tell on the Pope's republican policy in general. It surpassed the opposition that prevailed here during your stay and everybody was in it. To work on they had all the news of American papers, boundless private correspondence and a buzzing of whisperings. The head centre was Cardinal Parocchi. Then came the Society. The zeal of all these amounted to fury. . . . Well now it is no longer your fight nor mine, and it seems to me that it would be a mistake to make it so. It is the fight of the Pope for his delegate and you have no better time to retire. Certainly this opposition cannot be met forever, and peace will be obtained even at some cost, tho at very little. The victory remains, cannot be undone, and the laurels should not be risked for trifles. The newspaper controversy makes a bad impression here. Of course in America it may be necessary to vindicate one's reputation or to un-

mask others, but now it has gone beyond the limits of dignity. In all this you have lost nothing and in American public opinion I am sure there are many now trailing a broken wing. Your only friends are the American people; your last protection, their esteem. To count on anything but opposition for the Bps. & Abps. is a mistake. Another outcome of this controversy is the end of Irish predominance in America. It is now the adopted rule that the German character goes more in accord with the feeling of the Prop. Parocchi said: "The Irish in Am. are a bad set and the sooner the Prop. takes hold of them the better." . . . I am glad it is at an end. Now welcome peace. Brandi seems possessed by one idea, and everywhere, prudently and imprudently he is at work on it. The Pope, however, has imposed on the Jesuits to support his French and American policy. Abp. Corrigan has made it be believed at the Prop. that he was in favor of the delegation.[56]

Leo XIII followed up his January move with another letter to the American hierarchy on May 1, 1893, in answer to Gibbons' petition for an encyclical on the school question. The Pope stated that the new delegate's mission had the purpose of settling controversies, and he went on to declare that by giving toleration to the Minnesota school plan he had not abrogated the Baltimore legislation, but that the latter was still intact. At this point the school question of the 1890's ended and passed from the scene as an issue in the American Church. Those who had favored opposite sides of the question could

[56] *AASP,* O'Connell to Ireland, Rome, Jan. 25, 1893. Keane later reported to Gibbons on an audience which he had with the Holy Father, in which he said concerning several matters: "We got at the University. First I explained our success and presented an album of photographic views. Then we came to our difficulties, and discussed fully the opposition 1° of the Germans, 2° of the Jesuits, 3° of N. Y. — 4° of all opposed to Mgr. Satolli and his policy, with which they identify the University. The last point launched us into the discussion of the delegation and Mgr. S. Here is where the Pope is most determined, because the delegation is simply an element in his 'policy,' which is, the breaking down of the influence of the Triple Alliance, — which means monarchism, militarism, and the oppression of the Papacy, — by embracing the influence of democratic France and democratic America — an influence which presages democratic Italy, or Federated Italy, with the Pope in a position suitable to him. On this policy he is inflexibly bent, and the welcome given to the representatives of the Pope in America was a most hopeful sign of the rallying of all democracy around the Pope. In this there may be an exaggeration, but there is also a great truth, — the Church and the Democracy are fast drawing nearer. Hence opposition to Satolli and the delegation was the worst hostility to the Pope and he is ready to discipline the opposition and to enhance the authority of the delegation. This is going to be the central feature and motive of what he will say and do, — and he told me plainly that he was going to speak and act. . . .

"He regards the University as bound up with the same 'policy,' as an integral part of it, and it too shall be absolutely sustained against all opposition. He intends to speak strongly of it in the Encyclical which he is preparing to send to America in the near future — *how* near we could not ascertain" (*AAB,* 93-J-7, Keane to Gibbons, Pegli, July 31, 1894).

feel that they had won their points.[57] The new delegate and the position he would take in regard to liberal or conservative policies in the United States had now become the issue of the hour.

At first Archbishop Satolli indicated open agreement with the so-called liberals. He moved to Washington and took up residence at the Catholic University of America, considered to be the intellectual center of progressive forces. His speedy reconciliation of Father Edward McGlynn, and removal of the censure of excommunication from the New York priest who had supported Henry George and who had entered into open rebellion against Archbishop Corrigan, seemed to evidence further leanings toward his friends from Baltimore, St. Paul, and Washington.

The first indication of a possible break between Satolli and the *avant-garde* liberals came about as a result of the participation by Gibbons, Ireland, Keane, O'Gorman, and others, in the Parliament of Religion held in connection with the Chicago World's Fair. Under the chairmanship of Reverend Henry Barrows, Presbyterian minister from Chicago, the parliament aimed at bringing together representatives of the principal forms of religion who would freely expose their various tenets. At the New York session of the archbishops in 1892 the invitation for Catholic participation, extended through Bishop Keane, was thoroughly discussed and agreed to by majority vote,[58] and Keane and Bouquillon arranged the Catholic program of twenty speeches. Keane himself delivered an address and read several papers at the gathering which was opened on September 11, 1893, attended by 168 delegates and thousands of observers.[59] Cardinal Gibbons opened the first session by leading the audience in the Our Father, a session which was attended by Archbishops Feehan and Ireland, Bishops James Ryan, of Alton, Joseph B. Cotter, of Winona, and Archbishop Francis M. Redwood, S.M., of Wellington, New Zealand.

[57] The Illinois *Staatszeitung,* June 26, 1893, insisted that the Pope's letter came not from Ireland's ideas but was based on the Third Plenary Council of Baltimore.

[58] *AAB,* 90-Q-3, Minutes of the Third Annual Conference of the Archbishops of the United States, New York, Nov. 16–19, 1892, Placide L. Chapelle, secretary. Gibbons was quoted as having declared to Barrows: "I deem this movement you are engaged in promoting worthy of all encouragement and praise. If conducted with moderation and good-will, such a congress may result, by the blessing of Divine Providence, in benefits more far-reaching than the most sanguine could dare to hope for" (*ACUA,* Keane Papers, Barrows to "Dear Sir," Chicago, Jan. 27, 1893).

[59] John Henry Barrows, *The World Parliament of Religions* (Chicago, 1893), II, pp. 1407–1416. Corrigan, Gibbons, and many others attended the Catholic Congress, one of the separate religious congresses held before the parliament itself.

Bishop John Moore, of St. Augustine, attended the closing of the parliament along with Keane.[60]

But the more conservative-minded churchmen judged this participation to have been excessive broad-mindedness and a recognition of dogmatic indifferentism. Keane reported to O'Connell:

> I think he [Satolli] looks askance at our part in the Parliament of Religions, as do, no doubt, all the ultra conservatives. I got into it, first at the urgent solicitation of Abp. Ireland — then at the request of the Abps. at their meeting in N.Y. — and I am confident that the result is an enormous advantage to the Church. But I take it for granted that I shall be denounced for it. So be it.[61]

There was no doubt, indeed, that Catholic participation in this congress was denounced to the Holy See, and apparently with good reason, for the speeches at the sessions in great part extolled God's providence which, it was stated, opened more than one path on which men may rise from darkness to light. The thesis was also advanced at the parliament that the broadest religion was the one that had the greatest vitality.[62] The Catholics who entered into the congress had

[60] *Ibid.*, II, p. 1560; Barrows declared that "a new era of religious fraternity has dawned."

[61] *ADR,* Keane to O'Connell, Washington, Oct. 10, 1893. For fuller treatment of Keane's participation in this parliament, cf. Ahern, *The Catholic University of America, 1887–1896. The Rectorship of John J. Keane* (Washington, 1948), pp. 67–70, 142. Ireland philosophized on the parliament to O'Connell: "Manifestly the new democratic era is setting in for church and world. The changes are wonderful. Our hope is that Leo will push matters, that no reaction will be possible. This the bright side — but there is the other side — and I ask myself with you is the game worth the arrogance we have to suffer" (*ADR,* Ireland to O'Connell, Chicago, Oct. 4, 1893). Cf. also *Western Watchman,* Oct. 28, 1893, for a denunciation of Catholic participation in the parliament.

[62] Cf. Anton Gisler, *Der Modernismus* (Einsiedeln, 1912), pp. 77–89, for an unfavorable interpretation on theological grounds of American Catholic participation in the World Parliament of Religions. Tappert journeyed to the Cologne *Katholikentag* in 1894 and there delivered another of the German American denunciations of liberals in the American Church, this time with the added emphasis and unifying criticism of latitudinarianism based on Catholic participation in the recent Chicago parliament. He stated: "Since our enemies keep up their sorry courage by concentrating their criminal attacks on a man from the Center, who has been highly useful to the German emigrants, you will permit me to explain our attitude toward the ecclesiastical and religio-political questions which have so prominently occupied the Catholic mind in the United States of late. . . . Our great enemy is liberalism, the denial of the social kingdom of Christ on earth. This great heresy of our time is threefold: first, avowed unbelief; second, social rationalism; last, but not least, an ecclesiastical liberalism which here and there blocks our way. It holds sway over certain Catholics who have inscribed on their banner: 'Union of the Church with the age, with modern ideas, with Americanism.' Hence the extolling of modern liberties, not as a requisite for a justified

evident good will, a sincere desire to expose the doctrines of the Church to interested hearers, and their speeches were sound and uncompromising on dogmatic truths. But the American bishops who participated had misjudged the religious effects of the Chicago Parliament, and on September 15, 1895, Leo XIII sent a letter to Satolli in which he ordered discontinuance of such participation in the future. The Pope said:

> We have learned that in the United States of America assemblies are held in which Catholics unite indiscriminately with those who are separated from the Church, in order to treat of religious and moral questions. In that We willingly recognize the interest in religious matters which continues more and more to animate that nation. But, although these mixed gatherings have been hitherto tolerated in prudent silence, it would seem better that Catholics should hold their congresses by themselves; at the same time, that the advantages accruing from them may not redound solely to their own profit, they may so order these congresses that even those separated from the Catholic Church may be admitted as auditors.[63]

---

tolerance, but as the ideal of political and ecclesiastical wisdom; hence the cautiousness of preaching Catholic truth, under which truth and Catholicity suffer; hence the more than sparing attitude of this third kind of liberalism toward secret societies; hence the unreasonable breaking away from some Catholic traditions in the temperance and liquor question; hence, finally, that coquetting with a more or less general, all-embracing christianity to which a far-reaching expression was given at the Chicago parliament of unholy memory. From the same source originates those fulsome praises for the public schools . . . and that ridiculous boastfulness about Americanism, which is not ashamed to reproach foreign-born co-religionists with an attachment to the language and customs of their fathers, and brand them publicly as being opposed to the English language, and devoid of love of country" (*Verhandlungen der 39. General-Versammlung der katholischen Vereine Deutschlands in Köln a. Rhein, 26–30. August 1894* [Köln, 1894], pp. 264–271).

Keane answered Tappert in the *Journal de Bruxelles,* in which he denied that Tappert was a representative of German American Catholics, but rather of a fanatical group which had sent him to Cologne. Tappert desired not only national parishes but also national bishops; he represented the group that opposed the apostolic delegation in the United States and strove to bring it to naught, that forgot the United States was not a colonial land but that it was a new fatherland whose customs and usages they should adopt. Tappert and his group, Keane continued, forgot that a country should have one tongue, such as Germany itself was striving to implant in both east and west (Poland and Lorraine), and that many tongues harm the work of the Church. It was unhistorical to insist that the Catholic Church should have anything but a national character in a country, certainly not a foreign marking. The *SRB,* IX (Oct., 1894), p. 84, did not agree with Keane in any way. Here an American missionary termed the Irish Americans the real fanatics, and the editors then proceeded to moralize: "If the men of the various nationalities were inspired with the true Christian spirit of brotherly love, unity and zeal for the salvation of their brethren, this endless strife would have accomplished much good, prevented much scandal and prevented the loss of many to the faith."

[63] Buffalo *Catholic Union and Times,* Oct. 24, 1895.

Another indication that the tide was turning against those of liberal views came in August, 1894, when Rome, announcing that a stricter outlook on secret societies must be observed, condemned membership of Catholics in the Odd Fellows, Knights of Pythias, and the Sons of Temperance. But the clearest sign was Archbishop Satolli's sudden, definite, and public turning from his friends of the first two years, and his clear defense of the position that German Catholics had been defending through all previous controversies. This *volte-face* took place in dramatic fashion.

On April 21, 1895, Reverend Frederic W. Longinus, pastor of St. John the Baptist Church in Pottsville, Pennsylvania, had arranged a public ceremony connected with the laying of the cornerstone for his new parochial school. Satolli, accompanied by Monsignor Schröder, journeyed to Pottsville for this occasion, and created a sensation across the country by the address which he delivered that day. Before Satolli spoke, however, Schröder had delivered the sermon in the morning at a solemn Mass, presided over by the apostolic delegate. There he had announced that the delegate had taken the opportunity of a not-too-important event to give to the Catholics of German origin evidence of his good will, to show before the whole land "that the horrible picture of so-called Cahenslyism had thoroughly exhausted itself," to give evidence of appreciation for German maintenance and development of parochial schools, and to make known how he treasured and appreciated the works and merits of German Catholics.[64] At three o'clock in the afternoon, at the actual laying of the cornerstone, Archbishop Satolli delivered his address in Latin, which was in turn translated into German and English. He praised the sincerity, unity, steadfast Catholic faith and morals of the German American Catholics, their devotion to the Holy See, and he then announced that they rightly defended their usages and customs, their language and their schools, while as good citizens they stood second to none.[65]

Comment on the delegate's address at Pottsville was rather slow in coming because the move was totally unexpected. Gradually the full significance became apparent. The German Catholic press generally

[64] Baltimore *Katholische Volkzeitung,* May 4, 1895, observed that Schröder spoke with an openness that left nothing to be desired.

[65] Cf. Appendix VII (pp. 320–322) for the full text of this important address of the Delegate. At the banquet in the evening Longinus extolled Schröder with these words: "His name is dear to all the German Catholics in America. In him we salute an ornament to the Catholic University in Washington. Him we honor not only as our friend, but also as our guide, and we look upon him with just pride, because we see his devotedness to the Holy See, and always behold him in the front ranks defending the rights of our holy Church" (*Church News,* Apr. 20, 1895).

acclaimed it as evidence that in the eyes of the delegate, as in those of the Holy Father, there existed no difference of nationality or language when the welfare of the Church and salvation of souls was promoted.[66] On the other hand, the American secular press interpreted the speech as a broad change in policy, and the Washington *Post,* October 28, 1896, spoke of it in a manner that was fairly general among the secular dailies:

> Pope Leo in all his acts towards France and America has displayed favoritism for liberalism.
>
> On the other hand, it is undeniable that Rome, and especially Catholic Rome, including the Sacred College of Cardinals, looks with horror on liberalism. To retain his favor with Leo XIII, it is claimed, and to assure himself the support of the College of Cardinals was the difficult task of Cardinal Satolli. Previous to Satolli's coming to America as delegate, Archbishop Ireland and the liberal party enjoyed especial favor at the hands of Pope Leo.
>
> Cardinal Satolli came, as was expected, to reconcile the two parties in the church and it was supposed he would favor the liberal party. He came under the personal direction of Mgr. O'Connell, who has been for years the representative of the liberal party in Rome. Satolli took up his residence at the Catholic University, surrounded by Bishop Keane, Dr. Bouquillon, and Dr. O'Gorman, now Bishop of Sioux Falls. In his address to the Archbishops of the U.S., dealing with the school question, his position was claimed to be a support of the liberal party and Archbishop Ireland. So far he had carried out the policy of Leo XIII.
>
> Now, to conciliate the powerful metropolitan of New York, the Germans, the Jesuits, and all others who looked upon the rise of liberalism as disastrous to the best interests of the church, Cardinal Satolli removed from the Catholic University and took up residence in the Jesuit parish of St. Aloysius. His secretary, Dr. Papi, resigned and entered the Jesuit order. He became a great friend of Mgr. Schroeder, the German professor of Dogmatic Theology at the Catholic University and the powerful opponent of Bishop Keane's policy. Mgr. Schroeder accompanied Cardinal Satolli to Pottsville, Pa., when Satolli made the speech which gave the first intimation of his change of policy.[67]

[66] *Herold des Glaubens,* May 3, 1895; *SRB,* X (Apr., 1895), pp. 34–37. The *Civiltà Cattolica* of July 8, 1895, reported favorably on Satolli's Pottsville speech in conjunction with his participation in the opening of a new church for Italians in New York under the direction of Reverend Peter Bandini, secretary of the Italian St. Raphael Society in that city.

[67] This was a major change of affairs since the early days of Satolli's arrival when Schröder told Corrigan he could only hope that Satolli "would be susceptible to ideas other than those which he has taken from those suspect sources" (*AANY,* Schröder to Corrigan, Washington, Dec. 4, 1892).

In the same year as that of the Pottsville speech, Leo XIII sent his promised encyclical letter to the Catholics of the United States, *Longinqua oceani,* of January 6, 1895. In this message he expressed his love for the young and vigorous American nation, alluded to the simultaneous beginning of nation and Church in 1790 as evidence that the two societies should get along together, spoke admiringly of the work of the various councils held in the United States and finally praised the freedom extended by the State to the Church. But the Holy Father then went on to warn that it was erroneous to believe that this American system of separation of Church and State was an ideal one for all countries. The encyclical was variously interpreted by Catholics of the United States, both from the viewpoint of a continuation of his French American friendship and of an open manifestation of appreciation for American conditions, while, on the other hand, it was held to be a definite reminder that excessive idealization of their system had been advanced by American Catholics.[68]

But it was the announcement of June 7, following close upon Pottsville, which came as the major blow of 1895 to the so-called liberals of the United States. On this spring day, upon the request of the Prefect of Propaganda, Monsignor Denis O'Connell submitted his resignation as rector of the American College into the hands of a heartbroken Cardinal Gibbons. Continued protests had come to the Propaganda that the college was not being properly managed, that the rector was traveling around Europe on protracted journeys, and that his concerns were not primarily associated with his duties as rector. When he had been named rector in 1885 he had also been engaged by some of the bishops to serve as their Roman intermediary or agent, to impart information to the Propaganda and to expedite administrative matters by personal contacts. But gradually as the years went by, and the lines of difference within the American hierarchy became more clearly delineated, O'Connell more and more affiliated himself with Gibbons, Ireland, Keane, and their supporters. He had received his Roman office in good measure through the patronage of Cardinal Gibbons, and his allegiance had first and always been to the Archbishop of Baltimore. But his maneuvering and defense of the Faribault-Stillwater Plan and of the Catholic University of America, his tutoring of Delegate Satolli, and, especially, his part in the Cahensly-

[68] Cf. A. F. Hewitt, C.P., "Encyclical of Leo XIII to the Bishops of the United States," *CW,* LX (Mar., 1895), pp. 721–726, and Joseph Schröder, "Leo XIII and the Encyclical 'Longinqua,'" *ACQR,* XX (Apr., 1895), pp. 69–89, for interpretations of each party.

ism affair marked him as a partisan adviser. Years later Archbishop Messmer expressed the feeling which had existed against O'Connell in 1895 when he told him:

> I was angry with you, very angry, for the prominent and active part you took in the so-called liberal movement of American prelates. Common report, never contradicted, had it that you were the most active and influential agent of that party in Rome. True, I never doubted your good intention, but on the other hand I had my firmly set convictions regarding the consequences of that movement upon the Church in America. As I thought and felt, so felt thousands of our German Catholics, as you know.[69]

By such activity O'Connell had destroyed the good effects which should have resulted from his services at Rome for the whole American hierarchy. He furthermore contributed to the belief on the part of some that the need for an apostolic delegate in the United States was an urgent necessity. Brandi informed Corrigan that O'Connell's resignation had surprised no one in Rome, that it was requested by the Pope, to whom complaints had been made by the cardinals of the Propaganda, that he had neglected his duties by long absences from Rome, and that the "great majority" of American bishops lacked confidence in him.[70] Bishop McDonnell, of Brooklyn, likewise reported to New York that when the Holy Father had asked him if the bishops were satisfied with the management of the American college, he had replied in the negative.[71] Gibbons continued O'Connell as the vicar of his titular church of Santa Maria in Trastevere in Rome, and in this rather secondary post he remained in the Eternal City for eight years in exile and under a cloud. Gibbons had planned on his *ad limina* visit to Rome in 1895 to dispel, as Keane told O'Connell:

> . . . these clouds of whispers & suspicion which so assiduously are gathered around the Holy Father in regard to Mgr. Satolli, in regard to the University, in regard to the general tendency of so-called "liberalism" among us. The cardinal himself so appreciated the position of the venerable old Pope, so assailed on all sides with attacks on the principles which he has thus far so nobly upheld, he came to so appreciate the need of the Pope's hearing something of the right side and getting some moral encouragement & moral support in the stand

[69] *ACUA,* Messmer to O'Connell, Milwaukee, Jan. 26, 1904. For fuller treatment of the Roman days of O'Connell, cf. Barry, *The Catholic University of America, 1903–1909. The Rectorship of Denis J. O'Connell* (Washington, 1950), pp. 14–33.

[70] *APF,* Brandi to Corrigan, Rome, June 8, 1895, photostat.

[71] *AANY,* McDonnell to Corrigan, Rome, June 24, 1895.

he is making, that he was ready, as Mgr. Satolli urged, to start early in June.[72]

But Keane, too, apparently possessed a partisan outlook on "the right side of the question," as he himself was soon to learn.

In 1895 the blows fell at Pottsville and at the American College; in 1896 the third shock came at the Catholic University of America. On September 15 of that year Leo XIII informed Keane through Gibbons that his resignation as rector would be accepted, while due regard to his person and dignity would be recognized by his elevation to the rank of archbishop.[73] Keane accepted this abrupt dismissal without hesitation and with his customary magnanimity, while around him a national and international storm arose of sympathetic defense and of violent accusations against the source of the move. The removal was interpreted as a victory for the conservative and anti-American party in the Church, another blow at "home rule" in American affairs. The opposition viewed the move as another proof of the Holy Father's constant solicitude to maintain integrity of doctrine. Satolli, Schröder, and the Jesuits were openly accused of responsibility for the change at the University, and Schröder hastened to issue a public statement in which he vigorously denied that he was at the head of any opposition party.[74] The influential New York *Staatszeitung* on October 14 attributed Keane's downfall to his stand on the school question, but the next day the *World*, of the same city, attributed the removal as only an incident in what was called the "German Crusade." Cardinal Gibbons strove as usual to keep peace by denying that there existed any antagonism or want of harmony in the University's board of trustees, but the agitation was slow to die. Archbishops Ireland and Riordan were "very gloomy" and concerned, while Bishop McQuaid, with his usual candor, exclaimed:

The news from Rome is astounding. The failure of the University is known in Rome at last, and the blame is thrown on Keane. Much

[72] *ADR*, Keane to O'Connell, Washington, May 9, 1895. Cf. Ahern, *op. cit.*, pp. 162–198, for complete coverage of Keane's resignation and the resulting reaction.

[73] Buffalo *Enquirer*, Oct. 5, 1896; New York *Herald*, Oct. 6; *Catholic Citizen*, Oct. 10; *Courrier des Bruxelles*, Oct. 25. Protestant journals seized the occasion to decry the move as arbitrary papal action and an indication that Leo XIII had played with liberalism only as long as it served his interests. Cf. Boston *Congregationalist*, Oct. 15, 1896.

[74] Cleveland *Catholic Universe*, Oct. 9, 1898. Bishop Horstmann, one of the trustees of the University, expressed himself to Schröder on Keane's removal: "You know I will be blamed for the action that has been taken. You are blamed as the major cause — the Germans and the Jesuits come in for their share also . . ." (*ADC*, Horstmann to Schröder, Cleveland, Oct. 10, 1896, copy).

of it is due to him, but other causes are there. These causes are irremediable now. The failure implicated the Holy Father, who was made to father the undertaking from the beginning.

What collapses on every side. Gibbons, Ireland, and Keane!!! They were cocks of the walk for a while and dictated to the country and thought to run our dioceses for us. They may change their policy and repent. They can never repair the harm done in the past.[75]

The trustees of the University at their fall meeting proceeded to nominate a new rector in the person of Reverend Thomas J. Conaty, of the Diocese of Springfield, who was accepted by the Holy See as Keane's successor. The trustees attested their appreciation to Keane for his services and issued a public statement of denial to the press that accusations of factions or parties based on liberalism, nationalism, or Americanism separated the board of trustees, or that any party had won a triumph.[76] By January 15, 1897, Keane was named Archbishop of Damascus, Canon of St. John Lateran Basilica in Rome, consultor of the Congregation of Studies, and consultor at the Propaganda for American affairs. This was accomplished through the instrumentality of Vincenzo Cardinal Vannutelli and his friend Monsignor O'Connell, despite, as Keane stated, "strong efforts by all the hostile influences, especially American."[77] Keane humbly accepted his new duties and, after his position was clearly defined, he issued a statement to the press aimed at the "mischief bureau" in the United States:

The Pope said to me: "I am greatly shocked and grieved by these mischief makers who are so busy in the American press. I protest against this malice and falsehood. The idea that anyone would try to

[75] *AANY,* McQuaid to Corrigan, Rochester, Oct. 3, 1896. Cf. also *AAB,* 94-R-6, Keane to Gibbons, Chicago, Oct. 7, 1896.

[76] *ACUA,* Minutes of the Meetings of the Board of Trustees, Oct. 21, 1896; New York *Tribune,* Oct. 23, 1896. *The Independent,* leading Protestant weekly of New York in its day, proceeded on Jan. 14, 1897, however, to associate Keane's removal with his participation in the anti-Abbelen campaign: "This German faction of conspirators received a crushing defeat at Rome; yet . . . they still do business at the old stand.

"For ten years the wound dealt them in Rome by Bishops Ireland and Keane had rankled in their hearts. They have constantly tried to harass and to injure Archbishop Ireland. . . . Bishop Keane has not fared better at their hands. No prelate belonging to this faction ever had a kind or encouraging word for him. The German party never contributed to the Catholic University; they persistently opposed its success, because Bishop Keane was at its head. Their newspapers now boast that they have brought about the downfall of this enlightened and progressive American bishop; they also boast that Ireland will be their next victim." Cf. also *The Independent,* Aug. 13, 1891; Oct. 6, 1892; Nov. 17, 1892; Feb. 9, 1893; June 3, 1897, for similar unfavorable comment against German Catholics.

[77] *AAB,* 95-B-9, Keane to Gibbons, Rome, Jan. 15, 1897.

put me in the position of disapproving the splendid service of Cardinal Satolli or of publicly disgracing you would never occur to me. The change in the rectorship at the Washington University was submitted to me as a purely pedagogical routine matter. I was astonished and indignant when I learned that mischief makers had misrepresented the meaning of my act. I desire to denounce their statements and to give evidence of my love and esteem for you. My answer to your enemies will be a substantial one. The policy of the Holy See is unchanged!"

It is remarkable that when the so-called liberals are dominant in America no one is attacked by them, but when the so-called conservatives appear to have gained a victory the mischief bureau in New York suddenly starts into activity, and the whole press of the country teems with scandal, falsehood and venomous abuse.

All these stories originating in New York are pure inventions of malignant minds. I would be sorry to hold Archbishop Corrigan responsible for all that has been said or written by those who appear to be his friends, and cannot be brought to believe that he would consent to or authorize all of this mischief work.[78]

Reverend Thomas Gambon, of St. Paul's Church, Owensboro, Kentucky, friend of both Satolli and Corrigan, commented on Keane's public statement to the Archbishop of New York:

> You will learn from the enclosed clippings that there is a financial blizzard in the North West and a loud mouthed Canon by the Tiber.
>
> From the tone of the Canon's utterances one can easily fancy that Keane feels that he is in tight traces but this roar across the waters will make the Archpriest of St. John's [Satolli] keep his eye on some of his Canons and he is the man that will do so.[79]

Gambon was referring to Archbishop Satolli's new position in Rome to which he had returned in 1896 after having been elevated to the College of Cardinals on November 29, 1895. Reports continued to circulate in the United States that Satolli had not only influenced Keane's removal from the University, but that both Gibbons and Ireland were to be called to Rome for the purpose of removing them from their high posts, and that Bouquillon, Shahan, and Pace were to be asked to resign because of the former delegate's unfavorable reports on their teaching and progressivism.[80] These assertions were so persistent that the new delegate, Archbishop Sebastiano Martinelli, O.S.A., inquired from Rome as to the truth of the statements, and was happy to report to Gibbons that the Holy Father had authorized him to con-

[78] New York *Journal,* Feb. 12, 1897.
[79] *AANY,* Gambon to Corrigan, Louisville, Feb. 20, 1897.
[80] New York *Tribune,* Nov. 13, 14, 20, 1896.

tradict the assertions as a lie and to express his grief at hearing these false rumors.[81] Gibbons, deeply distressed at all these events and longing for peace, communicated this information to Archbishop Ireland, who had wrathfully written just before the delegate's letter:

> But, really, what is to become of religion — if things continue as they have come. There is, no doubt, a well-organized conspiracy. A villainous letter from Paris appears in the N.Y. *Sun* of Nov. 29 — and an article in the same strain in the *Germania,* of Berlin.
>
> Many Americans are beginning to believe that there is some truth in all these reports of papal disfavor. Something is to be done to stop this dreadful and diabolical conspiracy. . . . Nothing but stern courage on our part will avert disaster from us. We are timid children, & we are treated as children. Our enemies are not timid.
>
> The university is dead; nothing can revive it. The Jesuits have triumphed there for good.[82]

The opponents of Schröder soon became convinced, however, that something could be done. It was persistently maintained that the Monsignor, when in Rome during the summer of 1896, had worked against Keane through the instrumentality of Andreas Cardinal Steinhuber, S.J., and other German and pro-German supporters there. For years Schröder's resignation from his professorship had been desired, but he had determined that he would not voluntarily acquiesce. He did, however, follow Corrigan's advice after 1892 to keep out of all polemics — difficult as he found that to be[83] — and steeled himself for what he knew was coming. He told the Archbishop of New York:

> Meanwhile the day which will decide my fate and that of Dr. Pohle draws near. I have many reasons to believe that my silence in the controversies of the day was not enough for Mgr. Keane or his friends

[81] *AAB,* 94-U-2, Martinelli to Gibbons, Washington, Dec. 3, 1896.

[82] *AAB,* 94-U-1, Ireland to Gibbons, St. Paul, Dec. 2, 1896. Bishop John Lancaster Spalding expressed himself to his friend, Reverend Daniel Hudson, C.S.C., editor of *Ave Maria,* as follows: "A more disgusting state of things than our ecclesiastical situation is hardly conceivable. The only important question, it seems, is whether Abp. Ireland is falling or rising in favor with Rome. If we could only hear nothing more of him, it matters little whether he rise or fall. I am sick of it all and only wish I were away from it all" (*AUND,* Spalding to Hudson, Peoria, Dec. 6, 1896).

[83] *AANY,* Schröder to Corrigan, Washington, Dec. 4, 1892. Cahensly reported to Corrigan in his shaky English: "I also know from every good authority, that Msgr. Ireland, during his stay in Rome, passed unfair remarks about Msgr. Dr. Schröder and Dr. Pohle, professors at the Catholic University in Washington, saying that they must quit their chairs. He now will surely use all his endeavors with his friend Msgr. Keane, in order to get these men removed as soon as possible. . . . In the interest of the Catholic Church of America would I be sorry, were these learned men to get lost to the University" (*AANY,* Cahensly to Corrigan, Limburg, Oct. 31, 1892).

and they are still determined to have their victim. . . . Nevertheless, those gentlemen of the University are badly mistaken if they think that I am going to resign without being forced to do so.[84]

Throughout the early months of 1897 the lines of battle were drawn for what came to be known as the "War of 1897." After Professors Shahan, Bouquillon, Edward A. Pace, and Charles P. Grannan, of the University, along with John A. Zahm, C.S.C., had spent the summer in Europe with O'Connell, the plan of attack was ready. They had secured the support and assistance of Reverend Franz Xavier Kraus, author and professor of ecclesiastical history at the University of Freiburg im Breisgau. Kraus was an admirer of the progressive forces among American Catholics. He also was scarcely friendly to Schröder as a result of the latter's delation of his books to Rome as deserving of condemnation, and his frequent use of Kraus' name in previous controversies as a liberal and minimizer.[85] Documents were assembled, and affidavits were signed by prominent Washington citizens, attesting to a fact disturbing to the temperance advocates, namely, that Schröder had frequented saloons. Here the old conflict between continental customs and the Irish American defense of temperance — termed a Puritanical fanaticism by the Germans — came to play an important part in a major issue of these years. Archbishop

[84] *AANY,* Schröder to Corrigan, Staten Island, June 23, 1893. In January of 1894 an imperial appointment to a chair of dogma in Münster was offered to Dr. Joseph Pohle, who accepted the position. Before leaving, however, and in his letter of resignation he justified the part he and Schröder had taken in public questions of the day, because he said they had felt obliged to do so. He stated Schröder had been abused, and then added: "I pass a similar judgment upon his [Schröder's] attitude in the s.c. movement against Cahenslyism. Whilst condemning in common with him the policy falsely ascribed to Mr. Cahensly, I have publicly protested in common with him against such a scandalous crusade, based upon calumnious misrepresentations. I do not regret it; I even declare that this unchristian agitation influenced not a little my determination to leave America. Certain parties have accused us of a narrow national spirit, from which we were and are still far removed, perhaps more so, than our accusers themselves" (*AAB,* 93-D-9, Pohle to the Board of Trustees, Washington, Mar., 1894).

[85] Among the O'Connell Papers are a large number of messages from Kraus, who respected Ireland, Gibbons, Keane, and O'Connell and who was deeply convinced that Germany and the United States should be allies. His American friends informed him about the differences that had arisen in regard to ecclesiastical policy, and Kraus felt that the Germans had made a mistake in looking upon the advocates of Jesuit ultramontanism, to which he was strongly opposed, as the representatives of the German cause. Kraus invited his American friends to visit Germany and to become better acquainted with that land. On their part, O'Connell, Ireland, and Keane, much interested in the project, journeyed to Germany, explained American political traditions there, and received strong support from Kraus and his circle in their Cahenslyism and Americanism struggles.

Ireland entered the arena prepared for battle, as he informed O'Connell:

> Abp. Riordan will spend a week in St. Paul on his way to Washington. . . . He & I are not against Schroeder: he will lead the fight. The obstacle is C. Gibbons, who talks of giving a monitum to Schr. I wish you would at once write to the Cardinal a very strong letter, giving him an idea of the support we have in Germany. . . . If Maes stands with us, I have hopes: Corrigan and Ryan will vote to gain friends—and not for the University; Williams & Gibbons will want peace.[86]

At the same time Bishop Horstmann, of Cleveland, was preparing the opposition to this attack, as he informed Corrigan: "I depend on you to be present at the meeting of the University Board Oct. 20 to support me if any action is taken against Mons. Schröder."[87]

When the directors assembled for the board meeting at Washington the Schröder battle got under way at once, with Corrigan, Horstmann, and Ryan arrayed against Ireland, Maes, Riordan, Chapelle, and Keane who returned each year for the meetings because the board would not allow him to resign his position as trustee. All involved were motivated by sincere convictions. The defense maintained that Schröder had been maligned; that it was absurd to claim he ever drank to excess; that his classwork had always been of an advanced graduate character and according to regulations of the administration; that he absented himself from the University whenever possible only because of the treatment he had received from the majority of the faculty. Those against the professor were convinced that he was the

[86] *ADR,* Ireland to O'Connell, St. Paul, Sept. 13, 1897. O'Connell also informed his friends that at the International Congress at Fribourg, Switzerland, in 1897, at which he had given a defense of American relations of Church and State, the German delegates showed great interest in following the Americans, and had no sympathy with Schröder and his "narrow American faction." They were surprised that Schröder was kept at Washington, regarded him as a kind of fanatic who could never remain more than three years in one position, and twitted the Washington professors on being "intimidated by a poorly educated man who remains there only for the sake of his salary." O'Connell sent this letter to his friends on the board of trustees of the University (*AASP,* O'Connell to "My dear Friends," Freiburg i. Br., Aug. 27, 1897).

[87] *ACUA,* Horstmann to Conaty, Philadelphia, Feb. 26, 1897. Cf. Hogan, *The Catholic University of America, 1896–1903. The Rectorship of Thomas J. Conaty* (Washington, 1949), for a complete treatment of the Schröder removal, pp. 35–36, 148, 153–156. Rt. Rev. William J. Kerby, former professor of sociology at the Catholic University of America, wrote a letter while he was studying at Louvain to his brother Edward in the United States. This letter clearly traces the underlying differences between the liberals and conservatives in the American Church of these years, and is included in Appendix VIII (pp. 323–325) (*ACUA,* William J. Kerby to Edward Kerby, Louvain, Apr. 11, 1892).

center of a conspiracy; that peace and harmony as well as the advancement of the University was impossible as long as he remained; that he consistently suggested that the American Church was tending toward heterodoxy, and sometimes even heresy; that he sought ecclesiastical leadership; that he criticized at Rome prelates, professors, and the delegate; that he made these charges as well in the German press, especially in Arthur Preuss' *Fortnightly Review;* and that his classwork was not scientific.[88]

Obviously there were exaggerations and prejudices on both sides, but Schröder had become such a source of contention by this time that objectivity gave way to deeper, underlying differences. After a heated discussion the resolution for Schröder's resignation was put to a vote. Then Cardinal Gibbons read a telegram he had received from Cardinal Rampolla to the effect that it would be unfitting for the board to force Schröder's resignation, since the Holy Father himself had directed him to return to the University in the summer of 1897. The vote was then taken, with the result that Schröder was asked to resign by a ten to four majority, but it was also voted to delay action until the reasons for the professor's dismissal could be laid before the Holy Father. The next morning Gibbons returned to the matter and suggested that the affair could be more easily settled if some assurance was received from Schröder himself that he would resign. Horstmann proceeded to investigate this proposal, and in the afternoon he returned with a letter from Schröder who stated he would resign when Leo XIII gave his permission, because he had returned only at the insistence of the Holy Father and of Cardinal Steinhuber. The entire documented case was then forwarded to Rome, and on November 13, 1897, Rampolla informed Martinelli that Leo XIII had given permission for Schröder to resign, provided his good name be preserved. At first it was reported that Schröder would join the faculty of Monsignor Joseph Jessing's Pontifical College Josephinum in Ohio, but then it was announced on December 5, 1897, from the Prussian Minister of Education and Ecclesiastical Affairs in Berlin, that Schröder had been appointed professor of dogma at the Catholic Academy of Münster by Emperor Wilhelm II.[89]

[88] Cf. *ibid.*, pp. 182–190, for documentation of charges and defenses in the Schröder case.

[89] Professor Paul Gleiss, head of the Department of German in the Catholic University of America, declared in an interview that during his student days in Germany the imperial appointments of Pohle and Schröder were looked upon in university circles as justification by the regime of two scholars who had been mistreated in the United States. Reverend Johann Valerius, S.A.C., former director of

A farewell testimonial dinner was held for Monsignor Schröder at Columbus, Ohio, just before his departure, with forty-five German American priests from various parts of the country in attendance. Here, as a valedictory, Schröder struck out for the last time against the liberals. He denied that the Germans were a party in the Church; they were rather the real Catholics who must continue and uphold the one and only Church without false tolerance. They must, he asserted, refrain from going to the state for education, abstain from religious parliaments such as the one in Chicago, remain children of their mother tongue, preserve unity with the Papacy, and oppose exaggerated liberalism, excessive patriotism, state schools, and Americanism.[90]

With these explosive and challenging words the unfortunate and imprudent Monsignor departed for his homeland from which he had been driven by Bismarckian liberals and to which he was returning because of a campaign leveled against him by those he considered to be American liberals. Archbishop Keane, expressing the viewpoint of the opposition, considered that the University had ended the chapter of its first and greatest difficulties. He reported from Rome that the Pope had been convinced, especially by Martinelli's statement even before the documents arrived, that he himself had been led into an untenable position, and with simple dignity he had stepped out of it. Henceforth, Keane felt, there ought to be nothing but unity, harmony, and concerted energy for the higher purposes of the University.[91] The German Catholics in the United States viewed the treatment of their champion and intellectual leader with deep resentment,

---

the St. Raphaelsverein in Bremen, also informed the author that it was commonly held that Emperor Wilhelm II had personally made these appointments.

[90] Ohio *Waisenfreund,* Feb. 24, 1898. Ireland informed O'Connell: "The downfall of Schröder is the end of anti-liberalism, & of Cahenslyism, and a great defeat for Corrigan" (*ADR,* Ireland to O'Connell, St. Paul, Dec. 3, 1897); and again: "The 'Germania' comments on the promptness with which the Centrum & the Prussian Minister took up Schröder. You see, Germany is grateful to him. He was doing her work in America. He was a Cahenslyite — but the last of the Mohicans. The greatest and last battle of the war has been fought and won" (*ADR,* Ireland to O'Connell, St. Paul, Jan. 8, 1897). Shahan and Grannan also informed the ex-rector of "the terrible siege" (*ADR,* Shahan to O'Connell, Washington, Oct. 23, 1897; Grannan to O'Connell, Philadelphia, Oct. 25, 1897).

[91] *ACUA,* Keane to Corrigan, Rome, Dec. 16, 1897. An American reaction to Monsignor Schröder is found in Margaret B. Downing, "Kultur and American Catholicism," *Reedy's Mirror,* Aug. 31, 1897. Here it was asserted that Schröder was head of a "Kultur plot," and that his was a "huge political plot he concealed under the guise of zeal for the faith," in which he worked to centralize German Catholics under German pastors to keep alive their allegiance to the fatherland while remaining hostile to the ideals and aspirations of their adopted country.

however, and they were slow, as Archbishop Messmer said, to recover from an act which they considered to be unjustified.[92] Especially in reference to the Catholic University of America was this German resentment evidenced in the years following the removal.

As the resignations of O'Connell and Keane had not brought about the much needed harmony among American Catholics, so would the removal of Schröder from the scene of controversy fail to affect the reconciliation of two opposing groups of liberals and conservatives in understanding and mutual trust. Ideals and aims were directed at the same end, the advancement of the Church, but they ran in distinctly different lines of endeavor. This difference in outlook on the means best suited to advance American Catholicism was strikingly apparent in the statements of two leaders of each position. On the one hand, Archbishop Ireland's powerful vindication of his life philosophy at the centennial of the American hierarchy on November 10, 1889; on the other hand, President Henry Spaunhorst's farewell tribute in the name of the Central Verein to Monsignor Schröder. They read:

IRELAND

Success is not the test of valor or merit. The conservatism which wishes to be safe is dry-rot. . . . The timid move in crowds, the brave in single file. . . . The Church in America must be, of course, as Catholic as in Jerusalem or Rome; but so far as her garments may be colored to suit environment, she must be American.

There is danger: we receive large accessions of Catholics from foreign countries. God witnesses that they are welcome. I will not intrude on their personal affections and tastes; but these, if foreign, shall not encrust themselves upon the church.[93]

SPAUNHORST

When in 1883 Herr Cahensly, the protector of the emigrant, made a visit to America in the interest of the St. Raphaelsverein, a result of which was the establishment of the Leo House, dark clouds appeared on the horizon. Unfortunately, truly unfortunately, diversified opinions formed into separate camps which threatened a nationality war. Finally it became apparent in several dioceses, because of an attachment for secular education of youth, that some were ready to give our parish schools over to the unbelieving for a price. But the lawful successor of Christ, Leo XIII, has spoken. Our brave German Catholics stood firm and undaunted with their Holy Father, united — that made them strong.

They would have nothing to do

[92] *ACUA,* Messmer to O'Connell, Milwaukee, Jan. 21, 1904.

[93] John Ireland, *The Church and Modern Society* (Chicago, 1897), I, pp. 71–73;

IRELAND	SPAUNHORST
	with a liberalism which had developed. They wished to preserve their faith as pure, to conserve parishes with their school and mother tongue. To you, Monsignor, we — all American Germans — are indeed filled with a sense of deepest appreciation for what you have done through your speeches and warnings, your firmness and attention, the discernment which you evidenced in Catholic journals, the unceasing labors and personal activity by which you have shown the German Catholics what unity and common action can accomplish.[93]

Such remained the irreconcilable position of the two camps in 1897. Cardinal Satolli's *volte-face* would be influential in bringing another development in 1899 which overshadowed the "war of 1897," and qualified it as being in any way a clear-cut victory.

ACV, Spaunhorst to Schröder, Feb. 20, 1898, copy. In the Arthur Preuss Papers there are numerous letters from Schröder to "Dear Arthur," in which the former discussed his articles, his visits with the apostolic delegate in which he presented the German Catholic position in the United States, his translation of documents and of convention proceedings which he forwarded to curial officials at Rome. There are also included a number of letters to Schröder's confidant and close friend, Reverend F. Meifuss, pastor of Immaculate Conception Church, Centreville Station, Illinois, in which Schröder also details his plans and projects in the struggles of those days.

On May 12, 1897, the Sacred Congregation of Propaganda issued a decree, communicated to the American bishops by the apostolic delegate, concerning the problem of spiritual care of various national groups in the United States. By this legislation it was decided that when children born in the United States of immigrant parents reach their maturity, they were not to be held bound to attendance in a national parish to which their parents belong, and erected in the same territory as an English parish, but they could join an English parish. Furthermore, it was declared that immigrant Catholics who knew English had the right to become members of English churches and were not obliged to attend national churches for immigrants (*AER*, XVII [July, 1897], p. 87). In this manner the problem of these years, concerning attendance at national churches, was resolved by the Holy See.

CHAPTER VI

A House United

ON JANUARY 22, 1899, Leo XIII forwarded to Cardinal Gibbons an apostolic brief, *Testem benevolentiae,* in which the opinions comprised under the heading of "Americanism" were rejected by the Holy See. While the Pope reiterated his former assurances of love for American institutions, this letter was not one of praise but rather one of warning against certain contentions then rife in the Church of the United States. The immediate occasion of the papal brief was the public controversy resulting from a French translation of the *Life of Father Hecker,* by Walter Elliott, C.S.P., with a preface by Abbé Félix Klein, professor at the Catholic Institute of Paris.[1] Leo XIII repudiated Hecker's views of the ascetical life as presented in the French translation to the effect that a new age demanded new moral emphasis; that external spiritual guidance should be set aside in the modern age; that the religious vows were alien to the spirit of the time; that the natural virtues be emphasized over the supernatural virtues, and that the active and passive virtues be divided. The Holy Father stated, however:

> If, indeed, by that name ["Americanism"] be designated the characteristic qualities which reflect honor on the people of America, just as the other nations have what is special to them; or if it implies the condition of your commonwealth, or the laws and customs which prevail in them, there is surely no reason why we should deem it ought to be discarded.[2]

Both the beginning and the ending of this letter had been tempered by Leo XIII and Cardinal Rampolla, while the body of the document

[1] *Le Père Hecker. Fondateur des "Paulists" Américains 1819–1888, par Le Père W. Elliott de la même Compagnie. Traduit et adapté de l'anglais avec autorisation de l'auteur. Introduction par Mgr. Ireland. Préface par l'Abbé Félix Klein* (Paris, 1897).

[2] John J. Wynne, S.J. (Ed.), *The Great Encyclical Letters of Pope Leo XIII* (New York, 1903), pp. 441–454.

had been drawn up by Cardinal Mazella, S.J., and Reverend Alberto Lepidi, O.P., master of the Sacred Palace in Rome. Two years earlier Lepidi had given his *imprimatur* to Magnien's heated attack on "Americanism." Cardinal Satolli also gave advice on the document.

This important document addressed to American Catholics through the Cardinal of Baltimore came as a result of the accumulating controversies of previous years which had so deeply divided Catholics in the United States. The desire of the so-called liberals to impress the American character of their Catholicism, to prevent the immigration flood from giving a foreign coloring to the Church and to support the distinctive, independent, and favorable position of the Church in relation to the American body politic brought in its wake a sharp reaction. In the United States itself opposition had gradually crystallized against what the so-called conservatives considered to be excessive nationalism, exaggerated accommodation to the spirit of the age, and even, at times, a compromise of traditional Catholicism in order to win modern man to the Church.[3] In the original English version of the Hecker biography Elliott had written a popular appreciation of the founder of his society, a convert, who with Orestes Brownson had worked during the years of the mid-century to win Americans to Catholicism and to prevent the Church from being isolated in new-world society as a foreign island. But in his preface Abbé Klein had idealized the virtues and message of Isaac Hecker for modern times in terms which he later admitted were excessive. It was Klein's remarks which especially gave a handle on dogmatic grounds to European opponents of democracy and American Catholic idealization of their participation in the new order, an idealization which was often intemperate and strident if deeply sincere.[4]

[3] Cf. Thomas S. Preston, "American Catholicity," *ACQR,* XVI (Apr., 1891), pp. 396–408, in which the following theses are attacked: that the American Church had taken to itself "the wings of progress" and was more consonant with the spirit of the age while being less hostile to those differing from Catholics in faith and morals; that the American form of government was the best possible and most suited to Catholicism; that all religions were good, while the Catholic religion was only better and more complete. Also "The Chapter 'De Fide Catholica' in the Third Plenary Council of Baltimore," *AER,* XVI (Feb., 1897), pp. 147–154, in which a danger to the Church of the United States was seen in a growing disrespect for authority both in doctrine and discipline, e.g.: "Yet leaders in the Church are found appealing to the masses and the popular prejudices of those who are supposed to need correction and direction. . . . It is this constant appeal to the judgment of the American people which, however flattering to our national self-love, is at the same time wholly inconsistent with the divine plan of governing the Church; it is appeal without necessity which in reality weakens the basis of authority" (p. 153).

[4] Cf. the address of Bishop Keane at laying of cornerstone of Church of the Holy Name in Washington, October 18, 1891 (*Church News,* Oct. 22, 1891); Walter

In Europe interest had been growing in the remarkable development of the Church in the United States, ever since the Third Plenary Council of Baltimore, and an increasing number of Catholics on the continent turned to the new Republic of the West to discover the nature of a constitutional relationship which afforded liberty and progress to the degree manifested in the American Union. Italian Catholics, at the time, including a number of curial cardinals and officials termed *Concilionisti,* were searching for a pattern by which they could heal the serious break between the ruling House of Savoy and the Vatican, especially in regard to confiscated temporal properties of the Pope. Likewise certain German Catholics, such as Professor Franz X. Kraus and his circle at the University of Freiburg in Baden, as well as Professor Hermann Schell at the University of Würzburg, saw in American Catholicism a possible solution of German Catholic problems over against Bismarckian and Prussian nationalism. In France, too, a number of Catholics who were republican in sympathy were working for a policy of *ralliement* to their government in the hope of instilling Catholic principles and philosophy into the policies of the liberal republic. Other French Catholics, the legitimatists, were convinced, however, that the Church must adhere to its monarchical moorings of earlier days. It was in France, therefore, that "Americanism" became a national controversy. Here conservatives and legitimatists began a vigorous campaign against "Heckerism" on theological grounds, but with the accompanying political conviction that a blow could be struck at such Americanizers as Archbishop Ireland who had written the preface to Elliott's orginal volume on Hecker, and who had lectured them at Paris in 1892 on the virtues of American democracy and the necessity of accommodating themselves to the spirit of the age.

Only the German and conservative opposition to "Americanism" is *ad rem* here, and the full details of the events leading up to *Testem benevolentiae* must be passed over.[5] But in this respect the outlook of the intransigents in the United States had significance only as part

---

Elliott, C.S.P., sermon at the consecration of Bishops Shanley, McGolrick, and Cotter, St. Paul, December 27, 1889 (*Catholic Sentinel* [Portland], Jan. 27, 1890); John Ireland, "American Citizenship," *Church and Modern Society* (New York, 1903), I, pp. 185–214; Denis J. O'Connell, *A New Idea in the Life of Father Hecker* (Freiburg i. Br., 1897), an address given at the International Catholic Scientific Congress in Fribourg, Switzerland, August 20, 1897.

[5] For works on "Americanism," cf. Chapter III, footnote 1. Reverend Thomas T. McAvoy, C.S.C., of the University of Notre Dame, is presently at work on a definitive study of "Americanism."

of the whole background of the question, both European and American. After Klein's translation of Elliott's book came out in 1897 strong conservative criticism appeared, especially in the pages of *La Vérité,* by two writers, "Martel" and "Saint-Clement," who were identified in time as the Abbé Charles Magnien, of the Congregation of the Brothers of St. Vincent de Paul, and the Abbé George Périès, former professor of canon law in the Catholic University of America who had been removed from his post in 1896, and who had threatened retaliation because of his dismissal.[6] Magnien's caustic articles were later published in book form in 1898 under the title: *Etudes sur l'Américanisme, le Père Hecker: est-il un saint?,* and bore the *imprimatur* of the Dominican, Alberto Lepidi, master of the Sacred Palace in Rome. When he learned of this, Cardinal Gibbons protested to the Holy See that such action left the impression that Magnien's book had papal approval. But Archbishop Corrigan at the same time wrote to congratulate Lepidi and to approve his action, while Bishop Messmer, on a visit to Rome, spoke out against Heckerism to Leo XIII and to the cardinals. Rampolla assured Gibbons that Lepidi had meant no insult to the American hierarchy, and that the Holy Father was preparing a personal letter on the subject for the American cardinal. In the meantime both Keane and O'Connell were informing their friends in the United States to what an extent all opponents of the Americanizers — Satolli, the Germans, and members of religious orders in Rome — were urging the Pope to be severe with the Americanizers. At their annual meeting in New York, October, 1898, the metropolitans, following the motion of Archbishop Corrigan who had read a convincing memorial by Very Reverend George Deshon, superior general of the Paulists, exonerating his society of the French charges, voted not to take any action since the Pontiff was preparing an encyclical on the subject.

But Archbishop Ireland who was not at the meeting considered this action as timid and unjust to the Paulists, and he determined to go to Rome to ward off any possible condemnation of Elliott's book or of the American hierarchy itself. Although the Archbishop of St. Paul hurried to Rome his mission on this occasion was not successful, for the letter was issued shortly after his arrival. A crestfallen Ireland informed the Paulists: "Fanatics conjured up an 'Americanism' — & put such before the Pope. Lepidi & Mazzela [*sic*] wrote the body of

[6] Ahern, *The Catholic University of America, 1887–1896. The Rectorship of John J. Keane* (Washington, 1948), pp. 153–156; *APF,* Keane to Elliott, Rome, Apr. 19, 1898; *ADR,* Magnien to Ireland, Baltimore, Mar. 9, 1899.

the letter — I cannot pray that God forgive them."[7] The papal Secretary of State encouraged Ireland not to feel that the teachings condemned were ever held in the United States or propagated by Hecker, but rather that they were initiated in France, and Rampolla gave permission for this interpretation of the document to be made known. In their sincere and immediate letters of submission to the Holy Father, the American prelates for the most part followed this interpretation of Rampolla, as did the greater part of the Catholic and secular press. Press comment on the encyclical was surprisingly light, to the delight of Cardinal Gibbons, and no major controversy broke out because of it, perhaps because the majority felt that it was French errors that were being reprimanded.

There were exceptions, however. The French conservatives considered themselves responsible for the encyclical and rejoiced in its publication. Archbishop Corrigan sent a letter to Leo XIII, thanking him for saving the American Catholics from a heresy that threatened. Moreover, Bishop McQuaid ascended the pulpit of his cathedral, disagreed with those excusing themselves, and declared that there had been a species of Americanism which McQuaid said had four distinguishing marks: participation by liberals in the Chicago World Parliament of Religions; liberal advance of the Faribault-Stillwater School Plan; liberal defense of secret societies; and Keane's speeches in the chapels and halls of Cornell and Harvard Universities while wearing his clerical robes. Meanwhile the bishops of the Province of Milwaukee also thanked the Holy Father for his warning, and then went on to condemn those who, as they said, like Jansenists followed the letter rather than the spirit of the document by excusing themselves as having not been guilty of any of the errors listed. When the archbishops assembled for their 1899 session in Baltimore, Archbishop Riordon, of San Francisco, wanted the metropolitans to inform Rome that the implications of heresy in the Milwaukee letter were unfounded. Archbishop Ireland was, in turn, eager to have the whole hierarchy circulated to discover if such errors ever existed in any diocese. But

[7] *APF,* Ireland to Deshon, Rome, Feb. 24, 1899. In this letter Ireland also informed Deshon that the forces against the Americans in Rome were particularly the religious orders — Jesuits, Dominicans, and Redemptorists. It was from the last that the Paulists had separated earlier in the century. Much was made also of Archbishop Corrigan's letter to Lepidi as an indication that the American episcopate was divided on the question. Cardinal Gibbons told O'Connell: "It is very discouraging to us that the American Church is not understood abroad, & that its enemies are listened to, & that they can lie with impunity. I do not think that any of the questions discussed was a living question here. But I suppose H. Father had to act."

Corrigan strongly deprecated this suggestion on the grounds that it was disrespectful to the Holy See. The Archbishop of St. Paul had the support of his colleagues from San Francisco, St. Louis, and Portland, but Cardinal Gibbons begged: "Peace, peace, death even for the sake of peace," and voted with the opposition against the resolution to defeat it five to four. As a compromise Archbishop Ryan, of Philadelphia, suggested that all bishops who had not done so should write to the Holy See, and this motion received a carrying tie vote.[8]

Some time after *Testem benevolentiae* had appeared, Archbishop Corrigan forwarded an English translation of the apostolic letter to Cahensly in Limburg, who replied, with gratitude, that although he was already in possession of the document in the Latin and German languages, he was pleased to have it in English also. Then he continued:

> I conceive, that the Catholics in the United-States had been troubled very much by the proceedings of Msgr. Ireland and his friends. The magnificent letter has — I hope — calmed the minds and the catholicisme will progress.[9]

The *St. Raphaels Blatt* came out with strong approval of the papal letter and stated that the errors existed not only in France but also in the United States, where the Holy Father had prevented a great error from acquiring strength. The error the *St. Raphaels Blatt* particularly had in mind was that Anglicizing of the immigrants which the nativists had aimed at accomplishing. This liberal nativistic party, according to the German journal, consisted of Ireland, Gibbons, and Keane, who had opposed the Germans under the title of Cahenslyism with the special support of the Paulists. The Minnesota school plan, they said, had been a part of this effort and had it endured it would have undermined the whole parish school system. The St. Raphaels-

[8] *AAB,* 97-R-5, Minutes of Meeting of the Archbishops of the United States, Baltimore, Oct. 12, 1899; *ADR,* Ireland to O'Connell, New York, Oct. 21.

[9] *AANY,* Cahensly to Corrigan, Limburg an der Lahn, Apr. 10, 1899. Cahensly also detailed for Corrigan the most recent attack made on him by M. Brunnetière, editor of the Parisian *Revue des deux mondes,* in that journal on November 1, 1898. Brunnetière claimed that Cahensly had worked for national bishops in the United States with the support of the German, Italian, and Austrian regimes. Cahensly sent a letter justifying his actions to Brunnetière, whom he considered to be a friend and fellow liberal of Keane and other nativistic Church leaders in the United States, but Brunnetière refused to publish it. The Cahensly letter was published in *La Vérité* and *Revue canonique* of Paris, and Arthur Preuss vigorously defended his friend Cahensly in the *Fortnightly Review* of March 9, 1899, called Brunnetière a liberal and declared that the French journalist had learned a lesson in method from Cahensly.

verein editors had high praise for prelates like Katzer, Messmer, Schwebach, Zardetti, Corrigan, and Monsignor Frederick Eis, administrator of the vacant See of Marquette; for the bishops of the Province of Cincinnati; and for McQuaid whom, it was said, "for many years we have come to know as a sharp censor of Ireland's exclusive Republicanism."[10]

In the United States the German Catholic press generally viewed *Testem benevolentiae* as a vindication of their position of previous years. In *Der Wanderer* of St. Paul, for example, the theological ideas involved in "Americanism" were analyzed as follows: the writings of Hecker had minimized the sufferings of Christ; the liberals had placed too much reliance on the cultivation of independence and self-reliance; the Paulists, an "Order of Hustlers," had glorified initiative, activity, and native independence, and had also disturbed the work and interest of some of the American clergy in the policy they were employing for immigrant Catholics. The St. Paul German paper stated that Americans should save themselves according to American practices, but the immigrants should be allowed to worship according to their old-world customs.[11] The *Luxemburger Gazette,* of Dubuque, thought that "Americanism" ought to be a dead and buried phenomenon as a result of the Pope's letter. National pride had been growing with a reformation fire, the Church was supposed to have a new life in the new world, but actually "Americanism" had been a specimen of Gallicanism, Josephinism, and liberalism. But the editors felt also that this national pride would not die, for they said:

> The liberal and nativist spirit will push that party on in the future, to hate and oppress their opponents as Ultramontanes, Jesuits, foreigners, fanatics. In their eyes they alone are the representatives of the American Church; their opponents are enemies, are foreigners, who must be

[10] *SRB,* XIV (July, 1899), the entire issue. Maria Longworth Storer cabled Governor Theodore Roosevelt at this time, encouraging him to recommend Archbishop Ireland for the cardinalate. Roosevelt replied that he thought highly of Ireland and that as a private citizen he would recommend him, but that he was hesitant to use his office for that purpose. Roosevelt did not know who was against Ireland, but he observed that just then in the United States it was being claimed that Leo XIII had been converted to the Cahensly view because of his recent letter. Roosevelt did not believe this assertion. Cf. *The Letters of Theodore Roosevelt* [ed. Elting E. Morison] (Cambridge, 1951), II, p. 954.

[11] *Der Wanderer,* Jan. 4, 1899; Jan. 18; Feb. 1; Feb. 22; Mar. 8. These articles were signed by "W.H." On March 15 the editors of *Der Wanderer* commented on the condemnation of the theological works of Dr. Hermann Schell, professor of apologetics at the University of Würzburg, whom they named as the only outstanding supporter of "Americanism" in Germany.

> kept as far as possible from all Church offices. The war against the Cahensly, German and Jesuit spectre will thus survive. How much longer? Who can say?[12]

When charges such as these — and, fortunately, they were few — had died down, it was apparent that Leo XIII had wisely interjected a note of warning for the young American Church. Although the letter, both in content and method of origin, appeared to be a preventive measure, since no condemnations were enforced, yet hasty accommodation to the spirit of the age and idealization of a particular relationship of Church and State were tempered and evaluated in proper proportions. In other words, American Catholics in an encyclical letter addressed to them, and not to Catholics of France, had been directed not to place more value on their Americanism than on their Catholicism. While the recognized leaders of the Church in the United States firmly denied that they personally had ever been guilty of such exaggeration, yet the conservative American and French reception of their writings and ideas evidenced that such an interpretation had, in fact, been placed on their words. Beyond this, the conservative and immigrant section of American Catholics found assurance in the encyclical that their position was not as untenable as some Catholics in the United States had made it out to be. Accordingly, liberals could be satisfied that no condemnation had been issued, and that the letter had explicitly been directed at French interpretation of "Americanism," while their conservative opponents rejoiced that a warning had been given by the Holy See concerning policies and practices of the opposite camp. In this way the basis of a *rapprochement* was achieved which could not, perhaps, have otherwise been effected. The peace and harmony which gradually descended on the American Church in the years after *Testem benevolentiae* was ample justification in the area of practical affairs alone for the admonition of Leo XIII.[13]

[12] Quoted in *SRB,* XIV (Jan., 1899), p. 63. In reference to the Catholic University of America, the editors of the California *Volksfreund,* on April 16, 1898, stated: "That Americanism was from the beginning interwoven with the plan for the establishment of a Catholic University in America, was clear enough from the beginning, and therefore, the conservatives withdrew steadily from it. . . . We want a Catholic University with CATHOLIC professors, and indeed, capable ones who are to be found without distinction of nationality. We want a Catholic University in which the doctrine of the *Catholic,* and not of an *American* Church, are taught. We want a Catholic University in which the young are formed and educated in genuine Catholic spirit, and not chiefly and before all, in Americanism and Patriotism, and nothing else."

[13] Seven years after *Testem benevolentiae,* Pius X condemned the false doctrines of Modernism then rife in certain sections of the intellectual world. In an encyclical,

Monsignor O'Connell had informed Ireland that the general impression was current on both sides of the ocean that he was a crushed man as a result of *Testem benevolentiae.* This judgment was, however, not an accurate one. In the wake of the American occupation of the Philippine Islands, the Holy See had called upon Archbishop Ireland to give his support in solving the question of the lands of the Church there. And a year and a half after the papal letter on Americanism, Ireland informed his friend, Mrs. Bellamy Storer, wife of the American ambassador at Vienna:

> Well, "*mon accueil*" could not possibly be better. It surprises me. The evident purpose is to make me understand beyond a possible doubt that I am in highest favor, that they are all delighted with me, that they need my cooperation, and are resolved to have it.
>
> The Pope told me to forget that letter on Americanism, which has no application except in a few dioceses in France![14]

Pascendi dominici gregis, of September 8, 1907; a syllabus of errors, *Lamentabili sane,* of July 3, 1907; and a motu proprio, *Praestantia Scripturae Sacrae,* of November 18, 1907, the Pontiff condemned efforts to subject divine revelation to a test of purely scientific arbitration disguised as "higher criticism." Dr. Anton Gisler, professor of dogma at the University of Fribourg, in a comprehensive study of Modernism, associated Americanism with Modernism as a manifestation and one of the original sources of the philosophical-theological errors condemned in 1907. Cf. Gisler's *Der Modernismus* (Einsiedeln, 1912), pp. 27–212. Gisler's approach to Americanism as insipient Modernism was also advanced by Dr. Max Grösser, S.A.C., "Die deutschamerikanischen Katholiken im Kampf mit den Nativisten," *Gelbe Hefte,* V (1928–1929), and most recently by Joseph Matt in a series of articles on "A Century of Catholic Life in Minnesota," in *Der Wanderer,* Oct. 12, 1950 — Sept. 6, 1951. While exposing the false association of Cahenslyism with all previous German American attempts from 1883 on to obtain what they considered to be their rights in the Church of the United States, yet these writers go on to associate in a similar manner the writings and actions of the Americanizers with Modernism in an equally broad generalization. It would appear to be an unjustified association of the leaders of the Church in the United States, in the brick and mortar stage of development, with the explicitly condemned theories of scholars in theological and scriptural studies. A more careful application of the encyclical's condemnation is found in A. Vieban, S.S., "Who are the Modernists of the Encyclical," *AER,* XXXVIII (May, 1908), pp. 489–508; "The Encyclical on the Teachings of Modernists in our Seminaries," *AER,* XXXVII (Nov., 1907), pp. 504–535; "Modernism in the Church in America," *AER,* XXXVIII (Jan., 1908), pp. 1–10. In the latter article, Editor Heuser stated that there was perceptible adherence to modernist profession of faith in America, evidenced by more or less open criticism of the Pope's methods, certain assumptions of sympathy with the position of an Italian ruler of the Church who did not know what goes on in the world of science and atmosphere of American free thought, and criticism of the action of the Biblical Commission. Heuser, like Vieban, however, carefully applied the strictures of the encyclical to theological and scriptural theses. In no American theological, philosophical, or scriptural journal was Americanism associated with the condemnations of the encyclical on Modernism.

[14] Ireland to Maria Storer, Rome, Aug. 5, 1900; Maria Longworth Storer, *In*

It was also a striking vindication and obvious tribute to Archbishop Ireland and his Americanizing friends that, when the Holy See needed an acceptable intermediary with the Federal Government on a delicate matter, it should have turned to one who had stood forth for Catholic participation in American democracy, and to one who was accepted by political representatives as a leader of position and worth in American society.

During that same first year after the encyclical another manifestation that the so-called liberals were, to say the least, not entirely repudiated came when Archbishop Keane was appointed to the metropolitan See of Dubuque. His friends had recommended to the Holy See that he should be allowed to return to the United States, and both the Holy Father and the Secretary of State agreed to his promotion. Leo XIII personally forwarded his instructions to the Propaganda in regard to Keane, and the appointment was made. When the matter had become a certainty, Keane told O'Connell: "I must and do say *Deo Gratias* from the depth of my heart for this solution to my life problem."[15]

There remained, then, only Monsignor O'Connell among the principal Americanizers. His large number of friends, with Cardinal Gibbons at the head, had deeply felt his exile ever since 1895 and had worked to remove the cloud from his name. An opportunity offered itself as the term of the second rector at the Catholic University of America, Bishop Thomas J. Conaty, drew to an end. Conaty was a quiet, peaceful man who had striven to unify the university community and to restore confidence in that institution after Keane's removal. But he possessed no special talents for the position, the student body continued to decrease, financial support was inadequate, the faculties were incomplete, and the institution did not have the interested backing of the Catholic body in the United States. Both a number of the trustees and several of the professors, therefore, began activity in 1902 to bring O'Connell home as third rector of the university. Gibbons, Ireland, Keane, Riordan, and Spalding, on the board, and Grannan, Hyvernat, Shahan, and Pace, on the faculty, desired O'Connell's appointment both for the welfare of the national university and as a

Memoriam Bellamy Storer (privately printed, 1923), p. 46. Archbishop Ireland had also worked in 1898 under Vatican direction with the Republican administration, of which he was a strong supporter, to prevent the Spanish-American War. Cf. John T. Farrell, "Archbishop Ireland and Manifest Destiny," *CHR,* XXXIII (Oct., 1947), pp. 269–301; "Background of the Taft Mission to Rome," *CHR,* XXXVII (Apr., 1951), pp. 1–23.

[15] *ADR,* Keane to O'Connell, Bad Nauheim, Germany, Aug. 22, 1900.

further vindication of their position. At this juncture Cardinal Satolli, by now Prefect of the Congregation of Studies, surprised everyone by another *volte-face,* this time in favor of O'Connell. Satolli informed Grannan, during the latter's visit to Rome to advance the Monsignor's cause, that O'Connell was the man who could most perfectly meet the conditions of the university because of his intelligence, courage, integrity of character, and prudence. Grannan informed Gibbons that the conviction was strong in Rome that O'Connell had not been properly treated, and that public satisfaction was due him, while the Cardinal, to whom this joyful intelligence brought new life, rushed a message to O'Connell in which he said: "I know of few events which could give me more satisfaction than to have you near me and in an honorable position. It gave me satisfaction also as indicating your gradual return to favor in Rome."[16] When the trustees assembled at Washington in November, 1902, a majority of six votes out of ten was secured for O'Connell, and on January 12, 1903, Leo XIII approved O'Connell's nomination as third rector of the Catholic University of America. When the news reached Baltimore Gibbons expressed his great joy: "I believe that in the Providence of God you have a great and glorious career before you which will atone for your dark days and will compensate for my many sorrows on account of your distress." To Archbishop Ireland it was the "victory of victories for the dear old cause," as he exclaimed to Gibbons:

> And so we have Mgr. O'Connell. What a revolution in the temper of Rome there is implied in his nomination. Even at this late date it is difficult for me to realize it. In a letter I received not long ago from Card. Satolli, in which mention is made of this change of manner in Rome, he says in explanation — "certain prelates having gone to a better life." It would look as if Satolli himself had not been in his heart so much of an enemy of ours — but had rather yielded to pressure from others, from which he is now glad to recover.[17]

When the Associated Press announced the appointment of O'Connell on January 14, Ireland was even more exultant in his message to the rector-elect when he said: "The associated-press dispatch from Rome this morning tells of the significance in Rome of your appointment. And the significance in America! . . . O'Connell in Washington — Simply impossible! Well, he is here — *Viva l'Americanismo! Viva*

[16] *ADR,* Gibbons to O'Connell, Baltimore, Sept. 1, 1902; *AAB,* 99-W-5, Grannan to Gibbons, Rigi-Sheidegg, Switzerland, Aug. 20, 1902.

[17] *AAB,* 100-J-1, Ireland to Gibbons, St. Paul, Mar. 2, 1903; *ADR,* Gibbons to O'Connell, Baltimore, Jan. 11, 1903.

sempre!"[18] O'Connell, although deeply moved by his promotion, yet hastened to explain to the University's chancellor his determination to retain a neutral position in the future, in as much as that was possible. He told Gibbons:

> I go to my new work with an experience accorded to few men: — to have known all the ups and downs of life on both sides of its medal, and then to be granted field and I hope years of labor, to profit by the golden experience.
>
> I was surprised myself to see how congratulations came up everywhere, as it were, out of the ground, and the gratification of the authorities at their nomination is great. Satolli says "it is a nomination of Providence" — *una nomina providenziale.*
>
> I think that all those persons who think that I will take up politics are destined to be disappointed. All I expect to know in the country is the University and its prosperity. My audience with the Holy Father was very surprising and pleasant. He received me smiling calling me by name with a bright little twinkle in both eyes. Then with no admonition, no counsel, no allusion to the past no more than if these seven years had never existed. He only spoke to me of securing the success of the University he had founded and with which his name and honor were connected. He bade me be seated beside him which he never did while I was at the College. Then with affectionate blessing and promise of continued support, he dismissed me for my work. Strange world this. Nothing in it is true but the Gospel. . . .[19]

One of O'Connell's first aims after he had assumed the rectorship was to inaugurate an annual collection throughout the dioceses of the United States for the support of the University. This collection, ordered by the Holy Father, was at first received rather coldly by German Catholics who had come to view the University as a center of opposition to German language and customs, as the place of origin for accusations and denunciations to Rome against them, as the institution that advocated temperance and prohibition doctrines, and finally as the battleground from which their defender Schröder had been unjustly removed.[20] Yet German prelates like Messmer and

[18] *ADR,* Ireland to O'Connell, St. Paul, Jan. 14, 1903. Cf. New York *Herald,* Jan. 14, 1903.

[19] *AAB,* 100-G-9, O'Connell to Gibbons, Rome, Jan. 31, 1903.

[20] Cf. *ACUA,* Keane Papers, A. S. Hesing to Keane, Chicago, May 21, 1890, for a summary letter of adverse German opinion on the University from the editor of the Illinois *Staatszeitung*. Archbishop Messmer, however, opened the door to O'Connell for new co-operation when he wrote him: "A few flattering phrases will not succeed nor any flattery even given wholesale. The Germans are not easily given to emotional outbursts. But they are firm and steady friends, and workers where they see good will and real proof of it. If you and the professors will confine yourselves to the University

Horstmann, always ardent defenders of the institution, rallied to the cause of the University, and as a consequence trust and confidence in the University as a Catholic institution for all elements in the American Church — not merely for Irish or eastern Catholics — was thus slowly built up. It was, however, Reverend Anton Walburg, pastor of St. Augustine's Church, Cincinnati, who came forward again with a farseeing proposal for winning more active German support and participation in the University's life. As early as 1892, at the height of the Faribault-Stillwater school controversy, Walburg had indicated his change from an ardent defender of German rights to the position of the Americanizers, when he wrote to Archbishop Ireland:

> I am a strong Cahenslyite and published my views in a pamphlet "The Question of Nationality." I observe, however, that Cahenslyism is not wanted here either in the church or the country. Its friends and defenders have lost courage and retreat at every point attacked, Americanism will prevail. . . . The Church wants to be American and must accept American institutions and do the best she can. People may deplore the loss of souls; but a battle cannot be fought or a change of base of operation made without loss. Our own loss may be retrieved by new recruits from the general American public. Our parochial schools served well as a scaffolding and will do good service for an indefinite time but they cannot exist when we shall have become one people. I consider the Faribault plan an experiment in the right direction. If it failed we must try some other mode till we do succeed. If all our children were sent at once to the public schools, ways and means no doubt would be devised for their religious instruction. Now no provision is made for the two thirds of our children who attend the public schools, while the one third, the chosen few who attend the parochial schools are well taken care of. It was a bold move to adopt the public school system, but it will make us one people, one nationality, and the faith that overcometh the world will overcome the obstacles to the conversion of the country and find an entrance into the hearts of the American people. I am still a Cahenslyite in feeling and principle but I cannot understand how they who were one with you in denouncing Cahenslyism and proclaiming Americanism now shrink from following you to the logical legitimate conclusion.[21]

---

work and leave other things, politics, ecclesiastical and civil, etc., out of your hands, and perhaps give the German Catholics a chance of having some of their students, priests or laymen, as teachers in your institution, you will get their hearty support" (*ACUA,* O'Connell Papers, Messmer to O'Connell, Milwaukee, Jan. 26, 1904). Cf. also *AAM,* letter of Archbishop Sebastian Messmer to Clergy of the Archdiocese of Milwaukee, Feb. 28, 1905, for a pastoral letter of support for the University from Messmer.

[21] *AASP,* Walburg to Ireland, Cincinnati, Dec. 29, 1892.

In reference to the University, Walburg's generous overture was for the establishment of a chair of German literature, which he planned to erect from his own money and from donations he hoped to collect over a period of years. From 1904 until 1907 Walburg worked on this project, and at the trustees' meeting in November, 1907, O'Connell was proud to report to the board that the Cincinnati priest had presented $50,000 to the University. It was stated:

> A Chair of German Literature will soon be opened in this University. With a noble spirit of devotion, Father Walburg has undertaken this work alone and has already carried it so far that now its happy consummation is only a short question of time.
>
> Then shall be thrown open to our people the rich treasures of German literature and opportunities be offered our graduate students of making themselves familiar with a language, the knowledge of which is indispensable to progress in science. I love to consider this Chair as a common source of ever flowing blessings to a very large portion of our Catholic people.[22]

Walburg asked Gibbons and O'Connell to issue a statement that the University was advocating and insisting on at least two languages being learned, and he requested Gibbons to head a petition, along with President Theodore Roosevelt, to Emperor William II, requesting his support for the movement of preserving German language in the new world. Both the Cardinal and the Rector were sympathetic to Walburg's suggestions. Walburg aimed at engrafting German culture and literature on the American tree, removing the stigma of foreignism, and thereby broadening and enriching American culture. He felt that the Church had missed this opportunity through quarrels and misunderstandings in the past, and that as a result Catholics were behind other Americans, such as Presidents Harrison, Cleveland, and Roosevelt, all of whom had engaged German governesses for their children. To Walburg this was the proper assimilation of all that was good from the many nationalities that made up the nation. He stated:

> The chief end I have in view is to open the eyes of the German people here, and to show them that the unreasonable, childish and malicious hostility of the German press against the University is un-

[22] *ACUA,* Report of the Rector to the Board of Trustees, Nov. 16, 1907. Walburg's effort was not the first, however, along these lines. The Central Verein, at its annual meeting in Detroit in 1896, had resolved to establish a chair of German literature at the University, but the plan did not materialize due to misunderstandings and alienation arising from the Schröder case. Monsignor Schröder himself had promised to work for a German chair at the University before his break with the rector and the majority of the faculty.

> founded and a base calamity. To attain this the friendly press should be instructed to direct their efforts to out-German the Germans. As nothing succeeds like success, they may change their base of operations and fall in line when they see your untiring, heroic efforts for the University crowned with success. The German chair is safe and assured.[23]

In this effort Father Walburg was very successful, as he secured funds at German assemblies and obtained the support of German Catholic papers which began to swing behind the project. His contribution was a major step in uniting Catholics of German origin with the supporters of a national University where all the groups that went to make up the American Church could mutually contribute to the advancement of truth and science in the United States.

Not only at the University, but also in several dioceses during the years that followed *Testem benevolentiae* there were indications that bishops made a conscious effort to speak out against hasty and total assimilation of the English language by immigrant groups in the Church. It appeared that instead of creating suspicion and fear by speaking in glowing terms of Americanization, several Catholic leaders left the adjustment to time, and encouraged German Catholics to preserve their mother tongue both as a safeguard of their faith and as a cultural heritage for their children. Bishop Horstmann declared in 1907 that of all modern languages German was the most important, the most ideal, and the richest in literature. If a man would be successful and attain to the heights of his profession, the bishop stated, he must be able to speak German; doctors and professors traveled to Germany if they wished to learn the fundamentals of their professions. He then continued:

> I must truly wonder at our German parents, who themselves speak German, for not preserving the German language as precious in their families. They rather speak English to their children. Such parents sin against flesh and blood, they rob their children of the opportunity, given to them as to no one else, of having intercourse in later life with their professional associates. How easily and effortlessly, how playfully the child learns German when his parents insist that in the family circle only German will be spoken. The children learn English by themselves, they pick it up on the street, and it is taught to them in school. But they will never be able to master the German language if they do not learn it from childhood, if it is not spoken in the family. Yankees send their children to Germany at great cost so that they may learn

[23] *AAB,* 102-R, Walburg to Gibbons, Cincinnati, Oct. 14, 1905. Cf. also *ACUA,* O'Connell Papers, Walburg to O'Connell, Cincinnati, Mar. 15, 1904.

German, and here there are German parents who exclude German from their families. It is incomprehensible. . . .

I cannot close my address better than with this admonition: Hold firmly to your mother tongue, speak German in your families, insist that your children speak only German with you. Fail to do this and you have not fulfilled your parental obligation.[24]

In a similar vein the new Bishop of Peoria, Edmund M. Dunne, successor to the retired John Lancaster Spalding, declared in 1910, the year of his consecration, when addressing a Peoria district committee of the Central Verein:

Most of my student companions were Germans, and I always am happy to visit German parishes because I find all there in beautiful order. I especially rejoice at the good parochial schools in German parishes. I cannot encourage you Germans enough to teach your children as much German as possible; for a German who values his language lightly, as a rule abandons his religion without thinking. Hold to your language, and I will make it a point to see that there will be instruction in German conversation in the parish schools. I personally know how hard it is to speak fluent German if one has no practice.[25]

However, Henry Möller, successor to Archbishop Elder in Cincinnati, shocked the assembled delegates to the annual convention of the Central Verein in that city on January 28, 1906, by declaring that it would be best for religion if the different nationalities which made up the people of the United States became one nation with one language as soon as possible. German Catholics reacted immediately, and for a time it appeared that the days of the 1880's and 1890's might return. For instance, the Milwaukee *Excelsior* declared that the Church would actually be served very little if Anglicizing was enforced, thousands of Catholic churches would be deserted if priests were forced upon them who could not speak the people's language, and children would be alienated by force from the language of their parents. If the English language were adopted, the immigrants would lose their faith and customs. The editors then made a point by noting:

Our German forefathers who fought for the independence of this land and the hundreds of thousands of Germans who fought in the Civil War were unquestionably better patriots than the Tories who spoke only English. Anyone who forgets his language as quickly as possible in order to adopt a new one is never a good patriot.

Religion will not be advanced by all Catholics speaking English

[24] *SRB,* XXIII (Jan., 1908), p. 541.
[25] *Ibid.,* XXV (Jan., 1910), p. 15.

> without exception. On the contrary, the result would be only strife and loss, tepidity in religion and defection of the majority. The man who values his mother tongue and his home traditions is also a good Christian and a reliable citizen.[26]

On March 25, 1906, Archbishop Möller qualified his statement of two months before by declaring, at a confirmation ceremony at St. Francis Church in Cincinnati, that spiritual instruction should be given in English in all English-speaking parishes, but in German parishes German should be preached, while in mixed parishes the instruction should be in both tongues.[27] Here the incident ended.

Not only in regard to acceptance of the principle of language rights, but also in regard to the appointment of bishops representing various national groups and the advancement of colonizing projects, there were indications after *Testem benevolentiae* that the Cahenslyism controversy was subsiding. German Catholics, especially in the St. Raphael societies, saw in these moves an acceptance of proposals made in their Lucerne Memorial as well as a vindication of their name and position. In Cleveland, where Bishop Gilmour had earlier spoken out against Reverend Peter Abbelen's proposals, Reverend Joseph M. Koudelka, Bohemian pastor of St. Michael's Church, Cleveland, was appointed as auxiliary bishop to Horstmann on November 29, 1907, with special jurisdiction over the Slavic peoples of the diocese. Bishop Horstmann had requested this move only a few months before his death, and Koudelka thus became the first auxiliary bishop in the United States with special jurisdiction over a racial group. Likewise in

[26] Milwaukee *Excelsior,* Feb. 8, 1906.

[27] Archbishop Diomede Falconio, O.F.M., successor to Cardinal Satolli as apostolic delegate to the United States, confirmed the Pottsville position of his predecessor a number of times during these years. When speaking of the education of Italian American children, Falconio stated in 1904: "Let us try with all our power to make them good Americans without letting the love of Italy disappear from their hearts" (*Review of Reviews,* III [June, 1904], p. 593). Falconio attended the Central Verein conventions in Cincinnati, 1905; Dubuque, 1907; and Indianapolis, 1909. At Indianapolis he declared: "We are in need of Catholic societies of this kind, today more than ever, and particularly in the United States where the passion for worldly possessions and pleasure is shaking the foundations of a Christian social order. The material progress of the United States is indeed amazing, but material progress and prosperity is not sufficient to make individuals and families happy. The spirit of the Gospel must be revived in all of us and your society must set an example of Christian virtues, Christian faith and Christian fortitude. Of the Germans it is said that they are strong and dependable, that they know what they want, and that they have the perseverance to attain what they are striving for. I, therefore, have no doubt that your efforts will be crowned with success and that the strong German character will be of greatest benefit to the future welfare of America, in helping to preserve the Christian character of the American people."

Chicago, on May 22, 1908, Reverend Paul P. Rhode, pastor of St. Michael's Church in that city, was named auxiliary to Archbishop James E. Quigley. Rhode was the first Polish priest elevated to the episcopate in the United States, and his appointment accomplished much in meeting demands from Polish Catholics which were similar to those from German Catholics of two decades previous.[28] On February 28, 1907, Reverend Soter S. Ortynsky, O.S.B.M., was named first Ukrainian bishop in the United States with jurisdiction over all Greek-rite Catholics in the United States. With the large influx of Slavic peoples from Austria-Hungary, which in the years from 1904–1907 reached a total of 1,538,788, the need became pressing for priests who spoke the language of these immigrants. As early as 1890 the Ruthenians had petitioned Propaganda for their own vicars, and at first an appeal had been made to Ruthenian bishops in Austria-Hungary for mission priests. But when this did not alleviate conditions, the Holy See erected an apostolic vicariate for all Ruthenians in the United States.

While the *St. Raphaels Blatt* saw in this move a further vindication of their request of 1891,[29] yet it was apparent that this bishopric was erected on the basis of rite and not of nationality, as the Germans had requested, and that auxiliary bishops, not residential bishops, were appointed in Cleveland and Chicago for the care of Slavic and Polish Catholics. In this way a happy compromise was achieved. The hierarchy was developed along national American lines, according to the traditional policy of the Holy See and as the Americanizers had consistently requested, while the peculiar American condition of immigrant nationals living together was recognized and auxiliary bishops were appointed to meet that need. It was a striking fact also that priests of German nationality were never appointed auxiliaries over the German population, but were rather appointed to residential sees, such as Milwaukee, Cincinnati, or La Crosse, an indication, it would seem, that the German immigrants were fast becoming Americanized as the Americanizers had foretold would inevitably come about.

The leaders of the St. Raphael Society also saw in the emphasis on colonizing projects among Catholics after the turn of the century a fulfillment of their own earlier plans which had been stifled as a

[28] Bishop Rhode was transferred to Green Bay in 1915, where he died in 1945. Bishop Koudelka was named auxiliary at Milwaukee in 1911, and ended his life in 1921 as Ordinary of Superior, Wisconsin.

[29] *SRB,* XXIII (July, 1908), pp. 575–577. Cf. also "Ea Semper," *AER,* XXXVII (Nov., 1907), pp. 513–520.

result of the odium attached to Cahenslyism. Messmer pointed the way while he was still Bishop of Green Bay by encouraging the German Catholic Staatsverband of Wisconsin, an affiliate of the Central Verein, to declare that "a thorough Catholic rural life is badly needed by the Church to advance our Catholic interests." It was suggested that the society buy wooded farm land in the neighborhood of a Catholic church and school, and there establish a German Catholic community and parish. Messmer believed if the German Catholics of Wisconsin would only organize their forces much could be done to advance immigrant colonies. Good land was going fast to syndicates and Protestant organizations, and Messmer wanted the central committee to place a member in each county to watch for suitable land.[30] When he was promoted to the metropolitan See of Milwaukee in 1903, he established an Immigrant and Land Bureau, to be associated with the Staatsverband, which issued pamphlets and encouraged German immigrants to come to Wisconsin. In Minnesota the state branch of the Central Verein likewise established an Immigrant Bureau at St. Paul to attract Catholic Germans to the city of New Ulm and into the Minnesota River Valley. Archbishop Ireland, ever a firm advocate of Catholic colonizing projects, gave his support to this venture. Cahensly stated that when he had first come to the United States in 1883 to establish the Leo House he realized how little had been done in the western states for German colonizers. He had spoken privately with German Catholic leaders and encouraged them to organize, but the idea had not developed. The American branch of St. Raphael had begun such efforts, but the Cahenslyism misunderstanding had halted that work. Now Cahensly hoped that the project would be revived and the Catholic immigrant protected in his new home so that the Church could flourish on the land in the new world.[31]

But it was the establishment, in 1910, of the Catholic Colonization Society of the Church Extension Society of the United States which brought to fruition the dreams of Catholic colonizers of former years. This Society developed from earlier efforts of Belgian and Dutch priests to establish a society to aid their own Catholic immigrants. In May, 1910, the Archbishop of St. Louis, John J. Glennon, sponsored an organizational meeting in his see city of priests interested in such work. At that time statutes were drawn up on a broader basis for all

[30] *ADCV,* Messmer to President of Wisconsin German Catholic Staatsverband, Green Bay, Jan. 9, 1895, copy.

[31] *SRB,* XVIII (July, 1903), pp. 232–237. Cf. also *SRB,* XXV (July, 1909), pp. 715–718, for history of the Association of Belgian and Dutch Priests.

nationalities, a central bureau erected to be under the direction of the American archbishops, diocesan bureaus projected under local ordinaries, and a central committee established which was composed of Glennon as chancellor, Reverend Julius E. De Vos, pastor of St. John Berchmans Church, Chicago, president, Monsignor Denis J. MacMahon, pastor of the Church of Epiphany, New York, vice-president, and Reverend Edward J. Vattmann, apostolic missionary in residence at Willmette, Illinois, secretary. On April 27, 1910, the first national meeting was held in Chicago, with nine archbishops, several bishops and priests present. The aim of the society was to sponsor Catholic colonies in the West and South of the country where a priest could be supported, where immigrants could have their own language as long as they needed it, and where provision could be made for the spiritual and material security of incoming Catholics. Italians, Belgians, and Dutch were to be the first concern of the organization, and land sites were sought in Florida, Arkansas, Mississippi, Missouri, Wisconsin, and Minnesota. Archbishops Glennon, Ireland, Messmer, James H. Blenk, S.M., of New Orleans, and Bishop Joseph Schrembs, Auxiliary Bishop of Grand Rapids, were especially active in the work. Ten land companies offered to co-operate with the project, and the hierarchies of Belgium and Holland promised strong support to Glennon in an effort to secure chaplains from Europe. The Archbishop of St. Louis believed that, of the 700,000 Catholic immigrants each year, three fourths of that number were farmers who should be directed to colonies on the land rather than to large metropolitan and industrial centers. Archbishop Ireland further declared in Chicago at the first national meeting:

> We must labor in our country for the spiritual care and protection of the religious and moral welfare of those who come to us from the best sections of Europe. A recognized society should guide the colonists on their journey here; worthy immigrants should then be directed on their path to American citizenship. This is truly patriotic work as well as sound religious development. Two important foundations should be established: worship of God and Christian education in each colony which we establish. We aim to protect the immigrant from the perils of his arrival and from religious proselytizing. We are interested only in the Catholic whom we guide and protect, not with the land he acquires or the shop where he works.[32]

Both Glennon and De Vos sought the co-operation of Cahensly in the work, recognizing that it must first begin in Europe, and charac-

[32] *SRB,* XXVI (Jan., 1911), p. 753.

terizing immigrant care as a modern crusade for Christian leaders to meet the task of the times and protect the Church from serious losses. To Cahensly this was like hearing the echo of his own words coming back to him after forty years. De Vos further informed Cahensly that on a train from Washington to Chicago for the meeting, Archbishop Ireland had declared to him that Cahensly had been misunderstood and that he would now be pleased if they could obtain the St. Raphael leader's co-operation.[33] In turn, Cahensly declared that he was "not a little pleased" at this turn of events, and with his usual energy he immediately began to ask practical questions. He was just leaving for Austria and wanted exact instructions on where Slovenian, Slovak, Bohemian, Pole, or Lithuanian farmers could be sent, how much the land would cost, and so forth. Glennon suggested that both the German and American branches of the St. Raphaelsverein co-operate with the new society so that the Leo House could be utilized at the landing docks. From this time forward until his death Cahensly worked with the Catholic Colonization Society and directed immigrants, through his publications and missions, to settle in that society's western land projects. The co-operation he had so long sought had at length been achieved, but on a basis that was more in accord with the American situation than he had at first attempted. Now bishops representing dioceses with Catholics of several nationalities were involved in the effort, and in the United States the international co-operation he had asked for was realized through the joint efforts of one official society composed of all national groups making up the Catholic population.

Misunderstandings such as the St. Raphael Society suffered in former years were prevented because this association aimed at caring for all national elements together in one organization which, at the same time, recognized the particular differences and rights of each nationality involved. In this way a unity based on common Catholicity was achieved, and the processes of Americanization followed in due course. The new society recognized the contribution that national Catholic societies in Europe, such as the St. Raphaelsverein in both Austria-Hungary and Germany, could make to the effort. In addition the society in the United States also needed to have both a Catholic

[33] *ADCV,* Cahensly to De Vos, Limburg, Jan. 16, 1911, copy. Bishop Joseph P. Lynch, of Dallas, when visiting the Catholic Colonization Society of Wilmette, Illinois, in 1913, declared that the society was doing what Cahensly had aimed at twenty years earlier, i.e., establishing colonies for immigrants where they could use their mother tongue: "How many would have been saved had the pleas of the esteemed Mr. Cahensly been realized" (*FR,* XX [Apr., 1913], p. 118).

and a national character. It would have to be American, not a society of separate German, Italian, Belgian, or Austrian units as the original St. Raphael societies had been constituted.

The year 1910 also found Cahensly returning to the United States for his first visit in twenty-seven years. The occasion of this tour was his participation in the International Eucharistic Congress at Montreal, where he delivered an address on St. Raphael emigration work. The German leader crossed the ocean on the *Empress of Ireland* as a fellow passenger with the papal legate, Vincenzo Cardinal Vannutelli, and he was so enthusiastic at the reception accorded him on his arrival that he reported to his friend, Right Reverend Lorenz Werthmann at the Caritasverband in Freiburg im Breisgau: "we have 100,000 friends here in Montreal."[34] After the address of Cahensly both Bishops Richter and Schrembs, of Grand Rapids, rose to support his proposals. The latter spoke out for the preservation of the mother tongue among immigrants to the new world, and for priests to care for immigrants in their native language. He extended an invitation as well to immigrants to come to the Diocese of Grand Rapids, where they would find colonies already existing. After the congress was ended Cahensly toured the western provinces of Canada to view at firsthand the condition of German settlers there, in company with Abbot Bruno Dörfler, of St. Peter's Abbey and its colony in Saskatchewan.

From Toronto the St. Raphael leader moved on to the United States through Buffalo, Pittsburgh, Chicago, St. Louis, Washington, Baltimore, Philadelphia, and New York. In many ways it proved a triumphal tour, as German leaders, editors, and clergy welcomed him at every stop. Cahensly was pleased with conditions as he found them among the Germans in Buffalo, Rochester, Pittsburgh, and St. Louis. To him St. Louis was "the most important center of Catholic Germanism," while Rochester evidenced what he called an "indefatigable application of correctly understood Cahenslyism." In Chicago, while being received by Archbishop Quigley, he again met Cardinal Vannutelli who praised the work of the St. Raphael societies and expressed his good will toward German Catholics. Cahensly discussed

[34] *ADCV,* Cahensly to Werthmann, Montreal, Sept. 4, 1910. Rt. Rev. Count Vay de Vaya and Luskod, of Budapest, made journeys in 1905 and 1907 to the United States to study conditions among the growing numbers of Slavic immigrants. His reports were in the same vein as Cahensly's of former years, namely, that there would ensue a loss of faith if the mother tongue and pastors using the mother tongue were not employed in the United States for immigrants (*SRB,* XX [Oct., 1905], pp. 93–97).

German conditions with the editors of the Buffalo *Volksfreund,* with his personal friend Arthur Preuss in St. Louis, the editors of *Nord Amerika,* and the convert, Frederick P. Kenkel, who was director of the Central Bureau of the Verein and editor of *Amerika* and of the *Central Blatt.* When Cahensly arrived in Washington he received one of the most pleasant surprises of his trip. At the Catholic University of America where, as he said, Schröder and Pohle had for years brought German "Wissenschaft" to that institution, he found his "former sharp opponents now enthusiastically affirming that they had corrected their judgments on Cahenslyism." Monsignor Shahan, the rector, asked him to prepare a paper to be read at the first annual meeting of the National Conference of Catholic Charities in Washington on September 25–28, 1910, but, unfortunately, he could not delay his return until that date, although he did leave behind a memorandum for that purpose. In Baltimore he visited the St. Raphael mission at that port, and then was graciously received by Cardinal Gibbons who invited him to dine with him. Archbishop Ryan in Philadelphia likewise expressed warm sympathy, and when he arrived in New York to see his first foundation, the Leo House, not only was he given a public reception at the Catholic Club of New York, but Archbishop Farley, in an interview on October 3, asked him to draw up a report on his observations made during this journey through the United States, and to append to it suggestions for the betterment of conditions among Catholic immigrants from the various European countries. Five days later Cahensly had the report ready, having incorporated all his original points for immigrant care, but now pointed especially to the amelioration of conditions among the new immigrant groups, especially the Slavic and Italian Catholics.[35]

How different this tour and report had been from the first visit of 1883 or the Lucerne Memorial of 1891. The only unpleasant incident occurred when the Central Verein decided to cancel Cahensly's scheduled address at their annual session in Newark because of fear of unpleasant complications. Apart from that disappointment he had come in contact not only with German Catholics in the United States, but also with other groups and leaders of the many elements that at that time made up American Catholicism. He had visited the leading churchmen of the country and his report this time was presented at the suggestion of the Archbishop of New York to the American bishops themselves, and not to the Holy See as a memorial which could

[35] *AANY,* Cahensly to Farley, New York, Oct. 8, 1910. Cahensly's memorial of 1910 is contained in Appendix IX (pp. 326–328).

give any grounds for suspicion of interference. Nor could there be any interpretation on this occasion that he was reporting on the hierarchy of another country as had been the case with the international memorial that emanated from Lucerne.

In the written commentary on his trip which he published in the *St. Raphaels Blatt,* and in his oral report to the *Katholikentag* at Augsburg in 1911, Cahensly stressed what he had stated to Farley, namely, that the condition of the German Catholics was good in the United States, and that now it was the Slavic and Italian immigrants who occupied the unfavorable position that the Germans once held. He found that the Germans were rapidly abandoning their native language for English, a prophecy that the Americanizers had always advanced. But he still insisted that the mother tongue was an absolute necessity for the new immigrants, which would seem to indicate once again that his advocacy throughout previous controversies of the need of their native language for Catholic immigrants was never based on a desire to advance German interests, but rather to advance and to preserve the faith of these persons so far removed from their original homes. He also declared that there were not sufficient priests to care for foreign Catholics, a result of which, he said, was the very great losses suffered by the Catholic Church. Here also Cahensly refused to give ground; he now estimated the losses at six million, ten million less than the original estimate at Lucerne of sixteen million, but yet a large calculation. He moved at the annual assembly of German Catholic Societies that German Catholic literature should be sent to the Germans in the United States to help preserve the German language which was fast fading away, and as a means of sustaining a religious, national, cultural, and charitable bond between brothers in the faith.[36]

The question of losses to the Church in the United States continued throughout these years to be as a source of major differences among Catholics both at home and abroad. Jules Tardivel, editor of *La Vérité,* of Quebec, and ardent defender of Cahenslyism among French Canadians in the United States, made a critical survey in 1900 of the religious situation in the latter country. His unfavorable report on the character and practices of American Catholicism stated that the losses had been "prodigious," and at least ten million in total.[37] Some

[36] *SRB,* XXV (Oct., 1910), pp. 737–742. Cf. also *Central Blatt and Social Justice,* XXIV (July, 1932), p. 337, and *Caritas,* XVI (1911), p. 145.

[37] Jules Tardivel, *La situation religieuse aux États-Unis* (Montreal, 1900), pp. 251–268. One of the rare, and consequently strikingly interesting, alliances of French

years later Dr. Anton Gisler, professor of dogma at the University of Fribourg in Switzerland and later Coadjutor Bishop of Chur, in his book on modernism also supported the figures advanced by the Lucerne Memorial.[38] On the other hand, both Bishops J. Regis Canevin, of Pittsburgh, and Thomas O'Gorman, of Sioux Falls, published population studies of the Church in the United States, in which they strove to repudiate these figures which they considered unreliable. They defended the calculations of the Americanizers, such as Ireland or Shea, who had set Catholic losses at between one and one-half and two and one-half million during the nineteenth century.[39] But Arthur Preuss, in the columns of his *Fortnightly Review,* remained loyal to the European figures on American Catholic losses, and for years he published tabulations, statistical studies, and conclusions which stressed serious losses of at least one half and deprecated American boasting concerning the condition of the Church.[40] Martin I. J. Griffin, Philadelphia publicist, declared before an assembly of Catholic publishers at Columbus, Ohio, in 1911, that the assertion of great losses to the Church on American soil were unfounded, and he also joined the increasing number of speculators on this question with conclusions that corresponded to Shea's calculations of 1874 in the *Irish World,* and of 1884 and 1892 in the *Catholic News.*[41] The controversy was not conclusively settled in those years and it remained a largely

---

and Germans developed during these years between French Canadian and German immigrant groups in the Church of the United States. Throughout the whole period they both opposed Americanization and defended Cahenslyism. Cf., for example, Arthur Preuss in *FR,* XVI (May, 1909), pp. 260–262; and Worcester, Massachusetts, *L'Opinion Publique,* May 8, 1909; Fall River, Mass., *L'Independent,* Nov. 20, 1912.

[38] Gisler, *op. cit.,* pp. 89–102.

[39] J. Regis Canevin, *An Examination Historical and Statistical with Losses and Gains of the Catholic Church in the United States from 1790–1910* (Pittsburgh, 1912); Thomas O'Gorman, *A History of the Roman Catholic Church in the United States* (New York, 1907), *passim.*

Bishop John Lancaster Spalding, of Peoria, denied serious losses in his famous address at the Jesù Church in Rome on March 21, 1900. He stated: "There have doubtless been losses, but in the midst of struggle and battle loss is inevitable. Has there, then, been no falling away from the faith, no decay of spiritual life among the Catholics of other nations? Are not our losses in America to be attributed largely to the indifference or ignorance of many of those who come to us from countries that are called Catholic? Nevertheless, the history of the Church in the English-speaking world during the nineteenth century is one of real and great progress" (John Lancaster Spalding, *Education and the Future of Religion* [Chicago, 1900], p. 47).

[40] *FR,* XVI (July, 1909), pp. 389–391; XVIII (Mar., 1911), pp. 136–138; XVIII (Apr., 1911), pp. 227–230; XIX (June, 1912), pp. 360–362, 612–616; XX (Jan., 1913), pp. 17–19.

[41] Toledo *Record,* Sept. 1, 1911.

unsolved question until 1925, when Gerald Shaughnessy, S.M., prepared a scientific study at the Catholic University of America on the topic, *Has the Immigrant Kept the Faith?* Here the charges of Cahensly (sixteen, ten, or six million loss), Villeneuve (twenty million loss), Enzelberger and Walburg (two-thirds loss of the total Catholic population), as well as of those who quoted these men, were analyzed scientifically and rejected. Shaughnessy, unlike his predecessors, studied United States Government immigration statistics, the authorities on population, European emigration figures, census reports, and the rough estimates of Catholic numbers since no official Catholic census had ever been taken in the United States. After exhaustive analysis of each decade from 1820–1920, Shaughnessy concluded:

> 1. It is absolutely certain that there has been no enormous loss to the faith (that is, a loss of ten, fifteen, twenty, or thirty million Catholics) because of immigration to the United States during the past century.
>
> 2. There is no evidence of even an appreciable or measurable loss (two, three, five million) during the period.
>
> 3. It is very probable that there has been no loss at all, beyond that defection of Catholics which ordinarily takes place among any population, due to the weakness of human nature and the usual manifestations of the same.
>
> 4. If the Catholic immigration of the past century had not taken place, the Church in the United States, scattered over the immense expanse of the nation, would very probably today be a replica of the Church of 1790, a weak, anemic body, by the very force of circumstances, unable to conquer the insuperable, chiefly physical, obstacles which would prevent her growth.
>
> 5. It is due to immigration that the Catholic Church in America today stands out among her sister Churches of other nations, the equal of any, if not indeed superior to all, in loyalty, vitality, fidelity, and stability.[42]

The findings of Shaughnessy's study in good measure brought to an end the sharp and recriminatory aspects of a long and involved question in the history of the Church in the United States. True, the work did not settle the question to everyone's satisfaction, and flaws have been found in Shaughnessy's method, but at least after 1925 there

[42] Gerald Shaughnessy, S.M., *Has the Immigrant Kept the Faith?* (New York, 1925), pp. 221–222. Shaughnessy dedicated his effort to the "American hierarchy, the American priests, and the American peoples who under the guidance of the Holy See built the Church in the United States better than they knew." In 1933 Shaughnessy was appointed Bishop of Seattle.

was at hand for the first time a serious and scholastic analysis which lifted the discussion to a higher and more objective level. Both European and American students had advanced theories and figures to prove, it would seem, as a support for the attitude they held on the American Church, serious or minor losses to the faith. German Catholics had consistently maintained in their various petitions and in their press that great losses had occurred, and they advanced this thesis as a primary proof of the necessity for their language, customs, parishes, rights, and so forth in order to prevent further leakage. On the other hand, the Americanizers had insisted that the losses were not extraordinarily heavy, no more so than in other nations, nor more than the character and instruction of immigrant Catholics arriving from Europe would presuppose. In this contention the Americanizers were closer to statistical facts than the critics of conditions in the American Church. In time the St. Raphaelsverein itself, one of the most fervent proponents of large-scale leakage from the American Church, came to recognize that earlier figures had been exaggerated, that the calculations had been inaccurate, and that losses had often occurred even before many nominal or poorly instructed Catholics had left their home lands.[43] Earlier recognition of this fact would have prevented much misunderstanding.

Cahensly's triumphal tour of Canada and the United States in 1910 was not the only vindication he and his society enjoyed during the years before World War I. In Rome he was received by the Pope in a number of audiences, and a series of honors were bestowed upon him which left no doubt of his good standing. On December 28, 1902, the St. Raphael leader had the privilege of his last private audience with Leo XIII. In this lengthy conference the Pontiff stressed the importance of priests being acquainted with the language of the emigrants so that they might care for the growing number of Catholics in the United States. According to Cahensly, Leo XIII spoke with deep understanding of the immigrant character of the American

[43] Cahensly's co-worker and later editor of the *SRB,* Heinrich Herkenrath, wrote in 1914: "On the strength of all the fluctuating researches and studies today it may be said that losses in figures running into the millions, can by no means be charged arbitrarily to the New World. They belonged in large measure to branches of the tree of the Church which in Europe unfortunately had for a long time been dead, or retained but little vitality" (*Festschrift zum silbernen Jubiläum des Leo Hauses* [New York, 1914], p. 21).

Cf. also George A. Kelly and Thomas Coogan, "What is Our Total Catholic Population?" *AER,* CXI (May, 1944), pp. 368–377; George Anthony Kelly, *Catholics and the Practice of the Faith; a Census Study of the Diocese of Saint Augustine* (Washington, 1946).

Church, and mentioned the fact that in 1901 three fourths of the emigrants to the United States from ten different nations had been Catholics. The Pope termed the St. Raphael effort a "great work," and, after Cahensly had again denied the political motives which had been attributed to his program, the Holy Father stated: "Your work is good if you rescue the souls of others. It is a pledge of your eternal salvation."

On April 16, 1904, Cahensly was received in private audience by Leo's successor, Pius X, who asked for a full report of his activities, and gave approval of this work for what he called "the salvation of souls by priests using the language of the emigrants." Again in November, 1908, and on June 18, 1909, Cahensly had further audiences with Pius X. At the latter interview he presented a new memorandum to the Pope in which he explained that from July 1, 1899, to June 30, 1907, more than five million Europeans had gone to the United States, and, of these, four million were Catholics representing twenty different nations. In the previous ten years, 4,445,852 Catholics had emigrated, he affirmed, but the growth of the American Church in that period had been but two and a half million. He made reference to the Lucerne Memorial of 1891, and recommended anew that colonies be established, that pastors be obtained from the same nationality as the colonists, that pastors be required to use several languages in mixed parishes, and that parish schools be erected in which both English and the mother tongue of the emigrants should be taught. Cahensly also asked Pius X to encourage the establishment of new St. Raphael societies in nations where they were not already operating. It was said that the Pope received the petition "with much good will" and evidenced keen interest in furthering the work, especially among the growing number of Italian emigrants. He appointed Monsignor Cocolo to implement his desire that an Italian priest be on board every emigrant ship that carried Italian Catholics to the United States. At the end of the audience the Pontiff took a picture of himself from his desk drawer and presented it to Cahensly with the following inscription written in his own hand: "To our beloved sons, the President, Directors and Members of the St. Raphael Societies, who work for the protection of emigrants from all lands to America, best wishes from our soul. We bestow upon you from our heart the apostolic blessing as reward for your labors and for future accomplishment." The St. Raphael leaders likewise saw a further vindication of their efforts in Pius X's *motu proprio, De Catholicorum in exteras regiones emigratione,* of August 15, 1912, in which he spoke of the Church's traditional and special solicitude for emigrants, and thereupon proceeded to establish a special department of the Consistorial Congregation for emigrant care. As a result of this papal document, Arthur Preuss went so far as to term Pius X a Cahenslyite.[44]

Personal honors were now also coming to Cahensly. In 1899 he was awarded the papal gold cross *Pro Ecclesia et Pontifice;* in 1903, the star of St. Gregory, and knightship in the Order of St. Gregory with the rank of commander; in 1907, the distinction of papal chamberlain *di spada e cappa;* and personal apostolic blessings on the occasions of his seventy-fifth and eightieth birthdays. To his St. Raphael societies plenary indulgences for all members had been extended as early as 1894, 1901, and 1908. They were rendered automatic every seven years after the last date. There could no longer be any doubt, therefore, of the standing of Peter Paul Cahensly and his program at the Vatican.[45] Recognition came belatedly from his own government as well. Although no longer a member of the Reichstag, he was chosen by the government in 1897 to serve on the Committee for Emigration Affairs which drew up and saw through the imperial

[44] *FR,* XX (Feb., 1913), p. 118. Cahensly's audience was discussed in *SRB,* XVIII (Apr., 1903), pp. 20–23; XX (Jan., 1905), p. 346; *C,* VIII (1903), p. 143. Paul Maria Baumgarten reported in the *Allgemeine Rundschau,* Nov., 1910, on the significance of this interview as full papal recognition for the aims of Cahensly. He stated that he personally could confirm that in the future the Propaganda would be attentive "with an especially sharp eye" to appoint bishops in those American areas from the national background of the predominant element in the population. Of the Americanizers he wrote: "The nativistic exaggerators among the Catholics of the Union also begin to have their eyes opened, and to recognize that they have pulled on the wrong rope. The energy which they expended . . . would only produce astonishment and wonder.

"When the word 'Cahenslyism' has been entered in the American Standard Dictionary, and the definition given there cannot be consonant with the facts, then may the tireless president of the St. Raphael Society be consoled by the thought that Pope Pius X has recognized his excellent activity for the conservation and salvation of immortal souls from seduction and loss of faith by presenting him with a golden, silver and copper medal with his picture" (*SRB,* XX [Apr., 1905], p. 62). Modern day St. Raphael leaders saw in the concordats drawn up by the Holy See under Pius XI a further vindication of the Lucerne Memorial, because in these agreements between Church and State the right of spiritual care in the mother tongue of the people involved was always included (Nathem, *Peter Paul Cahensly. Ein Gedenkblatt zu seinem 100. Geburtstag. 1838* 28. October *1938* [Hamburg, 1938], p. 32). Archbishop Wilhelm Berning, bishop of Osnabrück, and present honorary president of the St. Raphaelsverein, declared in an interview with the author that Benedict XV in April, 1920, had praised the St. Raphael Society as the protector of faith and nationality, and that Pius XI had informed him in October, 1924, that the right of a people to Christian instruction and pastoral care in their mother tongue was a natural right.

[45] *DGH,* II, p. 1726.

parliament the first Reich emigration law for care and supervision of emigrants. Thus the law that Cahensly had advocated since the 1870's was finally enacted, but at a time when it served the needs of departing German citizens to an insignificant degree, and after the main emigration movement from the fatherland had ended, due to improved economic, political, and religious conditions at home. In 1902, as a recognition of his parliamentary services, he was awarded the Cross of the *Rote Adler-Orden IV. Classe,* and in 1903, on the occasion of the centenary of his Limburg commercial establishment, he was named to the Imperial Prussian Council of Commerce.

To Cahensly these distinctions were as nothing compared to the satisfaction he experienced at the growth and extension of new branches of the St. Raphael Society. As the character of emigration changed to southern European and Slavic peoples, the society's efforts were concentrated on the Austro-Hungarian and Italian branches. The problems of seasonal workers in Germany were met in 1896, care for unattached young women in 1897, protection of sailors in 1898, and provisions for Italian workers in Germany in 1899. The Spanish branch of the society was established in 1913, and that office assumed jurisdiction over the Spanish-speaking world. In 1898, at the second *Caritastag* in Wiesbaden, the St. Raphaelsverein in Germany was joined as a self-sustaining member to the *Caritas* organization, the central and official welfare conference of all German societies under the direction of the German hierarchy with headquarters at Freiburg im Breisgau. Monsignor Lorenz Werthmann, organizer and first director of the *Caritasverband,* worked closely with Cahensly during his declining years, and gradually assumed direction of the St. Raphael activities. Werthmann and Cahensly, who were both from Limburg, were close friends and shared similar ideals, especially in their desire to internationalize Catholic charity. In 1909 they established an International Conference for Emigration Problems, and through this medium they aimed at spreading the theory and techniques which Cahensly had learned and applied during the previous half century. In this broader mold of the *Caritasverband* he also found in Germany itself the international effort which he had contemplated from the beginning.

By 1913 the St. Raphael Society was able to report that since its beginning it had cared for 2,422,863 emigrants in the European ports of departure; offered religious services to 2,250,000, of whom 406,972 had confessed and received Holy Communion; banked 21,218,524 DM ($5,304,630); and written 156,867 letters for emigrants. In the year

1913 alone the society took in 28,928.16 DM ($7,232) through memberships, collections, and donations, of which 25,735.16 DM ($6,436) was paid out for its services.[46] This record spoke for itself and remained as a striking tribute to the accomplishment of the St. Raphael Society in social action. Before World War I temporarily interrupted immigration and the work of the St. Raphael societies, there were 109 agents of St. Raphael operating throughout the world: fifteen in Europe, fourteen in Canada, three in Argentina, twenty-two in Brazil, seventeen in Uruguay, twelve each in Africa and Australia, two in Chile, one each in Mexico and Peru, and twenty in the United States.

In the United States the first daughter branch of the society likewise continued its program of aid and service for German immigrants, but it, too, broadened its base of operation to include more and more of the Slavic peoples emigrating from the Austro-Hungarian Empire. After the United States Government took over direction of immigration affairs and transferred registration and inspection from Castle

[46] George Timpe, S.A.C., *Der St. Raphaelsverein, sein Gründer und seine Arbeit* (Hamburg, 1921), and "PP. Cahensly," *Staatslexikon der Görres Gesellschaft* (Freiburg i. Br., 1926), I, p. 1155; Lorenz Werthmann, *Das Auswandererproblem*. VII. *Fünfzig Jahre Raphaelsvereins* (Freiburg i. Br., 1919), pp. 9–15; *Rechenschafts Berichte des St. Raphaelsvereins zum Schutze katholischer deutscher Auswanderer für die Jähre 1881–1919* (Limburg a. d. Lahn, 1882–1920); *C*, I (1895), p. 270; II (1896), p. 35; III (1898), pp. 22, 166, 278, 279; IX (1904), p. 155; XVII (1912), p. 51; XVIII (1913), p. 47; XIX (1914), p. 45; *Nassauer Boten*, Apr. 28, 1903.

The St. Raphaelsverein did not only survive the death of its founder, but grew to high importance in the 1920's. The living force of Cahensly's ideas was carried on by Archbishop Berning of Osnabrück, honorary president of the society, and Reverend George Timpe, S.A.C., secretary-general. The Central Bureau, which Werthmann had taken over during Cahensly's disabilities, was transferred to Hamburg in 1921, and there under Father Timpe the society continued with renewed vigor its traditional activities in behalf of the Catholic emigrant. Reverend Max Grösser, S.A.C., succeeded Father Timpe upon the latter's retirement in 1930 from that post, and he directed activities during the years of growing Nazi domination and mistrust of any German emigrant organization. He died suddenly on March 19, 1940, after having been imprisoned for a month by the Nazis following a trip to the United States in which he besought co-operation from the American hierarchy in sponsorship of Jewish emigrants. The Nazis wanted to know who had financed the trip, and also thought he had made dollars in the United States. On June 25, 1941, the Nazis finally took over the Central Bureau and closed the office. But as soon as the war was over Archbishop Berning again requested a priest from the provincial of the Pallottine Fathers, and Reverend Friedrich Fröhling, S.A.C., was appointed new secretary-general, a post he still holds. Today the society is serving the millions of displaced persons who come to its doors.

The crowning aim of Cahensly was achieved on June 6, 1951, when Pius XII erected and blessed the endeavors of an International Catholic Migration Commission. Its original membership included Germany, Great Britain, Italy, The Netherlands, Argentina, Australia, Brazil, Canada, and the United States. Cf. *80 Jahre St. Raphaelsverein, 1871–1951* (Hamburg, 1951).

Garden to Ellis Island, government officials assumed full responsibility for the care of the immigrant. Besides a registration hall, the new landing place had waiting rooms, detention rooms, baggage and railroad rooms, department for exchanging money, hospitals, and the like, all under governmental direction. Third and fourth class passengers were placed under government jurisdiction until they were en route to their new destination, and thus many of the evils of former days were eliminated. Accordingly, the St. Raphael agents contacted immigrants only after they had passed inspection, but they still could aid them both spiritually and materially in many ways. The society in New York also extended its welfare work to embrace railroad travelers, religious and clergy who sought accommodations at the Leo House when traveling to and from Europe, and care for young women who arrived in second class from Europe and who were often subjected to the same dangers that earlier immigrants had undergone in steerage. In the years before World War I the Leo House corporation made plans to move to a location that would be closer to the landing docks and railroad stations, but it was not until after the war that the expansion and construction of the present house at 332 West 23 Street could be undertaken.

Not only in New York, but also in Philadelphia; Baltimore; Brooklyn; Buffalo; New Orleans; Pittsburgh; Washington; Galveston; Rockland Lake, New York; and Childs, Maryland, St. Raphael agents were active. In Galveston a mission was established in 1907 because of increasing German immigration into Texas and the southwestern sections of the country. In Milwaukee; Dubuque; St. Louis; Chicago; Mount Angel, Oregon; and Clarksville, Arkansas, six agents kept contact with German Catholics after they had reached their new homes in the West. Although German immigration decreased considerably after the turn of the century, the society continued its program as long as there were any settlers in need of assistance. Cahensly kept in close contact with American efforts at all times, and advertised their facilities and services throughout Europe. In 1908, when responding to greetings sent to him from the Leo House on the occasion of his seventieth birthday, the German leader reiterated his earnest desires of a lifetime in immigrant welfare when he said:

> I hope and desire that your house will always extend an open welcome to Germans who come to the United States of America, as well as a good home to those who intermittently travel between the homeland and their new homes. I earnestly intreat you to labor through your

agents so that the St. Raphael Society will enlarge, and expand and expand.[47]

Although international recognition and honors had come to Cahensly during the last years of his life, yet in the United States a cloud continued to surround his name and his aims even after his death. German Catholics in the United States gratefully acknowledged his contribution, but the charge of Cahenslyism in its traditional connotation appeared at regular intervals in secular papers and often, too, in Catholic publications. The accusation of political Pan-Germanism refused to die easily as the Brooklyn *Monitor* made evident in 1918 when it said:

> The simple truth is that there was an element in Cahenslyism which made it very distasteful to the American people. Whether it was meant or not, this element possessed the character of a German propaganda. No one would object to saving the souls of the immigrant, but what was objectionable was the introduction of the national and political element. A German episcopate throughout the United States in addition to the Bishops appointed over American sees was a political dream which the United States was certain to dissipate.[48]

Arthur Preuss never failed to answer all charges of this nature that came to his attention, and he had in mind to write a complete documentary history of Cahenslyism. Cahensly had requested him to undertake this project during his visit of 1911, but Preuss was too occupied with his publishing business to do more than answer charges and deny falsehoods. As late as February, 1922, Preuss declared:

> There is absolutely nothing in the career of Mr. P. P. Cahensly or the movement falsely branded as "Cahenslyism" that reflects the slightest discredit on either Germany or the Church. Cahensly's name will live in history, but it should not be held in reprobation, but in honor, because its possessor was an exceptionally enlightened and zealous

[47] *ALH,* Cahensly to Urban Nageleisen, Limburg, Nov. 4, 1908. Cf. also *Leo House Annual Report, 1889–1914* (New York, 1890–1915); *ADL,* Joseph Schäffer to Canon Eiffler, New York, July 26, 1894; *SRB,* XXVI (Jan., 1911), pp. 754–758. The Leo House issued an American counterpart of the *SRB* with its *Das Leo Haus Blatt,* which first appeared in January, 1902, and carried information on the activities of the society in the United States.

[48] XXXVIII, p. 4. Cf. also St. Paul *Bulletin,* Sept. 27, 1918, and rebuttal in *Amerika,* Nov. 11, 1918; Buffalo *Echo,* Oct. 9, 1918; Dubuque *Catholic Tribune,* Oct. 25, 1918; *Die Aurora und christliche Woche,* Oct. 18, 1918; New York *Times,* June 3, 1917, and rebuttal in Buffalo *Echo,* June 7, 1917; also *Freiburger Tagespost,* Jan. 4, 1934; *Der Wanderer,* Nov. 17, 1938; George Weibel, *Die katholische Missionen in nordöstl. Arkansas* (Little Rock, 1893), pp. 69, 70, 71.

Catholic, who sacrificed much time and no small part of his modest fortune for the benefit of his fellow men.[49]

Yet American Catholic writers, such as Maurice Francis Egan, who followed the lead of Allen Sinclair Will, as well as Michael Williams and Theodore Maynard, not only confused the historical facts of the case, but also handed down in their publications the fable of Cahensly's effort to retain German emigrants as part of a German state hegemony and to control the Church in the United States.[50] Even the News Service of the National Catholic Welfare Conference issued a release on a speech delivered by John A. Lapp, director of its Social Action Department, at the Mid-West Conference on Public Service in St. Louis on May 10, 1926, in which it was asserted that the Church had culminated its service to Americanizing the immigrant in what was called

> . . . the famous contest against the proposal to have the Church organized on a national basis, each nationality having its own pastors and bishops. In a memorable fight conducted by Cardinal Gibbons, this movement, known as Cahenslyism, was completely destroyed. What that meant in the time of the great World War can be readily imagined.[51]

[49] *FR,* XXIX (Feb., 1922), p. 55. Cf. *ACV,* Cahensly to Preuss, Limburg, Aug. 20, 1911, Sept. 23, 1911, and May 5, 1912, for examples of the close contacts Cahensly kept with developments in the United States on all problems concerning German Catholics. In the last letter Cahensly encouraged Preuss to write the history of Cahenslyism, and stated that he believed the articles by Joseph Matt in *Der Wanderer* of 1911 on Cahenslyism entitled, "Who Bears the Responsibility?" had presented the case as it should be understood. Cf. *Der Wanderer,* Nov. 16, 23, 30, and Dec. 14, 1911.

Cf. also *ACV* for a ninety-five page manuscript summary of Cahenslyism, "Beginnings of the So-Called Cahenslyism," by Rev. John M. Lenhart, O.F.M.Cap. Father Lenhart sent this document to the late F. P. Kenkel on April 21, 1943. Here the German nationality controversy of these years is compared to the dispute between St. Columbanus and the Frankish bishops in regard to Irish customs, as well as the Irish custom of establishing separate churches in Ireland for different clans. Cahensly is defended throughout the manuscript, and rather exhaustive documentation is supplied. Lenhart also declares that as early as the year 1902 Cardinal Gibbons expressed his regrets in a gathering of German American priests that he was influenced by Archbishop Ireland to champion his cause of Americanism; Bishop Shahan likewise corrected his earlier stand; and Cardinal Gibbons did not mention Cahensly or Americanism in his *Retrospect of Fifty Years* (New York, 1916). Lenhart further associates Archbishop Ireland's ideas with French liberal democracy "of the Lamennais type."

[50] Maurice Francis Egan, *Ten Years near the German Frontier* (New York, 1919), pp. 159, 166–167; Michael Williams, *American Catholics in the War* (New York, 1921), pp. 78–83; Theodore Maynard, *Story of American Catholicism* (New York, 1943), pp. 174, 509, 519.

[51] "Address of John A. Lapp to the Mid-West Conference on Public Service, St. Louis, May 10, 1926" (*News Service of NCWC,* Washington, May 10, 1926).

Archbishop Messmer collected materials on Cahenslyism and intended, like Preuss, to write an authentic history of the movement in the United States, but because of his advanced age and his numerous responsibilities he was unable to devote time to this project. Messmer declared publicly, however, at the sixty-seventh annual assembly of the Central Verein at Milwaukee in 1923 in praise of Cahensly and his work: "As I actually know, Cardinal Gibbons and Archbishop Ireland positively recognized that they had erred."[52]

Cahensly did not live to see his name cleared of the single serious charge attributed to one of the Church's most exemplary laymen of the nineteenth century. After a lingering illness he died on Christmas day, 1923, at the convalescent home of the Sisters of the Holy Ghost at Marienhof near Koblenz in his beloved Catholic Rhineland for which he had labored so long and so nobly. He was then in the eighty-fifth year of his life.[53]

[52] *Die 67 Generalversammlung des Deutschen Römisch-Katholischen Zentralvereins von Nordamerika* (St. Paul, 1923), pp. 19, 65. Cf. also Buffalo *Echo,* Jan. 9, 1922.

Recognition of Archbishop Ireland's contribution and position in the American Church also came from German Americans during these years. A German American Catholic Congress in Dubuque, Iowa, in September, 1892, paid tribute to Ireland and referred to him as "the much misunderstood and misrepresented prelate of St. Paul." On the occasion of Ireland's golden jubilee as a priest, Archbishop Messmer wrote him: "Permit me on this occasion to say how sorely disappointed I was at the news that the dignity of Cardinal had not been bestowed upon you. I made no secret of my deep regret & I am glad to say that in these sentiments I am not the only one among German American bishops in the U.S. Bishop Fox of Green Bay was quite strong in his expressions. While for many years, as you are well aware, German American Catholics had not very much love for the Archbishop of St. Paul, I am only happy to state that that sentiment has changed very much of late. There is more than one reason for that. I have spoken with a number of German American priests and laymen who were unanimous in expressing their disappointment that the red hat had not landed in St. Paul. I, for one, will hope for the happy event in the not far future" (*AASP,* Messmer to Ireland, Milwaukee, Dec. 20, 1911).

[53] Interviews of the author with Reverends Wilhelm Nathem, S.A.C., former director of the St. Raphaelsverein in Hamburg; Johann Valerius, S.A.C., former director of the St. Raphaelsverein in Bremen; Martin Rahsler, O.S.B., of Maria Laach Abbey, retreat master of Cahensly; and Right Reverend Kuno Jörger, director of Caritasverband in Freiburg, were all of the same tenor. Cahensly stood out in the history of nineteenth-century German Catholicism as a truly spiritual man of unbounded charity, deeply loved by all who came in contact with him, a practical Catholic leader in both political and social endeavor whose name and reputation were unquestioned.

Recorded testimony was obtained for the author by the late director of the library at Caritas in Freiburg, Heinrich Auer, from a fellow laborer of Cahensly at the Hamburg Station and from the nursing nun who cared for him at the time of his death. These two testimonies of Johann Friedrich, of Bremen, and of Sister M. Hedwigis, of Monikaheim, Frankfurt am Main, are eloquent descriptions of the

The German Catholics in the United States, for whom Cahensly had worked for some fifty years, continued their effort to preserve, as Joseph Matt characterized it, their "sturdy, rugged traditionalism."[54] Their parishes were models of order, efficiency, and pronounced liturgical emphasis. In their powerful societies, their songs, processions, and community consciousness they presented a united front, as well as a public manifestation of the faith they were determined to hand on to their children. Their first aim continued to be the erection and maintenance of parochial schools. In 1914, of parishes designated as "German" in the *Catholic Directory,* over 95 per cent had parish schools. This figure does not include mixed German and English-speaking parishes. Reverend George Timpe, S.A.C., former secretary-general of the St. Raphaelsverein, wrote of this record that "if today the American bishops give first position to German Catholics in the development of parish schools, it is due not only to the German spirit but also in a broader sense to the spirit of Cahenslyism."[55] Pius X recognized this contribution of German American Catholics on the occasion of the first pilgrimage from the United States to Rome of 200 German-speaking faithful for the celebration of his golden jubilee as a priest. In an audience on May 22, 1908, the president of the Central Verein, J. B. Ölkers, of Newark, first addressed the Holy Father in the name of the delegation:

> It was soon evident to German Catholic immigrants that Catholic schools and associations were needed to preserve and retain German Catholics and their progeny in the faith. Accordingly, German associations developed to meet this problem, to support one another and to establish churches and schools.
>
> These associations and congregations worked for a long time separated from each other. Gradually the idea developed: If all these societies of the entire country were united in one Central Society, then much more good could be accomplished for Holy Church. Thus the German Catholics were united in 1855 in the "German Roman Catholic Central Verein."
>
> It would take too long to detail all that this association has done for the Church in America. It only must be mentioned that the members of this association have stood firm by holy religion and their dear mother tongue, while yet being counted among the best citizens of their new fatherland. This association was never connected with "Amer-

life and death of a noble soul. Cf. also *Kölnische Volkszeitung,* Jan. 5, 1924; *Nassauer Boten,* Dec. 27, 1923.

[54] *Der Wanderer,* July 28, 1932.

[55] George Timpe, S.A.C., *Der St. Raphaelsverein* (Freiburg i. Br., 1921), p. 5.

icanism" nor with "Modernism" which your Holiness has recently condemned. It has established parish schools from the beginning in North America in which thousands of German Catholics and their offspring have been educated in holy religion. At this hour the members of the Central Verein are numbered among the truest Catholics in the United States of America.[56]

Pius X responded to this address in Italian, and his words were then translated into German. The Pontiff declared:

Your forefathers emigrated from their German homeland over the sea to the west, established Catholic schools where the young could learn the Catholic religion, constructed churches where at the altar God's graces and help could be obtained. Thus your accomplishment is worthy of all praise and recognition. You have followed in the footsteps of your countrymen in Europe. Yes, by your courage and perseverance in battle you are like them. As your German brethren have invincibly defended Catholic religion against the enemies of the faith in Europe, so have you resisted the enemy, and you have not been overcome. I pray God that your zeal for good may not grow cold in the future. May all members, whether immigrant or native, continue to strive for the noble aims of the society so that the banner of your association may ever flow in victory and glory as a symbol to your countrymen of your new nation, and of all nations, of your praiseworthy example. . . . May the Archangel Raphael guide you on your return journey and protect you in your homeland.[57]

This tribute of Pius X emphasized the deserving activity of previous years by German Catholics in the United States. They had left a land where liberals, infidels, and anticlericals had striven to destroy the Church. In their new home they continued to oppose Germans of this same character who had emigrated in considerable numbers after the revolution of 1848 and through the early 1850's. These liberals had echoed in the German American press the same arguments of their fellow liberals who later were to direct the *Kulturkampf* in Germany. From this defensive position German Catholics in the United States viewed their language, customs, usages, societies, and traditions as vital bastions to be defended at all cost. Gradually, however, social and cultural interests of the German immigrants became American, and with this change there arose new problems. It was as Archbishop Ireland and Cardinal Gibbons had foretold in 1888 and throughout the controversies of the 1880's and 1890's: German Catholics of the

[56] *SRB,* XXVIII (July, 1908), p. 570.

[57] *Ibid.,* p. 571. As the Pope left the hall of the consistory the delegates sang *"Grosser Gott, wir loben Dich."*

second generation would have to defend their religion and meet the challenge of American life from an American frame of reference. The spirit which had been handed on to them would be their strength, but their advancement in the new world would have to be in an American mold. German settlers themselves were not slow to realize this, as Arthur Preuss wrote, and traditionally in new lands they strove to become like their neighbors, to improve themselves, and to adopt native customs.[58] English was the accepted language of commercial and social intercourse, the special characteristic of American civil life and the language of the many nationals who came to the United States in the nineteenth century assumed the character of foreign tongues. German Catholic leaders themselves ultimately recognized and accepted this fact. Although many continued to consider it unfortunate, they gradually began to introduce English into their parishes for the younger people, while retaining the German language for the older generation.[59] Thus did the assimilation process inevitably work itself out in time. How different was the advice in 1930 of Right Reverend Karl Spohr, director of the Leo House during the years 1923 to 1929, from that advanced by his predecessors of the American St. Raphael Society such as Reuland, Tappert, Goller, Schäffer, or Mühlsiepen. Spohr stated:

> After the emigrant has found work, it is his greatest responsibility to learn the English language at once. Again and again he will realize how great a disadvantage he is at if he cannot speak the language of the land.
>
> It is not wise and farseeing for the emigrants to associate only with German-speaking people at their work. At first one feels very secure, and scarcely realizes that German-speaking families will therefore only associate with German emigrants, and the children of the family learn German. Jewish families hold firmly to German for many generations. They are able to do this easily by choosing to hire only German servant girls in their homes. The emigrant is accordingly the loser. . . .
>
> If we here advise that English be learned as soon as possible, we naturally do not say that the emigrant be "Americanized," or that he forget his homeland, or the German language. Of every immigrant who holds this we must say: "As for him the homeland has not lost, and America has not gained." On the contrary, every German emigrant must

[58] *Allgemeine Rundschau,* Apr. 28, 1906.

[59] Cf. the report of Reverend Laux, of the Congregation of the Holy Ghost, to the Erfurt *Katholikentag* in 1909 (*SRB,* XXV [Jan., 1910], pp. 676–679); "A report from one of the north eastern American dioceses," *SRB,* XXIII (July, 1908), pp. 571–574.

be proud of his homeland, for Germany belongs in every respect among the first nations of the world.[60]

Accordingly, German Catholics eventually came to accept the position of the Americanizers. The mother tongue was dying out, American national habits were being assimilated, the United States was becoming recognized by them as a nation. No more protesting memorials were forwarded to Rome, since German parishes gradually became mixed parishes, national parishes slowly gave way to territorial parishes, and the German parishes were distinguished only by a spirit of German Catholicism as practiced by American citizens of German origin. Interest in the appointment of bishops of German ancestry and tongue became an academic question as the American Germans took their place in American life as one of the many elements that went to make up one people. In this respect the opposition in 1905 of Archbishop Messmer, an ecclesiastic of Swiss German origin, in union with other members of the hierarchy, to efforts of the Polish Catholics of the United States for national bishops and rights was highly significant.[61]

In all this, however, it was apparent and worthy of note that the German Catholics acted freely and in circumstances where they felt that their faith would not be endangered by the assimilation process.

[60] Karl Spohr, *Der Auswanderer in Amerika. Vorteile und Nachteile* (Paderborn, 1930), pp. 105–107.

[61] "There is a petition from the Province of Milwaukee for a new diocese here. Now the paper brought the news today that the Polish are going to make new efforts to get one of their men elected bishop for the new diocese. The longer I think over it the more it seems to me a dangerous experiment at this stage to give the Polish people a bishop, for the very reason that he will be considered the bishop *for all the Poles* of the U.S. I know it. Wherever a bishop would have any difficulty with a Polish parish, *their bishop* would be appealed to. The Polish are not yet American enough & keep aloof too much from the rest of us" (*AAB,* 102-A, Messmer to Gibbons, Milwaukee, Jan. 19, 1905).

Throughout this whole period, and concomitant with the German question, there were manifold problems for the American bishops arising from demands of other nationality groups in the country, especially Italian and Polish Catholics, for rights and privileges. The German developments discussed in these pages were not isolated events, and other demands were not introduced only because of the limitation of topic. As late as June 28, 1920, the Polish legation at the Holy See, at the instigation of Polish priests in the United States, submitted a memorial to the Holy See charging the American bishops with neglect of their nationals in the United States, requesting Polish bishops in their states and protesting against Americanization. Archbishop George W. Mundelein, of Chicago, born in the United States of German ancestors, composed with Archbishop Denis J. Dougherty, of Philadelphia, at the request of Cardinal Gibbons, an answer to this attack in the name of the archbishops of the country. It was in terms reminiscent of the response in the name of the archbishops of 1892 to the Lucerne Memorial (*AAB,* 130-N, Gibbons to Gasparri, Baltimore, Nov. 18, 1920, copy).

The day was happily gone when, as in earlier years, they moved under compulsion and attack for resisting what they considered to be hasty Americanization at a tempo directed by too ardent nativists.[62]

On the other hand, the Americanizers saw their program accomplished and their prophecies fulfilled by this process of German assimilation. Their aims had unquestionably been progressive in the best sense of the word and they were of vital importance to the advancement of the American Church. But their means were sometimes questionable, means which were tempered in part by the *volte-face* of the first apostolic delegate to the United States, *Testem benevolentiae,* and by the blessing and recognition which the Holy See conferred on Peter Paul Cahensly. The Americanizers, on their side, ceased their intemperate charges about a conspiracy, came to realize more and more the valuable contributions of German Catholics to the deepening of Catholic life in the Church, and accepted and fostered the parochial schools as one of the best defenses of the faith. Several points of the Lucerne Memorial and of the St. Raphael program were also incorporated into American Catholic practice, such as colonizing projects and care for displaced persons. From the German example of a strong Catholic press and vigorous society activity American Catholics also drew inspiration. Although the Americanizers had never denied the natural right to the mother tongue of any foreign element in the Church, the more spirited emphasis on English of former days was left to time and environment rather than to stern admonitions which were open to misrepresentation and suspicion by immigrants not fully at home in American life. In this way the respective national Catholic elements that helped to make up the American nation could each contribute spiritual and cultural values from their own heritage to the enrichment of American society, rather than yield to the total assimilation of Anglo-Americanism with its increasingly materialistic and secular ideals.

Apart from these considerations, the leaders of the Church in the United States who had encouraged Americanization had made an important contribution to the nation. Some nine million Catholic immigrants from over twenty countries had flocked to American shores in the century from 1820–1920. This vast number of settlers, almost

[62] Cf. Dr. Max Grösser, S.A.C., "Der deutschamerikanische Katholizismus am Ausgang des neunzehnten Jahrhunderts," *Jahrbuch des Reichsverbandes für die katholischen Auslandsdeutschen. 1931–1932* (Münster, 1932), pp. 228–241; "Die deutschamerikanischen Katholiken im Kampf mit den Nativisten," *Gelbe Hefte,* V (1928–1929), pp. 281–295.

half of the total net immigration to the United States of that period, was introduced into the system of democratic government by the inspiration, encouragement, and direction which their new spiritual leaders gave them to love and to understand American political and civic ideals. Following in succession from the churchman-patriot, John Carroll, first American archbishop, the outstanding ecclesiastical leaders in the period under discussion worked to amalgamate divergent groups of people through a consistent and steady insistence on the moral responsibility of citizenship. The first responsibility of the Church was to care for the spiritual needs of the millions who had come to the new world, and who had scattered across the length and breadth of the land. In so doing it also sought the unity of the nation, especially through the training of a native American clergy, and through the legislation of provincial and plenary councils which would enable all national groups to live together in harmony. The Catholic Church was, in truth, also a "melting pot" for the millions of its faithful. In the Catholic climate of the Church the immigrants learned in time to abandon particular customs and traditions when those practices endangered the unity of the whole body. Adaptation and adjustment were made in the Church under the age-old direction and wisdom of the Holy See, while rights and duties were counterbalanced and directed for the common good. It was within the fold of the Catholic Church and there, perhaps, more than in any other sphere, that a significant number of immigrants from Europe learned to live together as Americans. There they formed a new unity which is today one of the dominant characteristics and special pride of both Church and State.

APPENDIX I

Address of the Catholic Committee for the Protection of the German Emigrant to President Ulysses S. Grant of the United States of America January, 1873

SOME SUGGESTIONS TOWARD INTERNATIONAL LEGISLATION REGARDING EMIGRATION

To His Excellency, Mr. Grant, the President of the United States

MR. PRESIDENT:

The physical and moral condition of the European emigrant has been for many decades a very sad one. The poorer classes especially, forced by reason of their limited means to travel in the lower deck, are, upon embarking and during the voyage as well as at their debarkation in the new world exposed to a very deplorable lot. The shipping agents, the owners of the European seaports, the persons who deal with the emigrants at the landing-places, are almost all, without exception, bent upon procuring advantages for themselves, upon enriching themselves at the expense of the emigrant.

The legislation of the various European countries, moreover, is chiefly to the material advantage of the owners, etc., in the seaports. The laws have been adapted to the ships and their cargo rather than to the well-being of the emigrant. There have arisen, accordingly, for the emigrant, physical and moral conditions that are indescribably evil.

New laws, it is true, have recently been enacted in France and Germany, most especially in England, which contribute very much toward removing the most vexing inconveniences. Despite this, however, almost everything still depends on the good will and caprice of the owners and captains of the ships, so that the immigrant's lot is still one worthy of the utmost compassion. Yet, let it be said here, the international legislation we have in mind will effect no essential improvement unless the government of the

United States intercedes resolutely for the well-being of the emigrant. It is, of course, quite natural that the European governments, even with the best of intentions, would be unfavorable to emigrants. Through emigration many thousands of laborers will be taken away from the countries of Europe and much capital lost to them. It is, therefore, not inconceivable that the European nations should take advantage of the fact that many of these, upon considering the great hardships of the voyage, etc., are deterred from emigrating. As to the United States of America the situation is different. The greatest advantages of emigration are hers; she ought, then, to have the greatest interest in good legislation that will take into consideration the welfare of the emigrant. The United States can intercede in an effective and successful way. A strict law coupled with careful execution will remedy most of the inconveniences. The European shipowners must and will adapt themselves. They will arrange their ships and conduct the same according to American laws, if only for their own material advantage. Nor is it to be feared that such a stringent law geared to the welfare of the emigrant would in any way hinder emigration to the United States. Your message to Congress last year on May 14, Mr. President, puts such legislation in proximate view and has, accordingly, filled all true friends of mankind with great joy. It clearly shows that the Union which courageously broke the chains of slavery from many millions is also determined to enter the lists for the welfare of the emigrants who will be its future citizens. The undersigned committee for the protection of the German emigrant thanks you, Mr. President, most warmly for the message and for the assurances made therein. At the same time, the committee presumes to present to you some suggestions for proposed legislation, confident not only that they are worthy of your attention, but also that they will be accepted with benevolence.

I. *Care for the welfare of the emigrant in general*

The legislation should first of all bring it about that sufficient room be assured to each emigrant, not only in the cabins, but in the lower decks as well. There are, of course, legal prescriptions in favor of this in the various countries. And yet, on this side of the ocean as well as on the other, complaints about overcrowding continually come in. During the year that has just expired, one of the New York newspapers censured the serious overcrowding of steamships as emigration increases. Universally accepted definitions in the legislation should, therefore, establish that the highest permissible number of passengers for each emigration ship be fixed by appointed officials; also the maximum number for each compartment in the lower deck. This should, as in the railroad cars, be declared in large ciphers over the entrance to each compartment, e.g., Compartment for Ladies and Girls — 150 Persons. For each passenger exceeding this maximum number the captain should be fined a definite sum. Obviously, overcrowding destroys the physical and moral well-being of the emigrant.

II. *Care for the physical welfare of the emigrant*

Special laws must be laid down for the physical health of the emigrant.

1. Persons afflicted with contagious diseases should not be permitted to make the voyage. Every emigrant must, therefore, be provided with a medical certificate or present himself before boarding ship to a doctor in the particular seaport appointed for examination of emigrants. The examinations of women by the doctor should take place only in the presence of persons of their sex.

2. Provisions are necessary and ought not to be perfunctorily controlled by the officials appointed for this purpose. Quality should be considered as well as quantity. Drinking water must especially be pure and wholesome. To facilitate this control before the voyage the owners must be obliged to submit to the authorities a list of provisions signed by them, the accuracy of which is to be attested to only after investigation by inspectors.

3. It is important for health that the lower deck be kept clean. The captain must see to it that it is frequently cleaned and carefully ventilated. At least once a day he himself should visit the lower deck, and, of course, not only as has been customary to date when the lower deck has just been cleaned and most all of the passengers are staying on the upper deck.

4. Ships which carry a large number of emigrants, e.g., over four hundred on board, ought always to be attended by a capable doctor, who should present his report to the proper authorities at the landing dock. It is a deplorable fact that ships carrying eight hundred to one thousand emigrants, on the ocean where sickness so easily strikes, frequently carry no more medical assistance than an incomplete drug dispensary, from which, according to the persuasions of thoroughly ignorant persons, things are taken or handed out.

5. For every one hundred lower-deck passengers a hospital with four beds should be prepared.

III. *Care for the moral welfare of the emigrant*

The most important matter in this international legislation is the maintenance of morality and decency among the emigrants. With regard to this, present arrangements are everywhere very bad. The owners and captains of the emigrant ships, of course, flatly deny that numerous outrages against morality occur. They appeal to the fact that Germans are very infrequently led before American courts for this complaint. But this proves absolutely nothing as far as the moral behavior of the emigrants is concerned, since:

1. Emigrants lack, for the most part, the means to pay the expenses for a lawsuit in American seaports. They cannot delay there a long time, but must hurry on to their destinations.

2. Further, a spirit of sacrifice is most often wanting. Complaint will not undo what has already happened, so that nothing useful is accomplished for oneself. The advantage would chiefly accrue to later emigrants, and

who among the lower-deck passengers wants to give up time and money for that?

3. Many emigrants do not want to bother about morality. They like the immoral excesses and desire unbridled freedom for that purpose.

4. Finally, the German emigrant, unlike the ones who come from Great Britain, is thoroughly unfamiliar with the sea, the arrangement of a ship and its voyage. It does not occur to him, therefore, to bring complaints before authorities whose language he does not understand.

In short, the excuse of the owners and captains that complaints are seldom brought forward by Germans in America concerning immoral attacks on the sea is a purely negative argument that actually proves nothing.

In point of fact, the outlook on emigrant ships, despite the new laws that have been issued in the seaports in France, etc., is very sad. It would be impossible for an ethical pen to describe all that goes on. We shall refer to one thing only, verifying it with witnesses.

There is absolutely no separation of the sexes in the lower deck. Frequently, the lower deck is nothing other than a single large room in which men and women, young people of both sexes, lie promiscuously near each other. Even when there is a special compartment for married and for single women in the lower deck, even then the separation of the sexes is not at all assured. Men and boys are to be found in the women's compartment and vice versa. Not infrequently are men and unmarried women to be found in the same bed, and in the sight of all. Quite naturally, things that are the shame of our century of culture take place there every day. Some eyewitnesses can attest to this:

On the steamer *Deutschland* Reverend Father Albrinck, of Reading (Archdiocese of Cincinnati), journeyed from Bremen to New York. He writes on March 12, 1868, after his arrival in America: "The sexes were not separated. Old and young, married and single, boys and girls — all lay about in disorder."

Gottlob Koehl, following his voyage from Le Havre to New York, writes on March 24, 1868, about the steamer *Cordova:* "Very close to me were groups of wicked men who reveled in the most atrocious unchastity."

Concerning the *Germania,* passengers gave similar reports to the Swiss consul in Le Havre when the ship was forced to return there because of damage.

How very much immorality there is to be found on ships leaving Antwerp can be learned from the reports made before the Swiss consul in Le Havre by those few passengers who were rescued from the emigrant ship *Nelson* which burned on the open sea.

Clement Gross (with residence at 552 S. 3rd Avenue in Philadelphia) sailed on May 25, 1872, on the *Main,* a Bremen steamer, from New York to Bremen. After his arrival in Germany he presented to the authorities a certified statement wherein he points out that, during the entire journey married and single persons of both sexes were placed without distinction beside and among each other and that the whole lower deck was one large room without compartments.

On the Hamburg steamer *Saxonia* an author, Mr. Kist, journeyed in August, 1868, to New York. In his book, *Amerikanisches* (Mainz, Kirchheim, 1871) he relates on pages 102–111 that there was no separation of the sexes in the lower deck, but that all were placed in disorder among each other without distinction. The most horrible obscenities resulted. And yet, a separation could very easily have been arranged, since an iron wall with iron doors separated the room of the lower deck.

Mr. Cahensly, a merchant from Limburg on the Lahn and a member of the undersigned committee, found, in June, 1872, in Bremerhaven on the steamer *Deutschland* no trace of separation of the sexes in the lower deck. Alongside unmarried young men lay single women and families as well. Women had to climb without ladders to the upper deck, under or opposite which men had their beds. Often young people of both sexes lay in the same bed. The same was true in the room set apart by boards and over which the title read: "For women traveling alone." This scandal was not considered at all.

The same gentleman found something similar in Hamburg on the steamer *Cimbria* in June, 1872. Here, too, separation of the sexes was not enforced. Everyone was placed anywhere, young girls had their beds placed beside young men.

Together with the witnesses we have just brought forward, to which we could add many more, numerous brochures prove — particularly that work which appeared under the Protectorate of the Austrian government, *Voyage of the Austrian Frigate "Novara" Around the World.* In the second volume of the popular edition, page 247 ff., it tells of the dreadful inconveniences that prevailed on emigrant ships bound for Australia. On page 250, we read: "There was not the slightest precaution taken toward separating the sexes. Male and female, old and young, single as well as married, all lived and slept together in the same room."

It is, therefore, well established that until recently very little was done on emigrant ships for the preservation of decency. That the most scandalous indecencies took place is an established fact. Only a stringent law, which leaves nothing to the discretion of the captain or shipowner, can put an end to this disgrace of our century.

The following points should be kept in mind:

1. In the lodging houses in which emigrants are sheltered often for two or three days before the voyage, a strict control should be introduced with respect to the separation of the sexes in the dormitories. Concessions should be taken away from housekeepers who formerly housed men, women, and unmarried persons of both sexes in the same dormitories.

2. On the emigrant ships, on steamers and frigates (these really ought

to be forbidden to transport emigrants), *separation of the sexes* must be *enforced* with inexorable strictness. Every emigrant ship — at least those to be constructed — ought to have *three* compartments in the lower deck separated from each other by solid walls and closed doors. Each of these compartments should have its own stairway to the upper deck.

a) *The men's compartment* should be in the prow, for men traveling alone and for unmarried persons of the male sex over fourteen years of age.

b) *The women's compartment* should be in the stern for women traveling alone and for all unmarried persons of the female sex over twelve years of age.

c) The compartment for families should be in the middle part of the ship for husbands and wives (who travel together or with their children), for their sons under fourteen years as well as for their daughters under twelve. Those children who have advanced beyond these ages should have their beds in one of the other two compartments.

No lower-deck passenger should be permitted to have his bed in any compartment other than the one to which he belongs. Only during the day and on the deck should free communication be allowed. This strict separation of the sexes among the many uneducated, even coarse and downright immoral lower-deck passengers, can only be maintained when no exceptions whatever are granted and nothing is left to the caprice of the ship's officers. The law must define the hour in the evening after which no one may tarry in any compartment other than his own. On English ships separation of the sexes is enforced by a law of August 14, 1855, Article XXII. As far as this committee knows it is strictly carried out.

This definition of the law must be expressly stated in contracts and handed by the agents to every emigrant at the conclusion of the contract. He should also remind them of it.

3. The ship's personnel should be forbidden under penalty to enter the women's compartment unless the services are necessary. The abduction of any woman by an officer or sailor for unchaste actions should be punished with a severe fine or imprisonment.

4. The ship's captain should be responsible for the proper lighting of the lower deck.

5. The sale of books on the ships should be forbidden, since only immoral literature is sold, a fact established by this committee during the year just passed. Immoral books in the ship's library should be strictly forbidden.

IV. *Necessary regulations for the carrying out of the laws in question*

All these and similar legal definitions will only attain their beneficent effects when their exact execution is observed. To this end, the following regulations are desirable:

1. When a contract is arranged which takes place for the most part in

the homeland, strict separation of the sexes must be kept in view. Every contract must keep persons of the same category in the same compartment of the lower deck. Accordingly, for the men's compartment, men traveling by themselves and boys over fourteen; for the women's compartment, women traveling alone and girls over twelve years; finally, for the family compartment, men traveling with their wives or men and their wives with children under fourteen years. If the contracts are issued according to these three categories, it will be easy to draw up lists in the ports of embarkation and to assign each one to his compartment upon boarding ship.

2. Before the ship goes to sea, special officials — in default of others, those who are to revise the provisions — must assure themselves that proper separation of the sexes in the three compartments of the lower deck has been taken care of. The officials must accept no gifts from the owners.

3. During the voyage, the government of the United States should have two American officials accompany every emigration boat bound for America, that is, a man for the men's compartment and an excellent woman for the woman's compartment. These should write down in a journal everything that takes place contrary to good morals or whatever is damaging to health. The first Austrian Union for the Protection of Emigrant also, and rightly, requests this in its address of August, 1872. Immigration is, after all, a national affair for the Union.

4. At the place of landing and before debarking, North American officials should board the ship and ascertain whether the passengers or persons of the ship's crew have any crimes against the emigration laws to report. Offenders should immediately be led before an International Court set up for this purpose in all seaports.

5. The owners and captains of the ships are responsible for keeping order in all moral and sanitary respects. Should separation of the sexes not be observed or coarse immoralities go unchecked, or health be impaired, through fault of the captain, then the captain's right to conduct an emigration ship should be taken from him.

These, Mr. President, are the suggestions which we, out of love for the well-being of the countless thousands of men who every year leave Europe to seek a better home in America, desire to submit for your kind consideration. May your Excellency cause these same to be considered in the drawing up of international legislation for emigration. It is surely of the greatest importance to the United States to put an end to the shameless outrages to which many, many thousands fall prey every year. Because immigration every year leads a tremendous number of new citizens to the Union, then, manifestly, this immigration is itself a conspicuous element in the life of the nation. Undeniably, it cannot be a matter of indifference to the future of the great republic what sort of elements settle every year upon its soil.

To be sure, the costs entailed in paying officials in the seaports as also those who are to accompany the emigrant ships, are not insignificant. But these will be more than counterbalanced by the material advantages which emigration will bring to the nation through the introduction of capital and labor power. Yet these costs must not even be considered when we consider the social advantages which these sound and humane institutions will bring to the United States. It is clear that the increase of honest, upright people alone can further the development of the gloriously flourishing and great union of states. On the other hand, an accumulation of morally depraved men can serve only to undermine the foundations of the nation's welfare. The great mass of those who yearly abandon Europe in order to establish a new home in the new world are certainly honest, upright people. How exceedingly useful, therefore, for the Union, nay how necessary to protect them against the wickedness and temptations of unchaste traveling companions or ship's crewmen. Any such protection rendered certain by severe legislation must win in advance the hearts of all good emigrants for the Union and fill the same with love for their new fatherland. Such protection by strict law and solicitude for the observance of these laws will secure for the Union the gratitude of all those who love and cherish true virtue and morality. And while the government of the United States prevents the unspeakable crimes and vicious excesses, of which the sea has thus far been the incessant witness, it will undoubtedly call down upon the republic the blessing of almighty God.

Be assured, Mr. President, of our most profound respect and esteem.

THE CATHOLIC COMMITTEE FOR THE
PROTECTION OF THE GERMAN EMIGRANT

Birstein bei Hanau am Main
January, 1873

APPENDIX II

Address of the Catholic Committee for the Protection of the German Emigrant to the Hierarchy of the United States of America March, 1873

MOST REVEREND ARCHBISHOP (BISHOP),

The undersigned president of the Catholic Emigration Committee in Germany takes the liberty of presenting to your Excellency the following.

The lamentable situation and the dangers encountered by our Catholic fellow citizens in emigrating from Germany to America has repeatedly constituted the subject of the discussions of the General Assembly of Catholic Associations of Germany which meets every year. At one of these meetings, that of 1868 held at Bamberg — at which also Mr. Joseph Kölble of New York, member of the German Roman Catholic Central-verein in America was present — the above-mentioned Committee was founded.

Before the Committee wished to begin its particular activity, the members thought it necessary to be assured of ecclesiastical approval. It was fortunate enough to obtain the approval of its undertaking from the Most Reverend Bishops of Germany, before whom it laid the project. Thirty of the episcopal ordinariates, accordingly, assigned representatives to the Committee.

In order to carry out its end the Committee needed money above all. At its suggestion, therefore, the St. Raphaelsverein was founded by the General Assembly of Catholic Associations of Germany at Mainz in 1871, copies of whose statutes are enclosed. A large number of Germany's Most Reverend Bishops approved the introduction of this society into their dioceses. At the same time, several of them granted permission for collections to be taken up in churches to assist the Committee. Some of these have already taken place and brought in considerable contributions.

With regard to providing for the emigrants, three periods of time are to be taken into consideration.

1. The delay of the emigrant in the port of embarkation and the departure;
2. The voyage on the ships;
3. The landing and the delay in the port of debarkation in America.

I am taking the liberty of sending to your Excellency a brochure drawn up by our Committee which treats of these three points in detail. Permit me briefly to call special attention to the following.

1. In the European ports of embarkation, that is, Bremen, Hamburg, Stettin, Antwerp, Rotterdam, Le Havre, and Liverpool, it will have to be the first and exclusive care of the Committee, with the help and approval of the Most Reverend Bishops, to remedy the extant inconveniences and to provide for the necessities of life. The first thing must be the erection of missions with priests in attendance for the emigrant, the appointment of lay agents for the support of the priests and for lending a helping hand to the emigrants in material ways. Your Excellency will learn from the enclosed brochures how the zeal of Father Lambert Rethmann, priest of the Order of the Sacred Hearts of Jesus and Mary, has already been effective in caring for the emigrants in Le Havre. In Hamburg and Bremen the Committee has within the past year paved the way for the erection of missions.

2. This point is essentially different. Here as also in the third point, the assistance must come chiefly from the American side; the decision lies with America. Your Excellency is surely not unaware of the dangers to which the emigrants in the lower decks of the ships are exposed during the voyage and to which they frequently succumb. Dangers to their health, yet far greater dangers to their morals and to the religion of these poor people. It is well-known that the numerous defections which the Catholic Church suffers in the United States are to be attributed in part to them. It is the duty first of all of the legislatures of the countries involved to relieve the situation here. England has made a praiseworthy beginning in her passenger act of August 14, 1855, of which Article XXII prescribes the separation of the sexes by compartments. This enactment is carried out on English vessels. Improvements have also been introduced into German legislation, but their execution is most ineffective. The laws are directed to the construction of the ships so that these must conform to the laws determined by the demands of health and morality. The government of the United States which, before all else, should have an interest in the welfare of its new citizens, has the deciding voice here. It lies within her power to say: We shall permit in our harbors only those ships whose entire arrangement measures up to the demands laid down by us. The President of the United States, in his address to Congress of May 14, 1872, has expressed his conviction of the importance of this matter. With regard to this, as well as to the circumstance that international legislation concerning this matter is just now being discussed between the governments of America and Germany, the Committee considered it appropriate to direct an appeal to President Grant. I have the honor of enclosing a copy of the same to your Excellency.

There can be no doubt that the voices of the Catholic Episcopate are not without influence in the conduct of the government there. For this reason, *I have presumed to ask your Excellency, together with the other Most Reverend Bishops of America, to support as best you can our petition to President Grant.*

3. The emigrants arrive ignorant of the language, ignorant of the local conditions of the seaport, very often without any acquaintance in his new home. Loss of possessions and loss of the Catholic faith are often the consequences. This latter is the more conceivable when one considers that alone in Castle Garden, New York's place of landing, there are stationed six Protestant preachers well provided with money and who have erected a mission right in the neighborhood, while the Catholic churches with their priests are a great distance away.

In order to protect arriving immigrants to some extent from the dangers that threaten them, the German Roman Catholic Central-Verein appointed three years ago two trusted men, Mr. Joseph Kölble, of New York, and Mr. Christian Bitter, in Baltimore. These gentlemen take care of those emigrants who are provided with recommendation cards from our committee, and these cards are distributed by our representatives at diocesan chancery offices and by pastors. But it is only too evident that one man alone cannot satisfy all the needs of so great a number of immigrants, cannot at the same time provide suitable lodging for one, the continuation of his journey for another, direct the sick to a hospital, etc. Above all, the erection of an asylum together with a church and a Catholic priest in the neighborhood of the place of landing are necessary.

The Immigrant Committee founded by the German Roman Catholic Central Verein in 1868 has, under the excellent direction of its president, Reverend L. Schwenninger, pastor of St. Louis' Church in Cincinnati, taken interest in this affair with genuine zeal. The transactions accomplished at the General Assembly give witness of this, yet because of insufficiency of money no major results can be obtained.

The undersigned has thus presumed to lay before your Excellency the urgent request that the Most Reverend Bishops of America intervene in this matter by promoting the aims of the Immigration Committee located there, which among other things has set for itself the task of erecting in New York an asylum for the sick and destitute in the vicinity of the place of debarkation. We ask this for those who up to now were our fellow citizens, but who, in the future, will be members of the Catholic Church in America.

May it please your Excellency to accept this request graciously as also the expression of my most respectful esteem. I have the honor to be, your Excellency,

FÜRST ZU ISENBURG-BIRSTEIN AM MAIN
President of the Committee for the
Protection of the German Emigrant

Offenbach
March, 1873

APPENDIX III

Abbelen Memorial and Letters of Bishops Keane and Ireland

MEMORIAL ON THE GERMAN QUESTION IN THE UNITED STATES WRITTEN BY REV. P. M. ABBELEN, PRIEST OF MILWAUKEE, APPROVED BY MOST REV. ARCHBISHOP OF MILWAUKEE, AND SUBMITTED TO THE SACRED CONGREGATION DE PROPAGANDA FIDE IN NOVEMBER, 1886

1. The question concerns the relation of non-English to English parishes, and especially the relation of German to Irish parishes in the United States of North America.

2. We ask of the Sacred Congregation de Propaganda Fide that it so define this relation that German parishes shall be entirely independent of Irish parishes, or on a par with them; that rectors of Irish parishes shall not be able to exercise any parochial jurisdiction over Germans enrolled in any German church, or who by right should be thus enrolled, whether they be newcomers from Germany or born in America of German parents.

3. We ask for this equality and independence because in many places they are denied to us. In some places, for example in St. Louis, German churches are called chapels of ease, in other places English churches only are called parish churches, while the others, that is to say, those of Canadians and of Germans, for instance in the Diocese of Albany, are called special churches, and in still other places, for instance in New Orleans, every distinction by name being omitted, German churches have no parochial rights. Finally, in other places, as in Baltimore, by law, that is, according to the diocesan statutes, German rectors have no jurisdiction over those born in America. It is true that in fact the Most Eminent Cardinal, with his great prudence and charity, grants them parochial rights, but this does not prevent Irish rectors from acting against the letter of the law, and meddling in various ways with the rights of Germans.[1]

Nearly everywhere the opinion prevails that Irish rectors are truly and

[1] After this was written, His Eminence, Cardinal Gibbons, was good enough to inform me by letter that, in a diocesan synod recently held, he had enacted a decree making German parishes equal to the English.

by right the parish priest of all those who were born in America, as if having over them an eminent domain; that German priests are, of course, necessary to take care of the souls of Germans while they speak the German language, but that it cannot fail to happen that they shall in the course of time lose their language and learn English, and that the sooner this happens the better; that the ecclesiastical status of the Germans is therefore a transitory one, and that German parishes should not be put on an equal footing with English parishes. There are also some who think that it is contrary to canon law that there should be two independent parishes in the same territory, and for this reason also that the English should be the only parish.

4. There are many and very grave reasons why it would seem this relation of dependence and subordination should be abolished, and entire independence and co-ordination established:

> *a*) Before our Civil Government foreigners, once they have been, as the saying is, "naturalized," are entirely equal among themselves, and even enjoy the same rights as Americans properly so-called, and they may attain to the same honors and offices with the one exception of the office of President; and shall there be a distinction before ecclesiastical law between children of the same mother so that a very great part of them shall be compelled to consider her not so much as a mother, as a step-mother, and to regard themselves as strangers more or less welcome, but not children of the family as dear as the others to the heart of the mother?
>
> *b*) It may well be inquired, whence do English Catholics derive the right to put themselves before non-English? If you except that very small number of Catholics who are and have been Americans for many generations, nearly all Catholics who use the English tongue are Irish, immigrants from Ireland and their descendants. Now they are no less foreigners and no less American than the Germans and other nationalities, newcomers from Europe. While in the Eastern States the Irish are more numerous and arrived earlier than the Germans, it is not so in the Middle States and still less in the Western States.[2]

For they [the Irish] live among their countrymen of whom many are Protestants, Rationalists, Free Thinkers, Masons, and numbers of other secret societies. All of these leave no stone unturned to pervert Catholics to their irreligious following, nor alas without success, especially where the necessary means are wanting to hold them to the practice of their religion. But the great majority of Germans have resisted and, God helping,

[2] By Western States in American geography are not commonly understood the states situated on the extreme western coast of the American Union, as for example, California, Oregon, which are rather known as Pacific States; but rather chiefly the interior states near the Mississippi river, such as Illinois, Missouri, Iowa, Minnesota, Wisconsin, etc.

will always resist their machinations and temptations. Their works make it clearer than the day that they are Catholics, since their churches, schools, and various charitable institutions are not surpassed in number or size by the others, and not infrequently surpass them. Their religious orders and congregations, both of men and women composed of Germans, occupy certainly no inferior place in works of charity and education. Their domestic life and civic virtues reveal their truly Christian spirit. They are of edification to all by their pious practices, frequent reception of the Sacraments, and the number of their pious sodalities. Equal to others in all things, in certain things they surpass them. For example, the only Normal School for the education of secular teachers is a German one. Only the Germans have daily Catholic papers, and they have five of them. There are more than 30,000 German men from different States united in one so-called "Central" Society. In almost every parish there are benefit societies. In the matter of education, and especially of parochial schools, no one who is not entirely ignorant of the origin and growth of these schools can deny that the system of parochial schools, which now flourishes, owes its origin to the zeal and perseverance of the Germans. You will hardly ever find a German church without a parochial school annexed, to which nearly all, if not all, parents send their children. There are some who say that the Germans in this matter are actuated not less by a love of their native tongue than of the Catholic religion. Be it so; the fact remains that the Germans most religiously care for the Christian education of their children.

5. Therefore, it is certainly not clear why Catholic Germans should be kept in a position inferior to that of the Irish. By granting the equal position which we ask, no right of the Irish would be impaired, while an injustice and a disgrace would be removed from the Germans.

6. But various objections are urged against the co-ordination: It is objected (*a*) — "It is against canon law that two or more independent parishes should be in the same territory." I deny this. Both authors and facts prove the contrary. As to facts: In Austria, in the Orient, in Canada, not rarely parishes, properly so-called, are to be found, independent one of the other, in the same territory. And authors, who are the most approved, explicitly teach that this system is not against canon law. The very distinguished Philip de Angelis, in the work *Lessons in Canon Law* etc. (Book III, Title II), discussing the condition "that [a parish] should have a population circumscribed within certain territorial limits within a diocese," so that it is clear that in the idea of a parish is comprised a population dwelling in or inhabiting a certain portion of a territory as commonly occurs in all civil and ecclesiastical jurisdiction, adds in express words: "But this in our case does not prove that in the same territory there may not be more than one parish; since there may be two and even three when the same territory is inhabited by populations of different nationalities and tongues. Thus in the United States of America in the

same territory and even in the same town there will be, say a parish of Irish and a parish of Canadians, the one comprising all those of that territory who are Irish or speak the English language; the other comprising all Canadians, that is, those who speak the French tongue, and so on; but each parish comprises all those of the same nationality who dwell there and not those who are settled there, unless they be of the same nation and tongue" (Vol. III, p. 37).

The very same argument is to be found in A. Bonal, S.J., *Institutions of Canon Law* (Vol. II, p. 8). And what these most learned authors say about Irish and Canadians are with much greater reason applicable to Irish and Germans in the United States in which there are at least twenty German Catholics for one Canadian.

It is objected (*b*) — "All this controversy is more theoretical than practical." If the dependence and subordination of which we are speaking existed only in law, and were not practiced in fact, perhaps they might be said to be merely theoretical, although even in such cases they would have no true and just cause for existing. But they are very far from not being reduced to practice. On the contrary, for this very purpose they are asserted, and, as we have already seen, they are supported with fallacious arguments in order that practical consequences may be made to flow therefrom. For example, Irish rectors without the knowledge and even in spite of German rectors may lease pews to Germans, collect money from them for churches, receive their children in their schools and admit them to First Communion, marry them, administer the last Sacraments to them, and bury them, but by no means vice versa, although the German rector may be perfectly familiar with the English language, and the Irish rector may speak hardly one or two words of German. All can see that this is a disturbance of good order, a cause of quarrels among priests, and takes on a scandalous appearance of sordid avarice. There is no end to well-ordered pastoral government and to the effectual care of souls if the faithful can run from one shepherd to the other at pleasure, withdraw themselves from the vigilance and the authority of their own pastor.

It is objected (*c*) — "The common welfare requires that Catholics shall be one in language and customs. Therefore, when the greater part of them is of English speech, and customs, the lesser part should conform. We are in America, we should be Americans." Certainly, and we wish to be. But the good of the Church above all things requires that each of her parts shall be good, faithful, united in love and reverence toward their common mother, and that they should prove themselves by their faith and morals to be true children of the Church. Now experience teaches that the only means by which Catholic Germans (and other foreigners) shall be able to preserve their Catholic faith and morals is that they shall have their own priests, who shall instruct them in the language and in the traditions of their fatherland. Wherever even Bishops have fallen into that most fatal of errors, I shall not say of heart and will, but of judgment and administration, of seeking to "Americanize" Germans as speedily as possible, refusing them, for instance, permission to build a school or church, committing them to the pastoral care of a priest ignorant of their language; wherever that most sad dictum, "let them learn English," has prevailed or now prevails, there has been and there will be, a truly deplorable falling away of them from the Church. Witnesses to this fact are the missionaries of the various orders. But even though the Germans should have their own priests and their own churches and schools, if they would be obliged to subordinate themselves to Catholics of another nationality, for instance to the Irish, as if they were Catholics of an inferior order of a worse character, they would never bear it with patience. They would feel that an injury had been inflicted upon them by the Church and that they were discredited among other Germans, non-Catholics, and they would be alienated from the Church. In matters political, social, and commercial, the Germans certainly hold no inferior place among American citizens — they are proud of their country, especially now after that celebrated *Kulturkampf* in which the Germans in Europe were made a spectacle to angels and to men. And shall they not be considered worthy here in America to enjoy the same rights as the Irish? Clearly, all those who know the German character, especially their tenacity, constancy, and their love of country, and, on the other hand, consider the dangers with which, as we said above, Catholic Germans are surrounded in the midst of their own countrymen, will surely do nothing, if they have love for souls, to render more difficult the perseverance of the Germans in the Catholic faith.

Moreover, they are entirely in error when they think that German bishops and priests, led by a certain want of sympathy for American institutions, are striving to prevent Germans from ever becoming Americans. This opinion of many is but a pretense and a delusion. Witness the innumerable schools, colleges, and academies, erected by Germans and directed by German priests and religious orders, in which the English language and English culture take, if not a first place, at least an equal place, with the German. Witness the material prosperity and the honorable position of the Germans among their American fellow citizens. All these things could not be if Germans did not adapt themselves to the language and manners of the Americans.

Let the "Americanization" of the Germans be a slow and natural process; let it not be hastened to the prejudice of the religion of the Germans. They will kick against the goad.

It is objected (*d*) — "But it happens that one or another German family may prefer to belong to the English church, and perhaps with so firm a purpose that if compelled to remain in the German church they may leave altogether. What then?" These cases are rare and will be most rare if Irish priests will not meddle in the affairs of Germans. If, however, there shall be sufficient cause for such a family to change to the English church, for instance, because the younger members of the family are more familiar with the English tongue, than with the German, let them go and let them be formally enrolled in the English parish. But it is by all means to be avoided, that members of the same family should belong to different churches. For instance, the parents to the German and the children to the English. In such cases there is an end of domestic devotions and the vigilance which parents should maintain as to the attendance of their children at divine services and reception of the Sacraments. Children, as long as they remain under parental authority in a parental home should by all means belong to the church of their parents; afterwards, if they have homes of their own, let them be free if they know the English language to pass over to the English church, but once and for all.

In all this controversy, besides a difference of language, we must not by any means make light of the difference and discrepancy of Catholic customs as they are to be found among Germans and Irish. The Irish, on account of the oppression and persecution which they suffered for religion's sake in their own land, love simplicity in divine service, and in all the practice of religion, and do not care much for pomp and splendor. But the Germans, from the liberty which as a rule they have enjoyed in the exercise of their religion from the earliest times, and the traditions of their fathers, love the beauty of the church edifice and the pomp of ceremonies, belfries and bells, organs and sacred music, processions, feast days, sodalities, and the most solemn celebration of First Communion and weddings. These and other like things, although not essential to Catholic faith and life, foster piety and are so dear and sacred to the faithful that not without great danger could they be taken away from them.

Then, again, Germans differ very much from the Irish in the administration of ecclesiastical goods and affairs. For nearly everywhere the former so manage their temporal affairs that the rectors, with a body of laymen, or even laymen alone, properly elected, carry on the administration, while the Irish leave all these things in the hands of the priests. It must be confessed, it sometimes happens among the Germans that the laymen meddle too much in such affairs, but this rarely happens; nearly everywhere the temporal affairs in German parishes are administered exceptionally well.

Finally, even manners and social customs of the two nationalities differ exceedingly. Thus it happens that scarcely ever will you find Germans and Irish united in matrimony. All this is here said neither to favor the Germans nor to disparage the Irish. Rather, these things are told by way of a narrative and as matters of fact, that it may be made clear how vastly one differs from the other, these two nationalities which are the principal parts of the Church in the United States, and how necessary it is that each should have its own priests and churches co-ordinate and independent. With the lapse of time, by a certain natural formative process one will become more assimilated to the other. But, God forbid that any one should dare, and most of all, that bishops and priests should endeavor to accelerate this assimilation by suppressing the language and customs of the Germans. The German temperament and a most sad experience demonstrate that their effort is not conducive to edification, but for the destruction and ruin of souls.

Since these things are so, we ask that the Sacred Congregation de Propaganda Fide shall define and decree:

1. That German parishes (and the others, French, Slovenian, etc.) shall be placed on an equal footing with the English (Irish) and shall be entirely independent of them. No distinction whatever either by general law or by episcopal precept to be made between them as to parochial rights and privileges.

2. Also, in the designation of irremovable rectorships, German parishes be under no disadvantage as compared with the Irish, provided the conditions prescribed by the Third Plenary Council, Baltimore, Title II, chapter v, be fulfilled.

3. All immigrants from Europe be assigned to the church of their own language whenever there is one in their place of residence, and be treated as members of that church, and the same hold good for their offspring born in America, as long as they remain under parental authority.

4. As to the descendants of German families who are their own masters and as to more remote generations, if they use the English language as their vernacular, according to the common acceptance of this term, let them be free to pass over to the English church, provided that the transference be made formally and forever, and that the consent of the rector be given in writing or even by the judgment of the bishop, if perchance, a contest should arise. The same also shall be permitted to the Irish who may be familiar with the German tongue.

5. Let bishops and priests be admonished on the one hand, not by any means to seek to suppress and root out the language, manners, customs, usages and devotional practices of the Germans, unless they shall be contrary to the Decalogue or the precepts, discipline, and rubrics of the Church; and on the other hand, to foster and promote the English language in the education of youth, and particularly in the parochial schools.

6. Let bishops be admonished to entrust mixed parishes and missions (Irish and German) to priests who know both languages, and to make it their conscientious duty to feed the people with the Word of God and to instruct the children, etc., in both languages.

7. Let bishops who are ignorant of the German language, and who govern mixed dioceses, be obliged besides an Irish vicar-general, to nominate also a German, or, if they should wish to have but one, to appoint such a one as shall have the knowledge and ready use also of the German language.

8. If, in course of time, especially when immigration ceases, in any church the use of the English language should be found more necessary than that of the German, the rector, either of his own motion or by the

judgment and order of the bishop, shall use the English tongue, and if it should perchance come to pass that on account of the proximity of an English church a new division of territory should be necessary, let the division be made with prudence, justice, and charity.

All and each of these things we ask.

First and second — Because we believe it to be right and just.

Third — Because the greater part of this request follows from No. 1, and the latter part seems to be necessary, to preserve families in the practice of religion.

Fourth — Because in this manner we think that provision is made for the personal liberty of each and the good of all.

Fifth — In the first part, lest the love of the Germans toward the Church and their confidence and love toward bishops and priests should be endangered; in the other part to promote even the material good of all.

Sixth — For the salvation of souls.

Seventh — Because of the justice of the thing in itself and for the salvation of souls.

Eighth — Because in the condition of our affairs the solution of doubts must be a sufficient and a sure one.

I have read and have approved.

✠ Michael Heiss
Archbishop of Milwaukee

Milwaukee
October, 1886

An Answer to the Memorial on the German Question in the United States Written by Rev. P. M. Abbelen, by Bishop John Ireland, of St. Paul, and Bishop John J. Keane, of Richmond, to His Eminence, Cardinal Simeoni, Prefect of the Holy Congregation of the Propaganda, Rome, December 6, 1886

The Congregation of the Propaganda will permit us to present a few observations upon the German Question in the Church in the United States. As we arrived in Rome, upon a mission to treat with the Propaganda concerning the project of the Catholic University, which the hierarchy of the United States desire to establish at Washington, we were very much surprised to find there a German representative, calling himself the delegate of bishops and of German Catholics of America, and asking in their name legislation altogether novel and exceptional, and of which the effects, we are convinced, would be disastrous to the Church in the United States. The American bishops of the English language, and some American bishops even of the German language, have no knowledge of the presence of this representative in Rome, nor of the demands, in their actual form, which he has submitted to the Propaganda. When the knowledge of this secret movement shall have come to them, the bishops of the

United States will be exceedingly indignant. We are convinced that they would never forgive us, if we did not hasten to expose the bad faith of this German party, and to communicate to the Propaganda the sentiments which we know to be those of a very great majority of the American Episcopate.

We shall first make some general observations upon the German Catholics in the United States, and then some more particular observations upon the demands presented by Rev. Father Abbelen to the Congregation of the Propaganda:

1. The question under consideration is styled, according to Father Abbelen, "The question in the United States between the German Catholics and the Irish Catholics." Presented in these terms, the question cannot be discussed; it has no existence. The only question that can be considered is this: "The question between the English language, which is the language of the United States, and the German language, which emigrants from Germany have brought to the United States." Why the Germans so often give to this question another form, as if to indicate that there is a conflict of races in America between the Germans and the Irish, we do not know. But neither the truth nor justice of the case permits us to accept what they seek to impose upon us. There is in the United States no Irish Church, nor are there any Irish parishes; no efforts are made in the United States to establish an Irish Church, or Irish parishes. What we find in the United States, instead of Irish parishes, are parishes of the English language, which are composed either of Catholics who are not at all of the Irish race, or of Catholics whose ancestors may have been Irish, but who today are, from every point of view, Americans, and they do not wish to be considered Irish; or, again, they may be composed of Catholics born in Ireland, or the immediate descendants of Irish emigrants. Our parishes of the English language are never called Irish parishes. The English-speaking bishops and priests, of which a large number are in no respect of the Irish race, have the interests of the Church in the United States too much at heart not to endeavor to eliminate from religious affairs Irish nationalism, and to impress them, as far as the circumstances of time, place, and sound principles will permit, with an elevated and Catholic character, against which no element, in a very heterogeneous population, could raise any objection. For the rest, let it be said to their praise, the Irish Catholics, even the recent emigrants, do not interpose any serious obstacle to these desires of their religious superiors. Whatever may be their attachment to the land of their birth, they hasten, on arriving in America, to adopt American ideas and manners, and they understand that, in regard to matters of religion, intermingled as they are with other Catholics, speaking like them the English language, but not like them of the Irish race, they must, for the general good, lay aside their national spirit. The sole question, then, which can be considered, in what regards the English-speaking bishops and priests in

America, is this — the question between the English language and the German language.

2. The Congregation of the Propaganda will permit us to state here, what is already well known, that the German language is far from being the only foreign language in use among Catholics in the United States. The French Canadians, Poles, Bohemians, Dutch are very numerous, and it is well to remark that, according to the present rate of emigration to the United States, it will not require many years for some of these nationalities to be more largely represented there than the German nationality. The concessions made to the Germans will, in course of time, be claimed by the French, Bohemians, and Poles for their languages, and the Church in the United States will be little more than *moles informis et indigesto* — without unity, without life, without authority. We have already had an intimation of what is threatening us. Last year, in a general reunion of Bohemian Catholic societies, the complaint was made, in language little respectful either to Rome or to the American hierarchy, that up to this time there had been no Bohemian in the American episcopate. The Canadians, as is well known, are exceedingly turbulent; and their cry, whether in the halls of their societies or in the offices of their papers, is that henceforth a decided regard must be had for their national spirit and language in diocesan administrations. A German bishop, the late Bishop of Green Bay, Mgr. F. Krautbauer, often spoke of the almost innumerable difficulties in the government of this diocese, on account of the preponderance there of French and Slav elements. On account of our heterogeneous population in the United States, we cannot have too much fear of legislation, however unexceptional, in favor of a particular nationality, or of the language of this nationality, and our wishes cannot bring about the time too soon when, without any detriment to our souls, there will be among us more unity of spirit and more unity of language.

3. We are bound to notice the fact that not all German Catholics or Catholics of German origin have the same ideas upon the question which is now engaging our attention. There exists what we may call the active party, whose object seems to be to preserve intact the German spirit among German emigrants and their descendants, and to prevent them from changing their language for the English language, and to give a preponderant position to German influence in the Church in America. This is the party of which Father Abbelen is now the representative at Rome. It is not for us to judge of the motive which is inspiring the action of this party; we merely wish to mark its line of conduct, and to point out the grievous results. This party is posing, in its public declarations in the United States and in its appeals to Rome, as the German people of America. This pretension is very far from the fact. There are a great number of Germans in America who entertain ideas altogether different. They oppose the establishment of a permanent Germany in America; they

approve of the use of the German language in so far as is useful or necessary for the welfare of souls, but they refuse to carry this usage to an extreme, merely for the sake of German patriotism, and they openly declare their conviction that in America *coeteris paribus,* the English language, as the language of the country, deserves the preference, and that religion is better served when this preference is accorded to it. We can cite in the episcopate Mgr. Marty, Vicar Apostolic of Dakota, and among the lower clergy, Mgr. Batz, domestic prelate of the Holy Father and Vicar-General of Milwaukee. Many priests of German origin, and many laymen especially, share the sentiments of these venerable personages. The number of adherents of this moderate party, which may be called the German American party, is increasing from day to day, according as the Germans have the time to Americanize themselves.

4. We desire to call the attention of the Propaganda to the manner in which this German party calculates its forces in the United States. Fr. Abbelen puts the number of German priests in the United States at 2067; this is the number given also by the editor of the *German Directory,* published by Herder, of St. Louis. But this number, as is admitted by this editor, who is more reliable than Fr. Abbelen, includes all the priests who speak German, whether they are Poles, Slavs, Bohemians, Dutch, or even English and Irish. The Poles and Bohemians very strenuously object to being classed with Germans. This number, we know, includes some priests who have a name of German origin, although, in fact, they would indignantly repel the idea of being Germans. Several years ago the German Catholic paper of Baltimore undertook to publish a list of the names of German priests. In this list, there appeared as German priests for the diocese of St. Paul, two French priests, and one Catholic layman who during the week sold beer and on Sunday taught catechism to the children of the village. What this editor was prepared to do for the other dioceses, we are not able to say. A writer in the *Pastoral Blatt,* of Saint Louis, enumerates eighteen German bishops; but in doing so he must count as Germans Mgr. Gross and Mgr. Becker, whose ancestors have been Americans for many generations, and some others who are Dutch or Slav, and who have no sympathy with the aggressive attitude of these Germans. The means by which they seek to find the number of the German laity are nonetheless false. All who are descendants of Germans, no matter whether they are now completely Americanized or not, are counted as Germans. Very often, parishes whose pastors have German names are passed off as German, although only a portion of the parishioners may be German, or even all may be English. In the *Deutscher Schematismus* or *German Directory,* published lately by Herder, the parish of Avoca, in the Diocese of St. Paul, which is an Irish colony, is set down as a German parish of 200 families, simply because the rector had a German name. Two other parishes in the same diocese were, for the same reason, counted as entirely German, although the Germans, in both, composed but a very

small part of the population. Often priests with a German name, or of German origin, but sufficiently Americanized, are placed at the head of English parishes by English bishops; mixed parishes have generally a German priest, if the German Catholics form a considerable part. Moreover, it is a well-known fact, that in certain dioceses, whose bishops are German, some English parishes are placed in charge of German priests, whether they are sufficiently Americanized or not. These facts show that from the number of German priests, no estimate can be formed as to the number of the Catholic laity.

Reference is often made to the number of German religious orders in the United States; to the number of colleges, and institutions for higher education, established by the Germans. They forget to say that a religious order introduced by the Germans always remains inscribed in the books of the party as German, although the members may after a few years be, to a great extent, English; which is especially the case with female religious orders. They forget to say that the institutions conducted by these orders, and in which they seek to place their English subjects as professors, generally have English Catholics for patrons. They forget, moreover, to say that several German religious orders have lately come to the United States, on account of persecutions in Germany, and not because the Germans in America asked for their assistance, and that in many cases it is Catholics of the English language who have generously received them, and have given them employment in the English hospitals and asylums maintained by the money of English Catholics. They boast considerably of the great number of German children found in parochial schools; a number equal, they say, to that of the English children in their parochial schools. More false premises. The *Pastoral Blatt,* of St. Louis, in its account of the diocese of St. Paul, dares to represent as German all the children of several mixed parishes, although a large number of these children are English (speaking). As for the rest, the German priests can easily build school houses, as they find among the new emigrants a great help in their love for the German language. The English have not this support, as the language of their parishioners is the language of the free schools of the State. For those who are acquainted with their motives, the numerous schools of the Germans prove, among other things, that the new emigrants naturally seek the German language, and that some German priests are a little too much attached to it; but they do not prove that German priests are more zealous than their English confreres, or that German Catholics are almost equal in number to English Catholics.

5. It is, indeed, evident to all that the German emigrants must have facilities for themselves and for their children, for the practice of religion, in the language most familiar to them. To this end, the bishops in the United States are multiplying churches as much as lies in their power, and the circumstances will permit, for the benefit of the different nationalities they are to serve. But for these and for such others as may be in-

terested in this question, to think that there is not a constant and very decided movement toward the English language, among the different nationalities, is to ignore the facts of circumstances. Their material and political circumstances are pushing the immigrants onward in this movement; the American people desire it and encourage it; the entourage of the foreigner in any country leads him, whether he wishes it or not, to identify himself with the common language. The immigrants are but a few years in America when they are able to conduct their commercial and political affairs in English, and excepting a few remote places, where foreigners are the only inhabitants, children born in America prefer to speak English. It is a recognized fact that German children who are taught German in their schools, speak English when they enter the recreation yard. Let us repeat, that religion should be taught the Germans in the German language, as far as may be necessary; but let it also be said that even religion sets a limit to this teaching, which must not, for evident reasons, go beyond the desires of the Germans themselves, nor beyond the spiritual and temporal needs of the people. The active party among the Germans of America, against whom we are complaining, is going far beyond just limits in its zeal for the German language. Let us cite some facts: The Congregation of the Sisters of Notre Dame, of which the mother house is in Milwaukee (Fr. Abbelen himself is its *Pater Spiritualis*) numbers 1100 members, employed in elementary teaching. Of these, some only were born in Europe; several hundred are of Irish or American origin. Well! the language of the prayers, of the meditations, of the retreats, of all the spiritual exercises for all these Sisters, is German, although the order has been established in America for thirty-five years. The Bishop of St. Paul has often heard it told that some sisters of this congregation understood German so little that they lost the time devoted to meditations and to retreats. Another community, that of the Sisters of Divine Love, was established in America at the beginning of the *Kulturkampf* in Germany. They are also employed in elementary teaching. Their councilors, certain bishops and German priests, have, as the superioress of Wilkes-Barre wrote to the Bishop of St. Paul in response to his protest against this practice so little American and so little Catholic, advised them to preserve everywhere the German language as the language of their community. These Sisters are following that advice, and while they propose to conduct schools for American girls, they receive as members of their community only such persons who may be sufficiently German, either by birth or by adoption, to consent to preserve German as their usual language. Priests who adhere to this active party persist in using the German language exclusively, always and everywhere in their catechism classes. Very frequently the children at home speak a dialect far removed from the German proper, and, on account of their surroundings, it is more difficult for them to learn German than English. But no matter; they must learn their religion in German. Often, especially in the country, where parochial schools are not possible because the farmers live so far apart, the children learn only English. But no matter; the teaching of religion must be in German. Later on these German children will perhaps change their residence, and find themselves in places where there is no German priest; in the English papers they will read objections to their faith, and their companions will repeat these objections in English. It would seem to be very useful for children, who know both languages, and learn arithmetic and geography in English, to learn catechism also in two languages. But no; religion must be German, and the bishops who would give advice differently would be treated as an enemy of the Germans, as happened to the Bishop of St. Paul among certain of his German priests.

Serious consequences result from these facts. The children do not know the catechism, on account of their imperfect knowledge of the German; whereas, it would have been otherwise had they been permitted to learn it in English. More than once the Bishop of St. Paul enquired of some religious, who were themselves German, why their students did not know their catechism better, and he was answered that the students found too much difficulty in learning it in German.

On the other hand, whatever the case may be with German children in their infant years, they will be in great danger of losing their faith later. They will be forced to Americanize themselves; sooner or later the English language will become their language almost exclusively; they will gradually detach themselves from everything that could point them out as foreigners. Religion having been taught to them in German, they will abandon it, in abandoning the German language. The transition from German to English is for them necessary and inevitable; their spiritual masters, with ever so little foresight, ought to have prepared them to save their faith in this transition. It is just the contrary which has come to pass. In the vain hope of keeping them Germans, they give a color thoroughly foreign to their religion, and they are lost to both language and faith. It cannot be denied that too many of the descendants of the Germans forsake the Church, especially when they have become rich, and have, moreover, intermingled with their American fellow citizens. If you enquire of certain German priests for the cause of this apostasy, they will very probably answer that they who lose their faith have not been sufficiently confirmed in their infancy in the use of the German language. The truth is, they have been confirmed too much in this usage. They could never be sufficiently persuaded to remain German, and they never learned how to save their faith from shipwreck in the transition from one language to another. If there is any city in the United States in which the Germans were, in a manner, supreme in the Church, it is the city of Milwaukee. It is a common saying in America, that in going to Milwaukee one goes to Germany. Very well! We are not afraid to say, and we have it from German priests, that there is not a city in the United States in which, in proportion to the German Catholic population, there are to be found so many persons who have lost their faith. Mgr. Marty, of Dakota, told his confreres of the episcopacy in the Provincial Council of Milwaukee, held six months ago, that thousands and thousands of Germans forsake the Church because they refuse to teach them the catechism in English, and to prepare them in this manner for the transition from one language to another. It is owing to the efforts of Mgr. Marty that the Council of Milwaukee has ordered that henceforth German children of an advanced age must learn their catechism in two languages. But this action of the Council was not pleasing to all the Germans. For several years past the German Jesuits of St. Louis have had the teaching of catechism in both languages as their rule, in spite of the protestations of some Germans, who complained that these Jesuits were endeavoring to Americanize their parishioners, and on this account little deserved the confidence of their compatriots. The children of darkness are wiser in their generation than the children of light, and lately the German Lutherans in the United States, assembled in synod, decided that in order to better preserve their people in the Lutheran belief, they would henceforth take particular care to teach religion in English no less than in German. It is, indeed, acknowledged that the obstinate love for the German language is much more noticeable among certain German Catholics than among German Protestants. A Catholic paper has with some emphasis declared that the great safeguard of the German language in the United States is the Catholic clergy.

6. Let us cite other facts, showing the spirit of aggression which distinguishes certain Germans; facts which, moreover, are exceedingly harmful to Catholics of American or of Irish origin, and against a repetition of which the latter are beginning to arm themselves. They have lately asked the Holy See to grant to the Germans in the United States a Cardinal Protector. This request had its object: it was intended to procure an exceptional position in the American Church, and to intimidate the English-speaking bishops and laity. Very fortunately, Rome did not accede to the request. In the city of La Crosse, the oldest and strongest parish was the English parish. When Mgr. Heiss was made bishop of this place, he chose the German Church for his Cathedral, and even to this day, under his successor, we behold this strange phenomenon, that the official language of a Catholic bishop in an American city is a language foreign to the country. The same state of affairs exists at Green Bay, where a sermon in English is never heard in the Cathedral on Sunday, the English Catholics being thus obliged to go to a neighboring city to receive religious instruction in the language of their country. Why this public establishment of the German Church as the Church of the American nation? In the diocese of Ft. Wayne, under Mgr. Luers, the predecessor of Mgr. Dwenger, the English-speaking priests were numerous. Mgr. Dwenger has reduced them to a dozen. It has more than once been said that there ought to be especially in the Western States, only priests of German origin. In the dioceses of Alton, of Milwaukee, of La Crosse, of Ft. Wayne,

some parishes, entirely or almost entirely English, have German rectors, who speak English very indifferently. The object of some German bishops seems to be to Germanize their dioceses, and that of many German priests to Germanize their parishes. As soon as one of these priests is placed over a mixed parish, the school becomes German; the German customs are introduced into the Church; the English people weary of a sermon in poor English, and gradually absent themselves from divine service. In this way American Protestants will never cross the threshold of a Catholic temple. Let this German element but once obtain a preponderance, and it will immediately inaugurate a warfare to perpetuate it. Mgr. Henni, lately Archbishop of Milwaukee, did not fear to declare openly that never would an Irishman sit upon his episcopal throne. In the Seminary of Milwaukee, twelve or thirteen professors have always been German, and that has been the case to this day, although the English-speaking priests of the diocese have never ceased to express their dissatisfaction at a state of things so manifestly unjust. Under Mgr. Henni, the English young men of the diocese, who aspired to the priesthood, were compelled to seek an asylum in some other diocese, so that the clergy of the Milwaukee diocese became almost exclusively German, and English Catholics in fairly large numbers emigrated to other parts of America, expressly to get away from a German Church, with which they had no sympathy, and under which they foresaw that their children would lose their faith. The Bishop of Cleveland, Mgr. Gilmour, told us, that before his time the Germans had come into control of the diocesan seminary, and that in consequence, all the students became Germans, until the English priests of the diocese rose in open rebellion against such injustice. We know for certain, that among certain German bishops and priests there is a determination, and systematic efforts are made, to extend the German episcopate over America. How they expect to open the way to success we are not able to say; but the fact is, that already, for certain dioceses where there are but very few Germans, and we may instance the diocese of Nashville, although the first candidates on the lists were English, yet Germans have been chosen. Preparations are now already being made on a grand scale to procure in the future German bishops for Cincinnati and for St. Louis, and more than once has the prediction been made that very soon all the States, of the West at least, will, without exception, have a German episcopate. It is openly boasted, to the mortification of other Catholics, that the German cause will be victorious at Rome, and in consequence of this idea, efforts are being made to Germanize the American Church. In late years several German papers have been overflowing in insolence toward what they call the Irish clergy and the Irish Catholics. The German paper of Detroit, whose editor is a priest, has especially distinguished itself by its repeated insults against everything that is not German. The object of the principal heads of this enraged German party, we cannot but think is, to make all the Germans believe that they are deprived of their rights; that they are even persecuted, and in this way to force them to range themselves on their side, and thus increase their force.

These facts are a cause of disaster to the Church in America; the Catholics of the English language get discouraged; their love for religion becomes cold; their character is not that of the Germans; they do not combine; they make no plans of resistance; except in extreme cases they do not bring their complaints to Rome; but they are beginning to see in the Church a step-mother, and little by little they separate from her; their children no longer frequent Catholic schools, of which the teachers but imperfectly understand the language of the country; they but reluctantly listen to sermons which are preached with foreign accents; the German habits and ideas are repelling to them. The more their American patriotism increases, the more difficulty they find in loving a religion of which all the forms are strange, and thus they withdraw — more and more from their duty. Often English Catholics, being the first to arrive in a certain locality, built at their own expense the church and rectory; later on a handful of Germans arrive; the war for the rights of the Germans is carried on with an obstinacy and a spirit of aggression characteristic of the compatriots of Bismarck; the English submit in order to have peace; a German priest is installed, and the parish is forever Germanized. The Germans speak of their rights; they are silent as to the rights of others, as if all those in America who are not Germans, had no rights. We can cite parishes and dioceses in which the number of Catholics lost to the Church, because in an English country they sought to Germanize them, is frightful; and if now we seem to raise our voice, it is because we feel the existence of a great danger for the Church, and that in the past, our fault has been to keep silent too patiently. If lately some appearances of opposition to the Germans have come to the surface in America, it is an opposition to these constant encroachments, so contrary in all justice, to all rights of English-speaking Catholics; it is an objection to this continued movement of the Germans to arrogate to themselves the entire government of the American Church. There is no objection to the Germans having all the rights which are due them, nor to their conducting their own affairs, whether religious or temporal, as they understand them. But it is desirable to remind them that America is not Germany, and that there are other Catholics there, besides the Germans.

With a German Church in America, there is no hope for the conversion of American Protestants. This is a vital question for religion. The Church will never be strong in America; she will never be sure of keeping within her fold the descendants of emigrants, Irish as well as others, until she has gained a decided ascendancy among the Americans themselves. Thank God, the times seem favorable for their conversion; prejudices are dissipating; the conservatory principles of the Catholic Church recommend her: There is a decided movement toward the Church. To accelerate it the Church naturally must, as far as it can be done without danger to other interests, be presented in a form attractive to Americans. The great objection which they have until now urged against her — an objection which at certain periods of their history they entertained so strongly as even to raise persecutions — is, that the Catholic Church is composed of foreigners; that it exists in America as a foreign institution, and that it is, consequently, a menace to the existence of the nation. Can we persuade them to lay aside this objection, and to receive our invitations to hear the Church, by spreading before them obstacles to the Americanization of the descendants of Catholic emigrants, and by placing in the first ranks, as the representatives of the Church, men who have no sympathy with the habits and legitimate ideas of the country, and who understand but imperfectly the language of the country? Will Americans, perhaps, find pleasure in temples in which even Catholics of the English language grow weary, and in which everything has the air of a foreign country? The Germans bring with them to America some noble qualities; but they also bring with them certain ideas and methods of action which the Americans fear. The Socialistic movements in the United States generally have Germans at their head; the Germans have little respect for Sunday; extend the German influence over the Church, and the Americans will see in her a powerful agent in spreading the ideas and manners which they like least in the Germans. It is very easy to create a stormy future for the Church; to accomplish this there is no means surer than to make her appear as the product of a European nationalism.

Is it desired, on the other hand, to give to the Church in our country the social prestige which will assure the public influence she needs for the enjoyment of all her rights, and to make her recognized in the legislation of the Nation? Give her, in her exterior forms, an American character, which moreover suits well with her divine catholicity; and above all, choose for her as her principal pastors, and great representatives, men whose sympathies and whose accent show that they understand the country and are devoted to its interests. A catholicity with the customs and language of America will not please in Germany; and a catholicity with the customs and language of Germany will please just as little in America.

7. The accusation has been made that Germans are neglected in dioceses presided over by bishops of the English language. Whether or not there exists some injustice toward Germans in some localities, we will not undertake to say. As for us, we know of none. But if they mean that this accusation is, in ever so small a degree, general, we deny it absolutely. In the past, the Germans, like the English, had to suffer from the scarcity of priests, which prevailed all over America. Until the beginning of the *Kulturkampf* which compelled many German priests to seek an asylum in America, it was a difficult matter for the American bishops to find German priests; those who had come here in consequence of the revolution of 1848 were suspect, and no confidence could be placed in them. But the bishops did all that was in their power to save the souls of Catholics of every

nationality. As regards the present time, let them point out the particular localities if they can; but let them not dare to bring a general accusation. It will no doubt be found sometimes that in particular localities, where the number of adherents of each language are not sufficient to have a separate church, that mixed parishes exist whose pastors are English without understanding German. But what is to be done? The rule followed by the bishops, is, when they have the choice of priests, they appoint a pastor who will at least correspond to the expressed desires of the largest majority of the parishioners, even if he cannot manage it so as to please all. If the Germans, Bohemians, or Canadians are in the minority and there is no priest of their language sufficiently Americanized to satisfy the English majority, the bishop chooses, if he can, an English priest who understands the foreign language, and if none is to be found, then he chooses an English priest who properly understands his own language, and who will please at least the majority of the parishioners. In the latter case there are some inconveniences; the bishop in his zeal for their souls seeks to remedy the matter; notwithstanding the fact that the Germans, Bohemians, or Canadians often understand the English, more or less, a law is made that the pastor must call to his aid, three or four times a year, a priest who understands the language of the minority! But, say they, why not always place a priest who understands English and German in charge of mixed parishes? The question would not even then be solved to the satisfaction of all; for often there are not less than four nationalities in the same parish, and without the gift of Pentecost some of them would always be dissatisfied. Moreover, English priests very rarely understand German, although this will not be the case in the future, the study of German having been made obligatory in several seminaries, as it is in the diocesan seminary of St. Paul. The German priest, it may be said, can ordinarily speak the English language, besides his own — the German language. We answer that he very rarely speaks it with elegance and grace. He is satisfied with a jargon of German and English, with which the English people will by no means be satisfied. Place such a German priest in a parish with an English majority, and there will be war, followed by the loss of souls and decay of faith. The bishops do the best they can, according to circumstances of time and place, and we ask the Congregation to trust to their zeal.

There exist also some mixed dioceses, with English bishops, and it is asked why are there not everywhere German bishops? To have German bishops everywhere would be the fulfillment of the wishes of this outraged German party; this is the ultimate object of all their intrigues. They always forget, that in these mixed dioceses there are several other foreign nationalities, each of whom is ever ready to claim, for the sake of its particular interest, a bishop of its own language. They always forget that there are English speaking Catholics who have their duties and rights as well as the Germans. They forget the general interests of the American

Church, which is loudly crying to be saved from German and foreign nationalism. It is not necessary to say anything more upon these important subjects, as we have now said sufficient.

However useful the knowledge of foreign languages may be to a bishop in America, it may be considered a fact that this is not necessary for him. People of foreign tongue like to confess in their own language, and to hear the sermon in this language; it is necessary, therefore, to have priests who speak these languages. But for all affairs of public life, the English language is used, as, for instance, in business, civil, and political life, and in judicial matters. In their relations with the bishop as supreme pastor of the diocese only public ecclesiastical life is concerned, and people of a foreign tongue never have any difficulty in coming to an understanding with him in English. We insist upon emphasizing this fact; it is very important in the discussion. We may add that the complaint that the bishop does not speak German, does not come from the German people as a people, but from their *soidisant* popular tribunes, from their journalists, who perceive in the continuation of their language the life of their papers and of certain German priests and prelates, who, we may also believe, imagine that they, German as they are to the very foundation of their being, would have neither occupation nor power in America, if there ceased to be a permanent Germany in America.

Far be it from us, indeed, to exclude Germans from the American episcopate. They have the right to be represented in the higher clergy, but only those ought to be bishops, in a country like America, who know the language of the country well; who well understand the needs of the Church in the country; who can eradicate from their hearts foreign nationalism, and who see in their new charges, occasion to serve the Church, to serve all her children, and not the occasion to make one particular element of the Catholic population dominant. We have, thank God, in the priesthood and episcopacy of America, some Germans, true ministers of the Catholic Church, and not servitors of a particular nationality, and we thank God for their presence among us.

It should no longer be necessary to place in the episcopate of any ecclesiastical province so many Germans as to cause the belief that the German is the favored race in the Church, or to lead Americans, either Catholic or Protestants, to suspect that a foreign element is seeking to prevail in the Church. A foreign character in the Church will always be a great danger to religion, and, we will say, we desire an Irish or French nationalism among us just as little as we do a German nationalism.

8. We believe we have said sufficient for the Congregation to understand that to the German question, as it has been presented by Fr. Abbelen and Mgr. Heiss, there is also a non-German side, which, in all justice, should not fail to be heard. We have said enough to show that in a country with a population as heterogeneous as ours, a legislation in favor of a particular

nationality is a most dangerous thing, and should be granted only in an extreme case, and after the bishops of that same country have had the time to present the views which their experience of the difficulties of the ministry have enabled them to form. We will now submit several brief observations upon the special demands made by Fr. Abbelen:

a) They demand that the German parishes have, in every respect, the same rights as the English-speaking parishes. We have no thought of disputing the justice of this demand. It is evident to us that there must be perfect equality among the parishes of every foreign language and the parishes of the English language. No privileges; equality in all; this is our doctrine and our practice.

But what astonishes us is that the demand should have been made as if there existed in the United States a state of things different from what this demand seeks to establish. We know a great number of American dioceses, and in all these dioceses, the same rights are scrupulously accorded to the German parishes that are accorded to others. Fr. Abbelen mentions St. Louis, New Orleans, Albany, and Baltimore. That is, after all, but four dioceses in seventy. We have heard, it is true, that there was some difficulty upon this subject in St. Louis and in New Orleans; not that they wished to mark the German churches as inferior, but because the decree, *Tametsi,* having been promulgated in these places, it was feared that it would suffer by recognizing several parishes in the same territory. As to Baltimore, we know that Fr. Abbelen is mistaken. For in the acts of the synod of 1876, we find: *"Quando uterque (parens) gente Germanus sit, rector Germanorum necessario erit adeundus ad sacramenta matrimonii vel baptismi suscipienda."* The Bishop of Richmond was a priest in the diocese of Baltimore for several years, and he is certain that German pastors enjoy the same rights there as English pastors, and that the latter never invade the rights of the former. We, therefore, object to the demand for a general legislation, made at Rome on this subject, because such a demand supposes a general state of affairs in America which does not exist, and the existence of which we would regret. If there is some local difficulty, let redress be sought from the local authorities, and if that should not prove satisfactory, let an appeal be taken for this particular locality; but let there be no general appeal, nor any general legislation.

b) They ask that in the establishment of *pastores inamovibiles,* German priests be placed on the same footing as English priests. We answer: The bishops of America have no other thought as to this subject, and any legislation in regard to it would be useless. We cannot but believe that these two demands have been made for no other object than to present with them to the Propaganda certain complaints, more or less imaginary, which the Germans have been wishing for some time to bring against the non-German clergy, and thus to follow them up with other demands which we will now mention:

c) They demand that all German emigrants, and their children, as long as they are under the control of their parents, be regarded as subjects of German parishes.

The demand in this form contains nothing that does not already exist in the United States. A formal approbation of this demand by the Propaganda would, however, give rise to difficulties. The demand being approved, the German pastors would not only reserve for themselves the right to baptize and to solemnize matrimony, but they would prevent their parishioners from ever sending their children to English Catholic schools, or from ever renting a pew in English churches. Great injustice would be caused by such claims.

Catholics, either English or German, believe that they have the right to send their children to any school, provided it is Catholic. The English Catholic sometimes desires his child to be instructed in German or French, and sends him to a school where these languages are taught. A German believes that his child can be taught German sufficiently at home, and he sends him to a school where English is thoroughly taught. Moreover, it is custom everywhere that the parishioner of one church may, if he wishes, rent a pew in another church, hear Mass and go to confession where he chooses. Why impose upon Germans restrictions which the English do not recognize? Let German and English parishes be equal in every respect but let there be no privileges for German parishes. It must also be said that in certain localities there are very few restrictions for Catholics in the choice of their parishes. This liberty the ecclesiastical authorities consider necessary, in order to make the practice of his duties easy to every Catholic. If a family, living in the immediate jurisdiction of a church, rents a pew in another church, it may call upon the pastor of the latter for all the offices of religion. In this case, that cannot be refused to Germans what is accorded to the English, and what some Germans would claim. There must always be equality, but not privileges; let each bishop dispose of all these matters as he may think best for his own diocese.

d) They demand that if the descendants of Germans wish to join English churches after they have adopted the English language, they be required to obtain formal permission of the German pastor, or of the bishop. This is an affair of too little importance to become the subject of general legislation. Let each bishop arrange such matters for his particular diocese. For the rest, it is sufficiently difficult to keep Catholics to their duty, without charging them with other annoying and useless regulations. The object of the demand is to make Americanization of German descendants more difficult, to permit the German pastor to decide when the time for such change has come, to interpose objections, should he wish to do so.

e) They demand that the Propaganda instruct English bishops and priests not to attempt, in any manner, to suppress the use of the German language, or to discourage German manners and customs. We answer: To give such an instruction would suppose that a serious injustice is being practiced in regard to the Germans. We deny this. To give such an instruction were to accord to the Germans a protection both special and odious, and to condemn and dishonor the bishops of the English tongue in America.

f) They demand that for mixed parishes the bishop appoint priests understanding English and German. We have already answered this demand, in showing the rule which the bishops in America follow in regard to mixed parishes.

g) They demand, finally, that when the bishop does not understand German, he be obliged to appoint a German vicar-general, at the same time with an Irish vicar-general. We answer: However desirable it may be supposed to be in particular cases to have a German vicar-general, a general rule upon this subject could not be made without serious injury. What would they do, for instance, in the diocese of St. Paul, where, according to the wishes of everybody, the vicar-general is a Frenchman? Must a German be appointed there? Then the Irish, Bohemians, Poles, and Dutch would want a vicar-general, and there would be six of them in a single diocese. What is to be done in the diocese of Richmond, where the only vicar-general is a Belgian? Let Rome order a German vicar-general, and an exceptional position would thereby be given to the Germans, which would so puff them up as to make the position of the English Catholics, whether clergy or lay, intolerable. And what rule would there be for German bishops, who, almost always in mixed dioceses, have only German vicar-generals? And, what is more, in America the vicar-general is of little importance, because the bishop attends directly to the diocesan administration. To impose upon the bishop a particular man, or a man of a particular race, would reduce to the smallest limits the liberty of the bishop in the administration of his diocese, and we have no fear that the Propaganda will encourage any such idea.

We have presented the foregoing observations to the Propaganda merely for the purpose of showing that the Catholics of English tongue deserve to be heard, and to obtain such delay in the consideration of all these questions as may enable the bishops of the United States to become acquainted with what is going on at Rome, and to allow them to communicate their ideas to the Propaganda. However wise the decisions may be which the Propaganda may make at present in regard to this subject, the American bishops will take offense, because they will perceive in these rules the success of the secret movements of a party. The bishops have, until now, believed that unity existed among them; that the members of the hierarchy had confidence in one another; that the questions affecting the interests of religion in their country could be discussed, at least in the first instance, between themselves in peace and fraternal love. With the most profound regret they will learn that they are mistaken, and that while all seemed calm around them, a tempest was rising and about to break forth. But, at least, we pray that the Congregation may not approve these sinister intrigues, and that before any decision is made it remand all these questions to the bishops of the United States.

The consultation which the Propaganda held some time ago with certain American bishops, related to only one of the questions submitted by Fr. Abbelen, and that one was of the least importance. Our confreres have no knowledge of the document which he has presented. Our prayer to the Congregation, then, is to suspend all deliberation upon this document until the necessary information of what is passing has been transmitted to the American bishops, and their advice has been heard.

JOHN IRELAND
Bishop of St. Paul
JOHN J. KEANE
Bishop of Richmond

To His Eminence,
Cardinal Simeoni, Prefect of the
Holy Congregation of the Propaganda
ROME, Dec. 6, 1886

Appendix IV

Memorial Drawn Up and Presented to His Holiness Pope Leo XIII by the First International Conference of St. Raphael Societies Lucerne, Switzerland December 9–10, 1890

February, 1891

Most Holy Father,

The presidents, secretaries general, and delegates of the societies under the protection of the Holy Archangel Raphael for the protection of emigrants, encouraged by the benevolence which Your Holiness has shown them, assembled on December 9 of last year at an international conference in Lucerne to deliberate upon means best suited to serve the spiritual and material well-being of their Catholic compatriots who have emigrated to America, the number of which is in excess of 400,000 yearly.

The above mentioned take the liberty to place before Your Holiness, with deepest respect, the fact that the numerous emigrants constitute a great strength, and could co-operate eminently in the expansion of the Catholic Church in the several states of America. In this way they could contribute to the moral stature of their new homeland, as well as to the stimulation of religious consciousness in the old European fatherlands.

Only the true Church, of which Your Holiness is the highest shepherd, can obtain these happy results because it is the true source of all progress and civilization.

But in order that European Catholics, in their adopted country, preserve and transmit to their children their faith and its inherent benefits, the undersigned have the honor to submit to Your Holiness the conditions, which in the light of experience and in the nature of things, appear to be indispensable for that purpose in the countries of immigration. The losses which the Church has suffered in the United States of North America number more than ten million souls.

1. It seems necessary to unite the emigrant groups of each nationality in separate parishes, congregations, or missions wherever their numbers and means make such a practice possible.

2. It seems necessary to entrust the administration of these parishes to priests of the same nationality to which the faithful belong. The sweetest and dearest memories of their homeland would be recalled every minute, and they would love all the more the holy Church which procures these benefits for them.

3. In areas settled by emigrants of several nationalities who are not numerous enough to organize separate national parishes, it is desirable as far as possible, that a pastor be chosen to guide them who understands the diverse languages of these groups. This priest should be strictly obliged to give catechetical instruction to each of the groups in its own language.

4. It will be especially necessary to establish parochial schools wherever Christian public schools are not available, and these schools should be separate, as far as possible, for each nationality.

The curriculum of these schools should always include the mother tongue as well as the language and history of the adopted country.

5. It seems necessary to grant to priests devoting themselves to the emigrants all rights, privileges, and prerogatives enjoyed by the priests of the country. This arrangement, which is only just, would have the result that zealous, pious, and apostolic priests of all nationalities will be attracted to immigrant work.

6. It seems desirable to establish and encourage societies of various kinds, confraternities, charitable organizations, mutual aid and protective associations, etc. By these means Catholics would be systematically organized and saved from the dangerous sects of Freemasons and organizations affiliated with it.

7. It seems very desirable that the Catholics of each nationality, wherever it is deemed possible, have in the episcopacy of the country where they immigrate, several bishops who are of the same origin. It seems that in this way the organization of the Church would be perfect, for in the assemblies of the bishops, every immigrant race would be represented, and its interests and needs would be protected.

8. Finally the undersigned wish to point out that for the attainment of the objectives which they have enumerated, it would be very desirable, and this they vigorously urge, that the Holy See foster and protect in the emigration countries: (*a*) special seminaries and apostolic schools for training missionaries for emigrants; (*b*) St. Raphael societies for the protection of emigrants, and that it recommend to the Most Rev. Bishops that they establish such societies in the emigration countries where they do not yet exist, and that the Holy See place them under the protection of a Cardinal Protector.

The undersigned hope for the happiest and most immediate results from this organization and these measures. Emigration missionaries trained under the direction of a distinguished Italian Bishop have already gone to America. Others, members of neighboring nations, are waiting, before entering, upon their important and holy calling, for the Supreme Shepherd .

of the Church, by a decree of his wisdom, to guarantee the free exercise of their mission. If the Holy See will lend its indispensable co-operation, wonderful results should result. The poor emigrants will find on American soil their priests, their parishes, their schools, their societies, their language, and thus cannot fail to extend the boundaries of the Kingdom of Jesus Christ on earth.

In giving solemn testimony of their loyal devotion to the Apostolic See, the undersigned humbly beg Your Holiness to grant paternal approbation to the proposals which they have proposed for the salvation of souls and the glory of our holy mother, the Church, in the different American nations. With the most loyal devotion, Your most devoted, humble, and obedient sons:

The board of directors of the German St. Raphael Society: Prince Karl zu Isenburg-Birstein; Representative Cahensly; Count von Preysing, Baron von Buol, Baron Franz von Schorlemer, Representative Josef Lingens, Count von Loë, Attorney Edward Müller, Eugene Haffner, Baron von Wendt.

The board of directors of the Austrian St. Raphael Society: Prince von Schwarzenberg; Dr. Wiard Klopp; Baron von Linde; Count zur Lippe; Count Chorinsky; Baron von Vittinghoff-Schell; Dr. von Sas-Krechowiecky; Count Zabeo; Count Sylva-Tarouca.

The board of directors of the Belgian St. Raphael Society: Senator Leon van Ockerhout; Count Waldbott-Bassenheim; Baron Ruzette; Prince de Rubempre; Count Albert de Ribiano; Duke d'Ursel; Count du Pre.

Delegate of the Swiss Society: Baron Rudolph von Reding-Biberegg.

The board of directors of the Italian St. Raphael Society: Marchese G. Battista Volpe-Landi; Marchese Frederico Landi; Count Medolaga di Bergamo; Count Alessandro Monandi; Marchese Balestrino del Caretto; Marchese Battista de Lucca; Prince Luigi Buoncompagni; Count Eduardo Soderini.

Delegate of the Catholic Committee of Paris: M. Charles Plista.*

* Plista signed the Memorial with the comment that he was endorsing it only on his own behalf, since the French St. Raphael Society was as yet only in its formative stages.

A duplicate copy of the Memorial was attached in the interest of the French-speaking Canadian Catholics living in the United States, and this manuscript bore the signatures of Prime Minister Henri Mercier, of Quebec, Minister of Finance Joseph Shehyn, and thirteen other Canadian Catholics.

Appendix V

Memorial Drawn Up and Presented to His Eminence Mariano Cardinal Rampolla Secretary of State to His Holiness by Representative Peter Paul Cahensly and Marchese Giovanni Battista Volpe-Landi

Your Eminence,

We obediently submit some considerations in respect to emigration to America. This important question involves interests of great consequence from the social as well as religious point of view. A continuously rising flood carries people of different countries to America, and will be more so in the future. Statistical figures indicate that in the year 1889, 439,400 Catholics emigrated to America from Europe. Of these, 178,000 went to North America which in addition received thousands of immigrants from Canada, Mexico, Brazil, and other South American countries. Calculations, based on most reliable informations, indicate that the Catholic immigrants and their descendants should have increased the Catholic population of North America to twenty-six million. The actual number of Catholics in that great country is hardly higher than ten million. Accordingly, Catholicism in that great American republic up to the present has suffered a loss of sixteen million souls. The following are the main reasons for this decrease in the Catholic ranks:

1. The lack of adequate protection for emigrants at the time of their departure from their native country, during the journey, and upon their arrival in America.
2. The lack of priests and parishes for different nationalities among immigrants.
3. The frequently exorbitant financial sacrifices which are asked from the faithful.
4. The public schools.
5. The lack of societies, Catholic and national unions, mutual aid and protection, etc., for laboring classes.
6. The lack of representatives of different nationalities of immigrants in the hierarchy.

Appendix VI

Defense of Their Position and Justification of the Manner in Which They and Their Predecessors Discharged Their Offices by the Archbishops of the United States of America to His Holiness Pope Leo XIII

November 16, 1892

Most Holy Father —

During the past year a suppliant memorial by Peter Paul Cahensly, presented to the Holy See, embarrassed us, the duly appointed bishops of the Church in the United States of North America, and sorely wounded the heart of Your Holiness. God so disposing, the Holy See did not concur with the petitioners. Although they tried their best, under the impulsion of right motives, to achieve their goal, they expended their energies in this direction to no avail.

It is true that at this moment we are able to contemplate with pleasure neither the elimination of serious errors set forth in the aforesaid petition, nor powerful support for our arguments. Wherefore we, the Archbishops of North America, gathered together in plenary session at New York for the consideration of Church affairs, consider it appropriate on this occasion that the several errors which were set forth in the said petition concerning our pastorate over the people be corrected, that our solicitude for the faithful be vindicated, and that the sorrow of Your Holiness be abated and be turned into joy by a statement of the truth.

Maintaining silence upon what does not concern us, or upon what is of slight importance, we shall turn our attention to the most serious part of the aforesaid petition, declared to be devoid of truth: namely, that sixteen million Catholics in the United States have been lost to the Faith.

It is impossible to conceive of a more serious and unfair accusation against the youngest branch of the Church; an inspection of the public records of the Republic of the United States proves beyond any shadow of a doubt that in the past seventy years the total number of immigrants who landed upon our shores did not exceed sixteen million people, who were neither of a single nation nor a single faith; before this period immigration was generally very slight.

Furthermore, it is worth noting that, unfortunately, the majority of Catholic immigrants belong neither to the closely-knit religious groups of Europe, nor have they all, in their fatherlands, been adequately supplied with the means for the fullest exercise of their religion.

On the contrary, the facts clearly show that the American regions in earlier unhappy times were the refuge of those who cried out most vehemently against crimes of the civil power or infringements of the sacred rights of individuals. This type of man, to whom the institutions of his native land appear fraudulent and criminal, and who is "wiser than the children of light," can most easily exercise influence over those who were raised in good conscience.

To all of these must be added the very great number of immigrants who have died because of severe and sometimes unhealthy climatic conditions, because of arduous labor, because of the lack of necessary subsistence, and particularly because of the activity of cholera and the general prevalence of yellow fever, which spread among the immigrants day and night.

Careful study of official documents on immigration, and diligent examination of the suggestions above noted indicate that the claim set forth in the aforementioned petition was without validity or was at best based upon specious arguments.

From about 1820 to the present, immigrants — Catholics, Protestants, and Jews combined — hardly reached the number claimed. And among the Catholic immigrants a large, if not the greatest number, were those who, in their native lands, were least solicitous about the exercise of their religion.

Is it therefore to be wondered at that a man who paid little if any attention to religious exercises at the time he was driven from his own country should, upon coming to America where he is continually fatigued as the result of heavy daily labor, gradually lose the faith without realizing it because he spends his life among Protestants, depends for his very existence upon them, and lives perhaps fifty miles from the nearest church? This remains among the mysteries of divine wisdom.

No one can deny, and we in all honesty admit, that indulgence toward original immigration resulted in certain losses to the Church, necessitated not by pastoral neglect, but by unfortunate conditions. Furthermore, according to historical evidence, it is equally impossible to deny that at that time there existed no episcopal seminary for the training of priests, and that the Sacred Congregation for the Propagation of the Faith ordered Bishop Carroll not to entrust the holy ministry in America to foreign priests.

Shining examples of the Church testify to the priests who supplied spiritual assistance to the early immigrants, multiplying themselves by their works and zeal, serving widely scattered areas, heroically undergoing the greatest dangers, and finally going forward cheerfully to their deaths for the salvation of the faithful.

Illustrious examples in point were Bishop-elect Grässel, Bishop Gartland, Bishop Barron, and innumerable priests who gave up their lives working for their brethren afflicted by the plague. Other examples were almost all the bishops of America who crossed the Atlantic to procure priests who might bring the consolations of the faith to the throngs of immigrants, and from whom our times can never withhold commendation.

Now that churches are built and workers are plentiful in the vineyard of the Lord, the things which unfortunately occurred, not from lack of zeal, but because of the peculiar conditions surrounding a growing Church, are no longer to be feared. Fifty years ago doubtless the harvest was great, but the laborers were few. Only the one Archiepiscopal See of Baltimore had been erected in the United States; sixteen episcopal chairs were set up, one with 528 priests, 512 churches, and thirty-three Catholic schools, so that a single diocese sometimes included an area almost as large as all of France.

And now, fifty years later, the aspect of affairs is definitely altered. The Catholic Church in the United States has grown marvelously; it now numbers eighty-eight consecrated bishops, almost 9000 priests, 9500 churches, and 303,000 students.

To these figures should be added, wherever they have been established, the seminaries for priests in which students from various areas are instructed in knowledge and the virtues in order that they may bring spiritual aid to the faithful.

What is of the greatest importance is that, as a result of all this it has become the especial care of the episcopate to supervise the allotment of functions, and to see to the increase of religion in the lands of America. Would that the future might be forecast in terms of these developments which, with God's help, have taken place in so short a period. On the other hand, consideration of the declining significance of the Protestant sects resulting from the competition engendered by division justifies, perhaps, the hope of an even greater expansion of the Catholic religion.

Faithfully obedient to the commands of Your Holiness, and guided by your advice, we are doing our utmost to bring our lands together in the Faith and in political order so that soon our country may acquire the name of a Catholic nation, as envisioned by Christopher Columbus whose memory we have formally commemorated with festivities during these recent days.

In the meantime, humbly prostrate at the feet of Your Holiness, we again profess obedience, and from our hearts beg the Apostolic Blessing upon us and upon the faithful people entrusted to our care.

APPENDIX VII

Address of Archbishop Francesco Satolli Apostolic Delegate to the United States Delivered at the Laying of the Cornerstone of St. John Baptist School, Pottsville, Pennsylvania April 25, 1895

Not only in my own name, but also in the name of him as whose envoy I stand before you, let me express my warmest gratitude and my sincere appreciation for the heartfelt and splendid reception prepared for me in this community, for the many manifestations of Catholic spirit of which I have been the witness in this city yesterday and today, for the sentiments of true attachment and devotion to which this manifestation is now added in so touching a manner.

I am entirely convinced of the sincerity of these sentiments which animate the German American Catholics, both clergy and people, and I happily take this opportunity of expressing my conviction before this public gathering of priests, whom to be with is true satisfaction for me.

Three things characterize in my eyes the work of the German Catholics in this country, in illustration of which I refer to three expressions of the Holy Spirit.

According to the Acts of the Apostles, the first Christians attracted the attention of the Jews and the heathens especially by the love which they had for one another. It is said of them: "See how they love one another!" Holy Scripture gives the basis of this spirit of fraternal love which possessed them all with these significant words: "They were all of one heart and one spirit"; in other words, they were one with each other. The experience of three years has proved to me that the German Catholics in the United States distinguish themselves in a special way by this spirit of unity and co-operation among themselves. They deserve for this expressive and well-merited praise. Those of other faiths say of them: See how they stand as one together! see how they are one heart and one spirit like the first Christians in public confession and courageous sharing of their faith, which they received from their fathers and forefathers, and which they have brought to this country. From this unity of the German Catholics in America arises the societies which exist among them and which are founded upon religious principles. The gatherings organized by these societies and the general Catholic conventions are the most eloquent witness of this unity. Upon this unity rests the great moral power which characterizes the German Catholics of America. It hangs together most intimately with the firm defense of pure, traditional doctrine, and — what I would especially emphasize in praise of you — your consistent and zealous work for Catholic education of youth, especially for the establishing, maintenance, and development of parochial schools.

We read in I Peter, 2, another word of Holy Scripture which I should like to mention here. It refers to certain charges which the heathens made against the first Christians in order to represent them as a stone of scandal. The Apostle teaches and encourages the first Christians by saying to them that they should oppose such accusations: "Behave yourselves honorably among the pagans; that, whereas they slander you as evildoers, they may through observing you by reason of your good works glorify God." In other words, the Apostle thus warns the faithful: so live among those who revile you that they may cite as your characteristic mark that you are Christians, Christians in the fullest sense of the word, that is courageous, steadfast and convinced professors of the teaching of the Lord. That will be your greatest honor and best defense.

I apply these words with the deepest conviction to the German Catholics of this country and their clergy since they are proved true in them. I know also that I may call upon the good sense and conviction of all those who judge the situation without prejudice. The German Catholics and their priests have throughout this land performed a tireless and worthy activity. They have become in many ways the subject of false charges and accusations. But let one consider the goal and the actual results of their restless zeal and tireless energy. It is the duty of justice to present them as the witness they have remained, true and steadfast in Catholic faith, morality, as one who give expression to their conviction of this spirit through their actions. They are always ready when it is important to support and genuinely advance Catholic movements. They rightly consider it to their honor to be called and recognized as Roman Catholic Christians, and they evidence their conviction in an unequivocal manner through their unfaltering devotion and attachment to the Holy See.

St. Paul, in the same way as St. Peter, warns the first Christians to give evidence of their belief: "in your manner of life," that is through their conduct and behavior in public as well as in private. Here in America the Catholics live among the most diversified sects. We must observe and follow this principle precisely in regard to them. I am convinced that the German Catholics of the country have also taken this apostolic principle as a guide in their efforts to maintain good and justifiable family traditions as well as their mother tongue. They rightly consider these customs and usages, inherited from their fathers along with their language, as an important and effective means of maintaining intact religious and domestic virtues as much as possible. They see them rightly as a strong aid to education. This does not prevent such education from being truly American and genuinely national since religion is the best and most certain foundation of all civic virtues. Thus youths learn in our parish schools the virtues which are the treasures of every good citizen. The accusation that our Catholic schools do not advance a genuinely national spirit is completely incomprehensible. It can only rest upon a complete lack of knowledge, or of intellectual misunderstanding of the good influence which religion exercises upon all facets of social life. Such an accusation would be doubly inconceivable in the mouth of a Catholic. The German American Catholics can point in this matter with confidence to the results which parochial school education has achieved. The history of America in the past as well as in the present testifies clearly that the German Catholics stand second to none as good citizens of this great republic. They truly observe the laws of their adopted fatherland; they cultivate the language of this country alongside that of their mother tongue; and under the protection of the Constitution, they are manfully responsible for their rights.

I repeat in conclusion the expression of my sincere thanks, and wish you, Reverend Father, happiness for the truly ecclesiastical spirit which your zeal for the Church and the welfare of souls has maintained and promotes among Catholic people with such success.

Appendix VIII

Letter of William Kerby to Edward Kerby Concerning Liberals and Conservatives in the American Church

LOUVAIN, BELGIUM, April 11, 1897

. . . Thanks for the clipping on Liberalism and Msgr. Schröder.

I have refrained from discussing that topic in my letters because I did not think you much interested, and it is unpleasant. But I'm going to make an exception today, at the risk of being dry.

Everyone talks of two tendencies in the Church. They are there, as they are everywhere. One clings to the old, and is slow to admit the new: the other welcomes the new and clings less warmly to accidentals in the old. Human nature is so inclined. Out of this grow revolutions. Democracy, a pure modern movement, had to fight down the old and spill oceans of blood. Out of these conditions we get the terms Liberal and Conservative, in politics, in science, in religion. Hence the presence of such tendencies in the Church is normal, ordinary, to be expected, to be welcomed. . . .

Now, to speak of U.S., we have a country where those modern liberties are cherished: with us, Church and State are separated (and both flourish). The question is: what attitude will the Church take to a State built up on such foundations and animated by that spirit!

The Liberal and the Conservative appear, and they answer.

The Liberal looks to present and future. He sees that the world cherishes what it calls its liberties and its supremacy of state over Church. He says to himself, ". . . seeing things as they are, the Church is well off separated. The constitution is all right: it lets us alone. We will flourish, hurrah for the flag, God bless America, let us be patriotic, we have a glorious country. Keep Church and state apart."

Thus you find the liberal, so to speak, in touch with the time.

The Conservative, however, looks back at the past and into books. He thinks of how much the world is out of plumb. He shudders at the recklessness of modern states, mourns over the heresies which develop daily: he can't love a country which cherishes what he despises, he has nothing good to say for it. Patriotism doesn't exist outside of the dictionary; he can't pray for the flag which doesn't carry above its stars and stripes, the Papal colors. But the liberal is at one disadvantage. Progressive, he is constantly lecturing, talking, writing. He has new ideas, he is full of zeal, he preaches his ideas. The Conservative has nothing new to say, he is merely stationary, if he talks or writes he does two things, no more, no less. He constantly repeats principles absolutely true and denied by no one Catholic; secondly, he insinuates that the Liberal denies those principles.

In the clipping you sent me, Msgr. Schröder says, "It is a great heresy to deny the supremacy of Christ and Church over modern state." Liberalism does that, "Liberalism is the creation of hell — No Catholic can be a Liberal." In themselves those statements are true, of another kind of liberalism, but who defends them? Is it Ireland the Archbishop, Gibbons the Cardinal, Keane the scholar? Not at all. Thus the Msgr. says what all believe and lets you draw the conclusion that the liberals in the Church are really heretics. That is mean, contemptible, and false.

Who preaches devotion to Leo and Rome more than Abp. Ireland? Who proved devotion to Rome more than Bp. Keane who, when crushed under the heel of the Pontiff, looked up, kissed the hand that smote him, and said while disgraced before America, "Holy Father, I recognize in your act, the will of God." Who is more Catholic than the gentle Cardinal! and who believes more earnestly in the duty of the Church to make America Catholic than those three?

The slurs, insinuations and machinations with which they are surrounded are simply diabolical. St. Paul was a liberal. He had to fight, and he did it with considerable force, to abolish old customs and ceremonies. He even tells us that he resisted St. Peter to his face. Pope Leo is a liberal. Take his attitude to France. In 1780, the Church owned half of France: clergy and nobility alone were educated, composed legislature, controlled the nation. Abuses entered. A third estate arose. The wealth and force and resources of the nation were in the third ignored class. What did it do? Simply swept clergy, Church and nobility to death in oceans of bright red blood in the French Revolution. That revolution was guilty of awful excesses, of unheard of cruelty. But in one way, it meant progress. Out of that revolution spring a number of things. It was officially atheistic. The Revolution took a famous ballet dancer, and crowned her goddess of reason in the finest church of Paris. Out of that period came the overthrow of royalty which made some struggles to regain power but seems buried under this present third republic in France: finally the modern liberties, referred to already, enter the continent by that door.

For evident reasons, the clergy never became reconciled. It was deposed. It became, was and is today, the enemy of the republic. It wants royalty. The Pope, seeing wisely that Democracy is here to stay, has forced that clergy and hierarchy to accept the Republic, and has given it his own sanction. He had to fight to do it. He did it, and we know, wisely. Did the Pope sanction the revolution: did he deny the supremacy of Christ: did he admit as desirable and ideal the modern liberties which, reason, revelation and Church condemn? No! absolutely. But he saw the trend of things, he said, we better be careful not to stir up hate, those things are facts; we must accept them to be able to end them, we cannot convert the world by making it hate us, we will be a little liberal, tolerate them for the present and trust in God.

That is exactly the condition in America and Msgr. Schröder in dubbing the so called Liberals as heretics is unfair, unjust, and blind. The Pope uses that policy, he has expressly approved it a dozen times in America.

Take Belgium. In 1831 she got her independence from Holland. Her constitution proclaimed the modern liberties, among them freedom of worship. Belgium has been and is Catholic. For years, Catholics fought bitterly against it: they refused to take oaths to defend that constitution; refused to serve in Parliament.

Their stupidity soon cured itself. Pope Leo has had to write again and again to tell Catholics here they must respect, accept and fight for the constitution. According to Msgr. Schröder again, that is equal to denying Christ's supremacy. Nonsense!

To resume. The two tendencies are legitimate and desirable when tempered with charity and common sense. Each emphasizes different sides of the same principle; life would be monstrous were either lacking.

The most fault is on the conservative side because it identifies liberalism with heresy. (There is a liberalism in protestantism and in political science of which I do not speak: there was a French Catholic Liberalism 50 years ago which was wrong and was condemned, the case of De La Mennais. I do not refer to it either). The conservative is constantly repeating principles which no one denies and he imputes the denial to his liberal enemy. He is in good faith, conscientious but unwise. Whether we become liberal or conservative depends upon temperament, youth and many other circumstances.

Take Msgr. Schröder. He is a warm hearted, sentimental, devotional German. As a young man in Germany, he witnessed the Kulturkampf, persecutions under Bismarck and Falk in the 70's. He necessarily came to despise his government and then slid into a scorn for any modern government: add to this his sentimental nature, and devotional character, to them a little natural narrowness, and mix all, out of the composition springs the Conservative German who tells America how to live, etc.

Reporters make things so much worse than they are that people are often scandalized without reason.

There is no cause for scandal in the existence of two tendencies. It is inevitable, to be welcomed. Extremes alone are wrong. So thoroughly is this seen in history that no one forgets it.

I have written hurriedly. Had I time, I would have put my thoughts into more respectable shape. But this will answer for you all at home, more is not necessary. . . .

Affectionately,
WILL

Appendix IX

Report of Peter Paul Cahensly President of the International St. Raphael Societies to Archbishop John Farley of New York at the Conclusion of His 1910 Tour October 8, 1910

I. During my sojourn in Canada and in the U.S. I have been repeatedly asked by Rt. Rev. Bishops, if I were in a position to recommend to them good priests speaking foreign languages.

It is an undeniable fact that in both these countries the bishops are very often unable to supply the Catholic immigrants with priests who can speak the languages of these foreigners; this is especially the case with the ten different nationalities of the dual monarchy, Austria-Hungary, that come to America to settle here.

In order to improve these conditions I beg to suggest the establishment of an international bureau where foreign-speaking priests who are without a pastorate or who desire a change may register, and where, on the other hand, the bishops may apply when in need of priests speaking foreign languages.

At the present time such a bureau could be temporarily established for the U.S. — in New York, as well as one for Germany — in Limburg on the Lahn.

II. The Department of Commerce and Labor, Bureau for Immigration and Naturalization in Washington, D. C., has furnished me with statistics according to which in the fiscal year from June 30, 1909, to July 1, 1910, 926,291 emigrants from Europe have come to the U.S., and in the past ten years a total of 8,136,000 persons.

The number of Catholics among these, according to the accompanying carefully prepared statistics, amounted to 637,894 in 1910, and to 5,331,-906 during the past ten years.

A large number of these immigrants to the U.S. — approximately half of them — found a home with their relatives or friends in the U.S.; the other half, however, are distributed over the immense territory of the

United States; a large percentage, chiefly Italians, Poles, and Hungarians, settling in large cities such as New York, Chicago, Pittsburgh, etc.

Means and ways must be found to direct these people, who are absolutely unfamiliar with the language and conditions of this country, to places where they will find countrymen and priests who speak their languages.

Better facilities, than now in existence, must be provided to improve communication between the native countries of the immigrants and the U.S.

It should be the special care of some person in the native country to announce in America the arrival of such persons who are suited to farm life so that the same may be sent to the settlements which the Catholic Colonization Society of the U.S. (Rev. Julius de Vos, 2517 Logan Boulevard, Chicago, Ill., president) has reserved for Catholic farmers.

To accomplish the aforesaid purposes Immigrant Homes for each nationality with a priest as director, should be erected in all ports of entry.

It is a well-known fact that in New York there are several well-equipped homes for immigrants. The erection of similar homes in the ports of Philadelphia, Boston, New Orleans, and Galveston should be considered. Offices should be established at once at all these ports with correspondents in all the large cities at which offices the newly arrived immigrants may obtain any information desired.

In order to put my plans into effect I should propose the establishment of a protective agency as described above, for a small nationality of Austria, for instance the Bohemians.

I have succeeded in securing for this purpose the co-operation of the clergy in the following cities:

Baltimore, Md., the Redemptorist Fathers of the Catholic Church for Bohemians, 2111 Ashland Ave.

Chicago, Ill., the Benedictine Fathers (Rev. Valentine Kohlbeck, editor), St. Procopius Abbey, 1641 Alfort Ave.

In New York City the Rev. Redemptorist Fathers of the Catholic Church for Bohemians, East 61 St., would willingly take care of the Bohemian immigrants if they were not already overburdened with pastoral work.

The Rev. Fathers are all conversant with the German and Bohemian languages.

After my return to Germany I shall communicate with the Austrian St. Raphael Society for the Protection of Catholic Emigrants, at Vienna (whose founder I am), in order that Bohemian emigrants may be instructed to apply to the above-mentioned addresses.

Concerning the protectorate over the other nationalities of the Austrian Empire immigrating to the U.S., especially Slavonians, Slovaks, Croatians, Magyars, I would suggest that the priests of these nationalities in this country should be admonished by Your Grace, to found religious, national (St. Raphael) societies. With these societies should be connected offices, with which the settlers as well as the newly arrived immigrants may consult.

To raise funds to sustain these offices an annual collection should be taken up in the churches attended by Catholics of said nationalities.

To insure success it would be essential that the Rt. Rev. Bishops of Philadelphia, Pittsburgh, Chicago, St. Louis, and other places of the U.S. would grant the same favor and propagate the organization of said Catholic societies.

EMIGRATION FROM EUROPE TO THE U. S. OF AMERICA

Race	*Persons* 1910	*Persons* 1901–1910	*Per Cent of Catholics*	*Catholics* 1910	*Catholics* 1901–1910
Bohemian–Moravian				8,462	94,693
Slavonian				39,562	309,727
Dalm.–Bosnia–Herzog.				4,911	30,654
Lithuanian				22,714	158,069
Polish				123,348	873,660
Ruthenian				27,907	143,143
Slovak				32,416	332,446
French				53,498	387,005
Irish				38,382,	371,772
Italian, North				30,780	342,261
Italian, South				192,673	1,761,948
Portuguese				7,657	66,560
Spanish				5,837	48,944
Syrian	6,317	50,281	50	3,159	25,141
Russian	17,294	80,602	33⅓	5,765	26,868
Dutch-Flemish	13,012	83,096	75	9,759	62,322
German	21,107	111,410	33⅓	7,039	37,137
Magyar	27,303	318,671	75	20,475	239,004
Romanian	14,200	82,210	25	3,550	20,552
			Total	637,894	5,331,906

The Sources

Since this study has been based in great part on manuscript sources, it is the use and value of manuscript collections which are emphasized in this essay. Bibliographical references for the printed books, newspapers, and periodical literature may be found in the footnotes, where indication has been given of their quality and pertinence for this study. The evaluations of the various archival materials that follow have been made solely in terms of the topic under investigation. There have also been included brief comments on the various libraries utilized, as well as a listing of the interviews granted by persons who had firsthand contact with the questions discussed in this book.

Manuscript Depositories

Archives and Library of the Caritasverband, Werthmannhaus, Werthmannplatz 4, Freiburg im Breisgau, Germany.

The most complete collection of documents on Cahenslyism, German Catholic emigration to the United States, the St. Raphaelsverein, German Catholic social welfare activity and international charitable work are in this depository. Under the direction of the German hierarchy, the Caritasverband is not only the clearing center for all Catholic welfare activity in Germany, but it also houses an excellent archives and library, both of which are rich in sources on modern German Catholic history. Contents of both archives and library were gathered with care over a long period of time and were hidden with keen foresight in the Schwartzwald during World War II by the late Heinrich Auer, director of the library. Director Auer, formerly interred in Dachau prison camp, was unstinted in his generosity by way of advice and information to the author. He collected pertinent books, journals, speeches, proceedings, reports, records, and statistics from his stacks and files; wrote many letters for desired transcripts; arranged contacts across Germany with librarians, ecclesiastics, and living associates of Peter Paul Cahensly; and instructed his entire staff to lend every assistance possible to the author. Besides the thousands of pages of printed background material on nineteenth-century Germany from this excellent library, which prides itself on having copies of all available German Catholic literature, the author also used the materials in the archives of the Caritasverband.

There the correspondence of Right Reverend Laurenz Werthmann, founder of Caritas, was investigated. Although these papers cover only the later years of Cahensly's life, they reveal his character and ideals in intimate detail. At the Caritasverband the only remaining complete file of *Der St. Raphaels Blatt* is preserved, as well as a collection of statistical and analytical German emigration literature.

Archives of the Ludwig Missionsverein, Munich.

Housed in the chancery building of the Archdiocese of Munich, this unusual collection contains thousands of reports, letters, and surveys from the United States, state by state, on the condition of German Catholics, as well as decisions on funds granted by the central council of the Bavarian Society for the Propagation of the Faith begun under King Ludwig I of Bavaria. Preserved as they are in excellent condition and order, these primary sources were helpful for the background on mid-century conditions of Germans in the United States. Most Reverend Johann Neuhäusler, Auxiliary Bishop of Munich and honorary president of the society, and Reverend Willibald Mathäser, O.S.B., archivist of the society, were helpful in every way, as were their staffs. Father Willibald likewise gave generously from his transcripts and from the knowledge of the subject which he enjoys as a recognized authority on Bavarian emigration and on the benefactions of the Wittelsbach family.

Archives of the Abbey of Metten, bei Deggendorf, Niederbayern, Germany.

From this ancient Bavarian Benedictine cloister Boniface Wimmer left for the United States to establish the first Benedictine monastery in 1846. All the Wimmer letters and reports to his superiors and confreres at Metten on German problems in the new world were available, and from the valuable old library of the abbey several secondary works not found elsewhere proved helpful. The letters of Wimmer to Abbot Benedict Braunmüller, O.S.B., of Metten, and Abbot Gregor Scherr, O.S.B., later Archbishop of Munich, were of special value.

Archives of the Diocese of Limburg an der Lahn, 16 Rossmarkt, Limburg an der Lahn, Germany.

The file on the St. Raphaelsverein in Peter Paul Cahensly's home diocese, letters of Cahensly, Prince Isenburg-Birstein, Christian Bitter, Joseph Kölble, and other leaders of the German and American branches of the society to both Bishops Peter J. Blum and Karl Klein of Limburg were valuable for early problems of the society. Documentary copies of Cahensly's first brochure on Catholic care for emigrants, his first appeal to the German government, to President Ulysses S. Grant, to the American hierarchy, and to the German hierarchy were all found here. It appeared that each move of the St. Raphael Society was reported to the Ordinaries of Limburg. Letters and reports of local leaders of the society, priests' comments on collections for the cause, copies of the responses of the bishops to the society's leaders, and Cahensly's explanations of the American attacks on Cahenslyism for the benefit and information of his bishop were also used to advantage.

Archives of the P.P. Cahensly Commercial Firm, 9 Kornmarkt, Limburg an der Lahn, Germany.

The major disappointment incurred on the author's research in Germany was met at Cahensly's Stein Haus. His nephew, Ernst Grandpré, current president of the corporation, stated that because of air-raid regulations during World War II the attic of the building, where all of Cahensly's incoming letters were retained, had to be cleared. After they were removed to the basement they were packed and shipped to the St. Raphael Mission at Hamburg. There the misfortunes of war overtook them and, as one of innumerable collections of cultural resources, they were destroyed in the air raids over that city which leveled the entire St. Raphael Mission. Herr Grandpré declared that Cahensly had preserved his entire correspondence, which was of an extensive character, so that posterity could some day make use of it. The Cahensly family had, however, retained in their possession several printed speeches, pictures, and reports which were of some value.

Archives of the Pallottine Mother House, I Wiesbadener Strasse, Limburg an der Lahn, Germany.

The Pallottine community, beneficiaries and personal friends of Cahensly, had a number of St. Raphael printed materials, magazine references to the activity of the organization, and the few library and archival items which were salvaged from the destroyed St. Raphael Hamburg Mission, of which Reverend Wilhelm Nathem, S.A.C., now resident at the house, was assistant director.

Archives of the Hamburg St. Raphaelsverein, 19 an der Alster, Hamburg, Germany.

Under the direction of Reverend Friedrich Fröhling, S.A.C., the society is again caring for the millions of displaced persons of central Europe and Germany at this new address. Driven from their former mission by the Gestapo on June 25, 1941, their records confiscated and then later destroyed in the bombings of the city, they have begun with energy to collect copies of St. Raphael materials from other depositories, as well as to assemble as many general emigration sources as possible. Here statistics and surveys not previously seen were very generously made available by the director and his assistant, Reverend Peter Hahn, S.A.C.

Archives of the Abbey of St. Paul Outside the Walls, Rome, Italy.

A chance visit to these archives uncovered the correspondence of Abbot Bernard Smith, O.S.B., where it had lain intact and untouched since his death in 1892. Smith had been consultor for three congregations of the Roman Curia, first pro-rector of the North American College in Rome, and Roman agent for a large number of the English, Irish, Canadian, Australian, and American churchmen from the early 1840's to 1892. His incoming American letters, numbering 3168, contained many important items on the German question in the United States from bishops and religious superiors who sought his advice and help. Reverend Ildefonso Panucci, O.S.B., archivist of St. Paul's, generously permitted the microfilming of the entire collection of the Smith Papers, which was done through the kindness of Reverend Hilario Grand, O.S.B., and the Benedictines at the Abbey of St. Jerome in Rome. The American clerics of the international Benedictine Collegio di Sant' Anselmo in Rome assisted most generously in classifying and arranging these documents for microfilming.

Archives and Library of the International Benedictine Collegio di Sant' Anselmo, Via di Porta Lavernale 19, Rome.

The library of Francesco Cardinal Satolli was bequeathed to Sant' Anselmo after his death in 1910. Among Satolli's books was a manuscript journal of his impressions on the Church in the United States written when he was first Apostolic Delegate to the United States. This sole personal document of 130 pages, dated 1896, supplied several items on the German question, and considerable background material. Reverend John Müller, O.S.B., librarian at Sant' Anselmo, graciously allowed full use of this document.

Archives of the Archdiocese of Baltimore, 408 N. Charles Street, Baltimore 1, Maryland.

The See of Baltimore held a prime position among American dioceses during the entire period covered by this investigation. Especially in the twenty-five years before the American Church was removed from the jurisdiction of the Congregation of Propaganda Fide in 1908, and during the administration of James Cardinal Gibbons (1877–1921), national questions were for the most part referred to Baltimore and from there often directly to Rome. The papers of Cardinal Gibbons were, therefore, of historical significance on German Catholic matters because, as the first ranking American bishop after 1886 and a member of the so-called Americanizing party, both the supporters and opponents of this group presented their views to him. Copies of his own communications with Rome and with fellow bishops of the American hierarchy; reports of the annual meetings of the archbishops; messages from the popes, the cardinals of the Roman Curia, and Gibbons' Roman agent, Monsignor Denis J. O'Connell; speeches, reports, and non-Catholic American viewpoints on the German immigrants — all were of significance for this study.

Archives of the Archdiocese of Boston, Lake Street, Brighton 35, Massachusetts.

A few letters were discovered here, but Archbishop John J. Williams' habit of penning his response in short notes on communications received, and his reserved participation in the controversies centering around the German question limited the quantity of original material. However, several documents from the Propaganda were found here, and a printed copy of the Abbelen Memorial, as well as the responses of the American hierarchy to that petition, were microfilmed here.

Archives of the Archdiocese of Milwaukee, 2000 W. Wisconsin Avenue, Milwaukee 3, Wisconsin.

Through the fraternal assistance of Reverends Vincent Tegeder, O.S.B., and Aelred Tegels, O.S.B., available materials in this depository were copied from the single correspondence file of the early archbishops. Pastorals, circulars, and speeches of the incumbents of this metropolitan see were of value, as were numerous items from the files of the *Catholic Herald Citizen,* the archdiocesan paper, and the Milwaukee German weekly, *Columbia.* A few letters from Giovanni Cardinal Simeoni, Prefect of Propaganda, to Archbishop John M. Henni, and a twenty-four page draft of Archbishop Frederick X. Katzer's report to the Holy See on the school question were found here.

Archives of the Archdiocese of New York, St. Joseph's Seminary, Yonkers 4, New York.

The Corrigan and Farley Papers were used to advantage, particularly the former. Archbishop Michael A. Corrigan, as the titular leader of the conservative group in the American Church of this period, played an important role in all the discussions, and Corrigan's position as honorary president of the American branch of the St. Raphael Society, as well as his rather frequent correspondence with Cahensly, were of help in obtaining a better appreciation of both sides of the Cahenslyism question.

Archives of the Archdiocese of St. Paul.

Right Reverend James H. Moynihan, who was in possession of the John Ireland Papers while preparing his biography of that churchman, generously allowed the author complete use of this significant collection of papers of the great Archbishop of St. Paul. They are at present housed in the rectory of Incarnation Parish, 3817 Pleasant Avenue, Minneapolis 9, Minnesota. The documentary evidence of Archbishop Ireland's principles and program as the most forceful protagonist of the Americanizing group, his many letters from Monsignor O'Connell in Rome, copies of his speeches, messages from Cardinal Gibbons, and evidences of Ireland's far-flung contacts in both American religious and secular circles proved to be valuable.

Archives of the Diocese of Cleveland, Cleveland Square, Cleveland 14, Ohio.

The papers of both Bishops Richard Gilmour and Ignatius Horstmann yielded a rich return in materials on the German question, and served as representative data from the Province of Cincinnati. These two bishops took definite, though opposite, stands on the question of the Church and

German nationality, and each played a role in the events connected with that topic on a local, regional, and national scale.

Collections of the American Catholic Historical Society of Philadelphia, St. Charles Borromeo Seminary, Philadelphia 31, Pennsylvania.

The author here met with one of his most profitable experiences during his research in the materials discovered in the correspondence and papers of Reverend Herman J. Heuser, editor for many years of the *American Ecclesiastical Review.* Heuser emerged as the key figure around whom there moved forces of the intellectual, journalistic, conservative opposition to hasty Americanization and the liberal position of the more progressive members of the Catholic Church in the United States. His voluminous correspondence had hitherto been untapped. Here, likewise, the unexcelled collection of Catholic newspapers and magazines supplied a large number of items of information. Moreover, some letters of John Gilmary Shea were used, as were many pamphlets, brochures, broadsides, journals, scrapbooks, and the correspondence of Catholic lay publishers like John T. Reilly and Martin I. J. Griffin. Personal newspaper scrapbooks assembled by Reilly and his editions of several volumes entitled — with variations — *Collections in the Life and Times of Cardinal Gibbons* (McSherrytown and Martinsburg, 1890–1905) were also helpful.

Archives of the Diocese of Richmond, 807 Cathedral Place, Richmond 20, Virginia.

The correspondence of the Bishops of Richmond through the administration of Denis J. O'Connell (1912–1926) have been microfilmed and are on file in the Department of Archives and Manuscripts of the Catholic University of America. O'Connell's Roman correspondence, which remained in Richmond after his death, completed the picture of the efforts of the Americanizers. As mentioned above, he served from 1885 to 1903 as an unofficial Roman agent for a number of prelates in American Catholic questions of the day.

Archives of the Catholic University of America, Washington 17, D. C.

In this archives are preserved some of O'Connell's letters from his days as rector of the University, and a few letters of Professors Shahan, Pace, Hyvernat, Grannan, and Kerby were found useful.

Archives of the Roman Catholic Central Verein, 3835 Westminster Place, St. Louis 8, Missouri.

Here is found the most important and extensive collection of German Catholic materials relating to the American Church. What the Freiburg Caritas collection supplied for the position of German Catholics in Germany, this Central Verein collection offered for the position of German Catholics in America. Moreover, for forty years the directors have made a concerted effort to assemble all available references to Cahenslyism. Files are maintained on every German Catholic topic for which materials could be assembled, for example, German bishops, priests, religious orders, nuns, parishes, colonies, charities, customs, language, pioneers, education, farmers, art, political influences, and so forth. German papers, pamphlets, convention proceedings, bulletins, and addresses were examined, as were the personal correspondence of Edward and Arthur Preuss, and the clippings collected by Reverend George J. Weber, former pastor of St. Mary's Church, Buffalo. Transcripts of Schröder and Cahensly letters were kindly prepared for the writer by Cyril Echele, of the staff of the Central Bureau.

Archives of the Leo House, 332 West 23rd Street, New York City 11.

Records of the American branch of the St. Raphael Society are preserved here, including minutes of meetings of the Board of Trustees, reports of the treasurer and of the Sisters who staff the house, journals, letter files, annual reports of all immigrants who passed through the mission, and a collection of newspaper clippings on the Leo House. Some Cahensly letters are also filed. The most enlightening item at the Leo House was Reverend John Reuland's manuscript and documented chronicle of the early days of the St. Raphael Society in the United States.

Archives of the Paulist Fathers, 415 West 59th Street, New York City 19.

The correspondence and printed materials on Americanism were consulted in this depository, and several letters from the friends of the Paulists among the American hierarchy proved pertinent.

Libraries

The Mullen Memorial Library of the Catholic University of America was used by the author at every step of the way. Eugene P. Willging, director of the library, advised the author and co-operated in many ways, even to the extent of conducting a preliminary survey of available German materials in both Europe and the United States through correspondence with Most Reverend Aloysius J. Muench, Apostolic Nuncio to Germany; Reverends Peter L. Johnson and Raymond A. Fetterer, of St. Francis Seminary, Milwaukee; and the late Frederick P. Kenkel, director of the Central Bureau of the Central Verein, St. Louis.

The Library of Congress was used for printed materials on immigration, United States census, and governmental literature. The New York Public Library contained files of the New York *Staatszeitung, Freiheit,* and *Freeman's Journal,* as well as background materials on New York state immigration history. The Library of the University of Freiburg im Breisgau offered valuable items on German Catholicism, among which were the only copies to be located of Kurd von Schlötzer's *Briefe,* and the complete records of the Landtag and Reichstag. At the libraries of the Universities of Munich, Heidelberg, Frankfurt, Louvain, and at the Vatican Library the author used with profit bibliographical references to Catholic emigration and statistics.

Interviews

Right Reverends Franz Müller, former president of Caritas, and Kuno Jörger, director of the Freiburg Caritasverband, gave the author invaluable direction and advice on the entire subject of this monograph. Most Reverend Wilhelm Berning, Archbishop of Osnabrück and honorary president of the St. Raphaelsverein, likewise discussed the development of that society with the author. Reverend Willibald Mathäser, O.S.B., archivist of the Ludwig Missionsverein, supplied many interesting insights on Bavarian emigration and aid. Reverends Johann Valerius, S.A.C., and Wilhelm Nathem, S.A.C., former directors of the Bremen and Hamburg St. Raphael Missions, detailed their personal reminiscences, while Adolph Statländer, former passenger agent of Nord Deutscher Lloyd, Bremen, explained Cahensly's labors for emigrants at that port. Reverends Albert Hammenstede, O.S.B., Martin Rahsler, O.S.B., and Brother Fintan Mai, O.S.B., of Maria Laach Abbey were helpful on the subject of German Catholicism and their personal associations with Cahensly. Reverend Friedrich Fröhling, S.A.C., present secretary-general of the St. Raphaelsverein, spent long hours supplying invaluable insights, and Ernst Grandpré, nephew of Cahensly, related family aspects of his uncle's life. The older fathers at the Pallottine Mother House in Limburg recollected numerous incidents of Cahensly's career, and Johann Friedrich, former member of the Hamburg St. Raphael Mission, and Sister M. Hedwigis furnished tape recordings of their experiences with Cahensly. Right Reverend Johann Schönhöffer, of the Agencia Fides of Propaganda Fide at Rome, discussed the history of overseas German emigration. Right Reverend John A. Nageleisen, late director of the Leo House in New York, related stories about the early days of that institution, and the same was true of Theobold Dengler, of the board of directors, Miss Lilian Cambeis, Miss Emma Messner, and the Sisters of St. Agnes at the Leo House. Professor Paul Gleiss, head of the Department of German in the Catholic University of America, gave the writer leads on German Catholicism in the United States, and the late Frederick P. Kenkel, director of the Central Bureau of the Central Verein, despite his illness, generously supplied revealing information. Reverend George Timpe, S.A.C., successor to Cahensly as secretary-general of the St. Raphaelsverein and at present resident at the Pallottine House of Studies in Washington, gave generously of his time and knowledge, not only in reading the manuscript critically, but also in mapping the author's German research itinerary. It was Father Timpe, more than anyone else, who in repeated conversations explained the major trends of German Catholic ideals and accomplishments.

As was to be expected in a work of this scope, the author encountered some disappointments in his research. For example, the Staats-Archiv in Berlin was decimated by the bombings of the German capital. The former archives of the papal nunciature in Munich, containing the papers of Antonio Cardinal Agliardi, Nuncio to Bavaria during the days of

Cahenslyism, had been removed to the Vatican Archives following the expulsion of the nuncio in 1938, and they are still restricted material. The rule of the Congregation of the Propaganda Fide that a hundred years must have elapsed from their date before documents are available to research students — according to Right Reverend Giuseppe Monticone, general archivist of the Propaganda — prohibited use of certain materials there which were not obtainable elsewhere. Likewise the papers of Reverend Franz Xavier Kraus in the Stadt Bibliothek in Trier were not, in accordance with the restriction in Kraus' will, opened until January, 1951, and they will not be available for at least another year until indexing and cataloguing are completed. The collections of the Volksverein für das katholische Deutschland at München-Gladbach, containing many of the remaining papers of the Center Party, suffered seriously during World War II. Finally, the Abbelen Papers, in the possession of the School Sisters of Notre Dame at their Milwaukee motherhouse, 1324 N. Milwaukee Street, were not available for use.

Index